Conservation Is Our Government Now

183-238

NEW ECOLOGIES FOR THE TWENTY-FIRST CENTURY

Series Editors: Arturo Escobar, University of North Carolina, Chapel Hill

Dianne Rocheleau, Clark University

Conservation Is

Our Government Now

The Politics of Ecology in

Papua New Guinea

PAIGE WEST

DUKE UNIVERSITY PRESS   *Durham and London 2006*

The author wishes to thank *Social Analysis* for permission to use material from West 2001. "Environmental Non-Governmental Organizations and the Nature of Ethnographic Inquiry," *Social Analysis* 45(2), November 2001. Copyright Berghahn Books.

The author also wishes to thank Desk Top Publishing and Anthropology in Action for permission to use part of the following: West, Paige 2003. Knowing the Fight: The Politics of Conservation in Papua New Guinea. 10(2). Special edition of *Anthropology and Activism*, edited by Nicola Frost.

For Patricia H. West

How we shape our understanding of others' lives is determined by what we find memorable in them, and that in turn is determined not by any potentially accurate overview of another's personality but rather by the tension and balance that exist in our daily relationships.
— Tom Robbins, *Even Cowgirls get the Blues*

I wonder if you have ever thought about this. Here we are — right now. This very minute. Now. But while we're talking right now, this minute is passing. And it will never come again. Never in all the world. When it is gone it is gone. No power on earth could bring it back again. It is gone. Have you ever thought about that?
— Carson McCullers, *The Member of the Wedding*

Contents

Preface

On 12 December 2003 an international oil and natural gas company announced that they would drill within the borders of the Crater Mountain Wildlife Management Area in Papua New Guinea. The company landed a helicopter, without warning, in a forest clearing located directly below the Sera Research Station, a station funded and maintained by the U.S.-based Wildlife Conservation Society and located in a bit of the forest that has been part of a social relationship between expatriate ecologists and Papua New Guinean landholders since 1987. The company did not alert the Wildlife Conservation Society's Papua New Guinea office, located in Goroka, a mountain town to the north of the Crater Mountain Wildlife Management Area, that they would carry in sixty helicopter loads of equipment and clear six hectares of forest. Rather, they just landed and began their work. The research station and the forest in which it is located are at the head of the Purari River system, a system that feeds life into villages, gardens, and forests across the lower half of the country. While there was some knowledge of the possibility of oil exploration in the area, this event was a surprise for the Pawaia peoples, who hold the land around the station in traditional tenure and for the conservation organization. It was not, however, the first shock of resource extraction exploration experienced by people who live and work within the Crater Mountain Wildlife Management Area (CMWMA) in the past few months.

On the other side of mountain, which has become known as Crater Mountain (the name's origin will be discussed later) there had been similar events earlier in the year. On 16 August 2003 a national alluvial mining company, landed in Maimafu village, one of the rural villages within the CMWMA, and announced that they would start an alluvial gold-mining project at the head of the Nimi River. The Nimi River begins high in the mountains where the Youha and the Nemeahlo Rivers meet, and it flows southward, giving life to a tropical forest that is the home to thousands of people. The land encompassed by the Nimi River prospect area is not held only in tenure by Gimi peoples, but also by Macmin, an international mining company with subsidiaries in Papua New Guinea, Australia, and Canada. Macmin had been dormant in the area for some years, due to the low price of gold on the international market, but upon hearing about the national mining company's activity, Macmin began to reassert its claims to the forest prospect area through bureaucratic actions such as press releases and well-placed articles in the national newspapers.[1]

In this book, I show the ways that Crater Mountain, a seemingly out-of-the-way place (Tsing 1993:10), and Gimi people, a seemingly less-than-developed people, actually exist within and at the same time generate what has come to be known as the transnational. Indeed, I will show that the transnational is a process through which Gimi and their interlocutors produce space, place, environment, society, and self. The two events described above are examples of the transnational nature of social and ecological life around Crater Mountain. The encounters and exchanges between Gimi people, Pawaia people (the Gimi's closest neighbors), and others have made the Crater Mountain Wildlife Management Area, and in turn the CMWMA has come to make the people that live and work within it.

The Crater Mountain Wildlife Management Area began as an integrated conservation and development project (ICDP or ICAD) based on the premise that environmental conservation can be achieved through the sustainable development of economic markets that are tied to in situ biological diversity. It was imagined that these markets would allow for the flow of cash income to people who live in highly biologically diverse places. In turn, these people would work to conserve the biological diversity on which the markets were based. This relationship between people, their environment, and the market was to be managed by a nongovernmental organization (NGO) as a part of the international push for neoliberal economic policies that attempt to meet the social and economic needs of rural peoples through doing away with the state and putting private industry and NGOs in its place (Hartwick and Peet 2003:189). Throughout this book, I refer to this project as a *conservation-as-development* project, and by this I mean that it was a project that assumed that *environmental conservation could be economic development* for rural peoples; that development needs, wants, and desires, on the part of rural peoples, could be met by the protection of "biodiversity" on their lands (MacDonald 2004).[2] In this project, as it was implemented from 1994 to 1999, conservation and conservation-related enterprises, were the development. So, what follows is also an examination of the processes and practices, the politics and economics that created a moment in which environmental conservation could be seen as the way in which people imagine they can have access to the things that they see as "development."

The conservation-as-development project established both the wildlife management area and a contract between villagers and outsiders. In this contract, outsiders — namely, conservation planners and practitioners[3] — understood that they would get conservation in exchange for development, while villagers understood that they would take part in social relationships that would allow them to access medicine, education, technology, and knowledge and wealth, the things they see as development, in exchange for their participation in conservation. That is, they would contribute land, labor, food, and friendship to the conservation planners and practitioners working with the NGOs that created the Crater Mountain Wildlife Management Area, and these contributions would be reciprocated in socially appropriate ways. This book shows that neither set of actors understood what they were supposed to be giving in this relationship and that different actors actually understood the contract in radically different ways. Villagers did not understand what "conservation" is, and conservation planners did not understand what villagers think of when they imagine "development." In addition, while villagers thought they were entering into an exchange relationship, conservation planners thought they were entering into a relationship in which villagers would work as a corporate unit (village and/or clan) in order to make money that would then be redistributed fairly to individuals and be used to buy commodities and services.

Throughout the book, I discuss the processes of commodification that have taken place in conjunction with the conservation-as-development project. Within anthropology there is a tendency to essentialize capitalism as a thing and to not understand capitalism as a process in which actors have agency and which can be changed in ways that make it more equitable. By discussing the commodification of the Gimi environment and their social relations, I am trying to make clear the ways in which this process is taking place at Crater Mountain and among Gimi. Understanding this process is crucial to understanding personhood among Gimi — how they see themselves and their relations with others and their environment—because capitalism as a process has begun to supplant exchange as a process, and it is through exchange relations that Gimi have, until very recently, made self, other, and the environment.

In addition to examining the encounter between villagers and conservation planners and practitioners that gave rise to the Crater Mountain Wildlife Management Area and the processes of commodification connected to this encounter, I also examine the multiple forms of production that have come about through the dialectical relationships between villagers and others. With this I will make clear how space (the CMWMA), place (Maimafu village), environment (the Gimi forests), and society (the Gimi), are social artifacts.[4]

Anthropologists and anthropology have had the effect of making "the Gimi." In 1973 cultural anthropologist Gillian Gillison, then a graduate student at the City University of New York, went to the Eastern Highlands Province of Papua New Guinea to conduct anthropological fieldwork among Gimi-speaking peoples (Gillison 1993:xiii).[5] The goal of her initial research was "to describe the society from a female point of view, to use women's own accounts, life histories, attitudes to men, etc., to portray the lives of both sexes" (ibid.). Her work over the past three decades has reflected this theme but has been more predominately focused on the relationship between mythology and cultural forms (Gillison 1980, 1983a, 1983b, 1987, 1991, 1993). During Gillian Gillison's initial fieldwork she was married to David Gillison, who, because of his interest in New Guinea birds of paradise, became a photographer and environmental conservationist (Gillison 1993:xiii). Because of a desire to protect birds of paradise from hunting and habitat loss, David Gillison, along with scientists and environmental activists, began the activities related to environmental conservation on Gimi lands that will be discussed throughout this book (Johnson 1997:398).

Gillian Gillison was not the first anthropologist to work with Gimi-speaking peoples. From 1960 to 1962, Leonard B. Glick and his wife, Nansi S. Glick, lived among Gimi in a village about twenty-five miles away from the Australian colonial post, or "station," at Lufa (Glick 1964:280 n. 1). Leonard Glick was particularly interested in Gimi medical categories, natural sciences, and kinship, with his work centering on understanding the ways Gimi categorize things, be they plants and animals, kin relations, or personality categories (Glick 1964, 1966, 1967a, 1967b, 1968a, 1968b). Sam and Nancy McBride, Summer Institute of Linguistics linguists, anthropologists, and missionaries, lived among Gimi-speakers in the late 1960s and early 1970s (McBride and McBride 1973).

And, finally the anthropologist and medical researcher Carleton D. Gajdusek passed through Gimi territory in March 1962 during a trek between the Lufa and Karimui stations (Gajdusek 1968).

I first arrived in Maimafu village to conduct anthropological research with Gimi speakers in November 1997. During my first year in Papua New Guinea, I conducted research on how Gimi understand their relations with the natural world and how they understand environmental conservation projects. During that year, and for the six months preceding it, I also conducted ethnographic fieldwork with conservation scientists, activists, and practitioners who work in Papua New Guinea, with the goal of understanding how they view the natural world and Gimi peoples. Although Gimi and Pawaia peoples hold the land that encompasses the Crater Mountain Wildlife Management Area, my work is predominantly concerned with Gimi peoples. David M. Ellis, another anthropologist, was living and working with Pawaia peoples while I conducted my initial fieldwork, and in his work he tells the story of their interactions with environmental conservation (Ellis 2002).

Since my initial research in Papua New Guinea, I have returned to the country several times: first from April to 1 September 2001, then during the North American academic summer breaks in 2002 and 2003, and during the fall term of 2004. Over the years since my initial fieldwork I have come to see Gimi peoples and Crater Mountain as both embedded in and as generative of transnational social and ecological relations and to understand anthropology as both a way of seeing and making sense of this complex world. I see it as a way of coming to terms with the relationship between social, ecological, political, and economic life and such concepts as history, agency, capitalism, culture, and the imagination. Anthropology also allows us to see the plurality of positions in any given situation. The story of the CMWMA is not a story of "good guys" and "bad guys" or even "the Gimi" and "the conservationists." It is a story about the social lives of people associated with a large bit of the forest in Papua New Guinea. Some of the people described in it live in that forest, and some of them live in other places but have a connection to it. But this book is not about "local people" and "others" as discreet categories or social groupings. The people who have moved through this forest over the past fifty years include those native to New Guinea, colonial officials, missionaries, agricultural development experts, and airplane and helicopter pilots. They also include biologists, ecologists, photographers, tourists, volunteers, gold miners, politicians, and anthropologists.

In what follows I hope to put into a historical context why they have all moved in and out of this forest, to ethnographically describe some of the social interactions between some of these actors, and to describe and analyze some of their ideas, beliefs, dreams, and desires.

The Gimi-speaking peoples I have worked with want as many different things out of life as there are people in Maimafu village. Some of them want to continue to live in and of the forest. They want to hunt on their ancestral lands, feel the heat of the sun as they work in their gardens, and hear the soft flap of the flying fox's wings late in the night. A few people are beginning to understand that this desire is connected to environmental conservation. They have, over the past thirty years, come to understand that conservation means seeing the world through a lens that imagines that things can be lost and destroyed, and that they can go away forever. Others, older people usually, cannot understand conservation at all. It is antithetical to the way that they see the world. For older Gimi, there is no such thing as the loss of something. All matter has been here for all eternity, and when things die or disappear, they are simply changing form. People's bodies and life forces go back to their ancestral forest, the reserve for matter, as do other things that seem to go away. For these people, conservation is completely alien. Some people, young men usually, want their village to look exactly like Goroka. They want cars and bars and markets and businesses. They want access to electricity and schools. They want to be able to go eat lunch at the Bird of Paradise Hotel every day. They want capitalism and modernity writ large. Others, women usually, want a kind of hybrid modern-village. They want schools and medical care and they want some way to make money, but they also see the value of a kind of village life that is safe. There are no roads to any of the villages around Crater Mountain right now, and for female residents that means that the threat of rape by outsiders, a constant threat in most of the country, is not part of their daily worry.

The other main actors in my research are conservation scientists, activists, planners, and practitioners, and they are as varied in their ways of seeing the world as Gimi are. For some reason, early on in my research, it was much easier to see these people through a lens of critical theory than it was to see Gimi that way. Once one of them asked me, after threatening me with expulsion from the country if I wrote or said anything bad about his work, "Why do you want us to fail?" I was stunned by this question because it was at that moment that I realized he had no idea what I was doing in terms of research. He did not understand that my project was to understand conservation as a process and hence to write ethnographically about it.

At its best, ethnography makes us feel like we were there when the events described took place and helps us to interpret those events in and of themselves and as they are tied to other events. When we read ethnography, we make judgments about the actors and their actions based not only on the story being told but also on the multiple simultaneous dialogues in which we take part. Vincent Crapanzano (1992) suggests that ethnographic conversations and interactions are not dyadic, but rather that their participants are continually taking part in multiple dialogues that shape both the ethnographic encounter and the end product. These dialogues, which he calls *shadow dialogues*, are grammatical and linguistic conventions, social rules of engagement, and internal conversations that the participants have with other places and people during the encounter (ibid.). Shadow dialogues are the kinds of dialogues that anthropologists and their subjects take part in during the dialogical engagement of ethnographic research (Crapanzano 1992:6). I like Crapanzano's idea of a continual dialogue with self and other during all encounters, and I think it extends nicely to describe what happens not only when we conduct fieldwork, but also when we read ethnography. We read something, and it immediately is engaged in a series of dialogues with our own experiences, the texts that we have read in the past, what we imagine we might write in the future, and the like. It also comes into contact with our imagination and politics.

In an analysis of the politics of ethnographic writing about development projects, David Mosse (2004:3) distinguishes between instrumental and critical approaches. Instrumental analyses work to examine policy and implementation and determine how to make them more effective, while critical analyses assume that development policy has failed and that behind the implementation of policy in the first place there was some sort of "conspiratorial ends" (Mosse 2004: 5).[6] The former examines policy documents, ideologies, and practices; while the latter examines the local social, economic, and political effects of policy. The former assumes that development is at its base policy to be implemented, and the latter that development is domination that should be resisted at all costs. Mosse (2004) argues that neither approach provides analysis that does justice to the complexity of the lived experiences of development and suggests that a new approach to the ethnography of development has begun to emerge.

Throughout my work in Papua New Guinea and my writing about the

Crater Mountain Wildlife Management Area, I have been torn between the two approaches that Mosse articulates. On the one hand, conservation activists, practitioners, planners, and scientists have wanted my work to focus on their projects in a way that can provide recommendations for future successful projects. I have been asked to provide a kind of translation or legibility-making service for them (Scott 1998). On the other hand, many of my colleagues in anthropology, geography, and the academy in general have assumed that my work will level a devastating critique of conservation as a way of knowing and producing knowledge. I have begun to see my role and the purpose of my work along the same lines that Mosse uses to describe this "new ethnography of development" (Mosse 2004:644). This new ethnography takes seriously the governmentality of projects—the fact that social lives, environments, and subjects come to make and be made by the productive power of the structures created by projects (Foucault 1977)—and the social interactions and transactions during all sorts of projects (be they conservation, development, or resource extraction) which create new communities (Golub 2005). This ethnography also examines the power of development narratives (Escobar 1995; Ferguson 1994; Hoben 1998; Roe 1991), and problematizes the role of the ethnographer in the creation of the "world described" by the ethnography (Mosse 2004:29).

In my research as a participant-observer in the community that produced and was produced by the CMWMA, the world I describe in this book, I have had several difficult conversations with conservationists in which I have tried to explain why anthropologists critically analyze conservation and development projects. It has been difficult to make some people see that I do not analyze the Crater Mountain project because I have any particular negative agenda with regard to this project. Rather, my goal is to provide an ethnography of the project and perhaps to persuade conservation practitioners, activists, scientists, and others to question the assumptions about nature, culture, and development that underlie many of today's biodiversity conservation efforts. Like many other conservation programs, the Crater Mountain Wildlife Management Area began with a focus on one kind of animal, expanded to cover a large area and many plants and animals, and ultimately encompassed the social lives of local people. Benjamin Orlove and Stephen Brush (1996:329) have pointed out that given this trend, anthropological research, which "documents local knowledge and practices . . . [and] . . . clarifies the different concerns and definitions of biodiversity held by local populations and international conservationists," is well suited to contribute to the conservation of biological diversity through ethnographic research.

The research on which this book is based was both multisited and multitemporal. In the past two decades, anthropologists have examined the role of anthropology, and ethnography in particular, in the production of the other and in silencing "subaltern voices." This critique of ethnography and anthropological practice is serious business and has forced the disciple to examine the power relations implicit in our profession (Appadurai 1988; Clifford and Marcus 1986; Friedman 1990; George 1995; Marcus and Fischer 1986).[7] One of the many responses to these criticisms is the disciplinary push for multisited research focusing on the connections between seemingly "local" sites and "global," or "transnational," processes (see Featherstone 1990a; Gupta and Ferguson 1992; Marcus 1995). I consider my research to fall squarely within this form of anthropological practice but hope to contribute to it by showing how, in the case of the Crater Mountain Wildlife Management Area, the seemingly local and the seemingly transnational were mutually produced.[8]

Multisited ethnography moves the ethnographer between sites and groups of differently situated individuals. Within the scope of a single project, an ethnographer might work with people from very different circumstances (Marcus 1997:121). Hence, the power relations in multisited ethnographic work are different from those in traditional ethnography, becoming more ambiguous than in the past, when anthropologists dealt with informants from one or two social or ethnic groups. Then, anthropologists may well have been in positions of power and dominance, or at least felt they were, with regard to the subjects of ethnographic research. Now that cannot always be assumed. Today, the anthropologist moves from subordinate to dominate and back again depending upon the informant or participant worked with at the time (Marcus 1997:121). In addition, multisited ethnography, in my reading of it, also means ethnography that takes seriously multiple sites of cultural production. So, although much of the "action" in the work that follows takes place in and around Maimafu village, the sites from which the mental, material, and social productions that work to make the CMWMA flow, are diverse and scattered. My multisited work moves between places in which I conducted research — Goroka, Port Moresby, Canberra, New York City, and others — even if they do not continuously appear in the text. I think it is an error to assume that because the "action" transpires mostly in Maimafu village in the shadow of Crater Mountain, that it is not multisited. Indeed, part of my argument is that "Maimafu" and "Crater Mountain" are spatial productions that are a hybrid artifact of multiple places: part New York City and part New Guinea.

The project is also multisited in terms of the differently situated people with whom I worked. I take "the Gimi" to be, in part, an anthropological invention in that Glick, G. Gillison, Gajdusek, the McBrides, and I have all written about them in ways they would never write about themselves (Keesing 1999:301). But I also take the categories of conservation biologist, conservation activist, conservation practitioner, Peace Corps volunteer, missionary, and so forth to be equally socially and anthropologically constituted. In my work I try to move between and among these categories, always holding them in tension as socially produced by ideas, actions, material relations, and imaginations, and I attempt to write about social selves as always in process, always being made and remade depending upon the circumstances.

By the multitemporal aspect of my work, I mean that the research presented here has been conducted over a period of seven years. The story in the pages that follow is a story that has taken all those years to unfold. The work is also multitemporal in that the polices, practices, and productions associated with the Crater Mountain Wildlife Management Area have worked to alter the ways people imagine the past and the future. So the book moves between the distant past, as reconstructed and imagined, and the future, as desired and imagined, and the present, that which we take to be "accessible" through our perceptions, experiences, and senses (Crapanzano 2004:17).

One of the threads that runs throughout this book is my story of imagining New Guinea. New Guinea, and places other than the United States, has been in my imagination for as long as I can remember the existence of words and meanings; indeed my grandmother taught me to read using *National Geographic* magazine. My story of imagining New Guinea and its peoples is intertwined with other threads of analysis that have to do with how other people have imagined New Guinea. Western writers, since the 1545 voyage of Spaniard Inigo Ortiz de Retes, have discursively produced the island of New Guinea and its inhabitants. Before that, Malay, Chinese, and Bugis traders and fishers knew the place and its peoples. This is a long history of representation and production. I want to weave these imaginings of New Guinea into an examination of how contemporary spaces get produced by a variety of processes. These processes are discursive, mental, material, and social (Lefebvre 1991).

The people in this ethnography are real, but they have all been given pseudonyms unless they have asked me to use their real names, they have published books or articles about Crater Mountain, or their names appear in other publications. Everyone that appears in the pages that follow gave their consent to be a part of this research, and I hope that I have done them all justice with my representations. The act of writing a book and then talking about it with many of the people represented in it, after they had read drafts of it, was terrifying, gratifying, and humbling. Writing about highly educated people who read and discuss your work is a curious position for an anthropologist to be in. I am not sure that if the tables were turned, and I was the one under the ethnographic lens, I would have handled it with the kind of grace and intellect that these people did. This book benefits from the many conversations I have had about my initial work with the people whom I was "studying." This includes both the highly literate readers mentioned above, and residents of Maimafu village who either read a manuscript version of this book, and there are a few, or who read or had read to them a summary of it written in Melanesian Pidgin.

Acknowledgments

The research that I conducted for this book was carried out in Papua New Guinea, the United States, and Australia and was funded by the Wenner-Gren Foundation for Anthropological Research, the United States National Science Foundation, Barnard College, and the Center for Environmental Research and Conservation at Columbia University. I wish to thank all four of these institutions for their support, especially the Wenner-Gren Foundation, who funded my doctoral research and awarded me a Richard Carley-Hunt postdoctoral research grant that allowed me to turn my dissertation into a book; and the Barnard College Office of the Provost and Provost Elizabeth Boylan. I also wish to thank Mr. Damon Dell, owner of the Hog Pitt, who gave me the bartending job that funded the portion of my research that was carried out in New York City between March 1997 and August 1997.

The debts that I owe to the people who participated in the research for this book are immeasurable, and I can only mention some of them here.

Every resident of Maimafu village deserves and has my gratitude. They allowed me to live with them, pester them with thousands of questions, follow them around their gardens and their forest, and make a general anthropological nuisance of myself. They took care of me, protected me, fed me, lifted me up when I fell down the sides of mountains, and taught me with kindness, patience, and humor. I would especially like to acknowledge Philip, Ine, Gilbert, Robert, Sarau, Moyha, Daniel, Waymane, Betty, Naomi, Kusiomo, Kalasaga, Seahnabe, Karo, Semi and her mother, Wallis, Thomas, Agua, Hamasabi, Little Daniel, Mybo, Kepsi, Anna, Tom, Carol, and Naison. Kawale took care of me like a father and Ebule protected me with old magic; not a day goes by that I do not feel the pain of our losing them. Jonah and Lukas saved my life one night, and for that kind of thing there is no way to adequately say thank you. Kobe gave me the food that sustained me, and so now, I feel her in my bones as I move through my life. I could not have written this book, conducted the research on which it is based, or lived in Maimafu without Ellen. Her labor and subtle readings of social behavior run throughout this book. She has taught me more about being Gimi, and sharing in the obligations of kinship and friendship, than anyone else has.

Robert Bino, Joe Egenae, John Ericho, and Phyllis Kanona patiently answered my questions and taught me about the complexities of being both conservation practitioners and Papua New Guineans. Robert deserves special thanks for helping me learn Melanesian Pidgin, being a good friend, and sharing both gossip and laughter. I would also like to thank Andrew Mack, Deborah Wright, Joshua Ginsberg, and Arlyne Johnson, who all showed a kind of patience with me during my first few years of fieldwork that was incredibly generous.

In the past few years the Wildlife Conservation Society's Papua New Guinea (WCS PNG) office and its employees, interns, and students have made Goroka feel like a second home. When you walk into their office, there is generally a flurry of activity. There are students getting ready to head off to the Sera Research Station, students entering data from previous fieldwork trips, and scientists discussing academic papers with students. The rhythm of the office is punctuated by shifts in cadence because the students, researchers, and scientists are skipping between Melanesian Pidgin and English. Almost all of the students and scientists are Papua New Guinean—a fact, a place, and a moment that could not have been the case when I first began my research in 1997. I am extremely grateful to the staff of WCS PNG for their logistical support and for the collegial atmosphere they offer visiting researchers.

I wish to thank the National Research Institute of Papua New Guinea and James Robins for their support and for allowing me to be a research affiliate, and David C. Wakefield at SIL International for help with the Gimi language.

The mission pilots who fly in and out of Maimafu save lives, make the local coffee business possible, and bring the world to the doorstep of the village. I could not have gotten to Maimafu so easily without them. I would especially like to thank and acknowledge Pastor Les Anderson and Brian Scarbrough.

Mal Smith and Brian Greathead both deserve thanks for taking care of me when I am in Goroka. They have both opened their homes to me numerous times over the past six years, and they have made both my research, and my breaks from research, richer. Mal deserves special thanks for helping me understand the geography of the Eastern Highlands, introducing me to the thrill of helicopter flight, and for being a constant supporter of research in Papua New Guinea.

I would also like to thank my friend and colleague David M. Ellis. We were separated by a magnificent mountain range, different "culture areas," different theoretical training in anthropology, and our own profoundly different cultures. A shortwave radio and an eerily similar way of being in the world connected us.

At Rutgers University, where this book began as a dissertation, Dorothy L. Hodgson, Neil Smith, George E. B. Morren, Bonnie J. McCay, and Richard A. Schroeder shaped both my intellectual and professional development. I also wish to acknowledge Cindi Katz, Andrew Bickford, Nelson Feliciano, Gavin Waters, Debra Curtis, and Rebecca Etz, all of whom made New Jersey more livable. While I was at Rutgers, a fellowship at the Center for the Critical Analysis of Contemporary Culture allowed me to write and think in ways that shaped both my initial research and this manuscript.

My colleagues Peter Brosius, James G. Carrier, Michael Dove, Frederick Errington, Colin Filer, Deborah Gewertz, Leonard Glick, Robin Hide, Dan Jorgensen, Bruce Knauft, Ben Orlove, Joel Robbins, Paul Roscoe, Diane Russell, and Andrew P. Vayda have all offered valuable comments on portions of this manuscript. I could not have written this book without the detailed comments provided by Aletta Biersack. Kathy Creely's help and advice were invaluable. During the spring of 2003, I attended a seminar that Vincent Crapanzano conducted on the imagination that helped tremendously in the writing of this book. The professors Ab Abercrombie, Gerry Ginocchio, James Gross, Charles Hudson, Robert Morgan, and Gerald Thurmond appear in the pages of the book in terms of their support early on in my academic training. I have benefited greatly from conversations concerning Papua New Guinea with Alex Golub, Jamon Halvaksz, Jerry Jacka, Thomas Strong, Flip Van Helden, and John Wagner. I feel privileged to have gotten to know Gillian Gillison, and I am constantly daunted by the task of writing about Gimi peoples in a way that measures up to her theoretically insightful and beautifully written ethnographic work.

At Barnard College and Columbia University, my colleagues Nan Rothschild, Lesley Sharp, Maxine Weisgrau, Marco Jacquemet, Lynn Meskell, Sherry Ortner, and Tim Taylor offered intellectual support and encouragement during the writing of this book. Amelia Moore, Patrick Gallagher, Michelle Murdock, and Leigh Johnson contributed to this book through their extraordinary work in my classes and in their own research projects. I would also like to acknowledge the following students: Scott Andrews, Shana Bromberg, David Fierman, Jamie Hodari, Sunita Kurra, Rebecca Jacobs, Averill Leslie, Phil Matricardi, Caroline McLoughlin, Mia Nathanson, Nuria Net, Brook Smith, Betsy Summers, and Allison Sudol. I wish to thank all of the students who have taken my Interpretation of Culture class over the past few years. They remind me in spectacular, hilarious, and odd ways why teaching is a way of changing the world, and they have helped, through their critical readings of many of the texts cited in what follows, shape this manuscript.

Valerie Millholland at Duke University Press has been a wonderful editor, and Arturo Escobar and Dianne Rocheleau have been extraordinary to work with as well. David Valentine's advice about publishing was invaluable. Three anonymous reviewers read and commented on this book. It is richer because of their work.

In New York, Lillian Martin, Andrew Steever, Angella Ahn, Alex Cone, and Sue Truitt provided social support during the long process of writing this book. Sensi Scott Zapfel taught me lessons about strength, endurance, patience, and how to defend myself—things that help me in my writing and in my research. Mike Moore began as one of my data but quickly became a friend. His friendship, knowledge of New Guinea's birds, ability to argue with me about anything and everything, and willingness to go drink a beer when writing became too much, have proved very valuable.

The writing of this book would not have been possible without the music of the Ahn Trio, Billy Bragg, the Replacements, George Michael, and Barry Manilow.

In the end, my family deserves much of my gratitude. My grandmother Mrs. Daisy Esta Whaley Henry taught me to read and to have a sense of humor, skills that I draw on every single day as an academic. My Aunt Ann taught me about nature, its fragility, beauty, and wonders. My mother's brothers and sisters and my cousins, especially Rick Wiley, have forced me to learn how to explain why anthropology matters, and, in ways that I have not always appreciated, taught me not to take myself or anything else so seriously that I lose the ability to see the darkly humorous underbelly of any situation. Robbie Ethridge, Sarah Lowthian Glover, Ashley Parham, and Marion Wilson are, by now, family, and their support and advice have been invaluable. John Clark Salyer III and Colleen Salyer became family slowly, but now I can't imagine it without them.

Before he was my husband, John Clark Salyer IV came to Papua New Guinea so he could understand me as an anthropologist and as his friend. Three years later, he came back to Papua New Guinea to pay my bride price and attend a wedding banquet celebrating our marriage. Our life together is richly permeated by Papua New Guinea. During the writing of this book he has suffered my moods, served as an editor, laughed with me, offered invaluable comments and suggestions, and made the whole process, and life in general, wonderful. My mother, Patricia H. West, is the most extraordinary person I know. Every day I strive to be half the woman she is, and I could not have done anything that I have without her love and support. This book is as much her accomplishment as it is mine.

Abbreviations and Acronyms

There are numerous abbreviations and acronyms used in environmental conservation and development. These appear in this book.

BCN	Biodiversity Conservation Network
BSP	Biodiversity Support Program
CBC	community-based conservation
CBNRM	community-based natural resource management
CMWMA	Crater Mountain Wildlife Management Area
DEC	Papua New Guinea Department of Environment and Conservation
ICAD or ICDP	integrated conservation and development project
ICCO	Interchurch Organization for Development Co-operation
IUCN	International Union for the Conservation of Nature and Natural Resources
MAF	Mission Aviation Fellowship
NGO	nongovernmental organization
PNG	Papua New Guinea
RCF	The Research and Conservation Foundation of Papua New Guinea
SDA	Seventh-Day Adventist
SDAA	Seventh-Day Adventist Aviation
UNEP	United Nations Environment Programme
US-AEP	United Sates–Asia Environmental Partnership
USAID	United States Agency for International Development
USPC	United States Peace Corps
USPCV	United States Peace Corps Volunteers

WCI   Wildlife Conservation International, previous division of the New York Zoological Society, primarily concerned with international conservation, now the WCS

WCS   Wildlife Conservation Society, formerly the New York Zoological Society

WCS PNG   Wildlife Conservation Society, Papua New Guinea Office

WMA   Wildlife Management Area

WWF   World Wide Fund for Nature, known in the United States and Canada as the World Wildlife Fund

CHAPTER I

New Guinea–New York

In the 4 February 1985 "Talk of the Town" section of the *New Yorker* magazine, sandwiched between an item about a man who translated *The Odyssey*, *The Iliad*, and *The Aeneid*, and a news item about fashionable hats, is a story entitled "Birds of Paradise." In the story, New Yorkers are introduced to Wildlife Conservation International (part of the New York Zoological Society), the island of New Guinea,[1] birds of paradise, and an ethnolinguistic group known as "the Gimi." Wildlife Conservation International had invited the magazine to an event at the Salon Vendome in the Hotel Parker Meridian to meet the anthropologist Gillian Gillison and the photographer David Gillison and to hear them talk about Papua New Guinea (PNG), birds of paradise, and "the Gimi." The invitation, as quoted in the *New Yorker*, reads, "Led through the dense tropical rain forest by a local Gimi guide, the researcher crouches inside a blind to observe the mating display of a bird of paradise. As they watch this splendid creature, the Gimi envisions the spirit of his ancestor; the scientist one of the last of a spectacular species" (*New Yorker* 1985:36). The article goes on to discuss the natural history of New Guinea, the conservation-related projects sponsored by Wildlife Conservation International, the New York Zoological Society's captive bird of paradise collection, and the mythological and ritual connections between Gimi social life and birds. At the end of the article, David Gillison cautions the mid-1980s Manhattan cocktail party audience that even with their "spirit of reverence toward birds," the Gimi, economically poor subsistence horticulturists, are strongly tempted to sell the birds' skins for profit (ibid.:38).

The location of the "Birds of Paradise" piece in the *New Yorker* between discussion of *The Odyssey* and of fashionable hats is both eerie and poignant, as is the invitation's invocation of "the Gimi" imagining kinship and the past and "the scientist" imagining the loss of spectacular nature in their future. The hero in *The Odyssey* travels in order to understand the meaning of life and to explore distant exotic lands. Milton was so moved by this narrative tradition that he used it as a model for his epic tale *Paradise Lost*, in which a man seeks to understand the meaning of his experience in life. *Paradise Lost*, in turn, became the basis for Western narrative forms, as its style and rhythm have captured the imaginations of generations of writers. Papua New Guinea, a country whose travel industry slogan was "The Land of the Unexpected," has for many years drawn writers, travelers, adventures, anthropologists, and others, who all wish to find themselves, their fortunes, and "spectacular" nature and culture.[2] Bird of paradise plumes first drew explorers to the island of New Guinea as early as 2,000 years ago (Swadling 1996:53), and their beauty took hold of the imaginations of European explores as early as 1522 (Cooper 1977:17). Their spectacular nature was inextricably tied to place early on, and indeed in Spain in 1523, there was a slippage in language concerning the birds, and they were referred to as "birds from paradise" (ibid.). These birds and this imagined "spectacular" nature in New Guinea have worked for over 2,000 years to create the transnational loops that envelop New Guinea today.

Throughout the seventeenth and eighteenth centuries, the trade in bird of paradise skins increased, as did the scientific study of the birds and their collection by various navigators, explorers, and naturalists. The Portuguese, Dutch, French, and British made significant commercial trips to the island during this time period and during these voyages; as was the case with other voyages during this period, collection for commerce and empire, and the collection for science, were intertwined (Pratt 1991; Swadling 1996). Alfred Russel Wallace, the well-known English naturalist and adventurer, was enamored of the birds and observed them extensively during the time he spent in the Malay Archipelago between 1854 and 1862 (Wallace 1880).[3] Wallace first visited New Guinea in March 1858, staying five months on the island and not having the collecting success he had initially expected (ibid.:492). Of his first view of New Guinea, Wallace writes, "I looked with intense interest on those rugged mountains, retreating ridge behind ridge into the interior, where the foot of civilized man had never trod. There was the country of the cassowary and the tree-kangaroo, and those dark forests produced the most extraordinary and the most beautiful of the feathered inhabitants of the earth — the varied species of Birds of Paradise" (ibid.:494). And later, when his foot was injured and he was confined to his house lamenting the days of collecting lost, he writes, "New Guinea! — a country which I might never visit again, — a country which no naturalist had ever resided in before, — a country which contains more strange and new and beautiful natural objects than any other part of the globe" (ibid.:504).

Wallace's desire for birds of paradise was, however, not to be fulfilled in Dorey or Mansinam, the villages on mainland New Guinea where he set up camp. After an initial few days, during which the locals he paid to hunt for his collections returned with a bird of paradise and several other "beautiful" birds, he faced ten days with no more birds of paradise, finally deciding that "Dorey is not the place for Birds of Paradise" (Wallace 1880:500). During his stay, however, several ships came into Dorey harbor, and Wallace, upon discussion with their crews, realized that bird of paradise skins came to coastal peoples through trade with peoples living farther in the interior of the island. Upon acquiring them, the coastal inhabitants sold them to Bugis or Ternate traders (ibid.:507).[4] These traders were already part of an existing international trade in plumes, and these interior parts of New Guinea, which Wallace imagined as untouched by civilization, were already connected to transnational commerce.

Even with his lack of success on the island of New Guinea, Wallace had profound collecting success on the Papuan islands to the northwest and southeast of the New Guinea bird's head peninsula. These collections, and his narration of his trip, inspired other naturalists and museum collectors to venture to New Guinea on collecting trips (Swadling 1996:74). For Wallace, New Guinea was an imagined frontier; it was "the beyond," a place that always turns on our images, ideas, and dreams, but that is also always destroyed by them (Crapanzano 2003:14). The beyond can never be found. Once it is constructed, it is immediately displaced; one can spend their whole life looking for it, and will never find what they are looking for.

While Wallace and others were collecting the birds for scientific study and to be housed in the collections of museums and private collectors, the ancient trade in skins for commercial purposes increased in the late 1800s as fashionable women began to wear the plumes in their hats. Indeed, by 1913 there may have been as many as 80,000 skins exported from New Guinea (Swadling 1996:91). In the summer of 1896, bird of paradise plumes were all the rage among fashion-conscious New Yorkers (ibid.:85).

A little over a hundred years later, in the summer of 1999, as I walked down

Madison Avenue in New York City, I was stopped dead in my tracks by the "flash" of an image in the window of a shoe store.[5] It was decorated with what seemed, at first glance, to be stuffed birds of paradise. I had just returned from PNG, where I had been conducting anthropological research while living with Gimi speakers in Maimafu village. The birds in the window were indeed modeled after the real birds of paradise — they were brightly colored with striking feathers displayed in wondrous ways. But these birds were a little bit strange, and it took me a couple of minutes to figure out what was wrong. The colors were a little too bright and the feathers a little too spectacular. They were copies of copies of copies, withdrawn from the objects on which they were based — birds that were squawking, displaying, and singing — they were drained of the lifeblood of the living (see Baudrillard 1981:169). Based on a model, the birds of paradise in the window had become a sign, an object and image with a particular kind of meaning (Baudrillard 1981:63). The birds themselves had become "hollowed out things" that worked to draw in meanings seemingly not connected to them at all (Taussig 2000:254). And these things that were once ritual objects, subjects of myth and religious practice, and even commodities themselves — things that had use- and exchange-value in and of themselves — were there being used to sell shoes, commodities that have nothing in the world to do with birds. Or so it seems.

In what follows I try to disentangle the connections between New Guinea and New York, conservation and development, and birds of paradise and commodities. The central arguments are (1) that ostensibly out-of-the-way places exist within, are made by, and help to make transnational loops;[6] (2) that in the past imaginaries of New Guinea and its nature and culture as untouched, exotic, and spectacular drove people who wished to protect it, sell it, explore it, and study it, and that these same imaginaries drive environmental conservation in Papua New Guinea today; (3) that the contradiction articulated in the 1985 invitation in the *New Yorker* — of the Gimi guide seeing a bird and imagining his family's past, and a scientist seeing it and imagining a future loss — is the central contradiction present in the integrated conservation and development project at Crater Mountain today; and (4) that there are profound differences in Gimi understandings of exchange and the social relations of exchange, on the one hand, and conservationists understandings of these relations, on the other.

CRATER MOUNTAIN

Places that are imagined as far from the historic reaches of capital hold much of the in situ biological diversity that is targeted for protection by environmental conservation organizations. These places are often geographically isolated and seemingly far from the prying eyes and actions of post-Fordist capital.[7] Deep in the forests of PNG, there is a mountain surrounded by a rugged and beautiful forested landscape. The people that live to the north of the mountain call its highest peak Bopoyana, after one of the bird species that lives on it.[8] Many of the other people who know the place call the entire mountain range the Crater Mountains and the highest peak in the range, rising to about 3,100 meters, Crater Mountain. Indeed, it has had this name since the 1950s, when the first Australian colonial patrol posts were established in Gimi territory (Carey 1950/ 1951; Eisenhauer 1950/1950; Young-Whitforde 1950/1951).[9] The mountain range is a group of peaks that are the remainders of a volcano that last erupted in the Pleistocene era. This mountain range and the lands that surround it have become a physical, discursive, and imaginative landscape in which the fields of conservation biology, cultural anthropology, and development studies have been drawn into conversations over the past, the present, and the future. It has also become a place where local and expert groups have been drawn into conversations, conflicts, and compromises about the environment and society and the appropriate relationship between the two.

Bopoyana, or Crater Mountain, is the centerpiece of the Crater Mountain Wildlife Management Area (see map 1). This Wildlife Management Area and the rural villages that it encompasses were the center of an externally funded integrated conservation and development project (ICAD or ICDP) from 1994 to 1999. The project was designed and implemented by three nongovernmental organizations (NGOs) made up of conservation scientists, conservation planners and practitioners, and environmental activists from the United States, Australia, and Papua New Guinea.[10] These actors entered into a set of social relationships with Gimi and Pawaia peoples in which it was promised that if Gimi and Pawaia gave their lands for inclusion in the Wildlife Management Area, they would derive cash benefits, access to economic markets for the forest products tied to local biological diversity, and "development." This was a conservation-as-development project in which conservation was to be the development.

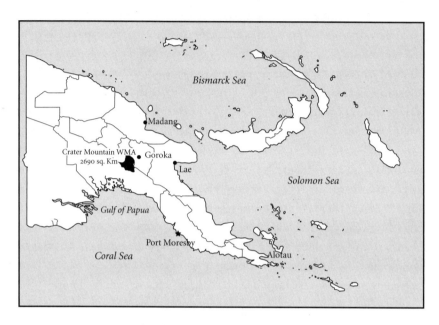

Map 1. Location of the Crater Mountain Wildlife Management Area (2,690 kilometers) in Papua New Guinea. Source: Mary Pearl, 1994. Local initiatives and the rewards for biodiversity conservation: Crater Mountain Wildlife Management Area, Papua New Guinea. In *Natural connections: Perspectives in community-based conservation*, edited by David Western, R. Michael Wright, and Shirley C. Strum. Washington, D.C.: Island Press.

Within this Wildlife Management Area (WMA), at the edge of the Lufa District and close to the borders of the Eastern Highlands, Gulf, and Chimbu (or Simbu) Provinces, lies Maimafu, one of the rural settlements whose traditional lands and lives have been subsumed by this conservation-as-development project (see map 2). It is easy to imagine Maimafu as cut off from the rest of the world, but this "out-of-the-way-place" is not an example of a fixed and timeless periphery relative to a dynamic and changing core (Tsing 1993:10). Rather, like many other seemingly out-of-the-way places in PNG, it is a place where its inhabitants and their social institutions have a dynamic and fluid history that is tied to individual and community engagements with local, regional, national, and transnational influences (Biersack 1995a; J. Carrier 1992; Errington and Gewertz 1996; Foster 1995; Jacka 2003; Knauft 1999, 2002; Lederman 1998; LiPuma 2000; Morren 1986). For the past three decades, many of these engagements have been associated with and connected to the creation of this Wildlife Management Area. The Crater Mountain Wildlife Management Area (CMWMA) is tied materially, socially, politically, economically, and ideologically to the Research and Conservation Foundation of Papua New Guinea (RCF), a nongovernmental organization (NGO) located in Goroka, PNG; the Wildlife Conservation Society (WCS), an NGO located in New York City;[11] The Biodiversity Conservation Network (BCN), an NGO funded by United States Agency for International Development (USAID) and others, and located in Washington, D.C.; and a host of individuals living in the United States, Papua New Guinea, and Australia.[12]

Broadly, this book takes one conservation-as-development intervention and ethnographically examines how the NGOs and villagers associated with it understand the environment and society. In so doing, it looks at how they imagine the past, future, and the present and how they understand and participate in the contracts of conservation. I am also concerned with the production of spaces that have come to be known as Crater Mountain, the Crater Mountain Wildlife Management Area, and Maimafu village. By the production of space, I mean the ways space is appropriated, controlled, understood, and represented and the making of new material and representative systems to deal with that space (Harvey 1990:218–225). I examine the Crater Mountain Wildlife Management Area as a "rich site of cultural production" (Brosius 1999a:277) as well as a rich site of spatial production (Lefebvre 1991) that is made by and that makes the transnational. With this, the book offers an anthropological critique of conser-

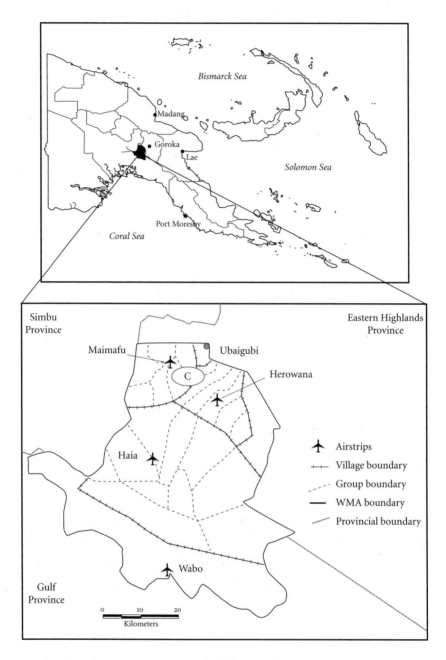

Map 2. Map of Crater Mountain Wildlife Management Area (CMWMA). Source: Johnson, Arlyne, Robert Bino, and Paul Igag (2004). A preliminary evaluation of the sustainability of cassowary (Aves: Casuariidae) capture and trade in Papua New Guinea, *Animal Conservation* 7 (2):129–137. Cambridge: Cambridge University Press.

vation-as-development interventions. Also, by demonstrating the ways in which anthropology and anthropological units of analysis are implicit in and complicit with conservation and development, it problematizes anthropology's role in both. More specifically, using history and ethnography, the book examines the discursive productions, practices, ideologies, and consequences of conservation-as-development as they have been articulated and carried out by people associated with the Crater Mountain project and people whose livelihoods have been affected by it.

Another level of analysis within this book is the relationship between anthropology and NGOs. These organizations have become key sites of analysis within anthropology—rightfully so given that NGOs often produce and circulate certain discourses about the relationship between nature and culture and then act upon their own discursive productions as if they were real (J. Carrier and Miller 1998). They produce the "problems" to be solved and then design and carry out the projects meant to solve them. Anthropologists, myself included, often articulate their critiques of NGOs using the language of the critical analysis of contemporary culture and veiling them in a progressive politics of human rights. But we often fail to discuss the relation between our critiques and the fact that NGOs have become the discursive and material terrain through which "indigenous," "native," and "other" peoples are known to outsiders and managed by statelike entities. While, in the past, this was the role of anthropology, NGOs, and conservation NGOs in particular, have usurped the traditional role of anthropology: speaking for and about "the other." They have also become the producers of the bureaucratic apparatuses that manage their productions (Said 1978). In what follows, I examine discursive and material productions with regard to the people who were the subjects of traditional anthropological inquiry. I also examine the environmentalists' and conservation practitioner's reliance on Western-derived notions of nature and culture in projects where they work with people who have radically different notions about the environment and society and the relations between the two.

This book is about places and people that are both real and imagined. To get to the real physical places from the Eastern Highlands provincial capital Goroka, you must take a car to where the road literally ends and walk for about a day and a half. Alternatively, if you have enough money, you can fly in on a small fix-winged airplane. Or, if you are very wealthy or the recipient of a free ride from a friendly helicopter pilot, you can fly into the area in a helicopter. Maimafu is real in that people live along a series of ridgetops on the northern edge of Bopoyana and in that biologists, missionaries, Peace Corps volunteers, aid workers, tourists, and anthropologists visit this place and the people that live there. It is imagined in that it is, at least in part, a production of space that has little local social salience for many of the people who live there and one that is intimately tied to an imaginary nature and culture. This social imaginary, a set of ideas that have come to be taken as common sense by some, and on which those with power act in ways that make the real world conform to the imagined one (Anderson 1983; Appadurai 1996; Carrier and Miller 1998; Crapanzano 2004:7; Taylor 2002; see also chapter 5 in this book), is connected to the images of people and place held by the individuals who move through the physical and discursive spaces of Crater Mountain. In many ways, it is also a production of space in order to render place and people knowable to outsiders. The people living along these ridges and the people that visit them engage in practices and hold ideologies that are produced by multiple scales of influence: the local and the regional; the national, international, transnational, and global; all these influences intertwine in place and space, in culture and politics, to create social relations between people and between people and nature. The story of these intertwining threads is complex and can only be understood through historic and ethnographic analysis. This is also the case if we wish to understand the social impacts of biological conservation and economic development projects, given that they are often located in areas considered culturally marginal and historically isolated. All of this is made even more complicated by the fact that the residents of Maimafu do not see the aforementioned scales as vertical or as encompassing (Gupta and Ferguson 2002). Indeed, they "jump scale" (N. Smith 1993) all the time, and with this, they confound the predictive tendencies of neoliberal conservation-as-development models.

MAKING MAIMAFU

"Maimafu village" is a settlement of approximately 600–800 people located along ridgetops in the mountains of PNG's Eastern Highlands Province.[13] The land surrounding the settlement, and the land held traditionally by residents of Maimafu, spans a topographic range from lowland rain forest to montane cloud forest and it lies in the shadow of Bopoyana, the mountain known to many as Crater Mountain. Motai, Tulai, Biabitai, Abigarima, Kolatai, Harontai, Lasoa-

1. (All photos/figures are by author.) Maimafu village airstrip.

bei, Kuseri, Atobatai, Bayabei, Iyahaetai, Wayoarabirai, Kalopayahaetai, Hala-baebitai, and Aeyahaepi are all place-names of the ridgetop hamlets that have become Maimafu village. This transformation occurred over the past fifty-five years, through the discourses and bureaucratic practices of governments, missions, and NGOs (Foucault 1972:49). *Spaces* have been transformed into *a place*, and Maimafu is now both a spatial production and an object; it is a thing created and sustained through a shifting set of power relations (Foucault 1986). This object/thing/place, Maimafu, is an externally imposed demarcation that is a way of producing local rural space and groups of people to meet the needs of outsiders. Australian colonial officials who carried out early patrols into the area named the group of small hamlets "Maimafu" when it was still an uncontrolled area.

In 1950 the district's administrator, George Greathead, sent patrol officers D. W. Eisenhauer, Dudley Young-Whitforde, and Arthur T. Carey out on a "three-pronged" patrol over the last portion of the Central Highlands District that was unmapped and unvisited; the area south and west of the Kratke Range and south of Mount Michael (Eisenhauer 1950/1951:3). The three men all took divergent routes and intersected along the way. These patrols were the first into the Gimi territory surrounding Crater Mountain, and they are the first significant mention of Crater Mountain in the colonial record. By 1952 several patrol rest houses had been established between Goroka and Mount Karimui, and in December of that year J. R. McArthur, a patrol officer, eight native policemen, one native interpreter, and sixteen native carriers began a patrol between Goroka and Mount Karimui. On Wednesday, 21 January 1953 McArthur arrived at a hamlet he called Maimafu (McArthur 1952/1953:5).

The naming of this place was part of a larger project of social simplification meant to make the Highlands "legible" to the colonial government (Scott 1998).[14] In the 1950s these hamlets were not a cohesive "village" at all. Rather, they were a set of settlements based on extended families and lying along adjacent ridgetops. These families were related by marriages and were often either in political alliance with each other or at war with each other. At this time, Maimafu was the place-name for the southern end of the settlement Wayoara- birai.[15] It is likely that the patrol officer McArthur asked someone at Maimafu what the name of the place was and then used it to demarcate all of the hamlets that McArthur could see from that spot. The southern end of Wayoarabirai is a flat plateau between two high ridges. From this spot, one can see all of the ridgetop settlements that are a part of the so-called Maimafu village. The colonial government, then, by treating people and places "according to its schemata" made this category stick (Scott 1998:82). In every patrol report that follows McArthur's first patrol through the area, the name Maimafu is used. During the 1950s it is used along with other names such as Abiagerima, Lioni, and Haununamu, clan names that the patrol officers used as census unit names and as the names of the hamlets in which the clans resided. By the 1960s Maimafu was used as a shorthand place-name that encompasses all of these hamlets.

Today, although the people who live in these hamlets use the name Maimafu for ease of communication when talking to outsiders, they do not use it when talking among themselves. Instead, they use the place-names above; names that mean things in their language and that encode bits of history and ecology: the place of a certain kind of tree, the place of a settlement that was founded after a tragic death in the 1950s, the place of the cool wind. So Maimafu is a place and not a place; it is a place when the world is being made by interactions between its residents and outsiders, or between outsiders, like me, who have some stake in this place's being real.[16] But Maimafu is not a place when the people who live in these rural hamlets make their world for themselves.

The people who live in Maimafu speak a language that was introduced into the anthropological literature by Stephen Wurm in a 1961 article in *Current Anthropology* (Wurm 1961:114–116).[17] Previously, until 1963, they had been classified by the Australian colonial administration as belonging to the Hogabie'-Unabi linguistic group (McArthur 1952/1953:16). After assessing the materials available on Highlands languages, and publishing a synthesis in 1957 (Wurm 1957) — in which the term Gimi did not appear[18] — Wurm traveled to the Highlands to conduct his own fieldwork from May 1958 to January 1959 (Wurm 1960:15). During this trip, he became acquainted with the language that he called Gimi, and he estimated that there were 16,735 people speaking the language (ibid:18). In literature published by the government, anthropologists, missions, and conservationists, *Gimi* has been used to discuss the people who speak it.[19] The name first appears in the colonial patrol record in 1963 with R. W. Cleary's patrol through the Labogai census division (Cleary 1962/1963:10) and is used consistently afterward to describe the languages spoken to the southwest of Mount Michael. Today, there are about 34,000 speakers of Gimi dialects (National Statistical Office 1983; DeLoach and Troolin 1988:14).[20]

Maimafu is located in the Unavi census division of the Lufa District, on the border of the Gimi-speaking area, and people in Maimafu speak a subdialect of Gimi that linguists call Unavisa Gimi.[21] This subdialect is also spoken in Gaiyani, Guasa, Guwasa, Kusi, Labugino, Nauga, Orei, Nobi, Rahakumo, Lauli, Mekino 2, and Ninwabamorai (DeLoach and Troolin 1998:8). It is different from the subdialects spoken in the two other Gimi-speaking villages in the CMWMA. The subdialect in Ubaigubi is Hagavisa Gimi, and in Herowana it is Herowana Gimi (DeLoach and Troolin 1998:8). Summer Institute of Linguistics research shows that the subdialects spoken within the CMWMA (Unavisa, Herowana, and Hagavisa) have a close level of mutual intelligibility. Herowana and Unavisa share a 94 percent similarity, while Hagavisa shares an 85 percent similarly score with the other two.[22] Residents of Maimafu make these and similar linguistic distinctions between the different dialects of Gimi. Although, in general, people from Maimafu see Pawaia peoples and Fore peoples as "more different" than people from settlements where other subdialects of Gimi are spoken, they do occasionally categorize people who speak other subdialects as "speaking a different language." So, like Maimafu, Gimi, a term first introduced by Wurm in 1961 in his analysis and classification of New Guinea Highlands languages (Glick 1967a:372), is a legibility-making tool; a name used to refer to both people and a set of related languages that because of its deployment by those with power, has come to be an object or thing.[23]

INTRODUCING SOCIAL LIFE IN MAIMAFU

The residents of Maimafu practice shifting cultivation on their ancestral lands, and gardening is their main subsistence activity. There is some seasonal variation in subsistence practices, but the climate is wet throughout the year. New gardens are cleared during the drier season, from April or May to August or September. Maimafu is known throughout the region for its abundance of garden foods, notably sweet potatoes, other tubers such as taro, green vegetables, onions, tomatoes, corn, pumpkins, beans, peanuts, pitpit (asparagus; *Saccharum edule*), ginger, and pineapples. In addition, people cultivate several species of bananas, red and white pandanus (*Pandanus conoidus*), sugar cane, papaya, oranges, and avocados. These gardening activities take place both close to the village and farther away, on both ancestral hunting and gardening lands. People also collect "wild" foods from the forest, including fruits, nuts, mushrooms, and other fungi. Coffee, the only significant cash crop, is tended year round, and is harvested from July through October.

Most individuals in Maimafu claim membership in the Seventh-Day Adventist (SDA) Church, and there are, as of 2004, five community church buildings in the village. Saturday church services are conducted by lay ministers and are attended by a small core group of men along with many women and children. The SDA Church forbids fighting, wife beating, premarital sex, lying, smoking, drinking, card playing, nose or ear piercing, and tattooing, as well as the consumption of certain foods. There are religious prohibitions against eating pork, tree kangaroo, cuscus (a marsupial), lizards, and snakes, and there are no pigs raised in Maimafu. Chickens, "lamb flaps," cassowaries, and other birds can be eaten.[24]

While there is no road to Maimafu, the nearest one being in Ubaigubi, the Maimafu community currently maintains a small airstrip, which is serviced several times a week by SDA Aviation (SDAA) and by Mission Aviation Fellowship (MAF). Since the village has no trade stores, all outside products and goods must be ordered through SDAA or purchased by individuals elsewhere and then brought back to the village. Residents maintain both a government school and a village aid post, but during the periods that I have lived in Maimafu, there have rarely been teachers present, and there have almost never been medical supplies in the aid post. Maimafu has two elected village ward councilors who hold seats in the provincial government that meets in Goroka. In the past ten years, there have been three U.S. Peace Corps volunteer couples there.

THE FIGHT

Listen. There is a noise in the distance. It sounds like crying. Wait. It's moving closer. It is crying. It's crying and screaming and wailing. The scene that follows seems surreal. It is set against a backdrop of seemingly endless green. The mountains stretch as far as you can see, and they rise into the blue of the tropical sky in a sharp relief that looks unreal to a television and media-trained eye. All around you there is green: the green of the tropical forest and the green of peanut gardens, sweet potato gardens, banana plants, avocado trees, and coffee gardens. What, when you first arrive at this place, appears to be endless un-touched green, upon a closer look and a conversation, becomes a forested landscape with a history of occupation, use, and myth.

But wait — the crying is moving closer. A crowd of men rushes toward us. Kelego is covered in blood, and yells that his wife is dying. Lasini is chasing him screaming that he is going to kill him. The two men face each other in the middle of a small circle of men. They are both in their late thirties and are dressed in what would be considered rags in the United States. Kelego is wear-ing a worn-out striped bath towel around his neck. A biologist gave it to him, along with a flashlight, a few years ago, and he cherishes that exchange. It is not the material nature of the towel that is most important to him, although it has served him well and he has found many uses for it. Rather, the importance of this towel is the meaning of the exchange with the biologist. That relationship, in Kelego's eyes, shows that he has a tie to conservation and to someone who is somewhere else.

Kelego's dreadlocks shake as he runs. Usually when he runs, it is to the delight of his nieces and nephews. They yell, "lik lik snek bilong em singsing i stap" (his little snakes are dancing), laugh, and wriggle their little bodies imitating his shaking hair. This is a generation of children who speak Unavisa Gimi, the local language, and Melanesian Pidgin. From the beginning of their lives in modern-day Papua New Guinea, they have an advantage that their parents, for the most part, did not. Although English is the official language of the country, Melanesian Pidgin, or Tok Pisin, is the language that one must know in order to travel, conduct small business transactions in cities, and communicate with the many biologists who now come to their lands.

Lasini has a long, dark pointed beard, the kind in pictures of "New Guinea Highlanders" in old travel narratives written by explorers. He is wearing a blue-and-white striped shirt with an Australian rugby team logo on it and a pair of construction overalls. He bought the shirt in a secondhand store in Goroka, the capital of the Eastern Highlands Province. He says he likes it because it has the Australian patch on it and because Australians taught Papua New Guineans how to play rugby. Usually when you see Lasini he is carrying his young son on his shoulders and smiling. He is a man who helps his wife.

Lasini and Kelego each yell that they are the rightful landowners of the ground on which we are standing. They scream that they are in charge of conservation in their village. As the fight escalates, strong young men hold the two older men back as they threaten and strike out at each other with bush knives. The knives gleam in their cold hard steel as the burning midday sun hits them as they lash out at the sky. An Australian photographer grabs his camera and runs toward the fight. He ducks into the circle of men and begins to snap photographs. He moves expertly with the ebb and flow of the gathering crowd. He has done this before. He has taken thousands of photographs of Papua New Guineans and their forests, and he knows how to work a fight. He gets close to Kelego and Lasini, close enough to catch the sweat streaming from their foreheads and to see the lines near their eyes as they scream. It is as if he has become lost in the moment.

An American Peace Corps volunteer, fresh in his second week of village life, jumps into the fray attempting to calm the men. He is twenty-three years old and had never been out of the United States before he came to this place. Joining the Peace Corps was his wife's lifelong dream, and over the years that they dated in college she brought him into her imagination and now it is his dream too. He has a tattoo of a mountain bike on his shoulder. During the fight, some of his imagined glamour of "saving the world" seems to drain from him.

Another Peace Corps volunteer sits motionless with three village women, under the overhang of a house. The women hold her hands and stroke her hair and whisper to her in an attempt to calm her. She is also fresh to village life, straight from the New York fashion industry. This life is her husband's dream, and she came along to remind herself that New York City is not the center of the universe. The women pet her and wipe the tears from her face. The discomfort she feels in their attention and touch registers in her eyes. I will have lunch with her a year later at a bar on the Upper East Side in New York City after she and her husband have quit the Peace Corps. We will talk about this day, and her eyes will shine with tears and her memories of this place and these people. She will say to me in an e-mail two years later, in 2000, "Paige, please, when you go back to Maimafu let the people know that I am sad I left and that I have big regrets." Four years later she will tell me about her medical school classes and ask me if I can help her figure out a way to work PNG into her residency. Over the years I will e-mail with her and see her become someone new, a doctor. She will be profoundly changed by her time in Maimafu, but on this day, sitting under the overhang of the house, she seems to be lost and scared.

Four male Papua New Guinean biologists rush to find male village elders. They have been here before too, perhaps not in their communities, as they are all from cities, but in their jobs as field biologists living for long periods of time in rural Papua New Guinean villages. They know that when the fight stops, there will be compensation to pay and that they will have to be a part of the negotiation. Female Papua New Guinean employees of a conservation organization go inside a house, removing themselves completely from the scene. They know the violence that can occur during a fight. One of the male biologists will tell me three years later that Kelego has died of cancer, even though we paid to send him to the hospital in Goroka. He will tell me this at the end of an e-mail exchange concerning his plans to take the Graduate Record Exam so that he can come to the United States for graduate school. I think of Kelego and his towel every time I see dreadlocks or a shop with watches in it. (He wore a watch that did not work for several years but was loath to give it up because it had been a gift from a biologist.)

A group of American and Australian biologists and conservation practitioners look on, and one can be heard to say, "welcome to conservation in Papua New Guinea." At the time that I hear this statement, I will become annoyed with her. I'll write it off as a sarcastic portrayal of Papua New Guineans out of some sort of neocolonial racism. In 2003 when I am in Maimafu with students from the University of PNG, we will witness a significant argument over our hunting study and who will derive benefits from our visit to Maimafu, and I will think about the person who made this statement. I will see her in a new light, not as a neocolonizer but as a person trying to do a job and constantly being faced with an argument or a fight that will, while working to level and stabilize local social relations, stop work for days on end and endanger her Papua New Guinean field staff.

The day of the fight, the biologists and conservation practitioners gather under a bright blue tent that was constructed for their visit. The tent is close to the village airstrip. Before all the visitors came, village leaders met and decided that it would be best for them to hold their meetings away from the airstrip at a neighboring ridgetop hamlet. The village men decided that the families living near the airstrip had derived too much from the conservation-as-development project that is currently being implemented in their area, and that it was time to spread the benefits to others in the community. But when the conservation organization employees got off the plane and heard the village plans for the meetings, they argued that the other ridgetop was "too far to walk to." So, the meeting tent was built at the airstrip.

Behind this scene, away from the circle of men and the onlookers, a small seemingly frail woman named Henano stumbles toward Lasini's house. Lasini's wife sees her and runs to help her. Other women quickly gather. Henano, Kelego's wife, has been hit in the head with a bush knife. There is blood running down her face and she is holding her scalp. Her blue-and-white dress, her best dress, her church dress, is covered in dark red blood. Her eyes are glassy, and she is no longer screaming. She seems quite calm.

Quickly and silently, the group of women starts to work on Henano's injury. Some go for water to wash the wound, while others go into the house to get rags. An American woman with some first-aid training runs to get her medical kit. When she returns, she washes the wound and pours peroxide and other medicines on it. Henano is in shock. She cannot speak. Her eyes are open wide, and her breathing is labored and punctuated by gasps for air. She does not cry. She picks up her bag, reaches inside, and pulls out a netlike string bag made of natural fibers and dyes, called a *bilum* in Melanesian Pidgin, that she has been working on for weeks. It is beautiful, with rich earth-tone colors adorning the strings. Silently she begins to "work" her bilum, her hands moving rhythmically in a motion that is ancient and profoundly feminine. Three years later, I will take a picture of her hands as she works and hang the photo on the wall in my office.

2. Henano (woman injured in knife fight).

Four years later after the death of Kelego, I will go see Henano at her house. I'll take dried beans, two nice new dresses for her to wear to church, vitamins, a copy of the photograph of her hands, and pictures of Kelego. We will reminisce about him, and she will tell me that I am their daughter and that it is good that I've come and brought her things. Then she will yell at me for not learning the Gimi language fast enough.

Close by, years earlier, the fight rages on. Now both Kelego's and Lasini's male relatives have joined in, and the crowd is ebbing and flowing with insults, threats, and accusations. Bush knives are being waved and bows and arrows pointed. The men sweat and scream, alternating between their language and Melanesian Pidgin—the latter so the white audience can "know the fight." Kelego is accused of hoarding the benefits from the conservation project and the outside visitors for himself and his family. Lasini is accused of not working for conservation and therefore not being entitled to any benefits. People are coming from all around to see the trouble. Shouts ring out over the ridgetops in a series of sounds that catch the wind and fly over the mountains. Young men can be seen running from the ridgetop to the north, their bodies moving swiftly down the mountain. They cross the river and reach the fight area. Women come behind more slowly, carrying huge bags full of sweet potatoes, children, and shovels.

The women sit around the edge of the fight now, whispering and giving commentary on the fight and its participants. Their words are biting and brilliant, sometimes hilarious. As the women make their way toward the fight, they all stop to see Henano. They touch her face and say Eetau (mother) as they pass. They call her this since she is old and wise and well liked. They have seen this scene before too. Many of them will tell me later that while it is always entertaining to see a fight, it just means that they have more work to do later in the day. They will also say that the men will be occupied with working out the compensation issues and will therefore not be able or willing to help their wives in the gardens that afternoon.

During all of this I am watching and listening. I am doing what it is that I came here, to the Lufa District of the Eastern Highlands Province in Papua New Guinea, to do. I am a participant who is observing the life around and within me. Early this very morning, I sat quietly with Henano under an avocado tree. She is one of my many village "mothers" and was concerned when she saw me sitting alone. She came upon me as she emerged from a garden in fallow. I was sitting trying to pull myself together, to be professional and document the conservation meeting that was taking place in Maimafu.

After having lived for almost a year in Maimafu, and having spent well over a year studying the consequences of a transnational environmental conservation project, I was having a moment of overload. All I wanted was to not be in a rural village in PNG or perhaps even to be at home and speaking English. At the least, I wanted my feet to be clean and for some thought in my mind that did not have to do with Maimafu or ICAD projects. Immersion in the life of a rural village with little communication with my own life at home was, on some days, living a dream that I had had since childhood. On other days, it was like being dead and floating within my own memories of family and friends, of home.

Henano, my mother, after sharing her sweet potato with me, had stroked my hair, and wiped the dirt off of my forehead. She had said that I would be fine because "Lave haputa bayaha biliama namolelena hanitali" (Where there is a woman, there is magic). When Henano spoke those words to me, I laughed. Before I came to know her, hearing this speech might have fit the image that I had in my head as a child of the wisdom of indigenousness, an image no doubt in some part produced by the television commercial from the 1970s in which a native North American man shed a tear over the trash generated by consumption in the United States. But instead of letting the wisdom of her words wash over me, I laughed. At first it was a little giggle pushing through my throat. Then it was a well of laughter so deep and full that I had to sit down again. You see, "Where there is a woman, there is magic" is the first sentence in a book about women in South Carolina. It is not some ancient and sacred bit of women's knowledge from Maimafu; it is a saying from my home, the American South. I will find out four years later that the book was written by one of the most famous graduates of the college where I teach. Multiple connections between time and space, between people and place, converge to create moments documented by ethnography. There is no ethnographic present; time slips and ruptures to make life. The present grows out of the past, but the past is remembered depending upon present experiences and future expectations.[25]

The book, *Sassafras, Cypress and Indigo,* a novel about the experiences of African American women, by Ntozake Shange, was left in the village by past Peace Corps volunteers. One day a few weeks earlier, my research assistant Esta had finished reading the book, having read everything else in the village written in English and now turning to the American literature left by the volunteers. We had a conversation about it with a group of village women. Henano had been in that group.

Esta had finished reading the book late one night, and the next day she came to the garden of a woman named Dabi to find me and return it. I was spending the day with Dabi, her daughter Patricia, her husband's aunt, and Henano, who is Dabi's husband's first cousin's wife. Esta found us sitting in the shade working on our string bags while eating a pineapple. She sat down, handed me the book, and in English told me that she had loved it but that she had some questions about it. Patricia asked, "What is the book about?" in Melanesian Pidgin. We then spent a couple of hours telling the story and discussing the differences between the lives of African American women in the American South and women in rural Papua New Guinea.

When Esta translated the first sentence of the book "Where there is a woman, there is magic" into Unavisa Gimi, Henano, who is a woman widely suspected of knowing much about sorcery in a society where women are not supposed to practice magic, laughed. She said, "Where there is a woman, there is magic. . . . No, where there is a woman, there is work. . . . Where there is a woman, there is a child. . . . Where there is a woman, there is a . . . sweet potato." We then all joined in: "Where there is a woman, there is a bush knife," "Where there is a woman, there is a lazy man," "Where there is woman, there is . . ." Ultimately, the conversation grew hilarious and graphic and in the days afterward, we all greeted each other with a variation on the translation. "*Mahalora* (good morning), where there is a woman there is a pile of clothing to be washed!"

On the morning before the fight, Henano's use of our shared joke made me laugh, reminding me that I did not really want to leave Maimafu yet. It also reminded me of the impact that a simple action can have. The Peace Corps volunteers left that book in their house when they left the village. Perhaps they left it for an imagined future Peace Corps couple to read, or perhaps they left it because they were traveling light and did not have room for it. Reading the book opened the world of African American experiences in the American South to Esta and others. Dabi and Henano did not know that there were "black women" in the United States until our conversation about the book. The discussion about where those women came from opened what was to be a long and ongoing conversation in the last months of my fieldwork about the African diaspora, a conversation complete with a torn and dirty map of the world and late-night discussions around fires between very old men about how Europeans got so much power. How do Europeans have the power to change other people's lives?[26]

The everydayness of village life had been shattered a few days before the fight, when about twenty people associated with the RCF, the WCS, and the BCN descended upon the village for their annual meeting. They arrived en mass with cartons of trade-store food, tents, and equipment. Along with the RCF's staff and associates came individuals from three other villages—Haia, Herowana, and Ubaigubi—also within the boundaries of the CMWMA.

The fight started when Kelego got a conservation organization identification card from a man that lives in another village. The card became a symbol of status. He took the card around with him that morning, saying "I am the boss of conservation now. This card means you have to listen to me and do what I say." Eventually, Lasini began to mimic and make fun of Kelego, and a crowd gathered. Kelego became angry. He drew his bush knife and began to cut down *tanget* plants (*Cordyline terminalis*) around a conservation organization building.[27] He did this to show that he owned that land. These plants are a traditional marker of boundaries and sacred areas and they delineate land claims. Lasini grabbed his hand and told him to stop. Henano then came from the sidelines and tried to pull Lasini off of her husband. Her injury occurred as the fight escalated.

The morning of the fight, my anthropological authority had been challenged. This challenge caused a part of the unhappiness I was feeling when I sat down with Henano to share her sweet potato. The challenge topped my long-standing frustration of trying to make recommendations to project managers about how to better address the needs and development desires of villagers. Although none of the funding for my research had come from conservation organizations, many conservation practitioners saw my role as providing them with data about "the Gimi," as translating Gimi social life for them so they could better manage them, and as providing useful recommendations for their project so it could be counted as a success. This challenge also rearticulated within me the anthropological problem of having two often diametrically opposed sets of "informants." Anthropologists often become political and social advocates for the people they work with. Conducting a research project in which my informants, friends, and confidants were both residents of Maimafu and people associated with the creation of and implementation of the CMWMA was a profound challenge.

That morning also seemed, at the time, to be the culmination of a year of hearing some conservation practitioners say, "What right do you have to tell us how we should be doing this?"; "Social science is not a real science so it has no place in conservation"; "What do you know? You are only a white woman; you don't know about my Papua New Guinean culture"; "No one else is trying to help these people, so what if we make a few mistakes"; and, the most upsetting, "If you say anything bad about our project we can make it so you can't ever come back to Maimafu again."

After the fight, an expatriate biologist, who had become a good friend during the course of my fieldwork, asked me, "So, what was that all about?" and then, before I could begin my answer, he added, "fifty words or less, OK?" His question and his description of how he wanted the information presented are instructive. The fight was "about" many things. It touched on property rights and relations, local and regional social relations. Included also were history, ideas about progress and development, the desire for status, local and regional development, and women's worth in the community. The fight was also "about" social impacts, both local and regional, of the actions and practices of conservation and development over the past thirty years, incorporating multiple understandings of how one appropriately reciprocates in social relationships.

THE ANTHROPOLOGY OF CONSERVATION-AS-DEVELOPMENT

I came to be interested in conservation in PNG through an attempt to rethink the relationship between the environment and society, in terms of the recent proliferation of biodiversity conservation interventions that purport to bring development to rural peoples living in highly biologically diverse areas. Reading the then-emergent literature on political ecology inspired this.[28] The methods and theories of political ecology have become the refractors through which many anthropologists now approach questions concerning relations between people and nature. While similar to political economy with its focus on power (Bates and Lees 1996:9), political ecology is far more focused on the role of discourse (Adger, et al. 2001; Brosius 1999a:277; Escobar 1998:54). With political ecology, we see local-global articulations that were not visible with earlier anthropological approaches to environmental issues, and we see capital's demand for both cheap labor and cheap natural resources (Biersack 1999:10; Harvey 1996). Political ecology examines and elucidates the ways in which multiscaled political and economic processes affect people living in rural and or biologically diverse areas, and the discipline takes seriously the production of nature (Katz 1995; N. Smith 1990). Biersack argues that it can be "understood as a merger of political economy with cultural studies" (Biersack 1999: 10). This set of theories lends itself to explanation, but in my mind its focus on theory often obscures the importance of ethnography in anthropological analysis. The challenge to anthropologists today is to maintain the multiscaled focus of political ecology but understand that there is agency at or within each scale and do ethnographic research that is multiscaled and multisited so that we can have a richer understanding of transnational processes.

Biodiversity conservation interventions are now the intellectual and material terrain through which the practices of economic development are often carried out. They engage transnational movements of ideologies and discourses, and serve as sites for the cross-cultural contact between variously situated sets of actors. Integrated conservation and development projects inextricably tie conservation to development, and the environment to the market economy (Escobar 1999; Sachs 1993).

Environmental interventions in PNG and elsewhere are not only acts of conservation, but also complex processes of social engineering and development where "fundamental" notions of self, social relations, and the environment are engaged (Robbins 1995:221). Theoretical and ethnographic work in political ecology has shown us that biodiversity conservation interventions generally engage transnational movements of ideas, capital, and people with culturally specific locales (Escobar 1999; Peluso 1993). It has also demonstrated that in particular, they serve as sites where social, environmental, and material relations can be examined within larger political-economic and historical contexts (Escobar 1998, 1999; Peluso 1992, 1993).[29]

Many of the recent analyses of development within anthropology and the social sciences more generally have acknowledged the "greening" of development (Sachs 1993). The discourses and practices of development have been analyzed and theorized by anthropologists since the 1960s (see J. W. Bennett 1988; Caulfield 1969; Gunder Frank 2000; Wallerstein 1974). Recent treatments of development (Escobar 1995; Ferguson 1994; Hodgson 1995, 2001; Pigg 1992) have been influenced by anthropological analyses of culture, power, history, and transnationalism (Appadurai 1991; Dirks, Eley, and Ortner 1994; Friedman 1990, 1994; Gupta 1992). Theories of transnational processes and globalization have been particularly influential (see Featherstone 1990a, 1990b; Gupta and Ferguson 1992; Kearney 1995; Rouse 1995). The proliferation of the motifs of sustainability, as well as climate and atmospheric changes, within the development discourse has prompted development and conservation practitioners to rework the practices and discourses of development appropriately (Elkins 1993; Sachs 1993; Worster 1993). Social scientists have responded with a proliferation of critical analyses of conservation-as-development projects.[30] Underexplored in these analyses are the multiple cross-cultural understandings of and productions of environment and society through the discourses and practices of conservation and development, and the historical circumstances in which these productions came about. Nevertheless, the use of methods and theories associated with cultural anthropology to examine conservation and environmentalism grows out of the longtime engagement of anthropologists with environmental issues (Brosius 1999a, 1999b; Kottak1999, Moran 1979, Orlove 1980).

This book builds on this tradition and draws from other recent anthropological work on transnational processes and the critical analysis of development (Escobar 1995; Ferguson 1994, Tsing 1993). In addition, following Neil Smith (1990, 1996a), this analysis takes nature, place, and space as social products, and their production is seen as intimately tied to the production of social difference.

In addition to documenting "local" responses to conservation, the environment, and development, I also document and analyze the ideas and practices of the project's American, Australian, and European participants (see Brosius 1999a; Dove 1993; Peluso 1992, 1993; 1995; Schroeder 1993, 1995). Anthropologists and conservation practitioners who rely on analyses of conservation and development projects that do not recognize the multiple agencies and ideologies of differently positioned actors only see part of the complex story of environmental conservation in sites where there is much biological diversity.

CHAPTER 2

Making Crater Mountain

In 2003, Professor Leonard Glick, the first anthropologist to work with Gimi speakers, sent me a package. In it, there were reprints, unpublished papers, and maps. One of the maps, from 24 November 1953, is a carbon copy of the hand-drafted "Base Compilation New Guinea and Papua Map" issued by the National Mapping Section of Australia's Department of the Interior. Its scale is 1:600,000, and in the bottom right-hand corner it reads: "Names Shown on this Map Approved for Official Use." The space on the map between Crater Mountain and Mount Karimui is virtually empty. There are a few rivers, nameless, flowing between the two named points on the landscape, but there are no place-names at all.

How is it that "Crater Mountain" and "the Crater Mountain Wildlife Management Area" came into being? I want to argue that it was through spatial practice, representations of space, and representational spaces; thus, through the production of space (Lefebvre 1991:33). These mental, material, and social practices, which Lefebvre characterizes as experience, perception, and imagination (Harvey 1990:219), are historical, discursive, ideological, legislative, and imaginative. Space comes to be constituted, produced, and made, through a process that is like a balloon being blown up.[1] It starts from an idea (mental), a location (material), or a relationship between people (social) and radiates out, all the while drawing in particles from similar processes elsewhere; hence, "The production of space examines how new systems (actual or imagined) of land use, transport and communications, territorial organization, etc. are produced, and how new modes of representation (e.g. information technology, computerized mapping, or design) arise" (Harvey 1990:222). Perhaps oversimplifying, what I mean to say is that nothing *is*, but that everything *comes to be*. Then, once brought into the world, space is always in process of becoming something else and contributing to the production of other spaces, objects, and subjects.

Lefebvre argues that once a space is produced, it "serves as a tool of thought and of action; that in addition to being a means of production it is also a means of control, and hence domination, of power, yet that, as such, it escapes in part from those who would make use of it" (1991:26). So once the product is out there, it comes to be something in and of itself that works to produce more space, place, people, society, environment, and so on; it comes to take part in the process of production.

Crater Mountain, Maimafu, and the other spatial productions in this book are not a given, not locations that came into being with ecology and evolution, but rather, they are produced by the social and material relations between peoples. Part of my goal with the present work is to "read" these spaces (Lefebvre 1991:8–9). In New Guinea, land comes into being; it is produced through the physical, psychological, and material relations that people bring to it (Lefebvre 1991). For Gimi, land is made by past, present, and future social relations; by mythology, which is both the past and the imaginary; use (so productive meaningful actions); ideas about the future (so the imagined frontier, the space beyond); and sensorial experiences (Feld 1996).[2] Crater Mountain has also come into being because of the scientific research conducted around it. Since 1987, when ecologists began working on land held by Pawaia peoples, numerous researchers have worked within the Wildlife Management Area. In their publications, these scientists have discursively located their field sites near Crater Mountain and within the Crater Mountain Wildlife Management Area (CMWMA), hence contributing to this production.[3]

Conventional concepts of space assumed it to be a static field in which activities took place and actors existed but which itself was not made or altered by social action. Lefebvre (1991), and others demonstrated that the nature of space itself was constitutive of those actors and actions. Hence, space has come to be seen as a process. In understanding space as a process, we must take into account that it is constituted within the same processes that shape and define "the environment" and "nature" (Harvey 1996:263). Thus, nature is produced right along with space (Smith 1990). In his "production of nature" thesis, N. Smith (1996a:50) attempts to move away from nature as fetishized or as seen as dominated by humans, to focus on the social relationships producing nature and the social relationships we have with nature. The key to the production of nature argument is that it brings together sociocultural constructions of nature with material productions of nature. This sort of analysis allows for a political theory of nature that expresses

> the inevitability and creativity of the social relationship with nature; the very real project of domination embodied in the capitalist mode of production; the differentiate relationship with nature according to gender, class, race, sexual preference; the implausibility of an autonomous nature; and a strong response to the almost instinctive romanticism which pervades most treatments of nature in bourgeois and patriarchal society. If we are to take seriously the centrality of labor in the relationship with nature then we need to begin to think in terms of the social production of nature. (N. Smith 1996a:50)

Thinking about the environment, which Smith calls nature, and the relationships between the environment and society as a process of production, allows us to think about the relationship between how we make ourselves and how we make our world (Harvey 1996:131). It allows us to see the shared mechanisms of the production of environment, selves, society, and space.

For Smith, the emergence of industrial capitalism is the thing that structures contemporary Western conceptualizations of the environment, and capitalism has even co-opted older understandings of nature for its purposes (Smith 1990:1). While there have historically been many ways of understanding nature, these conceptualizations are organized into a dualism today (ibid.:2). Tracing this dualism to Immanuel Kant, Smith shows that nature is seen as external, as outside the social, and as universal or internal, as what is inside us. The nature/culture dichotomy is derived from this dualism in Kant's thinking and is cemented as the bourgeois way of knowing and being in nature (Smith 1990:3).

In addition to its dualistic vision of nature and the natural, the capitalist way of seeing nature is also tied to the idea of the domination of nature by humans. Tracing this line of thought back to Francis Bacon, Smith argues that dominating or mastering nature was seen historically as a way to balance the relationship between nature and culture (Smith 1990:3). The mastery of nature was seen as a means of social control and as the impetus for scientific research (ibid.:4). External nature became the object of inquiry for the hard sciences and the scientific method began to abstract from the lived experience of social life to produce scientific laws (ibid.:4). Internal nature became the object of inquiry for the social sciences. But, although this distinction was adhered to discursively, as Donna Haraway shows, the external/internal dualism was not a reality in the ways that scientific theories really got produced or in the ways that the objects of study were imagined by scientists (1991:8).

The key for Smith and Haraway is that material nature, and its discursive production vis-à-vis scientific inquiry, is a social product. As a concept—wilderness, for example[4]—it is historically situated and constituted and always has a "clear social and political function" (Smith 1990:15). Internal and external natures are taken to be real, as fixed, as separate from the social. When this happens, they are used to justify domination of people and places. Ideologies are built on conceptualizations of nature in which nature is fetishized and the social relations that have gone into its production (discursive and material) are made invisible. Ideologically, under capitalism, nature has been seen as external and hostile and therefore as something out there in need of taming or mastery. This domination has become to be seen as natural. In addition, and this is where the production of social difference merges with the production of nature,

> The overriding function of the universal (internal) conception today is to invest certain social behaviors with the status of natural events by which is meant that these behaviors and characteristics are normal, God-given, unchangeable. Competition, profit, war, private property, sexism, heterosexism, racism, the existence of haves and have nots or of "chiefs and Indians"—the list is endless—are all deemed natural. Nature, not human history is made responsible. (Smith 1990:15)

So difference is seen as natural, and the social relations that have gone into nature are not seen at all.

In addition, place—like space, time, nature, and culture—is a social construct (Harvey 1996:293). Places are points on a map that are the "locus" of particular practices, social relations, and power relations. They represent such abstractions as institutional forms, discourses, imaginaries, sensorial experiences, and the outcomes of particular histories (Harvey 1996:294). I take *place* to be the fixing of a process in time and space, but not necessarily an enduring one.[5] This is perfectly illustrated by in *Creek Country* (Ethridge 2003). In it Robbie Ethridge shows how the Creek Indians' world—the social and political, the economic and ecological—came into being and then passed out of being.

She shows the struggle involved in the creation of a "middle ground" (White 1991) between whites and Indians, and then the slipping away of that middle ground, when Creek land became the desired location for the investment of surplus capital. Ethridge's book is one of the few that shows the history of a place both coming into being and ending. Neil Smith (1990) and David Harvey (1990, 1996) theorize this process through analyses of the circulation of surplus capital and the annihilation of space through time (Marx 1973:524), but Ethridge demonstrates how it takes place. We see capital "drive beyond every spatial barrier" because production has come to depend on exchange (ibid.). Exchange value, circulation, communication, transportation, and new frontiers for capital become key to the continuation of the system (ibid.).

G. Gillison has argued that Gimi have no nature and no culture; by this she means that the categories of nature and culture as derived from the Western philosophical and historical traditions do not exist as social categories for Gimi (Gillison 1980). But for the biologists and the conservation activists and practitioners that come to Crater Mountain, these categories do exist. They shape the ways that they see the landscape and Gimi. Given this, How should we understand the production of nature at Crater Mountain and within the CMWMA? Are Gimi producing a landscape in one way and the biologists in another given their histories and subjectivity? Is there a hybrid production of nature going on at Crater Mountain? Is the CMWMA a site where Gimi ways of knowing and being in the world are coming into contact with other ways of knowing and being in the world and the interactions producing a new kind of place? Nature now exists at Crater Mountain as does culture. Both nature and culture have, to use Eric Wolf's phrase (1982:3) become "things" (Gupta and Ferguson 2001:2).

In all of these examinations of how space is produced, but especially in Harvey (1990) and N. Smith (1990), dialectical process between space, place, time, environment, and the social are theorized. But the question is, How do we get at this ethnographically? How do we demonstrate these processes at work? Arturo Escobar argues that by focusing on specificity of places (natures, cultures, economies, practices), we will notice and track the kinds of articulations between these specifics of daily social lives and the movements of modernity and capital (2001:141), and he calls for a kind of ethnography that shows the production of place by capitalism and global forces and the sensorial production of place described by Steven Feld and Keith Basso (1996). And Akhil Gupta and James Ferguson (2001:4) argue that the processes by which places get made and "cultures" get tied to places are important topics for anthropological research. My argument is that the CMWMA is a spatial production in which "Crater Mountain," "Maimafu," and "the Gimi" have been made and folded into each other, through a conservation-as-development project that was based on the integrated conservation-and-development (ICAD) model.

INTEGRATED CONSERVATION AND DEVELOPMENT PROJECTS

The production of the global scale in environmental discourse and practice has silenced, or in extreme cases erased, other scales of analysis and the voices of certain social groups. This process has taken place even with the discursive production of "local people" and "local participation" in conservation rhetoric (Brosius, Tsing, and Zerner 1998). The urgency of the global environmental crisis has given conservation activists and practitioners a sort of moral high ground to stand on when making decisions about local peoples and the global environment. This series of practices and rhetorics has come about in the past two decades and has created new kinds of communities and new zones of transnational contact. One of these zones of contact is the Integrated Conservation and Development Project (ICDP). With ICDPs, conservation is supposedly enhanced or achieved in highly biologically diverse areas by tying it to small-scale economic development projects intended to benefit local landholders.

From the turn of the century through the two decades after World War II, national parks and wildlife reserves were the methods used by conservation practitioners in their efforts to conserve biodiversity (Oates 1999:45). These interventions were based on models derived from conservation interventions in the United States dating from the turn of the century (Hecht and Cockburn 1990). John Oates (1999) argues that beginning in the 1960s, there was a subtle shift in conservation circles concerning the *value* of nature (ibid.). While national parks and wildlife reserves were based on the conservation of nature because of an ideology of *intrinsic value* in nature, the social and environmental politics surrounding pollution, nuclear wastes, pesticides, and large dam and mining projects in the 1960s shifted the focus to an ideology in which the value of nature was seen as deeply connected to human life and well-being (Oates 1999:45).[6] Oates goes on to lay out a succinct summary of the history of the bureaucracy of conservation (ibid.:46–58). In doing so, he demonstrates the powerful roles certain individuals had in the creation of the modern-day conservation bureaucracy and the ways in which the push to constantly raise capital has altered the landscape of conservation over the past fifty years. Oates's argument is that conservation "fell in love with development" in part due to the social politics of the 1960s but mostly due to the rapacious desire for more money and the bureaucracy that grew up around conservation to feed that desire. This bureaucracy overlapped with the development bureaucracy that was also burgeoning in the post–World War II era (Escobar 1995).

Wolfgang Sachs (1993) argues that the post–World War II policy landscape was one in which the ideas of "progress" embedded in the notion of economic development became inextricably tied to the environment. While Sachs's argument is less clearly about shifts in ideologies regarding the value of nature and more about shifts in the ways economic growth came to be justified as the goal for societies (ibid.:5), he links the focus on continued growth with a focus on the desire for long-term availability of natural resources (ibid.:9). Nature became valuable because it was the raw material for growth, and growth came to be articulated as "development."

The transportation of American conservation practices abroad came under public international scrutiny in the early 1980s — directly after a series of meetings between the United Nations Environment Programme (UNEP) and the International Union for the Conservation of Nature and Natural Resources (IUCN) that had been begun in 1972 at the United Nations Conference on the Human Environment (Oates 1999:47). Conservation activists and practitioners argued that these projects were not successful, because the "local people" living on the edges of the protected areas did not recognize their boundaries while conducting their traditional subsistence practices (Wells, Brandon, and Hannah 1992:ix). With this, discourses concerning "local people" and their impact on biological diversity became popular in conservation rhetoric.

One of the responses to this emerging critical analysis of international environmental conservation projects was the development of the ICDP. The concept, although it existed in practice earlier (Bonner 1993:253–270), was discussed widely after a January 1992 World Bank publication that began the production of discourse depicting local people as excluded from protected areas and thus as posing a threat to those areas in the bureaucratic literature (Wells, Brandon, and Hannah 1992; Brown and Wyckoff-Baird 1992).[7]

Conservation publications argued that projects that combined conservation with income-generation projects aimed at "local people" represented the "vanguard" in conservation practice and that conservation should, whenever possible, be linked to economic development (Brandon and Wells 1992:557). Those who advocated that indigenous peoples work in conservation circles began to argue that "top-down" approaches to conservation were not working and that conservation organizations should foster community participation within conservation projects (Brosius n.d.:3; see also Borrini-Feyeraband 1996).

The recognition of ICDPs by conservation practitioners as a "new" way of doing conservation became entrenched in the conservation and development bureaucracy when the World Bank, U.S. Agency for International Development (USAID), and World Wildlife Fund (WWF) funded a team to study twenty-three conservation projects whose practitioners argued that their goal was to promote social and economic development around protected areas (Brandon and Wells 1992; Wells, Brandon, and Hannah 1992). This supposedly new approach was thought to be both cutting-edge conservation practice and socially just political practice. But early on in the history of ICDPs, the complexity of rural development was recognized, and it was made clear that the end goal of biodiversity conservation could not be thwarted by the social or development needs of rural peoples (Wells, Brandon, and Hannah 1992:x).

Beginning when various international conservation agencies began to rely on ICDPs as a method for conservation, local development was meant to take a backseat to the conservation of biodiversity and the strengthening of protected areas. Providing economic development options for local people was a means toward the end of biodiversity conservation and not an end in itself. Richard Schroeder (1995:326) has called this reliance by environmentalists on "positive economic incentives to promote sound land use practices" the "commodity road to stabilization" and critiqued the use of capital-intensive strategies as a tool for environmental preservation or stabilization.

The first review of ICDPs identified a number of areas in which conservationists were attempting to link conservation to economic benefit.[8] These included "natural resource management outside protected areas," "community social services," "nature tourism," "road construction for market access," and "direct employment generation" (Wells, Brandon, and Hannah 1992:x).

Despite some success in generating income and access to services for rural peoples, the early analysis was that "in virtually all of the projects, the critical linkage between development and conservation is either missing or obscure" (Wells, Brandon, and Hannah 1992:xi). From the beginning, it was recognized that making a link between conservation and development through the market and through the further introduction of capitalist institutions into village life was almost impossible. Yet, this method for the design and implementation of conservation projects was used worldwide. These strategies have included policies concerned with extractive reserves, ecotourism, nontimber forest products, green marketing, and adventure tourism.

The rationale for this interest in ICDPs, even when the existing data demonstrated their problems, was that biological diversity was suffering from human actions, and that the disenfranchised local communities who were policed out of these protected areas were a threat to the biodiversity on their lands.[9] Conservationists argued that "communities next to protected area boundaries frequently bear substantial costs — as a result of lost access — while receiving little in return" (Wells, Brandon, and Hannah 1992:2). They also argued that these "costs," coupled with population pressure and "unsustainable land use practices outside protected areas," cause local people to turn to "illegal and destructive encroachment" (ibid.) They concluded that if local economic needs were met by development initiatives, local people would not be such a threat to biodiversity conservation (Brandon and Wells 1992; Wells, Brandon, and Hannah 1992).

These projects were at their base about changing the actions and practices of local people in order to meet the end goal of conservation. They were about the integration of local peoples into commodity-based systems of production as a strategy for the conservation of biological diversity. Local historic subsistence practices were curtailed or were to be curtailed so that the local people, who through these practices were a threat to biodiversity, could engage in economic and subsistence practices sanctioned by conservation biologists and development practitioners as environmentally appropriate. In lieu of a language of exclusion, like the language used in previous models for conservation, the conservation rhetoric now incorporated development discourses as the central method for achieving biodiversity conservation globally.[10]

Peter Wilshusen et al. (2002), Steven Brechin et al. (2002), and Peter Brosius (n.d.) all argue that we are now experiencing a kind of backlash against CBC and ICDPs. In the late 1990s, Brosius, Anna L. Tsing, and Charles Zerner (1998) began to raise questions about the nature of the usage of the term *community* in these projects, among other critiques. From a similar critical perspective in the social sciences, Jessie Ribot (1999, 2000) raised questions about the legality of projects and the politics of practitioner understandings of their legality. Schroeder (1999), in addition to his aforementioned critiques of the commodity focus of the projects, raised questions about access and rights, and Jill Belsky (1999) raised questions about accountability in projects. In policy circles Michael Wells et al. (1999) and P. Larson, M. Freudenberger, and B. Wyckoff-Baird (1997) published books evaluating the effectiveness of these projects in terms of con-servation — although it was acknowledged that effectiveness is difficult to mea-sure, given that many of the projects had no baseline ecological data before their inception. Others in policy circles published manuals on how to evaluate and "monitor" CBC projects (Margoluis and Salafsky 1998; Salafsky and Margoluis 1999).[11] Natural scientists began to critique community-based approaches in the late 1990s as well. John Oates (1999) and John Terborgh (1999) both level devastating critiques concerning the "failures" of the approach.[12] I do not wish to jump on the critique-of-CBC bandwagon. Rather, I wish to call into question the ideology that using neoliberal market-based development strategies either conserves or develops rural or out-of-the-way places. I do, however, drawing on Harvey (1990:204), wish to point out that the idea of community works to disguise differential abilities to access power. When taken as a real social group-ing, and not an artifact of a series of spatiotemporal processes, "communities" can come to be seen as commensurable. By this, I mean the language of "stake-holders" can emerge, and conservation biologists, landowners, and the mining company, can all be seen as communities with similar positions in social nego-tiations. When seen as a kind of social conglomeration produced in space over time, however, a community is a more complex social configuration. So, for instance, the community around a gold mine might consist of local people, environmental activists, and mining company officials (Golub 2005). Under-standing community in this way allows us to see the intersubjective processes by which communities come into being across spaces and through time. Thus, the community around Crater Mountain becomes less about "the Gimi" or "the Pawaia" as opposed to "the conservation practitioners" and more about a shared social process and product.

THE CRATER MOUNTAIN WILDLIFE MANAGEMENT AREA

The CMWMA is the product of a series of local, national, and transnational exchanges between individuals and institutions. While the history of the project will be discussed fully in following chapters, in this section I will offer a brief introduction to the history and to the physical area encompassed by the project. The project began in the late 1970s with the work of David Gillison, who has worked tirelessly to get transnational conservation organizations interested in conserving the birds of paradise living in forests located near Ubaigubi, Herowana, Maimafu, and Haia. The land held by families in these four villages crosses the boundaries of the Eastern Highlands Province, the Gulf Province, and the Chimbu Province. The CMWMA was officially established in 1994 (A. Johnson 1997:397). In October of that year, the Papua New Guinea Department of Environment and Conservation (DEC) declared it a national Wildlife Management Area under the Faunal (Protection and Control) Act of 1976. The act establishes the mechanisms by which "Wildlife Management Areas, Sanctuaries, and Protected Areas" are set up and maintained. It provides for a set of formal institutionalized mechanisms to regulate wildlife harvesting, possession, and trade in these areas, and comes under the umbrella of the Fourth Directive Principle of the National Constitution, which states: "We declare our Fourth Goal to be for Papua New Guinea's natural resources and environment to be conserved and used for the collective benefit of us all, and be replenished for the benefit of future generations" (PNG National Constitution 1975, section four, Natural Resources and Environment).

For an area to be "gazetted," or officially made a part a national Wildlife Management Area, the "customary landowners" must provide the DEC with a "legal description of the boundaries of their area to be gazatted," a list of "clan leaders who will sit on the local Wildlife Management Committees," and a list of conservation rules or laws that will be used to govern the WMA (Johnson 2000:5; PNG National Constitution 1975). Since the majority of people living around Crater Mountain had, at the time of the CMWMA's inception, little knowledge of the mechanisms by which the national laws work, a Wildlife Conservation Society (WCS) employee, Jamie James, went to the area to help people establish the boundaries and determine who would sit on the legally mandated Wildlife Management Committees (A. Johnson 1997:399). He was the first, and only, expatriate "field coordinator" in the WMA, beginning his work in 1993, though U.S. Peace Corps volunteers were "utilized" by the project beginning in 1990 (ibid.).

Crater Mountain and the landscape surrounding it are seen by those in conservation fields as biologically significant for three main reasons. First, it is seen as forested with "primary forest," that is, highly biologically diverse in terms of floral and faunal species. Second, because the area encompassed by the WMA is large enough to cover the landscape between lowland rain forest on the Purari River and montane cloud forest on Crater Mountain (A. Johnson 1997:394), the CMWMA is seen as constituting "a natural resource of national and global importance" (ibid.:394). And third, even outside its forested areas, it has very high species diversity.

The Research and Conservation Foundation of Papua New Guinea (RCF), a nongovernmental environmental conservation organization officially incorporated in 1986 with the help of the Wildlife Conservation Society and the PNG Department of Environment and Conservation, now administers the Crater Mountain project. The RCF was founded by David Gillison because of his concern over the "declining populations" of birds of paradise in the forests near Crater Mountain. The stated goals of the RCF with regard to the CMWMA during the period of my initial research fell directly in line with the stated goals of ICDPs in general (RCF/WCS 1995:4–6).[13] The RCF attempted to meet these goals by implementing a series of programs within the four villages located in the WMA. These programs included creating local businesses that revolve around biological research, tourism, and handicraft production; training local men to work with biologists; teaching local men and children about biological diversity and conservation; and implementing a monitoring system to measure the results of biodiversity conservation.

The Biodiversity Conservation Network (BCN) was the major donor for the Crater Project and RCF during the period of my initial fieldwork. The largest single grant was the BCN implementation grant of $498,107, which was spread out over the three-year period of 1995 to 1998. As a BCN partner, the Wildlife Conservation Society committed $76,950 in funding to the Crater Mountain project. The Crater Mountain project is also linked to BCN ideologically through the CMWMA "conceptual model" and the BCN hypothesis. The conceptual model was designed with the help of a BCN planning grant and with the guidance of BCN staff (Ericho, Bino, and Johnson, A. 1999).

The BCN was designed to fund and study international conservation projects that linked biological conservation with economic development, and was based on the ideologies and practices of the aforementioned ICAD project analysis from the early 1990s. The ideology behind the BCN was that biodiversity is already linked to the economic "health" of the planet. Nature is discussed in BCN literature as biological capital, and BCN's statement of the "problem" of biological diversity conservation is as follows:

Biodiversity represents the very foundation of human existence. Yet by our heed-less actions we are eroding this biological capital at an alarming rate. Even today, despite the destruction that we have inflicted on the environment and its natural bounty, its resilience is taken for granted. But the more we learn of the workings of the natural world, the clearer it becomes that there is a limit to the disruption that the environment can endure.

Beside the profound ethical and aesthetic implications, it is clear that the loss of biodiversity has serious economic and social costs. The genes, species, eco-systems and human knowledge which are being lost represent a living library of options available for adapting to local and global change. Biodiversity is part of our daily lives and livelihood and constitutes the resources upon which families, communities, nations and future generations depend. (BSP 1996: iv)

The BCN program overview goes on to state:

Conservation efforts that ignore the economic needs of local communities are unlikely to succeed. The Biodiversity Conservation Network (BCN), a compo-nent of the Biodiversity Support Program (BSP), is an innovative USAID-funded program working in the Asia/Pacific Region to provide grants for community-based enterprises that directly depend on biodiversity. BCN is testing the hypoth-esis that if local communities receive sufficient benefits from a biodiversity-linked enterprise, then they will act to conserve it. (BSP 1997:iii)

The BCN took as its premise that commodity production and economic in-centives which tie people to commodity-based systems are the strategies that will promote the conservation of biological diversity. The BCN was a part of environmentalists' reliance on "the commodity road to stabilization," that is, using commodities, both harvested forest products and tourism as a forest product, to "provide short-term payoffs" in order to involve local people in projects and supposedly to enhance long-term conservation (Schroeder 1995: 326). This neoliberal approach to conservation favors export economies, priva-tization, trade liberalization, and "development" polices that bypass the state (Hartwick and Peet 2003:189).[14] The market is seen as both the savior of biological diversity and the most rational and efficient way to organize social and economic life (Hartwick and Peet 2003). And the seemingly "impassible divide" between growth and conservation is imagined to be bridged by market-oriented sustainable development (ibid.:189). The ideologies of "development" with which Truman began his 1949 speech on development and underdevelopment (Escobar 1995; Sachs 1993), and which came to an ideological frenzy when inextricably tied to issues of the environment during the Rio de Janeiro Earth Summit in 1992, have thus been implemented through these BCN-funded projects. Since the BCN project's end, those associated with it have published explanatory papers regarding its goals (Salafsky et al. 2001).[15] They argue that the BCN was conceptualized in order to determine, using scientific principles, the conditions that make for effective conservation intervention (ibid.:1586).

The BCN began in 1992 through the relationship between the Biodiversity Support Program (BSP) — a consortium made up of the WWF, Nature Conservancy, and World Resources Institute — and USAID. Through collaborations, BSP and USAID staff identified three factors that seemed to affect conservation efforts (BSP 1996:72). The first of these factors was that ICAD projects that did not establish a link between economic activity and biodiversity conservation often failed. The second factor was that there was an increase in consumer markets for products produced from rain forest items and that therefore people living in rain forest areas could take advantage of this marketplace recognition and "capture" some of these benefits. The final factor was that even though many conservation projects claimed to be "sustainable," there was little analysis of their long-term biological, economic, and social impacts (BSP 1996:72).

According to BCN-generated literature, based on these three factors, individuals at the BSP and USAID saw the opportunity to design a project that could implement and then evaluate "enterprise-based" approaches to conservation. Through the United States–Asia Environmental Partnership (US-AEP), the BCN could "test" their hypothesis in Asia and the Pacific.[16] They funded thirty-nine "community-based projects," each of which included at least one enterprise such as ecotourism lodges, extraction of nontimber forest products, small-scale sustainable timber harvesting, or collection of samples to be tested for pharmaceutical compounds (BSP 1999; Salafsky et al. 2001:1586). Each of the projects was defined using the spatial metaphor of *site*, and the people involved in the projects were termed *stakeholders*. The sites, stakeholders, and enterprises were given a temporal dimension in that they were funded and assessed over a period of four years (Salafsky et al. 2001:1587). As we will return to the idea of the spatial production of the "site" at Crater Mountain throughout this book, it is important to note the way in which the BCN defined the site in terms of spatial relations: "A site was defined spatially as the core area of natural habitats the project wanted to conserve, which was functionally equivalent to the area the stakeholders had the ability to manage or influence, either positively or negatively" (ibid.:1587).

The BCN devised what its literature refers to as the "core hypothesis." The BCN core hypothesis states that "if enterprise-oriented approaches to community-based conservation are going to be effective, they must: 1) have a direct link to biodiversity, 2) generate benefits, and 3) involve a community of stakeholders" (BSP 1996:1). In effect, the hypothesis is that "if local communities receive sufficient benefits from an enterprise that depends on biodiversity, then they will act to counter internal and external threats to that biodiversity" (ibid.). The BCN project of hypothesis testing began in earnest with a $20 million commitment from the USAID in 1992 and was planned to last for six and a half years ending in March 1999.

The BCN staff developed a series of monitoring tools in order to test their hypothesis and an "index of threat-reduction assessment," which was meant to assess "the percentage of identified threats at each project site addressed over the life of the project" (Salafsky et al. 2001:1587). They also developed a series of "models" to direct and assess the projects. Thus, the models for conservation-as-development were created at the same time that the models for assessment and the monitoring tools were designed — in 1995, at the beginning of most of the projects, when project field staff had little data about the actual on-the-ground social, political, ecological, and economic relations at the sites.

In 1995 the BCN also identified their "dependent variable" (conservation success) and a series of "independent variables." These independent variables include enterprise success, ownership, management, and linkages to biodiversity; distribution, amount, variability, timing, and frequency of cash benefits as well as "noncash" benefits; strength, leadership, and homogeneity of stakeholder groups, as well as resource governance and community policing; and "other factors," which include "chaos,"[17] and project effectiveness (Salafsky et al. 2001:1588).[18] All in all, the social lives of the people living within this series of biodiversity conservation experiments — people at thirty-nine different sites — are thus reduced to seventeen independent variables to be measured and evaluated in relation to the dependent variable of conservation success.

Several things are important to note at this point in the story regarding the

3. An RCF resident biologist distributes mail.

BCN, the RCF, and the Crater Mountain project. First, discussions about "conservation" began in Ubaigubi village in 1980, when David Gillison was "given" a bit of land, an event I will discuss at length later in this book (see chapter 4). Second, in addition to David Gillison's activity around the field site of Gillian Gillison, then his wife, in the 1970s and 1980s, there were beginning in 1987 scientists working on the southern side of Crater Mountain. Debra Wright and Andrew Mack, then graduate students, began their research on land held by Pawaia peoples in 1987, both eventually earning Ph.D. degrees.[19] From the beginning of their work there—which included building the Sera Research Station—these two scientists contributed to the local economy through the purchase of garden food and the hiring of scientific assistants, guides, and labor.[20] Third, as mentioned above, U.S. Peace Corps volunteers had been active in the villages around Crater Mountain since 1990. The volunteers were used as "field trainers," helping to train local people to work on small business development and the creation of community service committees (A. Johnson 1997:399). Finally, the RCF was created specifically for the management of the CMWMA. The RCF is an NGO that has grown out of the social interactions

4. Young man working with biologists in the forest.

between expatriates and Papua New Guineans that surround the creation of the Crater Mountain Wildlife Management Area.

The BCN has a central contradiction that merits discussion: The entire "BCN project," which tests the hypothesis that increased local participation in commodity-based systems relying on biodiversity will lead to higher levels of biological diversity (that the commodification of natural resources will ultimately save them) is based upon the BCN premise that nature or the environment is always already commodified in that it is "natural capital." The BCN "solution" to the "problem" of "the destruction that we have inflicted on the environment and its natural bounty" (as quoted earlier) through global commodity production is the further integration of "out-of-the-way" places where there is much biological diversity into commodity-based systems. Commodification apparently serves as the solution to environmental change as produced by late capitalism. This hypothesis was tested by the BCN, with the labor of staff from the RCF in Maimafu village. While Maimafu's residents were aware of the presence of conservation-related actors in Ubaigubi before Jamie James's arrival in their village, it was with his presence that they became fully incorporated into the Crater Mountain project, as the next section will discuss.

THE CONTRACTS OF CONSERVATION-AS-DEVELOPMENT

For the residents of Maimafu, when the WCS and RCF employee Jamie James arrived in their village to help choose the clan leaders who would sit on the Wildlife Management Committee for the CMWMA and to help demarcate its boundaries, his very presence formalized their social relationship with conservation-as-development actors and institutions. In the 1970s and 1980s some adult men from Maimafu had traveled to Ubaigubi to meet David Gillison and discuss conservation and development with him. They had heard him talk about the importance of conserving the birds of paradise on their lands and they had talked to him about the kinds of goods and services they thought they needed in the form of "development." Several of the men who were chosen, with the guidance of James, to be founding members of the Maimafu Management Committee, recount stories of their meetings with D. Gillison in ways that make clear that they see these meetings as forming the basis for what they expected to be long-term social relations with outsiders who would help them access goods and services in exchange for what was being called conservation.

From the beginning of the relationship between conservation professionals and Maimafu Gimi, conservation was explained to villagers in terms of regulating hunting, setting aside certain parts of their landscape for its conservation, creating Management Committees, serving on Management Committees, coming up with a set of conservation laws for their people and lands, and getting development. For the people of Maimafu, conservation was, and for the most part today is, the above list of actions. For the conservation professionals conservation was and is much more. At its most basic level, it is the maintenance of viable breeding populations of as many species as possible in any given area, but in as big an area as possible. It is also the maintenance and protection of ecosystem functions such as soil stabilization and watershed functions. When conservation professionals and activists talked to Gimi about conservation, the image they held was one of scientifically based maintenance and protection in which Gimi stopped being "threats" to animals, plants, and, through gardening, the forest in general. When they talked to them about development, they saw Gimi earning cash and participating in the market in ways that would allow them to access goods and services. When Gimi talked to conservation professionals and activists, the image they held of conservation comprised bureaucratic actions and functions such as serving on a committee and enforcing laws

5. Young men at a party for the arrival of Save the Children
representatives to Maimafu in 2001.

through the village court system. When they talked about development, they
imagined themselves in social relationships that would allow them to access
goods and services and ultimately accessing them in particular ways.

After the initial work of creating the Wildlife Management Area was completed, the RCF, through BCN funding, began to implement a series of programs
that the organization saw as its side of the conservation and development contract. These were, as mentioned above, setting up local businesses that would
bring cash to the community, training men to work with biologists for a wage,
teaching villagers about biological diversity, and monitoring the results of their
conservation-related actions. For conservation-related actors, the first two programs were "development," while the second two were "conservation." It was
thought that these programs would fulfill the RCF's side of the contract with
villagers, and that in exchange villagers would happily participate in the programs and "conserve" the biological diversity on their lands. The Maimafu Gimi
did not see these programs in the same light.

Maimafu villagers have numerous critiques of conservation-as-development
on their lands. But their biggest critique is that the people and institutions that

they have entered into exchange relationships with, because of the Crater Mountain Wildlife Management Area ICAD, do not fulfill their side of the relationships in socially appropriate ways. Here I mean "appropriate" in terms of how Gimi think the world does and should work. The outsiders (conservation biologists, activists, and practitioners, development experts, U.S. Peace Corps volunteers, and others) who have come to Maimafu because of the project, while understood by Gimi to be different from them in many ways, are assumed to be the same in that they are considered fully human. And for Gimi being fully human, or coming into existence as social beings, is intimately tied to reciprocal recognition though the exchange of objects, persons, labor, and services.[21]

Discussion and debates about the nature of exchange have occupied a great deal of thought in anthropology beginning with Marcel Mauss ([1925] 1990) and have especially engaged anthropologists working in Melanesia (Godelier 1999; Knauft 1999; M. Strathern 1988). Marilyn Strathern argues that Melanesians do not see objects and people as simply entities involved in exchange relations. Rather, people and objects come into being through the act of giving and exchange (M. Strathern 1988). People come into being as social actors through the use, possession, and exchange of objects, as they do across Melanesia (Robbins 2003; Strathern 1988). Conservation-as-development brings actions, or sets of actions, into this exchange equation. For example, a biologist promises a man from Maimafu that if he helps him find the nest of a New Guinea Harpy Eagle (*Harpyopsis novaeguineae*), then tourists will come and give him lots of money. The man from Maimafu helps the biologist find the nest and then awaits the reciprocation of this act, of his side of the exchange-related contract.

For Gimi, outside people who are nonetheless associated with the CMWMA are categorized as different from tourists and other one-time visitors to their village. Tourists are "wealthy curiosities" (Gewertz and Errington 1991:46) who are not seen as fully human. They exist only in terms of commodity relations and cash transactions. They are seen as entities that people will only interact with one time, a set of social relations that, until quite recently, was not part of the Gimi universe. Conservation-as-development actors, in contrast, are seen as entities that can and should enter into long-term social relations with Gimi. In other words, the Maimafu Gimi, because of their initial understanding of their contract with the conservation-as-development project, think that all of the actors and institutions associated with the CMWMA have an obligation to enter into a certain kind of relationship with them. This relationship is not one of barter. Barter relationships are one-time transactions, but conservation-related relations are thought to be long term.

While much Melanesianist anthropology has focused on the movement of objects and people in relation to the creation of social relations and social selves, my work with the Maimafu Gimi shows that both labor and services, as sets of actions, can also be seen in terms of exchange and social reproduction. Specifically, Gimi see their labor and cooperation as being given to the conservation-as-development project in exchange for "development." They see their participation as being given in exchange for long-term social relationships that will bring them development. This raises an important point with regard to how Gimi have come to see their relationships with conservation-as-development and its related actors. Gimi see themselves as entering into social relations with both individuals and institutions. So, for instance, a woman might well assume that because she has cooked dinner for a group of conservation biologists who are staying on her husband's land, she has entered into a social relationship with the individual biologists *and* with the institution for which they work (the RCF or WCS, for example). The biologists are expected to reciprocate with gifts and the like, thus paving the way for reciprocal gifts from the woman and her husband and strengthening the exchange bonds and alliances, and the institutions are expected to reciprocate with "development." The question thus becomes, To whom are the institutions expected to reciprocate?

When institutions, such as the RCF and WCS, reciprocate to an individual, they are criticized for it. If the RCF pays a man to do something, it is criticized for not paying someone else. If the WCS helps support a student through school fees, it is criticized for not paying school fees for each child in the village. Reciprocating by these institutions is always seen as unbalanced either in terms of someone else having gotten more than others or in terms of the perception that the RCF and WCS never reciprocate as much as they should given its resources. So while the RCF and WCS as institutions are expected to reciprocate to individuals on the one hand, on the other they are seen as having a social relationship on the village scale when it comes to their giving, in that everyone is seen as deserving of the benefits of development. But residents of Maimafu would say that it is absurd to image "Maimafu" as having a relationship with anything or anyone, because Maimafu is not the scale at which people see themselves as having social relations (those scales can be individual, extended family, subclan, or clan). They see it as perfectly reasonable that the RCF would have an obligation to both individuals and all larger corporate units (families, clans, and villages). So individuals and clans give to the CMWMA, which is almost always conflated with the RCF, and expect something in return. They do not, however, expect that that return will be given to the corporate unit of Maimafu, because to them Maimafu is not a social unit that can enter into exchange relations in that way.

In addition to seeing themselves as having given labor to the conservation-as-development project in order to establish the social relations that will facilitate development, Maimafu villagers see themselves as having given land. This exchange, or perceived exchange, on the part of many older Gimi is not about giving property but rather about giving themselves. These older people see themselves as coming into being not only through exchanges with other people but also through exchanges with their clan's forests and land. As G. Gillison has argued (1980, 1993), the conceptual categories of nature and culture do not exist for Gimi. Rather, what we conceive of as nature is for them a storehouse for matter that is in constant exchange with persons; with people making plants, animals, soil, and the like, and with all those things in turn making people. So for Gimi to give land to conservation so that they can create the social relations that will facilitate "getting development" is to literally give of themselves, to exchange their very being for the things they see as development. It is to exchange the social relations of the past, with the forests, ancestors, and spirits, for social relations that they imagine will be beneficial in the future.

Maimafu Gimi are perfectly willing, and indeed in some instances eager, to give up their past as they see it — the traditional ceremonies, myths, beliefs, and practices (what is thought of as "custom"), for instance, as well as the hard work, disease and death, difficulty with their businesses, lack of schools, lack of money, and all the "hardships" that they equate with the past — in exchange for what they imagine as a future full of development. Indeed, I have been told over and over since 1996 that people are more than willing to stop the practices they see as custom so that they can get development and services. Bruce Knauft has pointed out that among the Gebusi, this desire is about more than just an exchange in relation to things and people across time; it is an exchange "of time," one that is "an exchange between different ways of relating to time, different modes of temporality" that "entails new ways of relating to oneself, to others, and to material goods" (Knauft 2002:28).

At first glance, it appears that the Maimafu Gimi seem to want it both ways — they are willing, or say that they are willing, to give up the past and their customs if they can "get development," but they are not willing to stop being Gimi in that they are not willing to stop measuring everything in terms of exchange and what they get based on what they give. They make, see, and understand themselves and others in terms of the relations of exchange, but they clearly make the argument that they wish to give up custom for develop-ment. This is unsettling because while on the one hand arguing that they are willing to give up their past, they are still relying on very Gimi-of-the-past notions of exchange to make this offer. There is a dialectical relationship here between a "Giminess" of the past and a Giminess of the future that pivots around exchange. By being willing to give up the past for an imagined future, they are also saying that they are willing to enter into a whole other system of making place, people, and property, one that is based on contractual law and individual property rights.

When the conservation activists and professionals associated with the RCF and WCS first came to Maimafu, they were following the BCN ICAD model, one that is about creating relationships with people in rural places so that they can "capture" some of the benefits of the market through the conservation of bio-logical diversity on their lands. People in Maimafu read the actions, promises, and projects of conservation-as-development through a lens of Giminess, in which social relations are long-term exchange relationships and in which al-liances between themselves and conservation-as-development actors and in-stitutions were being created. The conservation activists and professionals saw their actions as creating the structures by which Gimi could eventually access markets and make cash on their own, with no help from outsiders.

PLACE AS IMAGINATION

The afternoon rain has a cadence that is hauntingly beautiful. It begins in the still hot of the day with the quiet sounds of the cicadas humming. The frogs join them, one by one, in an ever-expanding chorus that rises to a shrill pitch. As the sound grows, the water in the ditch next to the village airstrip begins to run.

Figure 6. View from Maimafu village airstrip.

You hear it as it grows in volume—rushing by as it pours down from the high mountain streams that are getting the rain before it comes to you. Then you hear the rain itself, as it comes over the backside of Bopoyana. Its patterned rumble moves across the forest top evenly, and it grows louder and louder as it approaches. It always comes from the same direction, from the high mountains to the southeast, moving in sheets, pushing rainbows in its path toward the Chimbu Valley to the northwest. As it comes to you, the center of the storm is a deafening torrential downpour, and as it leaves, much later, its sound begins to subside. You begin to hear the water running in the ditch again and the dripping of the rain from the plants and trees. As it recedes, you hear the soft buzzing of the bugs as they come back, and the slight shrill sound of the swifts as they emerge to catch the rain-loving mosquitoes. The other birds join in the dusk flights from forest to forest, and the dark rolls over you like the songs of the birds.

Some of the images that I have from spending time in Maimafu will always be with me, things such as the stark contrast between the still-dark outline of the mountains, and the clear blue of the morning sky. Daily, when I am there, I am amazed by how the views of the mountains change with the time of day and the kind of sunlight that pours down on them. There is a time in the late afternoon, after the rains and the return of the sun, when the sun is just about to fall behind the mountains to the west, that the light is almost indescribable in its beauty. It is like you can see every single tree on every mountain, but more than that even. You can see the individual leaves on every single tree on every single mountain. You can also see the ridge outlines and the tree patterns. It is like you can clearly see for the first time ever. It only lasts for a little while, and then the mountains start to get dark and lose their subtle features. It is easy to be seduced by the landscape around Maimafu. It is a kind of beauty that hits a cognitive spot that is not often stimulated in the daily lives of people who work and live in the more industrial parts of the world. But make no mistake, for Gimi this landscape has been made; it has been *produced by* the exchanges between people and the environment. Some of these exchanges are old: they are things that Gimi ancestors did to make place and produce space; but some of them are new: they are the exchanges of conservation-as-development.

CHAPTER 3

Articulations, Histories, Development

❀ There is a time in Maimafu, in the early morning, when the sun is just barely visible over the mountain behind the ridgetop settlements of Tulai and Motai. Before that first light, the world is veiled in a sheer sheet of darkness. All you can see in the predawn light is the black-green outline of the forest against the changing blue of the night sky. Then, as the sunlight finally reaches Tulai, it starts to pour down the ridge, and the world lights up with a golden-pink brightness. All of this is happening to the southeast. At the same time, in the deep valleys and low ridges of Chimbu to the northwest, the sunrise is turning the clouds, trapped between sloping ridges by the lowland night rains, a range of pinks that stretches from cashmere sweater baby-pink to Rosette Spoonbill scarlet-pink.

The first year I lived in Maimafu, I began my days watching the sunrise and marveling at its beauty. Almost every morning I sat on my doorstep, ate a sweet potato, listened to the receding sounds of night and the waking sounds of the village, and felt the morning chill turn to smooth bright tropical warmth. It is cold in Maimafu in the early morning. The altitude, about 1,500–1,700 meters, combines with the lack of cloud cover over the high mountains to make the air crisp and the dew icy. Chilly children scurry from their homes to fill bamboo tubes with water, and women start morning cooking fires to cut the cold and to bake sweet potatoes, taro, and yams. At 6:30 am people start passing by on their way to gardens, the airstrip, and the community school. By 7:00 am there is almost always a crowd of people at the junction of the four trails that meet at the north end of the hamlet of Motai.

One of these trails goes up the ridge to Tulai, Kolatai, Harontai, and Lasoabei. Another trail goes down a mountain and then up another to Kuseri,[1] Atobatai, Bayabei, Iyahaetai, and Wayoarabirai. The third trail goes down the ridge to Motai, and the final trail goes down to the river past Kalopayahaetai and Halabaebitai and then up the mountain to Aeyahaepi, Biabitai, Abigarima, and the airstrip. The trail junction is a gathering place and a resting place. It is a place where people catch up on the night's gossip or plan afternoon sporting events for when they have returned from their gardens. On many mornings, it is the spot where women and young children separate from their husbands and older children. On these days, the women and the young children, and the occasional dog or goat, go to the gardens. The older children, if there is a teacher in the village, go off to the airstrip, where the community school, some-times supported by the government, is located. The men sit at the junction and plan their day. They gossip about current issues in the village, discuss the coffee prices in Goroka, or go off to the airstrip to wait for the plane. By 8:30 am the majority of people have passed by, and Motai is almost empty. There are only very old women, young women with small babies, and a few young children left. By 9:00 am the women left in Motai are sitting outside their houses either making *bilum* (net string bags) or cleaning and drying coffee.

FAMILY

There are two main levels of group identification for individuals in Maimafu. These levels roughly correspond to the anthropological terms *clan* and *lineage*. The first level, clan, is that of an exogamous group of men who are related through patrilineal lines and who trace their relations back at least five genera-tions. Within these exogamous groups, there are smaller groups of men, lin-eages, who are more closely related patrilineally and who trace their relations back two or three generations. People in a lineage can trace their ancestry back to one individual, while clan members assume genealogical connections to a shared ancestor but cannot always recount them. All of the clans in Maimafu trace their ancestral origins to a migration from Labogai. This migration will be discussed later in this chapter in the section "Recounting Local History." For now it is important to say that these clans are thought to be related back between six and seven generations. Patriclans are exogamous, and a woman who has married into the clan bears children who belong to her husband's patriline. This seems to be consistent with other villages in which people speak Gimi language dialects (Gillison 1993:29; Glick 1963:20–25; and Mike and Barbara Howell, personal communication, from Faith Mission, August 1998).

The majority of people live in small thatched bamboo homes located in hamlets on high ridgetops. Although the pattern of occupation differs through-out the village in terms of familial makeup of the home, a few generalizations can be made.[2] First, a man builds a home that is then considered to belong to him. He may share it with his newly married adult sons and their wives, his unmarried children, his unmarried or widowed brother, and his wife, but there is still a notion of home ownership. Second, men tend to build their homes very close to men from their smaller extended family group and close to men from their lineage. So, for instance, an old man with five sons will have a home that is surrounded by his sons' homes and that is close to his brothers' homes and his brothers' sons' homes. Finally, home occupation is rather fluid. While a single nuclear family usually forms the basis of the household, members from other parts of the extended family move in and out of the household.

People in Maimafu draw on different scales of personal identification at dif-ferent times depending on the situation, their interest in it, and who they are interacting with. For instance, if there is a conflict between men from two different clans, men will identify with their clan, but if it is between two men within one clan, they will identify with their lineage. Similarly, if there is a conflict over something having to do with the Wildlife Management Area, men may identify with their village, saying things such as "mipela ol lain long Maim-afu" (we are one family from Maimafu). Additionally, they may identify as "Crater Mountain landowners" when dealing with mining companies or oil companies or as "Eastern Highlanders" when dealing with representatives of the national government. But these scales of identification, "Maimafu villagers" and "Crater Mountain landowners," that are tied to the spatial production of Maim-afu and Crater Mountain are never more salient to people than their kinship ties.

RECOUNTING LOCAL HISTORY

Now you listen daughter, I will tell you the truth. We are all the children of the men that came from Labogai. They lived in that place. One day, in the distant past, two brothers in Labogai got in a fight over the river stone that they used to sharpen axes. It was a big fight, but they were brothers, so they settled it with a contest. An important man from their village put a seed on the top of a wooden dish. The two men stood far away, and then both tried to shoot the seed. The man who shot the seed left Labogai. The man who missed stayed.

So this man, Honenabo, the son of Ohtakabayara and Ohkomebayapa, set out to the south with his family. He is the father of all of us, because he came first. But he came with other men and their families. They stopped along the way, but Honenabo came all the way to what is today Maimafu. Other people here will tell you that their ancestor was the first man to come here from Labogai, but my story is the true one. Honenabo came first.

First he went to Mane, and some of his line built houses there. Next he went near Kora, and some of his line stopped there. Some went to Kusi and Mount Michael, and some went to Mengino. The first people here, in what now people call Maimafu, lived in Abigarima. These people built houses, made gardens, looked after their pigs, and hunted. This is how they claimed the land. They were the first people here. My ancestors were the first men to build houses and to hunt here.

After they came here, they had a good life, they worked hard, and, when it was time to kill pigs, they had festivals and they played their bamboo flutes. We do not do any of this now. When they killed pigs, they shared with all of their mothers' brothers, fathers' brothers, and all of their good friends.

This was the time when many men fought. When there was going to be fighting, they would kill pigs, and then they would fight. When a man wanted to stop the fight, he would go to the bush and get the tree, the one I showed you that has white on the bottom of its leaves, and bring it back to the village and cut it in half. This would stop the fight. Friends and families helped each other when it was their time to fight. When it was over, they got compensation. Sometimes they got women; sometimes they got ground [land]. When a man was killed in battle, his family would bring his body home and cook it. The women and children would eat it. The hardness [strength] of his body would go inside them and make them hard [strong] like him. When I was a boy, we still ate the men who died in fights.

My father saw the first two airplanes to fly over our land. He saw them before I was born, but he told the story like this: "We saw the planes and we didn't know what to think, then some people said they must be spirits or devils. They said that if we looked at them we would die." So everyone covered their eyes and ran to the bush to hide.

After they saw these planes, the first white man came through our land. He walked along the river Wage and he walked to Karimui. Our people thought that he must have come from the things in the sky since they had never seen either before. They followed him as he walked to Karimui. But he did not know they were there. Some of the black men with him did, but they did not tell the white man. We thought that he lived in the clouds and that he had come down to earth. The people in Karimui were afraid of him, so they killed him.

Now listen; this is important. After all of this, the white men started to build roads to other places, but we did not get roads or services. This was where a white man had died. He was working on a report when he was walking, and since he was killed, the report was never finished. All of the other places inside the bush got roads and services, and we did not. All of the other white men finished their reports. The white men went to Moresby, Rabal, Lae, Hagen, and then Goroka. That is also why we don't have anything. They went to other places first. We were last.

Then another white man came. This time he came from Goroka, and he was welcomed. When he came, we gave him pigs and food from our gardens. He gave us salt and bush knives. I was a boy then; I remember him. My father walked to Karimui with him and carried his cargo. This white man said that we could not eat people anymore and that we would never get anything if we ate people. He also told us that we couldn't bury people the way that our fathers did [see Gillison 1993:127–34 for a detailed description of traditional Gimi burial and death rites] but that we had to plant them in the ground. He also told us that we couldn't fight anymore or kill birds anymore.

He came back a second time, and he marked men to be in charge of the area. He gave them a book he called a contract, and they made marks on it. The men who made the marks were the Kiap's policemen.[3] They stopped fights, and then reported people who fought. They came up as big-men [community leaders] after he appointed them. Before they had been just men. He also told people what the names of their clans were. He took the names of men from the past that the policemen told him, their ancestors' names, and he marked families with the names. Before we didn't have clan names.

My father had to go to a big meeting in Lufa once. It was for all the policemen. The Kiaps at the Lufa station held the meeting. My father and mother took lots of food, and they went to the meeting. They took pigs and gave them to the Kiap.

My father and the other policemen did not get paid for this. It was work, but they got no money. They worked hard for the Kiap — they killed pigs, and the women brought food from the gardens — and they got nothing in return. He promised services and development, and we are still waiting.[4]

After the Kiaps were done [after independence], they started the Eastern Highlands Province Council and the Lufa Council; now it is the same, but it is black men and not white men. They make promises and ask for our support; we give it and we get nothing in return. We don't have ways to get much money, and we don't have a way to get to town. We grow our coffee, and that is not development from somewhere else; it is a road that we found for ourselves. It is development that we gave ourselves; it did not come from another man. The Kiap told us that it was good to grow, but it is our work that got it this far.

Now what we want is some man who has an education to help us learn more about how to do this for ourselves. Coffee is good. We get money from it if the kilo price is good. But we can work more. We want to work. We want to earn money. We are not afraid of working hard; you have seen us. All we want is help to know what to do. Now, daughter, you put that in your book.

This is Natu's version, told in May 1998, of a story that each clan recounts.[5] The stories serve as both a group origin narrative and a narrative about the coming of whites. With this, villagers locate each clan on the landscape, through the repeating of the part about where people hunted, built houses, made gardens, and kept pigs. They also articulate the kinds of social relations that they have had over time with outsiders and the sorts of exchange relationships that they have entered into with them.

Natu is Honenabo, so he recounts the story from the Honenabo point of view. Sandra Bamford (1998:14) has argued that this class of narratives is particularly important in the creation of lineal continuity and in the social relations between people and nature. Among the residents of Maimafu and others in Melanesia, these stories are told as truth (ibid.; Munn 1973). They are perceived to be actual historical fact. The stories tend to follow ancestors, documenting their travels and their use and altering of the landscape. Bamford argues that these stories are about production, both the production of the tenure-related narratives that are called upon in land and resource disputes and the production of personhood (1998). These stories are powerful and they are invoked in disputes over land and resource access and in the case of disputes over historic relations between clans and families.

All of the origin stories in Maimafu start with trouble in a place called Labogai, either a disagreement between brothers or a dispute between male patrilateral parallel cousins.[6] After the dispute is settled, either by a contest or a fight, one man and his family have to leave Labogai. The man, who is in all cases termed the son of Ohtakabayara and Ohkomebayapa; his immediate family; and a group of other men, who always include other "first fathers" mentioned by other families in their version of the story, set off and subsequently populate the entire region inhabited by Unavisa Gimi speakers.

This story highlights a number of important issues. First, the story never includes Herowana or Ubaigubi, the two other Gimi-speaking villages that are part of the Crater Mountain Wildlife Management Area (CMWMA). Herowana and Ubaigubi are seen as having been populated at a different time, albeit by people similar to the people of Maimafu. Men and women say that the first fathers who beget the current residents of Herowana and Ubaigubi came from Labogai long after the first fathers came to Maimafu. This is particularly important because of the discursive land claims made by these stories. People from Maimafu see themselves as the first inhabitants of what is now the CMWMA. Therefore, their land claims are seen as primary and more salient. Men say, "Our graves are on the way between the places" to indicate very primary claims on the land. They also talk about their ancestors as building hunting homes in the forest and stalking marsupials on their way to the area that is now known as Maimafu. This is a way of claiming access to land through historic hunting practices. A man who can trace back in time to show that his ancestor was the first to kill kile and kama, two important tree-kangaroo species, on a piece of land holds a claim to that land.[7]

Second, the story highlights a cultural knowledge about historical change. People in Maimafu realize that their history is one of profound social change instigated by local agency as well as by regional and other pressures. They begin their group history with this story of migration and change. This makes it almost impossible to employ traditional Western tropes of "change" when writing about or attempting to understand Maimafu. Frederick Errington and Deborah Gewertz identify two "possible explanations of change" available in Western tradition and applied to understandings of history in the Pacific and Melanesia (1995:4). They term the first model "the myth of the fragile Eden" and the second "the myth of the inflexible tradition." The fragile Eden model is the idea that people living in remote, marginal, and/or rural "out of the way places" (Tsing 1993) are living in a pristine kind of "state of nature," unattached to, and unaware of, outside influences and cultural articulations, and which is often devastated by sudden change that is "likely to be demoralizing, catastrophic, and virtually inevitable" (Errington and Gewertz 1995:5). In this model change is seen as undesirable. The inflexible tradition model holds that these people are "frozen in time" and that they serve as a window on our own evolutionary past. It also holds that "change among 'remote' peoples is desirable but difficult to effect unless great and transforming pressure is applied; it is thereby likely to be either all or nothing" (Errington and Gewertz 1995:5).[8]

Third, as Aletta Biersack (1995b) argues, people in New Guinea, although often painted with the modernist brushstrokes of the "tribal" and bounded premodern, have in fact, never existed in isolation. Using the intercultural relations between the Duna, Ipili, and Huli, Biersack, and the other contributors to her volume, demonstrate the historic, and even some prehistoric, relations of trade, travel, marriage, and warfare that created the "hybrid cultural forms" of the present (Biersack 1995b:6).[9] Indeed, Biersack argues that "syncretism is the ordinary state of affairs" in Highland New Guinea and that while colonialism, missionization, and capitalism brought outsiders into contact with Highlanders — thus creating the possibility for new sorts of intercultural contacts — people had always been rather "cosmopolitan" on a regional scale (ibid.). These stories illustrate not only that Gimi have a social history that is full of movement and change, but also that this "syncretism" emerges in their cultural forms of expression, that is, stories and myths.[10]

Fourth, for people in Maimafu the narratives highlight a real-world beginning of the people. It is a story not of mythic origins but rather one of geographic and sociopolitical origins. People use these stories, and mythic stories, to garner rights to lands and to access power politically and socially. They also use them to set the stage for current events and local perceptions of why things are the way they are today.

Finally, this is also a story about exchange. Natu explains that his people thought that because the first "white man" who came across their land was not treated properly — he was spied on secretly by Gimi and then allegedly killed by the people in Karimui — they did not benefit from the kinds of things, roads, for instance, that whites could bring. The second white visitor was treated differently. People entered into what they thought were exchange relations with him. They gave him food and he gave them salt and bush knives. He told them what they were no longer allowed to do, and people thought that this was another kind of exchange. If they gave up these practices, they would get things in exchange. The entire second part of the narrative is about the sorts of exchange relations that the Gimi thought that they were entering into and the story of these deals gone wrong. The "white men" constantly breach the contracts of exchange. All of these social relations are tainted by nonreciprocity.

Gimi narratives, like those of their Fore neighbors, have changed over time (Lindenbaum 2002). These changes represent Gimi's having come to terms with social, political, economic, and environmental transformations taking place in their lives (ibid.:64). Gimi use these stories to help make sense out of the historical processes in which they are taking part (ibid.:64) and to make sense out of those stories from elsewhere that they do not understand. In this section, I will briefly recount a creation story that illustrates the melding of traditional mythology with Christian origin stories.[11] This mixing of traditions is another example of how people in Maimafu have been living for years with changes to both their social lives, to be discussed later in this section, and their notions of self. The following is a translation of a taped interview in which I asked the question, "How did people get here?" This question often evoked discussions of the aforementioned migration from Labogai, but it also often evoked other responses, including this one from March 1998:

One day God looked around the world and saw it. He saw tree kangaroos, cassowaries, pigs, flying foxes, and other animals. He saw trees and mountains and rivers. In the day he felt the heat of the sun, which is very hot. And at night he saw the light of the moon, where he sometimes goes. He had made it all before. It came from him. And he thought that the world was good, so he decided to make people. He made them so they could live in the world.

He made Adam and Eve first. Adam and Eve were brother and sister. They lived in Australia, and Eve had a garden at the head of three rivers. They lived in the forest and slept in caves like flying foxes! Adam slept all the time, so Eve did all the work. They were there and happy for a long, long, long time, with Eve working and Adam sleeping so he could be rested, until Bihu the snake came.[12]

Bihu is giant. He is huge. He can kill a man by taking him under the water. He lures him to the riverbank and then he grabs him with his belly and drags him down. When he comes up from the bottom of the river, when the man is almost dead from the water, he ties his tail around one tree and his head around another and then he pulls. The pulling kills the man.

So Bihu came, and he tried to take Eve away; he tried to lure her away with fruit from the forest. He tried to get her away from that place that God had made for them. He wanted to lure her away from Adam. So Bihu came, and she was asleep, and he bit her on the place where her vagina would be, and he made a hole there. She awoke, and she followed Bihu and went down the mountains away from the head of the three rivers. Down, down, down, she followed him until Adam found her and wrestled with the snake. Bihu squeezed him so much it hurt his ribs, but Adam won, and Bihu swam down, down, down even farther down the river. But after that they were afraid to live in the forest. That is when they moved out of the first place.

The "first place" in this story is not Labogai; these events happened in the "true time before." More important, Adam and Eve, according to this storyteller and others, have white skin. Repeatedly, people told me that the first people God made were white skinned and that "black men" were made later at a different time, either through the workings of God or through the social relations between birds. There was a different creation for white skin and for black skin, according to this lore. And there is a difference between the two, but as this story shows the creation of white skin is understood in terms of the melding of old stories and Christian myths.

In the "men's flute myth," a traditional origin story told by men, the first couple were also brother and sister (Gillison 1993:10; see also Herdt 1981). That story, a version of which is recounted below, as a key to gender relations, is an explanation of why men had flutes, and women did not, and why women menstruate. In the *nenekaina* stories, or traditional stories told by women to women, the first couple is an old man with a huge penis and a young girl (Gillison 1993:10). The man's penis goes alone one night to find the girl, and it creates her vagina by biting her in the spot where a woman's vagina is located. Bihu the snake appears often in contemporary stories. He is thought to be enormous and real and living in a river "near Chimbu." But he is also conflated with the giant penis of the first man in the nenekaina stories recorded by Gillison (1993). In this story, he is conflated with Satan in that he and the serpent in Christian myth are one. In other stories he is portrayed as ruler of an underwater realm where he takes his victims, and they are made to suffer eternally.

The whiteness of the original couple in this story is important. The Seventh-Day Adventist (SDA) missionaries who originally converted the residents of Maimafu to Christianity were Papua New Guinean.[13] Thus, the whiteness highlights the association between Christian myths and expatriates, even when Papua New Guineans are the source of the stories. It also highlights a kind of local understanding in which whites are "the first," and in which whites have both primary accesses to things as well as a kind of perceived original knowledge. This is important as these issues influence local understandings of development. Development is seen as coming from elsewhere, and in particular from the social relations forged with outsiders. "One day in 2002, an older person told me, 'When the whites and [then] the church came, customs changed; people stopped doing some things the way that they had done them in the past. Some of the things from the past were good and we miss them; some were bad so we are not sorry that they are gone.'" This statement of Korba's is representative of the things people told me when I asked about the impetus for, and consequences of, social change brought about by outsiders in Maimafu.[14] Paula Brown (1972:8) describes Gimi speakers' neighbors, the Chimbu, as "delighted" to accept both the material goods brought from the outside and "the new ways of the white man." She goes on to argue that this acceptance of change was in part due to the lack of local attention paid to notions of past and present, and the fact that the Chimbu lived in the present and were acutely aware that sociality changes over time (ibid.). Others (Gajdusek and Alpers 1972) argue that while the ethnic groups physically and culturally close to Gimi readily accepted change, that Gimi did not.

While it may have been the case that some people in the region readily accepted change and some did not, colonial administrators and patrol officers did not focus their efforts on the villages to the southwest of Kainantu and south of Mount Michael until the late 1940s and early 1950s (C. Berndt 1953: 112). Rather, they focused on the areas between Goroka and Kainantu and the areas directly to the east and west (ibid.). Maimafu, and Gimi lands in general, were to the southwest of Kainantu, and on the periphery of several administrative districts. In his 1953 report about his patrol through the area, and the patrol that includes the first mention of Maimafu, McArthur, in his discussion of the "native situation" in the area says that the "situation is excellent" (McArthur

1952/1953:15). He goes on to ask how the administration might improve on this already satisfactory situation. In answering his own question, he says,

> Past experience has shown that every disturbance in the area of any importance was the result of an introduced cause; and that the natives are peaceable and law-abiding if let live their own lives with guidance and advice from regular patrols. . . . With these thoughts in mind, and the ultimate welfare of the people, I strongly recommend that missions be restricted from entering the area as yet. A premature penetration of the area by mission evangelists will be attended by disaster. The natives of this region are a proud and free race. They will not willingly tolerate the destruction of their sacred relics. Destruction of such things as the sacred flutes will produce a wave of resentment, and quite possibly lead to open hostility against the destroying agent. (McArthur 1952/1953:15–16)

Gillison's account of life in Unavi villages indicates that there was a sort of "revival" of traditional practices in 1973 but that people associated with Faith Mission had begun working to curtail traditional religious practices southwest of Lufa in 1954 (Gillison 1993:5). This revival included the building of men's houses and the holding of initiations for boys (ibid.), both things forbidden by missionaries.[15] In addition, ritual theater, which had also been forbidden, was once again practiced (Gillison 1993; Glick 1968b).

Today, there are age differences in the ways people understand the "loss" associated with cultural change and assimilation into the Papua New Guinean nation-state and the larger process of nation-making (Foster 2002). The salient changes according to older men and women have to do with male initiation and marriage:

> The thing from the past that is over for good is about men and boys. When I was young, all the boys went around like they do today. They did not work, and they did not help their mothers in the garden. They went around, that's all.
>
> When the big-men in the village decided it was time, they put the boys in the men's house. They did it. They were the ones who decided. When they were in the house, they had a big ceremony to teach them how to be men. They told them about the customs and how to be good husbands. They killed pigs and cooked them on stones, and then they ate the pigs.[16] After they ate, the big-men sharpened a shinbone of a cassowary, and they pierced their noses: two holes on the side and one through the center.

When it was time for them to attract a woman, they would put Vulturine Parrot feathers in the sides and the Balot [King of Saxony Bird of Paradise] tail through the septum. This attracted women; without it, no women would come to them. After they worked these holes, they would go and have a festival and get a wife.

An old man surrounded by a group of men between the ages of seventeen and forty recounted the preceding story in June 1998.[17] Afterward, some of the men in the group showed me their pierced noses, and they pointed out that no man under about thirty, at the time, had a pierced nose. This correlates with the dates of conversion to Christianity, because, according to Gimi, the first SDA missionary arrived in the area in 1962.[18]

When I asked, in May 1998, why people stopped practicing traditional cultural practices and if the younger men were sorry about losing them, a man who was at the time nearly twenty answered:

We are sorry that parts of it are gone. We like the idea of dressing up and having a big festival and dance to attract women. That would have been fun. Also, in the past, men were stronger than they are today. They worked harder, and they worked with stone axes. Those are hard to cut with, and they made men strong.

We hear stories from old men about fights, and we are glad to not have to deal with huge fights. Sometimes they went on for a very long time. Now there are not so many. Every once and a while, but not so many. That is good.

We also hear stories about eating people (laughter in the crowd) and we think we prefer tinned fish to tinned . . . to tinned . . . to tinned man!

We stopped doing some of these things because God says they are wrong. For instance, we do not eat pigs now because Satan lives in the pig's ass (riotous laughter from the crowd). The bible says that one day Satan was in a man making him do very bad things. The man got rid of him, but he flew up a pig's ass, and that is where he lives today. You can tell that Satan lives in him because the pig is a thief. He will go to another man's garden and steal until someone beats him away.

Other things stopped because they were at odds with Christian traditions, and when our grandfathers heard the talk of [the first SDA missionary] they thought his talk was good and right so they stopped. They chose to stop.

We know that if you never stop some traditional practices, you will be *bus kanaka* forever.[19] We do not want that. We want to be modern and developed, so we stopped some of these things.

An older man, also in May 1998, when describing things he misses from the past, said:

> In the past we men would get our dogs and go to the bush [forest]. We killed kile and kama [tree kangaroos] and Cassowaries. Our bush is full of animals, and they were ours if we wanted to go get them, so when our wives' throats hurt from eating too much sweet potato, we would go to the bush and get the meat. Now because of SDA, God says that we can't eat some meat. RCF [the Research and Conservation Foundation of Papua New Guinea] tells us not to hunt at all.[20] I liked going to the bush. Now I feel like I have no work, and when my wife's throat hurts from garden food, there is no meat to go get for her.
>
> You white people have holidays. You have Christmas and things like that. In the past when we looked out for pigs and went to the bush, we also looked out for cassowaries for our daughters. When it was time to sell our daughters, we had this big festival; it was like your Christmas. It was a time of big happiness. Then we showed the cassowaries we had gotten, and we had a big festival.
>
> People from other places came; people from all over; people who were relatives of my wife's father, people from other villages, even people from Haia sometimes! We got to visit and see relatives who live far way. Now we don't do that anymore.

Another old man said:

> Before we didn't have people telling us what to do too much. Men were the men, and they made decisions. Now there is RCF and the government. But before them, the missions came, and before them the Kiaps. Some of the changes are good. The government makes sure that there are no fights now. That is good. But my father is dead now, and I have become the last of his sons alive. I am the one who remembers his stories of before the Kiaps came.

Older people miss the social relations of the past, while younger people often associate custom with an antimodern backwardness. People do not see their culture or their identities as static. While people invoke *kastom* (custom) at times, and this will be discussed in the section "Making Gender" in terms of the control of women, there is an awareness of cultural fluidity.[21] This awareness is juxtaposed with some conservationist's images of "Giminess," which tie "true" Gimi identity to past social practices which are no longer part of daily life in Maimafu.

The preceding speech also highlights the local understanding that change comes from outside — via missions and the colonizer in the past and via conservation, researchers, and tourists in the present — and from within. Local agency with regard to change is also expressed in that speech. People express the feeling that they had, and have, a choice about which "traditional" practices they wish to continue and which they wish to abolish.

When the first Australian colonial officer came to Maimafu, he appointed certain men as the "big-men" in the village. The names listed on the earliest patrol report, when shown to men in Maimafu, elicited a response of "oh yes, those men were big-men. He just marked them officially." Karubo appears in early patrol reports from the area and in Gajdusek's journals (1968:55, 58). He was one of the first men to be appointed as luluai (village leader) in the area. Most people in Maimafu today, who were alive in the late 1950s and early 1960s, remember Karubo as a strong leader in fights and as the most talented warrior they had ever seen. They also remember him as generous, kind to his kin and allies, and a man who could lead with intelligence. He seems to fit well with anthropological descriptions of big-men.[22]

This type of sociopolitical organization, organized around big-men, is the norm in Melanesia (Knauft 1999:10) and is a cultural complex based on exchange, oratory skills, aggression, and other signs of strength and knowledge (Meggitt 1971; Sahlins 1963; A. J. Strathern 1966, 1971). Instead of changing the sociopolitical and status system drastically, colonization and subsequent migration to the coasts by adult males to work on plantations supplemented the status requirements for big-men. It added another level for the measurement of strength and knowledge. Mr. Kayaguna, arguably one of the two most respected men in the village, derives much of his big-man status from having lived in other places, having been a member of government, and having completed some schooling. Many of the other older and well-respected men in the community worked as wage laborers on plantations in the 1960s and 1970s.

Twelve men with whom I conducted semistructured interviews went to work on plantations after the first colonial officials had come to the village. These men worked in Lae, Madang, Rabal, and Port Moresby, and they spent, on average, five years away from Maimafu. One of them, Joseph, went to Madang to work on a copra plantation. He worked there for about two years, first as a cutter and later as a cooker. He thinks that he left Maimafu when he was almost twenty. While in Madang, Joseph learned to speak Melanesian Pidgin fluently and to navigate the government and city systems. He gained knowledge about the rest of the world while he was away. When he came back to Maimafu, he was treated with respect. He told me in May 1998, "We have always had leaders here. They are leaders because they have knowledge and because of what they say and do. They come up in our village as big-men because of these things. They must be intelligent, strong, powerful, and they must know about how to get development to the people."

In the past there were different criteria for high-status positions in the community. Now many of the criteria have to do with access to, and knowledge about, development, the government, the conservation organization, and the outside world. However, this is not always the case; there are still important criteria of status other than long-distance travel and knowledge of other ways of life. Aside from Mr. Kayaguna, Kabi, the other most well-respected man in the community, did work on a plantation for about a year back in the 1960s, but aside from that, has not left his land. As mentioned earlier, Kabi's father was a powerful leader in the community, and Kabi is a renowned hunter, a strong orator, and a skillful political actor, but Kabi also has something else that makes him powerful: he is thought to be a sorcerer. He holds an older kind of knowledge than does Mr. Kayaguna, but he and his knowledge are equally respected. Even people who are Seventh-Day Adventists, and thus believe that practicing magic is a "sin," revere him.[23]

People in Maimafu tend to paint a rather idyllic picture of family relations before the Kiaps came, saying that everyone lived together and that they were all "one group." Glick, however, argues that there was intense and "endemic" intervillage fighting before the Australian pacification and that Gimi "heartily enjoyed" it (Glick 1967b:39). In contrast to their portrayal of family life as idyllic, elderly people in Maimafu tend to portray other parts of life, before the Australians, as difficult, such as this account, related to me in April 1998:

> Right before the first Kiap came to Maimafu, there was a big sickness that swept
> through the region. Our fathers and mothers did not know what was causing it

then. It was a terrible sickness. Many people died, and it was especially hard on children. It was a kind of sickness where you defecate blood and you throw up blood. Blood runs from both ends.[24]

Now we know that this sickness came because the Jews killed Jesus. They killed him, and the blood ran out of him. This blood running out of him caused the blood to run out of people here. The blood ran out of our ancestors just like it ran out of Jesus when he was on the cross. Right after this sickness ended, the first Kiap came.

That first white man, he told us the story that there would be some mission men coming after him. He said that they would come and give us new ways to do things. After he came, we waited a while, and then we heard about Master Ben.[25]

The first mission that the majority of people who now live in Maimafu can remember is the Faith Mission at Gona. Ben Wertz, an American, established the mission in 1954. His wife, Talila, joined him later that same year. Although the area was still "uncontrolled," and Talila was the first white woman in the area, they set up a small mission station, and Ben began wandering through the land to the south of Mount Michael converting people to his brand of Christianity. He remained on the outskirts of the Unavi census division until early 1962 (Gillison 1993:5). One adopted daughter of Ben and Talila said to me in August 1998:

Ben and Talila were brave. Especially Talila. I mean these people, the Gimi, were living in the Stone Age, and they went to live among them. I have seen the movies that Ben shot in 1953 and 1954, and they scare me. My birth mother is in them. She was Gimi and my father was a white Australian Kiap, and it is like looking at the ancient past to see her.

In June 2002, I had the pleasure of meeting another one of Ben's and Talila's adopted children. This woman, a Papua New Guinean, was running for the Lufa open seat during the 2002 national elections. She defined herself as their "adopted" daughter, even though she grew up with her own birth parents. Her father, a prominent political leader in the Lufa District right after independence, was a missionary trained by Ben. She recounted the following story about Ben:

After Ben returned home from the war [World War II], he got malaria. He was very very sick, and everyone around him thought that he was going to die. While

68

he was sick, he had a vision. God came to him and told him to go back to New Guinea. God told him to go to [a place called] Gona and begin a mission to spread the word of God. Ben himself was not a Godly man at the time, but Talila's father was a missionary. After he was healthy again he told Talila about his vision, and she was not surprised.

At first Ben went to New Ireland. He thought that he would find Gono there, but he did not so he came back to New Guinea, and he found out that there was a Gono in the Eastern Highlands. So he came here to Gono, and he began the Faith Mission. Talila was the first white woman to come here. She was the first one. There had been white men before, but she was the first white woman that my ancestors ever saw. Imagine that. Seeing a white woman for the first time [*she touches my face with her hand*]. Imagine seeing that pale skin for the first time!

Ben and Talila built the mission up over the years, and now Mike and Barbara are here. They, all of them, have brought all of the development that has come to these places. To Gona, Kora, Guwasa, and the other small bush places. Ben was a great man; he changed lives for the better. His ways were strict, but they brought us medicine and school. He was a great man.

Most people in Maimafu who remember Ben refer to him as Master Ben, and they remember him visiting nearby areas right before the total eclipse of the sun that occurred on 5 February 1962. One woman from Kora, a settlement to the north of Maimafu, recalled in May 1998 why she associated him with the eclipse:

Master Ben came in right before the eclipse. He said that God was going to show a sign. He said that God was trying people and that the sign was to show them that they had to become Christians. He said that if the people did not go with him in faith that God would destroy them with the power that makes the sun go dark.

A very old man, one who says that even before Ben came to settlements to the north of Maimafu, he had walked with his brothers to go see this white man in Gona, also remembers the story Ben told about the coming eclipse, which he conveyed to me in May 1998:

Master Ben said, "The God that I am telling you people about will give you a sign. He will make the sun go black in three days time. You must stay inside your house and eat there for the next three days. You must not go to the forest. You must not disbelieve. You should listen to the story that is in the Bible." We all went to our houses afraid, and then when the sun changed, and he was right we all believed. It was as he said. The sun went black, and we were afraid of what would happen if we did not listen to this white man.

In late 1961 people in New Guinea began to hear rumors and stories about the impending total eclipse of the sun (Glasse and Lindenbaum 1967:46). The colonial government distributed information about it to ensure that the people on the island understood what was about to come, but this government-issued information was in the form of radio broadcasts and press releases, and probably would not have reached Maimafu. Robert Glasse and Shirley Lindenbaum (1967) recount the reactions to the 1962 eclipse among Fore. Even though the Fore peoples, with whom Glasse and Lindenbaum lived and worked, knew well in advance that the eclipse was coming and had had it explained to them by many, their reaction on the morning of 5 February was one of profound fear and uncertainty (ibid.:50). They regarded the eclipse as intimately tied to whites and as "a religious phenomenon" (ibid.:52).[26]

In Maimafu, right after the eclipse, people built a house for Ben Wertz, but then another missionary came to the area. This man was a Papua New Guinean missionary and a Seventh-Day Adventist. His name was Mr. Kassa, and he lived in Maimafu from 1962 to 1977. One devout SDA said, in July 1998,

When he [Mr. Kassa] came, he showed pictures of missionaries in Australia. They were white people. When the adults — I was only a boy then — saw the pictures, they thought that all of the dead that they had buried had gone to this place. They thought that the people in the pictures were their dead relatives. They recognized people, their husbands and sons and fathers. They thought that all of the dead had gone to Australia. They cried and cried over the pictures.

They thought that the dead in Australia made all the cargo that the Kiaps and the white missionary [Ben Wertz] brought with them to New Guinea. They thought that the whites were keeping the cargo themselves. They thought that their ancestors made those things and the white people were keeping them. But Mr. Kassa said this was not true. The missionary finally cleared this up and taught people that when you die you go to heaven or hell, not to Australia.

Right after the sun went black, they built a house and a church for Mr. Kassa.

He told us that everything Master Ben said were lies and that we would burn in hell if we believed him. He stayed here a long time, many years. His house and the church were next to the place where the airstrip is now. That is the place that was originally where people lived, but Mr. Kassa said that we should move and that we should not live so close to the big mountain. He said that it might fall down on us. So he went and found a better place for us to live, and there is where Motai is now.

After they built a house for him and moved the village, he started teaching people the right ways of God.

Following strict SDA doctrine, Mr. Kassa told people that fighting, marrying more than one woman, eating pigs, eating other "taboo" animals, sex before marriage, drinking, smoking, and playing cards were all wrong in the eyes of God and that if they engaged in these behaviors, they would go to hell. He also told them that they must build and live in single-family homes. People say that they had built single-family homes when the Kiaps told them to build them, but that they still spent the majority of their time in single-sex men's and women's houses. Mr. Kassa also focused much of his attention on the lineage and "clan" level of society, telling people that it was not enough for one or two people to become SDAs, but rather that whole families had to make the choice to "go the way of God."[27]

Mr. Kassa also taught people that both initiation ceremonies and traditional marriage ceremonies were evil and must be stopped. When I asked in June 1998 why people believed this man and why they chose to give up the traditions he deemed as "sinful," one man answered,

Christianity has come to this place and taught us about heaven and hell. Mr. Kassa told us that our traditional customs were a sin and that we must forget them. The men's house, the women's house, hunting certain kinds of animals, keeping pigs, initiation, and our traditional marriage ceremonies, these things are all sinful. He told that this was a sin so we had to stop it or go to hell.

We believed him because of his knowledge about hell. But we also believed him because he had come to help us. He was the one who first sent Kayaguna to school. Kayaguna was the first. Mr. Kassa taught us that if we believed in God, things would come to us. Knowledge would come, education would come, and services would come.

Now you see, before he came to our place, but after the Kiaps started coming, some of the men, Soko, Natu, and others, had gone out to the coast to work on plantations. They had seen what development was. They had seen services and cargo that Christians got. We heard their talk about Madang and Rabal and Lae, and we knew that Mr. Kassa was speaking the truth. We saw that we had nothing here like the men described, and we knew it was because of our sins.

The combination of Christian stories of hell, with the very real fear that they engendered, and stories of coastal towns brought back to Maimafu by men who had worked on plantations made people see a "lack" in their own village. Some people tied this lack to their traditional practices, while others tied it to development. Many older men and women speak about Christianity as their salvation from the harsh life of "the time before" and as a viable avenue for "development."

Joel Robbins (2004:2–3) outlines two of the standard explanations for rapid transformations from historic systems of belief to Christianity. The first is that missionaries' intense activities, tied to the "compulsions and seductions of the colonial or Western orders the missionaries represent," worked to transform lives and beliefs (ibid.:2).[28] The second is that rapid Christianization occurs because of "radical socioeconomic dislocation" (ibid.). As people encounter new economic forms, take part in the market economy, move to new places in order to access markets, and the like, their older ways of being in the world are less apt to help them understand the new worlds in which they move (ibid.:3). Because of this, they turn to systems of belief and new "conceptual schemes" that allow them to better understand their new life circumstances (ibid.). Both of these explanations seems to indicate that people take up bits and pieces of culture to help understand and maneuver in their new modernities. In his explanation of Urapmin (an ethnic group and their language in PNG) Christianity and cultural change, however, Robbins argues that the Urapmin did not use Christianity to "patch" their "traditional cultural fabric," but rather that they took up Christianity as a culture in itself and that they now work with two simultaneous cultural logics (Robbins 2004). Gimi seem, however, to better fit with the first two explanations: those of intense mission activity and Western orders, and rapid socioeconomic dislocation or change. In many ways, the residents of Maimafu are correct about the connection between Seventh-Day Adventism and development. The missionaries associated with the religion have brought numerous services to the village. In fact, SDA missionaries and missionaries associated with Mission Aviation Fellowship (MAF) have been the key conduit for health, education, economic gain, and other aspects of development for the people of Maimafu.[29] The SDA mission in Papua New Guinea (PNG) has grown dramatically over the past fifty years. Organized in 1953, the Eastern Highlands SDA Mission began with 7 churches and 758 members. Today, in the Eastern Highlands Subdistrict of PNG, the church has 172 churches and 66,106 members.

THE SDA CHURCH

[handwritten: perpetuating fear IN ORDER TO ↓ CONTROL]

The SDA movement began in the 1840s in the northeastern New England states and was officially named in 1863.[30] The first SDA missionaries were sent to the Pacific in 1890, and today the church's Web site boasts that mission work is being done in over 207 countries. The church is focused on the end of the world as one of its central beliefs. At the end of "this time," according to SDAs in Maimafu, Christ will return to earth with his angels, and they will take all who are "saved" to heaven. Those who are left behind will be tormented by a thousand years of hell-on-earth by Satan,[31] who will return to earth from hell after the ascension of the saved to heaven. At the end of this thousand-year period, Christ will return, battle Satan, and win. God will then send a great fire to the earth that will kill all the unsaved souls and reform the earth into paradise. This paradise will be free of sin, and those who live there will be in perfect harmony with each other and with "God's other creations." God will come to earth and walk among the people and the animals. He will "walk about the bush, and talk to the sky and rivers and moon." This paradise will be perfect: there will be no fighting, no hunger, no poverty, no death, and no suffering. This phase of the earth will last forever. Before the dawn of the thousand years of hell-on-earth, people must prepare themselves for salvation. During this lifetime, death is inevitable since it is the "punishment for sin."[32]

The church officially recognizes "man" as God's steward on earth, and the church's members in Maimafu argue that "God made the forest; he made the trees and the birds, and the rivers. Because of this, we must look after the forest. It is God's, and he has entrusted it to us for safekeeping until he returns to us." The SDA Church prohibits the eating of most animals that have traditionally been important to Gimi diets; this includes pigs. There are no pigs in any of the ridgetop settlements that are included in the village of Maimafu, though there are pigs in settlements that are quite close. While this might seem unbelievable to those familiar with Papua New Guinean subsistence practices, I am convinced that it is the case. I visited all of the settlements numerous times, often unannounced. I also spent many nights at each settlement and never once saw a pig. This is not to say that people do not consume pork. On numerous occasions during 2001 and 2002, while I visited non-SDA villages with people from Maimafu, we consumed pork. These pigs had been killed in celebration of elected officials visiting in 2002, and they were simply bits of pork shared with us by extended family members in 2001.

The rationale behind getting rid of all of the pigs in the village is partially tied to religious prohibitions, but it is also tied to the difficulties of keeping pigs, as expressed in this account by a forty-year-old man in March 1998:

> In 1982 we got rid of all of our pigs because we are SDAs. But also because we were all tired of the work that has to go into pigs. They are lots of work. We had to build fences all of the time, and they still got in gardens. We had fights over them all the time, and now we don't. Now the place is nice; we have decoration around the houses, and we didn't have this before the pigs.

People argue that pigs are dirty and that they used to be the cause of many fights. They also attribute the beauty of their hamlets to the absence of pigs — arguing that it is easy to keep flowers and decorative shrubs now that there are not pigs to root them up.[33]

THE HISTORY OF DEVELOPMENT

The absence of pigs in Maimafu is tied to both religious prohibitions and real-world individual choices regarding "development." In 1982, when the village (adult men) "voted" to kill all their pigs and give up raising them forever, they also voted to build, with the help of the SDA Church, a community airstrip.[34] There are various stories about why people decided to build an airstrip, but the one told most often is about carrying coffee to the "head of the road" in Ubaigubi. This story resonates with the origin stories discussed earlier. When people tell the story, it is told as truth, and it is recounted as something that happened to them personally. Here is one version, communicated to me in August 1998:

In 1980 my wife and I carried seventy kilograms of coffee and our baby to Ubaigubi. We wanted to sell the coffee in Goroka, so we had to carry it to a place with a road. She carried fifty kilograms, and I carried twenty and the baby. It was a terrible walk. We went up over the mountains, and I hurt my back as we crossed. I sat down in the road and cried. I told my wife that if I made it to Ubaigubi alive, I would stand up for government election and build a road or an airstrip to Maimafu. I cried because the government forgot my people. I cried because they see us as useless, and they do not help us. I promised my wife that if I won, I would build an airstrip, build a road, start a school, and build a hospital.

The man who told me this version of the coffee-carrying story was Kelego Kayaguna. Mr. Kayaguna is, as mentioned above, one of the most well-respected men in Maimafu. In 1966, upon the urging of Mr. Kassa, whom Mr. Kayaguna had been working for in the village, Mr. Kayaguna was the first man from Maimafu to go out of the village for schooling. While Mr. Kassa had been teaching a few literacy classes in Maimafu, so people could read the Bible, there was no formal community school in place. Mr. Kayaguna left home in 1966 and attended mission school in Karimui. He then worked from 1970 to 1974 as a SDA missionary and returned to Maimafu in 1974.[35] Today, he is the elected village councilor for Maimafu and the leading advocate for gold mining in the area.

The building of the airstrip is one of the most salient events in the history of development in Maimafu. Both men and women mark its building as the beginning of "getting services" and development. Although the construction of the aid post began before the construction of the airstrip, and the building was completed before the first plane landed in Maimafu, people see the airstrip as their link to the rest of the country. Mr. Kayaguna, when discussing the first plane to land in Maimafu, said to me in January 1998,

> The first plane came in 1992. It was an SDA plane. The church had given us tools to build the airstrip. They brought them in on a helicopter, and we started working. They were the first to use the airstrip. When the plane landed, we sat down and cried. That airstrip is our link to development. All of what we have comes through it. People here believed me in 1982 when I sat down with the men and told them my idea of the airstrip. They started to build it. It took ten years to finish it. They worked hard. Not just men, but the whole village. We worked to make this happen, and it did.

The people here built it for nothing. They did not get paid for the first nine years of work. When I was elected in 1991, I got some money from the national government, but it was very little. One year's wages for ten years of work. Like I said, it is our link to the world. People can sell their coffee and get money now. People can go to Goroka if they are very sick. They can get things from stores now. They can get things that they need.

In many ways the airstrip is the center of modern community life in Maimafu. It is where all goods enter, all coffee exits, and most outsiders enter, and it is the conduit of information about the rest of the world. The plane landing is a big event every time. On days that it is scheduled to land — and people know this because there is an "agent" for both MAF and Seventh-Day Adventist Aviation (SDAA) in the village who calls the mission air services on the radio daily — people from all of the ridgetops go to the airstrip to wait. Waiting on the plane is a community event.

The point cannot be made too strongly — everything that comes to Maimafu comes on an airplane. The connection to these airplane landings and the airstrip as a conduit to the rest of the world can be seen in people's discussions about the pilots. Everyone in the village knows every pilot's name, where they live, what their family makeup is, what church they go to, whether they like peanuts or not, and myriad other personal facts. Although MAF and SDAA are the only planes that fly regular routes that include Maimafu, there are a few other planes that land sporadically in the village. Ian Leslie, an Australian pilot who owns his own charter airline, and New Tribes Mission, occasionally land in the village, as do Pacific Helicopters. When these unusual planes and helicopters land, the fervor over the landing is even greater than when it is a scheduled flight by MAF or SDAA.

The village airstrip is the site of new things, ideas, people, and money. All of the RCF activities are centered close to the airstrip, and all of the RCF and Wildlife Conservation Society (WCS) affiliates who come into the village enter that way. All of the teachers, though they rarely stay a full term in the village, come on planes and live next to the airstrip. The community school is immediately next to the airstrip. All coffee buyers come on planes and take purchased coffee to Goroka on planes. Finally, all trade-store goods come into the community on planes, and trade-store goods are a high marker of development.

In addition to the airstrip, the community aid post and the community school are seen as the two other historic sources of development in Maimafu. These three places are seen by most as the seats of what will lead to further development and as the places that can help people create social relationships that will lead to development. In most of my interviews in Maimafu, with both males and females, people said that better upkeep for the airstrip, medicine and a trained doctor for the aid post, and teachers who would stay in Maimafu are the keys to future development. Although there is a growing desire for personal economic gain, including jobs, money, and status, most people argue that the only way for "development" to flourish is with access to and from the rest of the country (airstrip), adequate health care (aid post), and education (school).

When I asked one man in 1998 where he thinks these kinds of development would come from, he answered with the following commentary on the outside sources of development options. This section of the interview highlights the frustrations that the residents of Maimafu feel in regard to promises made to them in the past about development and services:

> The national members [of Parliament] forget about us here in the rural areas, so we bring in people like RCF. They must help us and they must bring development. With one hand they bring their story of conservation, so with the other they must bring development. We hear their talk; we hear, "You must look out for your bush" all the time, but we do not see development. We work with them, and we do not sell or give our land to people who will destroy it, but if no development comes, if it is just talk, then we will be forced to find a way to make money. We will have to look to other sources, like oil, gold mines, and logging. We will be forced to do this.

He went on to say,

> I am not clear about what RCF is doing or has done. They say that they have brought development. What I see is that they have brought a few tourists, who would have perhaps come anyway, and many scientists. They bring them, and they take our knowledge and learn about our bush, but what do we get from them? We get some money, a little, for carrying their bags or for helping them, but it is not enough. I am just not clear what development they have brought to us, but I am clear that they said that if we do conservation, they would bring development. It is like the men who come here before they run for Provincia

77

government. They say, "vote for me and I will bring development," so we vote for them. But we never see anything from them. It is all the same.

POLITICS

He concluded his commentary with the following:

> But I have one big worry about development today. I think that RCF must find a way to help the children here go to school. They must make sure that we can give our children a decent education and some training. If they do this, our children will come back to their homes. They will come here and be doctors and teachers. They will not forget about us. If they [the RCF] and the government keep sending people in from other places [teachers and the like], they will always leave. This is not their home. It is our home.

The preceding speech also shows the difficult position that the RCF has come to hold. The organization is primarily concerned with the conservation of biological diversity. But since the RCF has become inextricably linked to local development, people expect it to take on the role of the government. The RCF is expected to help manage local disputes, bring teachers to the village, maintain the health center, help to maintain the airstrip, provide sources of income, provide access to services in Goroka, and many other services that belong in the realm of government services. The RCF is also supposed to take part in the social creation of children by contributing to their school fees. If one gives money to a parent to help pay for a child's school fees, if it is a girl, they are to receive part of her future bride price; and if it is a boy, they then have the obligation to help when he pays a bride price.

In some ways, the conservation practitioners who work for the RCF have gotten themselves into this position. Relying on the conservation-as-development discourses engendered by the Biodiversity Conservation Network (BCN) funding of the Crater Mountain project, they have tied themselves, a conservation organization, to local development desires. They have, in the past, promised development, and now they are expected to be the agency that brings it to Maimafu. People in Maimafu see conservation-as-development as another episode in the story of nonreciprocity on the part of outsiders. They feel like they have given what they agreed to give: land, labor, and support; but that they have not received what they wanted in exchange: development as they envision it.

MAKING THE FOREST

In this section, I introduce the ways in which Gimi understand the environment and their relationship to it. I begin with a brief discussion of how I asked people in Maimafu about how they understand the past and imagine the future. In order to do this, I explain Gimi linguistic conventions for talking about the imagination.

In the Gimi language, there are several ways to talk about the imagination and images. An "image" can be a visual image, such as a picture (*aona*, where *ao* is "eye" and *na* is "eat and thing"), an image created through language by someone else, such as a parable (*afae gaina* or *gaina*: "speaking that has taken place"), or an image that you create through language (*afae kaina* or *kaina*: "language"). An image that exists in your head that is not visual and not created through language, so a sense or a feeling, is *Iuna*. A dream that you have at night when you are asleep is *amo rana*, and "I dream" is "amo rano ago." In asking people about how they imagine things, in both the past and the future, I have tried to use these Gimi terms. I've distinguished between dreams that happen at night (*amo rana*) and dreams that happen during the day or imaginings (*amo rana kuna*, where *kuna* is "day"; and *amo rana fo*, where *fo* is "sun"). In order to understand how Gimi make their environment and make themselves through their relations with that environment, one must understand dreams.

Dreams that you have at night have different meanings to different generations of Gimi. Older people believe that their *auna* (life force)[36] leaves their body at night and flies through the village and to the forest and sometimes lodges in the bodies of birds or marsupials (Gillison 1993:108).[37] Before morning, the auna comes back to the sleeping person. When a person dies, his or her life force leaves the body as if it were leaving for a dream. This often takes several days, especially if the person is young. Until the auna has left the body — and the vicinity of the settlement in general — and has gone to the forest, the auna can be quite dangerous (ibid.:122). In the past, the ritual consumption of men's bodies by women and children and the subsequent taking of the large bones to the forest by men were crucial steps in this process.[38] A year after a man's death, the men from his family would carry his bones to the forest held by his clan (Gillison 1994:38). When the auna finally leaves the body for good, it goes to the person's clan's ground (the ancestral hunting grounds) and gradually turns into *kore* (spirit) and lodges itself in animals, plants, mountains, and every other part of the forest (Gillison 1993:122). The "wild" parts of the forest (*kore*: "wild"; *maha*: "ground") are filled with, and "animated by" the kore of Gimi who have passed away (ibid.:199). The forest as wild (kore) is literally the spirit of the dead (kore). There is a subtle transformation here—the life force becomes the spirit and then returns to the forest from which it came; the auna was the form the kore took while it was in the living person—but it was always, and always will be, the kore that animates the forests. People and forest have been, and will always be, for these older Gimi, one (Gillison 1980).

Older people also believe that dreams, auna, and kore are intimately tied to conception and childbirth (Gillison 1993:208). When a woman conceives, she must dream about some sort of animal that is the "ancestral incarnation of the fetus in a dream" (ibid.). Dreams of frogs, fish, and ground-dwelling animals will bring a female child, while dreams of birds will bring a male.[39] Gillison (ibid.:101) argues that "the dissolution of a man's bones enriches his clan forest, giving rise to new life forms in the way semen engenders life in a woman's body." In the past, when a woman was married she was forced to drink water from a river on the land held by her husband's family. This was the spirit of her husband's ancestors, and it made it possible for her to conceive her husband's child (Gillison 1980:160).[40] Gimi also believe that everything that comes from the forest is a "gift" from their ancestors (Gillison 1993:200) that is infused with the kore of their ancestors.

Younger Gimi do not recount the movements of auna and kore in the same way as older Gimi do. Indeed, kore has come to be seen as the "devil" or "evil spirit" because of the SDA missions. For younger Gimi, auna is your "soul," and when you die it will go to "heaven." A kore is always a bad or malfeasant entity, and it is not connected to the living in any way. If there are kore in the forest at all, they are devil-like tricksters who wish to lure people to their death or to "Satan," who is a constant danger to missionized Gimi. One must be constantly vigilant in the fight against him; he is always lurking, always waiting for you to make a mistake. One way to make a mistake and invite him into your "soul" is to pay too much attention to the old stories and beliefs and to pay heed to the lessons to be learned in myth and ritual. To believe that the forest *is literally your ancestors*, that there is a set of social ties and bonds between you and the forest, is to discount "God's" power on earth. Younger Gimi are beginning to believe that God created the forests and their inhabitants. To imagine that your ancestors made the forest and the forest made them is blasphemy for which you will go to "hell."

For older Gimi, they and their forests are in a constant cocreation with each other. Tim Ingold (2000), drawing on the idea of the *Umwelt* (environment) and on Martin Heidegger's (1971) ideas of building and dwelling, sees humans and animals as constituting their worlds and themselves through their activities in the world. His project is a radical rereading of life-on-earth in which humanity is not seen as separate from the environment, but rather as constituting itself through social relations with and in the environment (Ingold 2000). Ingold develops the idea of an "organism-in-its-environment" as opposed to the more traditional idea of an organism (person or beaver or parasite) in an environment (village or pond or human body). By this, he wishes to convey that the organism *is* only in relation to its environment, and its environment *is* only in relation to the organism (ibid.:172). This sort of relational notion of being-in-the-world by which an organism constitutes and is constituted by its environment is the way that older Gimi understand their life-in-the-world. When men place the bones of their dead into caves and the hollows of trees, they become part of the forest, and from them flows new growth, water from the high mountains, and the animals that sustain life (Gillison 1980:159).

For Gimi of the past, and for some Gimi today, the forest is an "exalted domain" of unlimited power (Gillison 1980:143) where past, present, and future intertwine to make the world and all the people in it. For these Gimi, the forest is a male space, one produced out of male actions and spirit, where "the male spirit, incarnate in birds and marsupials, acts out its secret desires away from the inhibiting presence of women" (ibid.).[41] The forest is a *source* of power and a *sink* for matter that is not at play elsewhere in the Gimi world or in the bodies of Gimi themselves (ibid.:145; 1993:101, 200). This conception of the forest as source and sink is articulated in historic Gimi myth and rituals, particularly in rites of initiation. Gillison (1980, 1993) examines the relation between myth and ritual in order to show that the logic of myth actually provides the motivation for ritual, and that the two, combined with Gimi ways of knowing the forest, literally make up what it is to be Gimi (1993:102).

In the past, Gimi rites of male initiation were intimately tied to knowledges concerning birds of paradise, especially the Raggiana bird of paradise (Gillison 1980:146; 1993:339).[42] Boys become birds during initiation ceremonies involving imitations of the behavior of birds (Gillison 1980:146) so that they may, through the embodying of the male perfection of the forest, become men. Gillison (1980) and M. Strathern (1988) read male rituals among Gimi as texts that lay out men's power with respect to women through detaching female characteristics from women and allowing men to "appropriate" them (ibid.: 111). But the appropriating goes both ways, in that women also through their roles in myth and through their actions work to make men at the same time that men work to make women. The point is that the transactions between men and women in myth, in the present, and in the imagined future, work to make "male" and "female" and hence these gender roles are not inscribed on bodies as identity, but rather lived through social interactions (M. Strathern 1988).

Kabi, one of the oldest men in Maimafu, recounted the story of his initiation to me in June 2003. As I asked him about the symbolism of the birds of paradise, he grew frustrated and finally told me that I was getting it wrong. He argued that initiates were not like birds, that they were birds. That for a second during the process, they were transmogrified into birds and that through their trans- mogrification, there was a moment in which their ancestors' spirit (which be- came them), their spirit (which will go back to the forest when they die), and the birds in which those spirits come to rest were all one. Men are also at one with the forest when they use it for hunting, fishing, or gathering (Gillison 1980:152). Men in the present become men in the past (their ancestors) as the forest, which houses past and future spirits, produces or gives forth the things needed for the present life. And although parts of the forests, marsupials, and the cavities of trees and rocks, are female, the forest itself is male. But the male is only "male" if it encompasses aspects of the female. It is through this constant dialectic of gender that each is made (M. Strathern 1988).

Like many Highlanders (Lindenbaum 1981:123), Gimi also have a notion that resides in forests, which is older than ideas about "Satan" and "evil." In Unavisa Gimi the term *neki maha* means "crazy ground" or "mad ground" (*neki*: "mad," "crazy," "not right"; *maha*: "ground" or "place"), and it is used in discussions of dangerous places in the forest.[43] McBride and McBride (1973:4) report that in the past, each Gimi clan had its own patch of "forbidden ground" which was inhabited by *neki kianak*, or "bush spirits." These spirits were thought to cause death, insanity, blindness, and dumbness to people who tres- passed on their lands (ibid.). They were also thought to cause birth defects in women who walked across their lands when pregnant, and in one instance to have caused a man to lose the ability to speak his own language (ibid.).

Gillison (1993:224) recounts that among Gimi she worked with, neki maha were "bad" places that spanned a range of environmental types from swampy marsh areas to high alpine bogs. If a man were to trespass into a neki maha while his wife was pregnant, there were almost certainly going to be consequences for the child (ibid.). And if the man had ever trespassed into one, there was a chance that this could still come back to affect his pregnant wife and his children (ibid.). The animals and plants that reside in a neki maha could also work sorcery against people who trespassed there or who were careless while hunting or gathering nearby (Gillison 1993:225). And the kore of unborn and young children who died tended to "gravitate" toward the neki maha because there was abundant food there — since no one hunted or gathered on the land — and their kore became lodged in the low and dark places there. (ibid.:226). In the past, neki maha were also of use to sorcerers. A sorcerer could leave something from his intended victim in a neki maha as a part of his technique of attack (ibid.:313). And finally, the neki maha was also used metaphorically by men to describe the dangerous interior of women's bodies (ibid.:211).

Today, the Maimafu Gimi see neki maha as specific, known places in the forest which one should avoid. They are described as dangerous, scary, and unclean. Everyone knows the story of Horara's father, a man who went hunting for cassowary in neki maha when his wife was pregnant. His son, Horara, was born like a normal child, "fat" and "happy," but when he was about two years old, he fell into a cooking fire. Instead of just burning the baby, although he was burned badly, the fire brought out the madness derived from the trespass in the neki maha, and Horara became *neki* (mad) himself.[44] The neki maha is so dangerous that if you fall down in the forest while walking by it, you, your unborn child, or your kin can be injured. I have been told repeatedly, while walking in the forest, that I cannot go anywhere near neki maha because of my tendency to fall down. Many older Gimi give explanations for what neki maha is that resonate with Gillison's work, but some young people say neki maha is full of devils sent by Satan.

In asking both men and women about the relationships between people and the forests and birds and people in particular, I was often told the two following stories (the first is a version told by "Little Rick" in 1997, the second by Kumpalahoyi in 1998):

Where Men Came From

Once there were three birds in the bush. There were Kokomo, Koke, and Feletae. Kokomo and Koke were at the river getting ready to take a bath. Feletae was high in the trees finding food. Koke said to Kokomo, "Kokomo, you wash first, and I will watch your feathers while you are in the water." Kokomo said, "No Koke, that is nice for you to offer, but you go first and I will watch your feathers while you are in the water." So Koke took Kokomo up on his offer. He took off his feathers, and he was a black man under them. He got in the water and began to wash. While he [Koke] was washing, Kokomo looked at Koke's beautiful feathers and decided to try them on. He put them on and liked the way that they looked. He strutted around and saw that the new feathers made his tail long and different from any other bird. He liked them so much that he slipped away with them while Koke was washing.

When Koke got out of the water, he looked for his feathers, but he could not find them. He looked and looked. He called out to all of the other birds in the forest, and he asked, "Has anyone seen my feathers?" No one had. Then Feletae came down and said that he had seen what happened to them.

So Feletae and Koke went to look for Kokomo. They looked everywhere. They looked in the hamlets where the birds lived. They looked near the water. Then they looked in the big bush. Kokomo was hiding in the bush. They caught him, and Feletae, who was small but had a big bush knife, cut him four times on the head. He put four marks on him. Then he got away, but they caught him again. Feletae put four marks again on his head in the same place as the first four. Then Feletae took his hand and put blood on the back of his own neck.

This is why today people exist. They came from Koke, who lost his feathers. And this is why when you see Kokomo, he has beautiful long feathers different from any other bird. And this is why Feletae has a red spot on the back of his black and white neck. This is also why we can kill Kokomo for his feathers; they belonged to us to begin with.

Where the Birds Came From [45]

One day a woman whose husband had been killed said to her two young children, a boy and a girl, "You stay here near the banana tree while I go to the forest." She told them to stay near, and if they heard ripe bananas falling from the tree that would be a sign that she was dead. She was going to the garden that her husband had been in when he was killed. She told them to listen hard, and then she went through the forest up to the garden.

The garden was on a river, and she decided to go up the river to the head. So she went out of the garden and went up, noticing along the way that it seemed that her husband had gone that way before he died. She went up and up into the mountains following the trail that her husband had made. Along the way, she caught frogs and collected ferns and other greens. As she climbed higher and higher, she thought she heard another person.

She came to a clearing, and there was an old man sitting by a fire as if he were waiting on her. She asked him who he was, and he answered with a question for her. He said, "Who are you, and why are you here on my ground?" She replied that she was gathering greens for herself and her children. He asked where her children were, and she told him they were at home, but she did not tell him they were under the banana tree. He said that she could collect greens there or she could follow him and he would show her where there were more greens and some yams for her to dig. She followed him higher and higher.

They came to a place where there were yams, and she began to dig. He went off to do other things. When she looked up, he was standing over her with a sharp stick. It was covered in blood, and she knew that he had killed her husband in the same way: by leading him to this place in the forest and tricking him. Then he brought the stick down and killed her. He killed her, and then he ate her. After he ate her he put her skin on, and he became her. He put her legs on like pants and put her arms on like a shirt. After he put her on, he put her clothes on and took up her bilum. Then he went back down the mountain. Because he was her now, he knew where her house was so he went there.

He went down and down and then came to her house. He called out to her children, "I am home with greens for you." The old woman's daughter ran out and said, "We were worried about you," but she did not say anything about the banana tree. The man, disguised as their mother, said, "I am fine, but I am thirsty from the walk up up up the mountain. You must go and get me water to drink. Water to quench my thirst." So the young girl left her still younger brother with the man who she thought was her mother. She walked to the river all the time still knowing that she had heard the bananas fall, but not knowing that her mother was dead.

While the young girl had gone to the river, the man killed the small boy. He killed him and put his body in the roof of the house. Then he returned to a fire he was building. When the girl came home with the water, the man was cooking the greens that her mother had gathered. He told her that her brother was asleep in the bilum that he was carrying on his head, the bilum he had stolen from the dead mother.

The young girl sat down at the fire with the man and soon the man fell asleep. He slept and he slept while the girl worked her bilum. As she worked she thought that she felt rain coming through the roof, but then she remembered it was not raining. She wiped the "water" away that was dripping on her, and she saw that it was blood falling from the roof of the house. She looked up and saw her brother. Immediately she knew that the person sleeping was Satan and that he had led both her father and her mother high into the mountains, killed them, and then eaten them. She took her brother down and then killed the old man as he slept.

She put her brother's body in a bilum. She called to the dog, and then she burned down her father's house. As she ran from the house she heard the old man's spirit scream as it burned, but she knew he was Satan for sure then because she had killed the old man before she set the fire.

She then went to the forest for a while alone with the dog and her dead brother. After a while in the forest she wanted to find a husband, so she sent the dog to look for him. She told the dog that he should run to the ridgetops in the distance and look for her husband. She told him that if he found her husband, he should come back and wag his tail to show her the way. She sent him off, and soon he returned wagging his tail. She was not suspicious, because the dog was a good hunter when it had gone with her father, so she followed him to a garden house that was close by. In the house she found her husband.

When she entered the house, the man inside asked her why she was there. She did not answer with a question. She told him the story of her father and mother and brother. She stayed with him from then on. He was her husband.

After they were married, they took the things from their wedding and they threw them in a tree. They also put the dead brother in the tree. Then the husband went hunting. He told the new wife that no matter what she heard, she should not try to get into the tree. Then he went on his way.

The woman stayed in the house until she heard the tree singing. She went outside to see it, and it sang and moved. She remembered her husband's warning, so she did not climb in the tree, but she hit it with a great stick, one that was to become a fence post. When she hit the tree once, nothing happened. When she hit the tree the second time, nothing happened, but then, when she hit it a third time, it burst open.

Out of the tree flew all of the birds! All of the birds! All of the birds came out at once. All of them. Some went to live near the He River. Some went to live near the Nimi River. Some went up high into the mountains. They went to the top of Bopoyana[Crater Mountain]. Some went to the place where the salt water begins. But that is where they came from. They came from here. They came from what this woman did. They came from here.

Even though Christian origin stories are now widely known in Maimafu, these two stories were told to me repeatedly by old men and women when I asked about the relationships between people and birds. Both stories illustrate the creative, synergistic relation between humans and animals. The birds literally come from the body of the baby boy, and the bodies of men literally come from those of birds.

The man who told me the first story and the woman who told me the second story both agreed that the stories were used in the past to "teach children." Little Rick told me that the first story was to show little boys what bird to kill and to set the stage for other parts of men's behavior that was modeled on bird behavior. Kumpalahoyi indicated that the second story was to teach women to plant banana trees near their homes, not to go to the garden alone, not to speak to strangers, to listen to what their mothers tell them to do, and a whole host of other childhood lessons. She also said that the story "shows that the girl and her true husband put the dead boy in the tree but that it was the girl who let the birds out of the tree." It teaches that women generate the environment as much as men, even though the environment is talked about as "men's business," and thus have similar use rights, if they choose to act upon them. Gillison's (1993: 165) analysis of this second story is brilliant and complex. She argues that it is also "about" the taming of the wildness in women through marriage to the right man (ibid.:159). I asked Kumpalahoyi about this analysis, and she said,

Ah oh, this woman is a woman who knows! I have never thought that before, but the story does say that the girl is alone and roaming in the forest like a wild woman [*kore badaha*]. She is with a dog, and in her grief and anger she is alone. But then she finds the true husband, and she makes the birds, a good act.[46]

The stories both show this very primary productive relationship between birds —the ultimate local symbol of the forest and environment—and humans. In one story, birds and the environment, with the practices of people already a part of

7. Man making pandanus paste.

8. Boy with a pandanus nut.

behavior, give birth to humans. In the other, humans, while working out social issues and through social practices, give birth to birds and the environment.

Dianne Rocheleau, Barbara Thomas-Slayter, and Esther Wangari (1996) argue that there are real differences in the ways men and women experience and participate in environmental conservation. What is particularly important about their work, for the purposes of this chapter, is their assertion that in their multiple roles as producers, reproducers, and consumers, women are required to integrate themselves within increasingly complex scales of social relations (ibid.: 8). Women move between different scales in ways that are particular to their experiences as women. Indeed, in the context of Gimi social life, gender makes the scales, and the scales in turn work to make social relations between men and women, relations that themselves make gender.[47] In the story and analysis that follow, I will show how gender and scale are made in Maimafu today.

Once in the past, when we still had menstrual huts, a group of young women were all in the menstrual hut at the same time. In the hut, the girls kept their bamboo flutes, and when they went there, they would play them. The flutes made a beautiful sound, music like the birds in the forest. The men in the men's house heard the women playing, but they didn't know what it was. They thought that it was some bird that they had never seen.

One day, some young boys came to the menstrual hut and put their ears to the wall and heard the musical sounds coming out. Later that day, when the women had gone out to get firewood, the boys broke into the hut and looked around. At first they didn't see the flutes; all they saw were beds, a fire pit, and bamboo. But when they looked closely, they saw that the bamboo was really flutes. They stole them right then and there.

When the girls came back, they put their firewood down and made a fire. When they were done, they looked for their flutes, and they couldn't find them. Then they heard them coming from the men's house. The girls worried for a while over the flutes, and then finally they went to the men's house, and they asked them about the sounds. The boys said "Yes, that is right. We heard them coming from the menstrual hut, and we came and stole them. We liked the music, so we took them. You women can't have them back; they are ours now."[48]

9. Man wrapping a banana plant to protect it
from flying foxes.

Gillison interprets this myth as the first sexual encounter between men and women, and she argues that this is the "central myth" around which Gimi life is arranged (1991, 1993).[49] While I do not disagree with this interpretation, Kobe, the woman who on a dark night told me the story, interpreted it as follows:

> Women create things. They produce them and make them. Women give life to things, and then men see what they have made and they want it. They don't ask for things, they just take what they want. But it is women who do the real making. Do not be fooled by men's big talk and show. We are the ones who make life work.

Kobe's interpretation is instructive in terms of present-day gender relations. Today, there is a wide range of diversity in gender relations in Maimafu. Many women are dissatisfied with what men add to the family upkeep, and they complain bitterly, and constantly, about the growing pressures on their labor and the lack of work done by men. But others are, in general, happy with their husbands and their relations. Nasi, a woman about my age — twenty-eight when it was collected in 1998 — and born in a settlement about a two-day walk from Maimafu, encapsulates the story of contemporary marriage and gender relations in the following:

When I was a girl, before I got breasts, I was in Kuseri. I lived with my mother and father and my second mother. I was one of the children. I went to the garden with my mother, and I learned about gardens. I dug sweet potatoes with her and with my grandmother. I picked greens with my mother and my sisters. I was a girl there.

Then when I started my period, I was a woman. My family, my father and his brothers, had a big festival for me. They got meat from the forest, they killed pigs, they got garden food, they got pandanus, and they had a big party. Every-one came from our line and from the lines around Kuseri, Moti, and Biabitai. It was quite a party. There I saw all of the boys for the first time. I had seen them before, but now I knew that I was going to get married someday. All of the boys offered money to my father for me. They all saw that I was a hard worker and that I was a good woman. They offered money, but I saw Jessie and I took his money. I took it and gave it to my father, so I was marked for him.

After that Jessie and his uncles worked to get the things to buy me. They got rice and tinned fish and clothes. They got pigs and money. They gave me pres-ents, and then they bought me from my father. When I went to live in Moti, they gave me plenty of beautiful things to wear and decorations. They gave me things to make me look good. I went there, and there was a big party, but it was Seventh Day now, so it was different than at the place my father lives. The people from Kuseri, my line, and from my husband's family all stood in rows and sang and danced. Then after it was over, I went to live with my husband and his father and mother.

We were like brother and sister for a while, and then one day when we were eating he grabbed at some food just as I did and he grabbed my hand. The next thing you know, Joseph [their first child] came up! [*lots of laughter*] Well, you know what I mean! Then when Joseph was big enough to run and play, Koleate [their second son] came up. Now I am their mother. I work in the garden with

10. Women making a *mumu*
(huge earthen oven).

my husband, and we decided those two children are enough. We don't want to
have more. We want to send them to school and have enough money for them,
so we go to the aid post and get the shots [birth control]).

Nasi's story of her life shows us the salient features of most women's day-to-day
existence. Their days revolve around taking care of their families through labor.

Women's day-to-day lives in Maimafu are made up of work. Women carry the
majority of the subsistence burdens now that there is little hunting on the part
of local men. They cook, clean, garden, take care of their children, look out for
old people who cannot gather their own food, carry water to their homes from
the river, produce net string bags to be sold by the RCF, produce bags for their
own use, find and carry firewood, care for chickens, do the majority of secular
work associated with the SDA Church, plant and tend peanut gardens for market, and share the work involved in coffee production with their husbands and

children. Of course, there are individual differences between families as to how much of the day-to-day burden of work is placed upon a woman. But the above list can be generalized in that both men and women term the above actions as "women's business."

While all of these tasks are important, one of the most salient tasks according to women is childbirth and child rearing. Women tend to tie marriage, and their relations with their husbands, to this set of responsibilities. Kobe called me to her house about a week after my now husband came to Maimafu to visit. She told me the following:

There are things that you have to know now that Tambu is here.[50] Now that a man is staying in your house, you must understand some things about men and women. I am your grandmother, and it is my role to tell you these things. You must be quiet and listen to my talk.

Now when you play around with Tambu, you know this: that is what causes children. And you know this: it will be painful. That is the most important thing to know. It is not a simple thing or an easy thing. It is like you come to the point of death. Before you have children, you are free, when you are a girl and you are not married yet. When you have children, it is a big thing; it is the thing that makes you a woman.

We all thought that it was a game with our husbands when we got married, but then comes the hard truth. All that fun becomes a baby, and then you are in for it.

In the past, a man knew that having a baby was hard; he would come and see the baby after it was born and feel sorry for all of the pain he had caused you. He would go and get lots of food and have a big cookout for you and the new baby. He felt responsible for it. Today it is different. Men don't know that having a child is a big thing. They think that it is easy. They think that they could do it [*about a fifteen-minute break for laughter here*]!

Now, since I am your grandmother, I am telling you all of this. It is not to scare you, but I'm just letting you know what can happen to you if you get pregnant. It is hard. You may experience it someday, and now that we have talked, you will be ready.

I had six children, four boys and two girls. None of them died; they are all healthy and alive. In the past, when a woman had enough children, her father would say to her, "that is enough," and she would stop. Today it is different.

Women go and get shots and pills to stop having children. In the past it was easier.

When you get married people expect you to have children. You do not have a choice; you have to have them. When you are married, you are not free. Now that my husband is dead and all of my children are grown, it is like I am a child again. I have no worries at all.

In the past, when a woman was close to her time, her husband would build her a little house for her to have the baby in. She would go there to get away from the rest of the village and all of her other children and go to the work of having the baby. When she was ready, she would come home.

Now I want to tell you something important about tradition/taboo here. When it is your time of the month, you cannot ever cook food for Tambu. In the past, when it was her time, a woman had to stay in the house and not go around. Today it is different, but it is still important that you not cook food during that time.

When all of you white people came here, we stopped many of the traditional taboos, and staying in the house at that time is one that died. But I have a secret; if you don't want to cook for a man, just tell him that it is that time, and he has to cook his own food. Then you can sit back and watch him work for once!

There is the general perception in Maimafu that women do more work than men. Both men and women articulate this; however, men tend to say that while they help their wives and share the burdens of the household equally, other men do not. Both men and women complain about groups of men in the village who spend the days sitting at the airstrip playing cards and gossiping while their wives are working. However, this does not stop the men who complained about this from themselves doing it.

In addition to heavy work burdens at home, women are restricted in their movements by the cumbersome job of taking care of children, by the constant threat of sorcery, and by their husband's arguments with men from other hamlets. This limitation on movement, when their husbands are at the airstrip or elsewhere, prohibits most women from taking part in the few "development" activities that have been carried out by past Peace Corps volunteers. The artificiality of "Maimafu" is apparent in situations with regard to the movement of women. People do not see that they live in a village that is a cohesive whole; they see the hamlets in which they reside as their communities. A woman is in danger if she leaves the hamlet or her gardens without her husband. She can, however, when it is time to go to distant gardens and her husband does not want to go, make the trip with other female relatives. These same-sex groups of women cannot, however, attend literacy classes offered in a different hamlet, walk to the aid post, or visit the Peace Corps house to take sewing lessons.

Both the government and RCF have used the fiction of "Maimafu village" to allocate services in the area. This is fine for men and boys but problematic for women. The government-run community school is in Biabitai, on land held by the most powerful sorcerer in the area if not the region. Women who live in Kuseri, Atobatai, Bayabei, Iyahaetai, Wayoarabirai, Kalopayahaetai, Halabaebi-tai, and Aeyahaepi—all hamlets that are a fair distance away from Biabitai, and all family groups that are not closely related to the man who holds the land—are prohibited from going to the community school alone. Women from Motai, Tulai, Abigarima, Kolatai, Harontai, and Lasoabei are allowed to make the walk from their homes to the community school either because of proximity or relations between their husbands, and the sorcerer and his sons.

In numerous interviews and focus groups, one of the two biggest complaints that women had about their lives was the lack of medical care in the village and, specifically, that the biggest problem in their community was women dying during pregnancy and childbirth and from general sickness. Women argue that there are a number of causes for these pre- and postnatal deaths. First, poisoning by sorcery is rampant in Maimafu. The jealousies created and fueled by the conservation project have added to an already high instance of local poison threats. During one focus group, women from Tulai said that they have had eight women from their hamlet die in the past four years. When a woman is pregnant, she is especially likely to suffer severely and die from sorcery. Second, women say that when a young woman gets pregnant now, she has so much work that her body just cannot keep the baby. Many women correlated the increase in labor demands upon women, the increase in bride price regionally, and pregnancy-related deaths.[51]

People consume little protein in Maimafu. With no pigs, a limited supply of hunted protein sources, and no easy access to tinned fish from trade stores, the majority of the protein in local diets comes from vegetable matter, peanuts, and a small number of chickens. Women have even less access to protein sources than do men. While men, when walking in the forest to visit other hamlets or check on land they hold, can consume hunted animal meat "on the sly," out of the watchful eyes of the SDA Church lay ministers, women, who generally do not go on these outings, cannot. In addition, women go back to work soon after childbirth. Finally, and this was pointed out by many women, although the government, missionaries, and past Peace Corps volunteers have instructed women that it is unsanitary to give birth next to the river, the traditional site of birthing, they have offered no sanitary alternatives.

An older woman named Fagokuna spent an afternoon in 1998 telling me the story of what it used to be like to have a child and recounting a story in which the Kiaps and missionaries tell women that they had to either give birth at home or at a village aid post. They told women that women's houses were a sin, so they could not use them for birthing. With the loss of the women's houses and the rituals that used to go along with birth, women lost the knowledge of how to be midwives. This has not been replaced here by adequate health care. Fagokuna said,

> We have lost our traditions for births, but we do not have a decent aid post now. What do we have now? What are we supposed to do? We don't have either. They gave us the building, and they told us what not to do, but now we don't have any guidance or supplies. My daughter had a child in Gona. There they have plastic gloves, antibacterial soap, clean razors [to cut the cord] that can be thrown away after one use, clean blankets for the babies, and clean cloth diapers.[52]

She then suggested that she and other women would like for four women from each hamlet to go to learn how to be midwifes. That way, if one of the skilled women were in a distant garden, there would still be someone in the hamlet who is skilled in midwifery. Fagokuna also suggested bringing back the women's houses. In terms of general illness in the village, the other big concern for women is that there is no medicine in the aid post. The village aid post is a large building with many rooms, a radio connected to the village aid-post network and to the medical office at the Lufa District headquarters, a supposedly on-duty aid worker trained to work at health posts, and no medical supplies.

Gillison recounts that during her initial fieldwork, bride price consisted of pigs, cooked pork and/or marsupial meat, marsupial fur, plumage from different birds, kina oyster shells, materials for making net string bags, taro, bananas, blankets, tinned fish, frozen meat, and money (1993:53). According to the McBrides, in the very early 1970s the average bride price among Gimi—

exchanged on the day of the ceremony — was 50 to 100 Australian dollars and six to ten pigs (McBride and McBride 1973:35). Today, only thirty years later, bride price can be as high as 6,000 kina.[53] It is, always at least 1,000 kina, and a woman with this sort of "low" bride price is considered a *discount meri*.[54]

One highly educated young woman from Maimafu was "marked" with a bride price of 6,000 kina. Her father, who had "invested" heavily in her education argued that since she had "eaten" so much of his money, she would have to "bring a good price" for him to get a "return on his investment."[55] The young man that she wished to marry, the son of a village big-man, wanted to marry her, and his father and male relatives were willing to "pay the price."[56] His mother, however, was less than ready to contribute to it.[57] The young woman's father had "marked" this price with the knowledge that she had been having clandestine relations with the young man, assuming that his parents would "pay the price." The young man's mother worked slowly through her husband's brother to spread rumors about the young woman. First, it was that she was having sexual relations with a man who worked for the RCF; next it was that she was stealing money from the community school — where she worked as a teacher, since there were no government teachers in the village at that time; finally, it was that she was having sexual relations with students at the community school. With all of this "gossip," the young man's father began to have second thoughts. And with this, the young man became frustrated and went to spend time in Goroka with business associates of his father's.

During the time that he was gone, the young woman worked hard, and her father decided to send her to Goroka to complete her schooling. While in Goroka, she discovered that her young man was in the middle of a relationship with another young woman from Maimafu who was living in Goroka. As retaliation, she began an affair with another young man from Maimafu. During this affair, she became pregnant, so she and her new young man had to return to Maimafu and tell their families. Her father, realizing that this young man's father could not pay 6,000 kina, "discounted" his daughter to 4,000 kina. The new young man's family balked at the "price" until his father's older brother made the argument that if they "bought" her, she could teach all of the lineage's children how to read and write. With this, contributions were made, and over the next two years, the bride price was paid.

In the past, bride price and head payments (transfers of wealth associated with various rites of passage) were the social glue of Gimi society (Gillison

11. Young women outside an RCF meeting.

1993). Today, it is often as if people have forgotten their importance in terms of the sorts of social reproduction that Gillison writes about. They are discussed in terms of economic transactions and not social exchanges, and they are negotiated in ways that are similar to negotiations over trade-store items in the market in Goroka. While in the past, wives given in exchange were regarded as "embodiments of affinal relationships of enduring inequality," today, because of their location in the hierarchy of exchange mediated by the money form, they have become similar to commodities, and affinal relations are becoming increasingly commercial (Errington and Gewertz 1987a:111–128). The monetization of these social relations works to "dilute" their meaning and their message (ibid.:115): it takes a set of relations that was about social reproduction and nurture—the highlighting of past, present, and future relations of nurturing—and turns all of the relations into equivalence and then makes them equivalent with the money form (ibid.).

FORGETTING GENDER

In the myths and stories that Gillian Gillison collected from her informants, the gender of the participants and actors is clear. Birds, snakes, people — every actor is gendered, and by this I mean that they are either male or female and that their gender has an importance in the myth. So, for instance, in a story about how the cassowary lost its flight, the cassowary is female (Gillison 1993:328). The fact that the cassowary is female in the story is central to the meaning of the myth. The story is not about birds, although they are the actors in it; it is about the meaning of *hot* and *cold* and an argument that women, although mostly "cold," could be and have been in the past "hot." She was powerful once; she did possess the things that men possess; she was not always low and on the ground.

One of the things that I've done over the past few years is collect from Gimi many of the stories in Gillison's 1993 book. I've done this to look at the changes in the ways that the stories are told and understood given the past thirty years of change that has taken place among Gimi peoples. In re-collecting Gimi stories, I've realized that there is a sort of forgetting of gender going on among Gimi. The ways in which gender relations were understood and maintained, and the things that kept men's violence directed (for the most part) against other men and not women, were tied to the stories, their understanding, and their replication (see Tuzin 1997). Today, the cassowary is male in the story — every time I've collected it, and everywhere I've collected it. These stories are not told much at all anymore — so they are slipping out of the collective memory of Gimi peoples. All of their ability to maintain a sort of (more) balanced set of relations between men and women is slipping away. I'm not saying that there was some sort of gender equality in the past, but that there were ways of balancing things.

During my research in PNG, I have employed several research assistants. One of them, Esta, was sent to school from Maimafu to Goroka when she was eight years old. Her father had been the second man from their village to attend mission school, and his pastor-mentor urged him to "give his daughter a better life" by sending her away to school. She was the first woman from her village to attend school, and she is the only woman currently living there with an education above fifth grade. She attended a SDA school for nine years. She likes Madonna, her favorite food is spaghetti, and she wants to be a nurse or an accountant when she grows up. In addition to the language spoken in her home village, she speaks fluent Melanesian Pidgin, English, and the languages spoken in Karimui and Goroka. She wanted to learn other languages during her final years at school, especially the language from the coastal city of Madang, where her roommate was from, but at the end of her ninth year, her father told her she had to come back home. He said that he was worried that a man from Goroka or elsewhere would take a liking to her and that she would be married outside their community. She says that on the day she came home, she thought she would die until she saw her grandmother waiting for her at the airstrip. Then she realized how much she had missed the old woman and the rest of her family.

On most days now, Esta goes to the garden with her new husband's mother and his brothers' wives. Esta was married in 1999 and had a beautiful baby girl in 2000. When I left Maimafu in 2002, the last thing that she said to me, in a whisper as I hugged her goodbye, was "When you come back next May, I will have a baby boy to show you." Her son was born in December, and she named him Patrick, after my mother (Pat) and my favorite cousin (Rick). Now that she is married she has, according to her grandmother, "finally learned how to make a good bilum."

Since the RCF has had a steady presence in Esta's village, her father has seen what he calls her "potential," and according to Esta, when I interviewed her in January 1998, he has begun to try and think of ways to connect her to the conservation project:

> It [the mountain] is called *Bopoyana* in our language. I've never been there. To the top I mean. My father says that a white man came in a helicopter and called it Crater Mountain. He worked for a mining company, and he came looking for gold. I think that was before I was born. My grandmother says that the tree I was named after grows only there. So, I'm a tree [*laughter*]! But you know, everyone, after I went away to Goroka for school, started calling me my school name, Esta, and not Pare. Only my grandmother and her friends called me Pare while I was in school. But now my father says Esta "when you go to get a job from the Research and Conservation Foundation, tell them your real name." He thinks that because the tree is on *Bopoyana*, they will give me a job.

When Esta's father sent her brother away to school in Goroka, there was not enough money for two children to attend the very expensive boarding school. Esta worked for both the first and the second set of RCF-supervised U.S. Peace Corps volunteers (USPCV) stationed in her village. She also continued to run the USPCV Pidgin classes after the second couple went home. She was suggested to me by the RCF as a research assistant and began working for me in 1997.

The story of Esta's life is intertwined with the story of her village's development. Her father's school attendance is directly linked to the first SDA missionary who came to the village. He taught Esta's father about the possibilities that existed outside of Maimafu. And with the missionaries' help, Esta's father went to school and then to a government program that trained people as health-care workers, where he earned a position in the village aid post health-care system. He worked all over the country including Goroka, where he met Esta's mother. Eventually because of his good work and long service, he was allowed to go back to his home village and run the Maimafu village aid post.

Esta's father sent his daughter away to school, but then, when the choice had to be made about keeping her in school or sending her younger brother, he made a calculated decision. Esta's potential income and labor would be his until she was married but after that, her husband's. He had already invested quite a bit of money in her and was worried about the return he would get. He worried that her bride price might not make up for this economic investment and that if she married far away from home, the social obligations of bride price would not be as readily met. He was also worried that she might never find a husband if she had too much education. His son's education seemed to him a better investment and less of a familial social burden, so he took Esta out of school. He is very open about the social and economic decisions he made with regard to her education.

Esta embodies the contradictions and articulations between the modern and the traditional that are so often evoked in academic discussions of development. Her life is made up partially of the continued valuing of the past and of old symbols engendered by her close relationship with her elderly grandmother, and partially by the rapid change that defines modernity (Giddens 1990). In addition, her life has been changed by transnational environmental-conservation initiatives on her ancestral lands and conservation-as-development in her village. She has moved through the complex social landscape of development as it has come to her place and as it has intertwined with and made her life. She sees no contradiction in believing in sorcery and garden magic, on the one hand, and being a devout SDA, on the other. Before she was married, she and other young women with whom I lived in 1997 and 1998 would stay up late at night talking, gossiping, working on our *bilum*, and listening to all sorts of music, both on my

12. House construction.

radio and on the tape player I brought with me to Maimafu. Esta sees nothing extraordinary about knowing who the Beastie Boys are, and not particularly liking them, participating in a system of social obligations such as bride price, and spending most of her time now working in gardens.

Experiences such as Esta's draw attention to how social changes that involve increasing objectification or commodification of people, activities, and the environment have led to reconfiguring of gender relationships in Maimafu. In *The Gender of the Gift*, Strathern stresses that "totalistic sexed identity of a Western type" and Western idioms, such as the concept of one sex's (i.e., male) control over the other (i.e., female), are inappropriate for analysis in the traditional Melanesian context (M. Strathern 1988:107). In part, Strathern's argument is that the Western notion of personhood conceptualizes characteristics or aspects of a person, such as gender identity, as immutably possessed by that individual. By contrast, in societies based on gift exchange relationships, such as in the Highlands, personhood and identity are the result of social relationships with others, and gender identity is produced from relationships between those engaged in social exchange.

By this argument, individuals' identities are understood to be made up of the sources that go into their making, and their capacities are seen as they relate to others (see M. Strathern 1988:131). Just as the Gimi flutes, which were originally women's flutes but were taken by men, are neither male or female but are identified by who plays them at a given point in time (ibid.:128), individual conceptions of self and other remain in flux. Throughout this section on gender, I have shown the ways in which contemporary life in Maimafu, as it is focused on development and Gimi imaginations of what the future might be like, is working to make gender in new ways. In Maimafu if, like elsewhere in Melanesia, personhood resides at a confluence of relationships that encompass specific social capacities, knowledges, and practices that can only be expressed and utilized with reference to other people, as social relationships change because of development and conservation-as-development, persons are changing. Conservation-as-development in Maimafu is making new kinds of men and women because it changes the sorts of social capacities people have, their knowledges and their actions.

MAKING A LIVING

Each adult woman in Maimafu has at least three gardens. When a woman feels that it is time to plant a new garden, she urges her husband to choose a piece of land on which to plant the garden. Her husband enters into discussions with other men in his family about where to locate this new garden. If there are large things to be cut down, or secondary or tertiary growth that has come up while the plot has been in fallow, men usually cut them down. Women "weed" the groundcover, cut undergrowth, and burn the brush.

Once garden plots have been cleared, women do the majority of daily garden work. Although Gillison (1993:39) argues that in the past in Ubaigubi, men decided when to plant and how to space crops and plants, my data from present-day Maimafu suggest a slightly different division of labor today. Women urge their husbands to choose new garden plots when they decide that the old ones are no longer yielding well. Men do make the final decision, and rules of patrilineal inheritance apply to new plots, but women seem to have more control than they may have had in the past. Women choose what to plant — no small matter, as the diversity of foods planted has greatly increased over the past twenty years—and where, within the new plots, to plant it. Gardens are either very large and far away from the ridgetop hamlets or very small and quite close to the settlements. Gillison has termed these two kinds of gardens "large supermarket gardens" and "kitchen gardens" (ibid.). This characterization seems to still hold true today. There are no fences around gardens today, but they are often marked off with lines of stones or with plants that serve as borders.

When I asked what garden plants are new, women generally answered peanuts, onions, tomatoes, certain varieties of pumpkins, certain beans, white potatoes, and chili peppers. Garden plants that are old or "from the past" are sweet potatoes, other tubers (i.e., taro), greens, corn, pumpkins, pitpit (*Saccharum edule*), ginger, and pineapples. Men also term the following as "traditional" foods: bananas, red and white pandanus (*Pandanus conoidus)*, sugar cane, papaya, oranges, and avocados. Although this is not a strictly accurate account of introduced plants, it probably reflects chronology. European foods such as potatoes, tomatoes, peanuts, and pumpkin had been traded up from the south and down from Goroka as early as 1952 (McArthur 1952/1953:19).

When women harvest the garden, they often gather food for a few days at one time. Things that will keep—peanuts, sweet potatoes, taro, corn, ginger, and pumpkins, for example—can be stored in cooking houses or in the rafters of the family home for a few days. More-perishable foods are gathered daily. Things mature at different times in different gardens, depending on when they were planted and the altitude. Gardens mature rapidly in Maimafu. Women argue that it is because of their superior gardening skills, while men say that it is because of the soil. Anecdotal evidence suggests that the volcanic soil does increase the abundance of food and the rapidity of growth and the number of crops yielded by a given garden.

One area of agriculture in Maimafu in which everyone contributes is coffee production. Coffee was first planted in Chimbu in early 1950, and in about 1956 Australian agricultural officers began to establish coffee growing blocks or collectives (P. Brown 1970:247). At about the same time, coffee production was beginning in the Eastern Highlands. George Greathead, former district commissioner, began working his own coffee plantation outside Goroka in the early 1950s (Brian Greathead, personal communication, June 2004). By 1964 there were at least 129 acres of coffee in the Labogai and Unavi census divisions, and they produced at least 64 tonnes of coffee (Campbell 1964/1965:6). In 1966,

13. Woman in garden.

patrol office Donne counted 16,098 seedlings and trees in the two divisions (Donne 1965/1966:appendix A). In 1968, within the Unavi census division, the census division adjacent to Labogai, there were 370 growers, with 32,962 mature trees and 14,924 immature trees (Foran 1967/1968:appendix H). By the 1970s, the patrol reports all offer detailed information on coffee production. They also connect the vast quantity of coffee produced with the need for a road into the area.

During the 1998 coffee season, residents of Maimafu reported selling 32,089 kilograms of coffee, and during the 2002 coffee season they sold 74,044 kilograms.[58] As of June 2003, there were 223,375 coffee trees there, with one man having as many as 7,000, and another having as few as 250; these trees were owned by 193 different growers. This coffee is harvested in Maimafu, cleaned, dried, and then sold to buyers from Goroka. The price per kilo offered by buyers fluctuates according to the price that they will receive for the coffee when they take it back to Goroka. That price in turn fluctuates according to the world coffee index price and according to the trading of coffee on major markets. In a very real way, coffee ties people in Maimafu to global markets.

During the 1998 coffee season, the price for coffee in Maimafu, offered by buyers, was on average 1.95 kina per kilo. In Goroka, it was on average 2.95 kina per kilo. In addition, all residents of Maimafu have to pay freight charges of 0.61 toea (100 toea = 1 kina) per kilo to the mission planes that pick the coffee up at the airstrip and take it to Goroka. During the 2003 season, the price dropped to as low as 1 kina per kilo in Maimafu, while the airfreight charges had risen to 1.54 kina per kilo. During that season, many people could not afford to pay the freight to get the coffee out to Goroka, so much of the crop rotted on the airstrip. The airfreight charges paid to the mission planes fluctuate according to the price of fuel, thus tying Maimafu and other rural places that grow "airstrip coffee," to the global political-economy of oil.

When a man marries, he and his wife plant a coffee garden on land allocated to him by his father or by his father's brothers. Unmarried people do not have coffee gardens in Maimafu. Occasionally, if a man who is from outside the Maimafu region and who is quite suited to grow coffee marries a woman from Maimafu, her father might allocate a plot of land for them to plant a garden. This happens most often if the man is from somewhere known for not having good coffee-growing conditions, such as Haia, or if the man is from Chimbu or Okapa, places with a shortage of land. People plant the seeds for coffee trees in old tin cans and then tend the seedlings until they are large enough to be planted. Both men and women work to clear secondary growth before the planting of a coffee garden. At first they are careful to get rid of all the other plants in the plot, but, over time, as the coffee trees mature, their shade creates optimal conditions for other plants. During the year, women weed and tend the coffee gardens, but during coffee season, everyone works to pick, clean, dry, and carry the coffee. Coffee is harvested from the trees beginning in late June, peaking in August, and ending in October. The number of trees per man varies according to circumstances: the amount of money he had to buy seedlings when he started, his experience in coffee growing, available family labor, and the amount of land he has allocated to these gardens.

People plant coffee gardens, with few exceptions, quite close to the occupied hamlets. Men argue that this prohibits others from stealing ripe coffee and that it makes it possible to work late and long hours picking the coffee when it is ripe. The coffee trees must be tended all year long, but the real work starts when the buds begin to come out in the spring. Men begin to go to the coffee garden daily to check on the trees. After the small white buds flower, a green, beanlike pod appears on the tree. Over the course of the next month, it turns bright red. When the coffee is ripe, people have only a few days to get the bean off the tree, otherwise it will become too ripe. The coffee trees do not ripen uniformly, and they are harvested over several months. Once harvested, the beans are soaked in water and the red skins removed. This is either done by hand, in most cases, or with a coffee-skinning machine. Next, the naked beans are washed again and placed in the sun to dry. At the end of about a two-day drying period, they are washed a final time and placed in the sun again. After this, they are stored in burlap bags that hold about fifty-five kilos each.

When a coffee buyer comes to Maimafu, word goes out to the hamlets, and people carry the coffee to the airstrip for purchase. There are, for weeks at a time, strings of men, women, and children carrying coffee across the mountains to the airstrip. Family groups make temporary shelters at the airstrip so that they can have a cool place to rest during the long hot days of carrying coffee and so that someone can stay at the airstrip overnight with the coffee. It is important to interject here again that all of the coffee is taken out of the village on small mission planes and that while the coffee season is going on in Maimafu, it is also going on all over the rest of the Highlands. These planes work all day every day, but it still takes a while for them to get all of the coffee out of the village.

Although people realize that they do not get the same price from a buyer who comes to Maimafu as they would if they carried the coffee themselves to Goroka or if they sent it with MAF, they still choose to go through a buyer. They argue that the cost of flying to Goroka, and of housing and food while in Goroka if they do not have family there, together with the stress of all the illegal activity in Goroka, dissuades them from accompanying their crop to the market. In response to MAF's offer to carry the coffee to market and then return with the cash, people say that they want money up front.

In addition to being the most important crop in terms of income in Maimafu, coffee also adds to justifying the villagewide choice to give up pig husbandry, as described by an older man in May 1998:

> When we had pigs, they spoiled the little trees, and it was hard for them to live. People also had to work with the pigs all the time, and they didn't have enough time to look out for coffee properly. They did not have enough time to clean the

gardens if the trees did get big, and then they didn't have enough time to process the coffee when it was time to sell it.

Coffee was introduced as a cash crop in the Maimafu area in the mid-1960s, and it is likely that, like their Fore neighbors, Gimi men left their villages in the late 1960s and early 1970s to work on coffee plantations in other places around the Highlands (Lindenbaum 2002:67 n. 5). Malo, an older man, speaking with me in July 1998, remembers the first seeds he heard about:

> The first coffee came here from Lufa. A *didiman* carried seeds to Lufa and told them to plant it.[59] Then the Kiap told people here that it was a good thing to do to get money. When all of the big-men went to Lufa for a meeting, they got coffee seeds, and they carried them back to Maimafu. They said that if we planted coffee we could make lots of money and get the things that we needed from the stores in Goroka.

He then continued with his version of the history of coffee production in the village:

> When the people here first started to look after coffee, they had to walk from here to Guwasa and spend the night. Then they had to walk to Maiva and spend the night. Then they walked to Mengino, and that is where they sold the coffee. That is when they got paid in Australian dollars and not in kina. Now we get paid in Papua New Guinea money.

The production of coffee in Maimafu has most likely increased rapidly in recent years because of the airstrip. When people had to carry it to the Lufa station or to Ubaigubi, they did not grow much because they could not transport it. In terms of future production, my observations lead me to believe that Maimafu is at peak coffee production capacity right now. I base this assessment on the labor time already involved in production at this level and on the ability to transport it out of the village before is spoils.

When a man dies, his coffee garden goes to his oldest living son. This is a steadfast rule unless there is an exception that must be made. If his oldest son is not married or widowed, he does not get the garden. If his oldest son does not live in a hamlet that is close to the garden, perhaps if he lives with his wife's family—also against cultural "rules" but sometimes broken if a man could not pay the full bride price or if there are some other confounding factors—then it might go to a younger brother who is closer by. This is an illustration of the contextual nature of land claims and tenure issues in Maimafu.

Land tenure and property relations are perhaps the most complex set of sociohistoric relations in Maimafu.[60] All property relations in Maimafu are tied to history, and most, on top of that, are tied to exchange. They are shifting, and the way that they are discussed can change depending on when and to whom you are talking. Stories about primary or first land claims seem to be both prototypical and archetypal, meaning that they both describe some event that the tellers believe really happened and illustrate how and when claims can be made under the given, and also most likely shifting and historic, set of social rules. When you ask people about who owns what, you do not get a fixed picture; you get a story of social relationships. The history of the place is written with this system, as is the history of local and regional social relations.

The way that people became the stewards of a particular plot of land is tied to the Labogai stories and other old stories of hunting trips and bush walks. When people went out to unclaimed lands, they would build a hunting house, cook and eat a meal, and plant things for future visits. These actions would mark the land as their own. A particularly strong claim comes from being related to the man who first killed a tree kangaroo on the land.

These primary stories, archetypal in nature, are supplemented by stories that tell of specific events in local social relations that may have caused the land to change hands. Marriages and compensation payments are two possibilities. This is where current disputes crop up. People seem rarely to argue with the primary stories. They simply tell a story that shows how a past social relationship caused the transfer of the land or the transfer of certain rights on it to their ancestor. The following story, recounted by an old man in June 1998, is about the first time someone from Maimafu learned about the existence of Pawaia peoples.

When my grandfather was a boy, he and some of his family went on a big hunting trip to the top of river Nimi [the river here] where it meets Youha [another river]. They went up the mountain that all the white people call Crater, and they went over it. They went a long way. When they had gone a long way, they found a tree kangaroo and they shot at it. They shot their arrows into a tall tree, and then the tree kangaroo came down with one of the shots. Some of the arrows were too high up in the tree to retrieve. They sat down and cooked the tree kangaroo, and then they hunted more and then came home.

A while later some people from Haia (we did not know them yet as from Haia; they were just people in the forest) were also hunting in this part of the forest. Someone saw the arrows that my family had shot up in the top of the tree. The line from Haia cut the tree down, and they got the arrows. They did not know how to make that kind, so they knew that they were from other people. They then shot arrows up into a tree in the same spot and went away.

Again my grandfather and his male relatives went to the bush to hunt. They came back to this same spot. This time they found arrows that they did not know how to make. They made their mark on the bush, and they went away thinking that the others would not come back.

This went on for some time, the two groups marking the bush with their marks. Finally, one day my grandfather's line was out, and they caught a man from Haia. They did not understand his language, so they talked with hand signs. They figured out that he was from behind the mountains. They did not know what to do with him, so they talked about it, and they decided to give him some bamboo to smoke and let him go. So they did that.

Since they now knew that men lived behind the mountain, some of them went to see. They went to the forest near Haia, but Haia was not Haia then. It only became a place like a village when the New Tribes people came [missionaries]. Before that, the people who live there now went around in the forest and lived that way. So my line went to see the people in that part of the bush, and they gave them things and they got things. They became brothers. They traded dogs, spears, and other things.

This story is an example of a prototypical and archetypal story. It is, as Mattanaba told it and understands it, a true story, and it illustrates some of the actions that allow a man and his family to claim land.

The beginning of the story of the journey into the forest by Mattanaba's grandfather and other relatives when his grandfather was young establishes that the land claim is old and that it might be a claim that can be made by any of the descendants of Mattanaba's grandfather and male family members of Mattanaba's generation. It shows that land could be originally claimed by hunting on it, killing something there, and eating it on the land. The arrows serve as a marker to anyone who might come through later saying that the land is already claimed. The "unknown" men came afterward to the land, and because they were from a different place, they did not understand that the land was already held or claimed. The return of Mattanaba's ancestors to the land, their property now, to hunt, and the evidence they find that other men hunt there show that infractions of this system will be found out. The shooting of the arrows as a sign for the claim shows that Mattanaba's ancestors were not "hotheaded" and that they knew that they were in the right with their initial claim.

Since the men from Haia and Mattanaba's ancestors went back and forth a number of times, the story illustrates that arguments over land claims are accepted and that the person who holds out the longest usually wins. The capture of the man from Haia and the subsequent inability to talk to him mark the locally understood profound differences between people from Haia and people from Maimafu. But the kindness shown to the man by Mattanaba's ancestors shows that they were good men and that they understood that the Haia man was different from them but that they did not judge him because of it. Finally, the trip to "behind the mountain" to look for the man and his family shows that Mattanaba's relatives were not fearful and that they were willing to make alliances and perhaps even share access to the land if it furthered possible future alliances.[61]

UNDERSTANDINGS OF DEVELOPMENT

As Maxine Weisgrau (1997:1) has perceptively argued, although development has been roundly decried by academics, in the realm of practice and local social life it is still much the focus of considerable thought, discussion, desire, and action. Among Gimi, development is something to be gotten, a set of social relations to be entered into; it is the way one discusses social changes tied to Christianity, governmentality, conservation, and the influx of the cash economy and commodities (Knauft 1999, 2002).[62] In her analysis of development interventions in Nepal, Stacy Pigg theorizes a framework for the analysis of development interventions as "social practices." She sees these practices as exporting certain ideologies and specific kinds of social relation configurations and cultural changes (1993). She effectively illustrates the ways that development interventions amplify existing social differences and in some situations have an "othering" effect that creates new social differences. She argues that development "provides a framework through which social relations and difference are discussed" and that "development institutions describe problems in a way that justifies their interventions" (ibid.:47). This notion of the institutional production of problems and solutions is also present in the work of Ferguson (1994) and Arturo Escobar (1995). For Pigg, Ferguson, and Escobar, development is a discourse that constructs "others" as requiring change, and it is a discursive practice that has profound material consequences. Caught up in these discursive and material consequences is the creation of social relations in terms of the development intervention. For each of these authors, development structures local perceptions and constructions of self and culture; and constructions of self are never free from power relations (Abu-Lughod 1993:7). If we remember Georg Hegel's notion that the self is created through interaction with another, and that it is within this kind of exchange that Edward Said's (1978) "us and them" is created, then we can clearly see the ways that the production of self, identity, and difference are tied to development.[63] I wish to extend this to include the production of images, imaginations, and imaginaries. These discourses and the materiality they engender create particular imaginaries of what it means to be "developed."[64] Sachs (1995:1) argues:

> For development is much more than just a socio-economic endeavor; it is a perception which models reality, a myth which comforts societies, and a fantasy which unleashes passions. Perceptions, myths and fantasies, however, rise and fall independent of empirical results and rational conclusions; they appear and vanish, not because they are proven right or wrong, but rather because they are pregnant with promise or become irrelevant.

Among Gimi, ideas about development are far from static. On 14 September 1998, I was approached by a group of men and given the following list. I was to give it to the director of the WCS Asia program upon my return to New York City. The men told me that they had consulted with everyone they knew and had come up with eleven things that they all agreed upon as the most important that could be given to them as "development." Here is the list:

1. We need a clean water supply for the village.
2. We need medicine and a doctor for the aid post.
3. We need someone to help us get a better price for coffee.

4. We need some sort of fund to help kids finish grade ten, to become teachers, community workers, and aid post workers.
5. We need more support for the church.
6. We want someone from Maimafu working in the RCF office in Goroka.
7. We want help finishing the guesthouse.
8. We need a good bridge over the river.
9. We need pay for the Management Committee.
10. We want a tin roof for the school.
11. We need a new pay rate for carrying cargo.
12. We need help with the maintenance of the airstrip.

In every interview and focus group that I conducted during 1997 and 1998, people said that they want the following: to be able to send their children to school (either in Maimafu, with new teachers at the community school, or to a mission school in Goroka), to have medicine and a doctor at the village aid post, and to have help maintaining the airstrip. Secondary concerns were a clean water supply, a bridge over the river, help with an animal husbandry business, help getting loans from the "rural development bank," help starting a coffee co-op and getting the local coffee certified as "organic," a road, and tin roofs.

Some quotations from interviews will illustrate local thinking about development needs in the 1990s. The first is from an adult male, approximately thirty-three years old:

People here get sick, and there is no medicine. There is no way to cure them. They get sick, and then they die. If we had a decent health care worker at the aid post and if we had some medicine, things would be better. RCF should pay for one of the students from here, like Esta or Nara, to go to school. They are smart. They could finish their grade ten and then go to aid post school and come back here to take care of people. Even though Esta is a girl, people would go to her to get medicine if she had training.

The following is from a school-age girl, approximately eleven years old, and was recorded in English:

I just want to finish third grade. My father sent me last year, but the teacher left after a few months and we had to stop. My father had to pay ten kina for me to go, and when the teacher left he lost it and said that it was wasted money. Now this year after you talked to him, he sent me again and the teacher left again. I just want to finish it so I can go on.

And this view comes from an adult female, approximately twenty-one years old.

RCF. RCF. Why should we listen to them? They forget about us the minute they get to Goroka. They forget. We go out of their minds. All they see is our forest in their eyes, and they forget that it is ours. They go to Goroka, and they have power because we gave it to them. They go there and they sleep in good houses with tin roofs, and their children can go to good mission schools so they forget about us. They have plenty of meat to eat so their stomachs do not rumble. Mark my words, every time my little girl's stomach rumbles from not having meat, I think about them. I think about them and their smiles and promises.

But development desires are tricky business, especially when nongovernmental organizations (NGOs) are involved as the most significant vehicle for local development (Weisgrau 1997). In 1997 and 1998, during my first fieldwork in PNG, those residents that I interviewed about their development desires almost without fail said that if the RCF helped them attain the list of things mentioned at the beginning of this section, then they would see the "hand mark" (*hanmak* in Melanesian Pidgin) of the RCF, and they would participate fully with the conservation initiatives begun by the NGO. By 2002, the RCF had secured community schoolteachers for Maimafu through a deal with the provincial government in which the RCF bought household items for the teachers and paid for them to visit their families on long school holidays. This deal made Maimafu a more desirable posting than other rural areas.[65] The RCF had also, with the help of a partner NGO devoted to rural development, built a water supply in Maimafu. Finally, through the creation of a scholarship fund for all children within the CMWMA who finish sixth grade, the RCF had directly affected the ability of people to send their children to school. When I returned to Maimafu in 2002 knowing, through e-mail correspondence with RCF staff during the academic year, about all of these changes, I was surprised to find that most of the men in the village were still complaining about the work that the RCF has done there.

In 1998 one of the biggest supporters of the RCF project at Crater Mountain was Morekey Topa. In 2002 when I interviewed him about the social, political, and economic changes that had taken place in the years between my initial work and the present, he had made a radical break with his earlier analysis of the conservation-as-development project. His gestures brimmed with anger as he told me that the RCF and all of the people working for them had come to Maimafu and taken pictures of the forests and animals belonging to the men from Maimafu. He said that they had taken the pictures back to "overseas" and sold them for "millions of kina." This was an expression of his feeling that he and others had not received what they deserved from conservation-as-development or from the social relations with conservation-related actors. He told me:

> Our big-men never signed an agreement with RCF, so in effect they have stolen our bush. They do not have the right or authorization to be here. We are in the process of doing the paperwork in Moresby so that we can sue them.
>
> RCF is like a company now. They have opened accounts in banks overseas, and they steal all of our money now. They steal from us in two ways. The first is with the pictures that they steal of our bush. The second is with the money they get using the Crater Mountain name that they keep and do not give to us.
>
> RCF is our second government and their *pasin* [tradition, way of being in the world] is no different than the government that came first. The first one gave us the school and the health post but then forgot about us. They said they would support these things, but now they both stand empty. They told us that if we planted our dead and we stopped fighting with each other, then we would get development, and look what we have now. RCF came and was the second government; they said if you look out after your bush, we will bring development, and then they forgot about us.
>
> Both the government and RCF get money from overseas to give to us, to do development here, and they both steal it. We are not stupid. We know that they are all lying to us.
>
> Every three months RCF gets money from the United States. RCF stays in Goroka and uses our name, the donors stay in the U.S. and use our name and we don't hold our name close enough, so we sit here with nothing. RCF is *namel* [between] us and the donors.
>
> RCF gets the money, and then they work a liar's report and tell the donors that they are sending all the money to us in the bush. The boss of RCF is a bullshit man. He has a huge bank account in Australia.
>
> They should set up a bank account for every clan and mark one big man to

hold the save card for the account. He should hold it and RCF should put the money from the donors directly into the account for each clan.

RCF pulls in big money from the United States and other overseas places. In the newspaper there was a story that they have gotten either 200,000 or 300,000 kina every three months for the last twenty-one years. [*Discussion here in the group about whether or not it is 200,000–300,000 or 2–3 million.*]

God gave us everything that we have, and he said that we should look after it; that we should take care of it and make sure our children have it. I am talking about the bush here. I am talking about the trees and the mountains and the animals and the birds and the water and the nice cool breezes. God gave us all of this, and he said that we had to save it. And we did.

RCF did not look after their own ground like God told them to, so now they want to steal ours. They want to steal it because they did not look after their own.

Our ancestors told us to keep our forest safe and sound before the missions came, but then when the missions did come we found out that our ancestors were right about some things. They [our ancestors] were wrong about many other things, but they were right about how we should take care of our bush.

The ancestors of the RCF people told them to look after their bush also, but they did not do it. They are *Bikhet* [stubborn] — they did not do what their ancestors told them to do, and now they have no bush and they want ours. Look at the people who work there; they are all from town where they have no bush.

We go to town and we see the *niupela niupela* [very new] things that they have in their office. We see them with our own eyes. We see how they hoard them. We see the cars and the computers, and we know they all live in nice houses. We heard our ancestors' talk, and our bush made these things come to us — these cars and computers and houses — but RCF has stolen these things from us.

Morekey's speech encompasses many of the salient local critiques of conservation interventions into the lands and lives of people in Maimafu village. It also illustrates some ways in which local understandings of the environment and society and the relations between the two have been transformed by the conservation project.

Morekey's first argument is a critique of the role of NGOs in contemporary conservation. The natural resources management legislation in Papua New Guinea is based on the Queensland and Commonwealth statutes, which were used as models during the colonial occupation of the eastern half of New Guinea by Australia[66] (Whimp 1997:352). The Australian statutes are in turn based on English common law, which was enforced during the British colonial period in Australia.[67] The Australian laws concerning natural resources and conservation had the chance to "evolve" between 1901 and 1975, the date of Papua New Guinean independence (ibid.:532). By this I mean that they were amended and altered over a period of seventy-five years, between the time of their initial implementation in Australia and their transportation to PNG in the form of the Papua New Guinean Constitution. The laws were crafted to fit the specific sociocultural context of Australia and transported to PNG by the colonial government.

The failure of the state of Papua New Guinea to enforce laws with regard to natural resources is well recognized and commented upon (see Filer and Sekhran 1998; Johnson 2000; West 2000; and Whimp 1997).[68] Kathy Whimp cogently argues that this failure is tied to the exportation of legal models and types of legislation from Australia and Britain to PNG (Whimp 1997). She suggests that the differences in the systems of land ownership between Papua New Guinea and its colonial powers are the key to this failure.

A. Johnson, one of the key players in the implementation of the Fauna (Protection and Control) Act at Crater Mountain, has argued that "effective conservation will require institutional arrangements to create rules, to monitor and sanction violations, and to arbitrate disputes" (2000:65). To these ends, she advocates "co-management," which she sees as melding the "knowledge and presence of local communities" with the "powers of the State" (2000:65). One challenge is that "there are high transaction costs" inherent in a model in which the state must interact with local people. Her solution is the participation of "an intermediate organization" that can serve to "represent and reconcile traditional practices of multiple groups in the resources use area" (A. Johnson 2000:65). The Fauna (Protection and Control) Act creates a space for these "intermediate organizations," and PNG serves as a kind of natural laboratory to test out this theory (ibid.:66).[69]

The idea behind Wildlife Management Areas is that the state will declare an area a WMA, thereby formalizing boundaries and regulating plant and animal use. This is to be done in consultation with the local landowners. Well-meaning conservation scientists, such as A. Johnson, take this to mean that "traditional" boundaries and "traditional rules for wildlife use" will thus be formalized by the state (2000:66). A Wildlife Management Committee that is made up of representative members of clans from the bounded area who will work with the state to codify boundaries and rules will supposedly do this. Johnson, who worked for the WCS and RCF, sees the legislation as allowing for "a non-governmental organization to assist the state in providing technical assistance to the management committee under the arrangement of co-management" (ibid.). This is, however, an interpretation of the act, as there is no mention of an outside institution of any kind in the act. The act positions the minister of environment and conservation as the intermediary between the local landholders and the state, even though the minister is an agent of the state. Indeed, the act states, "the Minister may, after consultation with a Wildlife Management Committee, make rules for the protection, propagation, encouragement, management, control, harvesting and destruction of the fauna in the Wildlife Management Area" (Fauna [Protection and Control] Act, 1966, part vi, section 17). The act also allows for the committee and the minister to create a set of "laws" or WMA rules with regard to the use of fauna. This set of laws, after posted for public review, goes into effect and sanctions behavior within the WMA. The state of PNG and the Wildlife Management Committee rarely enforce these laws, however. Instead, the committee expects the NGOs to enforce the laws and thus adds to the role slippage between NGOs and the state.

While this legislation is clear to conservation scientists and practitioners, it is much less clear to local people. Morekey's critique is tied to this. When the young man working for the WCS in the early 1990s walked around the area asking who the big-men were and talking with them about conservation, he got many of them to sign on as landholders who wanted to be part of the Wildlife Management Committees. This process is now seen as unfair in Maimafu. Men such as Morekey argue that they were never consulted and that the original agreements between "some of the men" in the village and the RCF are not valid.

In his critique Morekey uses the language of "business" (such as when he discusses bank accounts and companies) a language that existed around the WMA before the conservation project,[70] but that has been on the increase over the past few years. In 1951 a man named Bimai Noimbano from Watabung, a valley on the western border of Goroka, worked at the Aiyura Agricultural Experimental Station near Kainantu. He learned about coffee there, and in 1953, with the help of the first extension officer in Goroka, he developed the first nursery for coffee seedlings in the Goroka area (Finney 1987:5). People in Maimafu trace their first coffee seedlings directly to this man, by talking about how the seedlings first came from "the Watabung side." This means that the language and ideology of business have been in and around the Maimafu area since the mid- to late 1950s. So business is nothing new.

Ben Finney, in his discussion of business development in the 1960s in Goroka, citing Max Weber's *The Protestant Ethic and the Spirit of Capitalism*, argues, like many writers before him, that "entrepreneurs commonly arise from marginal, dissident, or reformist groups" (1987:8). This seems to have been the case when the young man from the WCS was walking around the Crater Mountain area and collecting participants for the conservation business. Many of the men who initially signed up for the committee were marginal characters who did not have big-man status in the community.

Flip Van Helden (2001:28) articulates another critique of conservation in PNG in his analysis of a conservation intervention in the Jimi and Ramu Valleys that was similar to the one at Crater Mountain with regard to "business."[71] While conservation practitioners want local communities to see conservation as the harbinger of economic stability, they also want to participate in exchange relations with the local people. Van Helden calls this an "assumption" of the conservation teams that he worked with in the Jimi and Ramu Valleys (ibid.). The assumption on the part of conservation practitioners is that since Melanesians have traditionally participated in exchange relations with one another, that in the face of major economic changes in social life that are directly tied to their integration into the market economy, they will continue to participate in exchange relations with one another. For example, conservation practitioners associated with the Crater Mountain project were dismayed to learn that members of the Wildlife Management Committees wanted to be paid a salary for their work. They expressed both confusion and outrage over this request. They assumed that since people were willing to share labor with extended family members in terms of garden work, coffee harvesting, the building of houses, and the like, that the entire "village" would be willing to work together for the conservation project and that when the project earned money, say in the form of tourist dollars, people would evenly distribute it among themselves. This disjuncture between the way the RCF works and the way local people see exchange relations is also apparent in Morekey's assertion that the RCF should create a bank account for each clan in the village and distribute the money evenly.

Another major critique in Morekey's speech is his assertion that the RCF has become both a "company" and the "government." This critique is tied to the local view that all companies are corrupt, that the government of PNG is corrupt, and that the nation-state has thus far failed the citizens of PNG. Since 1997, I have heard critiques of the government of PNG as a failure and, since 2001, local articulations of the sentiment that "conservation is our government now." Neoliberal policies and projects do away with the role of governments in favor of allowing the market to regulate and develop. Now, conservation and its organizations are seen by the residents of Maimafu as filling the role of government in some important ways.

The fourth and final critique voiced by Morekey involves the production of Crater Mountain and the use of that production to garner donor funding. In his discussion of how the RCF "uses our name" to get money, Morekey highlights the local understanding of the way the production of Crater Mountain and "Crater Peoples" is a highly politicized act meant to create and produce space and then to use that space to get the money to save it.[72] Just as Maimafu became a "place" through the trajectory of the colonial contact, mission contact, government contact, and then conservation contact, so too have the people living in Maimafu, Herowana, Ubaigubi, and Haia become Crater Peoples, through processes imbued with the power of discursive hegemony. If you say it enough, it becomes true enough to focus and filter interventions (Hodgson 2001; Said 1978). If you make Crater Mountain and Crater People, you are making "space, place, and culture" (Gupta and Ferguson 1992:7), and by making them you can then describe and solve the problem they pose.

Embedded in this final critique is the idea that the RCF has stolen money from the people of Maimafu and used that money to buy nice things for itself. This argument is derived from both personal experiences, seeing the nice things in the RCF office in Goroka, and from reading the national newspapers. In the 4 October 4 2002 edition of the *National* (4 October 2002), there is a letter to the editor that expresses the exact sentiment that Morekey expresses about the things the RCF does with donor dollars. The letter reads, "The Red Cross must justify why its employees drive around in flashy cars, and have a modern building and expensive office equipment/furniture."

In July 2001 at the RCF annual meetings, the same yearly event at which the fight occurred in 1998 (see chapter 1), Nanasuanna stood up and spoke to the crowd. This was the first time a woman from one of the rural villages located in the WMA had addressed these meetings. It was an extraordinary moment. At most of the previous annual meetings, the women's main role has been to cook for the meeting guests. In the early mornings they carry net bags full of sweet potatoes, greens, pumpkin, and other garden vegetables to the meeting site. Then they spend the day cooking breakfast, lunch, and dinner. They combine the locally grown produce with food flown in from Goroka, and they are paid for their labor. Women's secondary role at the Maimafu meeting in 2001 was to sell locally grown produce at a "market" just outside the meeting tent.

In the middle of the day, during a long discussion about the local critique of the RCF in Maimafu, Nanasuanna whispered to me that she was sick of hearing men talk. She wondered why only men got to speak and told me that I should stand up and tell "all the people in charge" what it is like to be a woman in Maimafu. This momentarily moved me, as it seemed to me that she was saying that I had achieved that mythical anthropological moment of knowing the truth about social life in a place that is not our own. This feeling was fleeting as I looked around me and literally saw the women that I had come to love over the past years at the margins on the meeting. They sat in groups working their bilum right outside the meeting tent, they sat in a row on the ground behind the bench on which their husbands who serve on the village Management Committee sat, and they worked in the distance in the *haus kuk* (cooking house).

It was at that moment that I think I became an anthropologist, not because of some privileged knowledge of "the other" but rather because I saw several of the texts that I had loved reading in graduate school become real before my eyes (see especially Abu-Lughod 1993; M. Strathern 1988). I saw inequality between the sexes in practice and saw that the social practices in which I was participating were fortifying this inequality. And then I looked at Nanasuanna, and I said, "You stand up and speak. I know you have more to say than anyone here does and that you are more capable than any man here. I can't do it for you, because no matter how hard I try, I can't show them what you really feel." And she did it.

Nanasuanna silently stood up. She stood until the director of the RCF noticed her and asked, "Wife of Nelson, do you have something to say?"[73] Nanasuanna cleared her throat, and still she stood silently. Then, after what seemed a very long time, Nima, her husband's brother's sister, stood up, walked across the room, and took her hand. As she did this, Nanasuanna began to speak. Her speech was slow and deliberate and her voice clear and strong. She spoke in Melanesian Pidgin and she said,[74]

We women of Maimafu, we are pleased that you have come here to hold your meeting. We are pleased that you are happy with the food that we have cooked. We are pleased that you like the guesthouse where you are staying. We are happy that you are going to bring development to us someday. I have to say something to you now. I have to say something to you and to all of the men on the Management Committees from all of the villages. We women are the backbone of the community.[75] We are the backbone of life.

You men tell us that we do not know things. You tell us that we know nothing. But we do. We know. We know gardens. We know houses. We know children. We know how to work. We know how to make a bilum. We know how to make a bilum.[76] [*As she speaks, she makes the motion of her hand making a bilum.*] These are the things that make life possible. So we know things. But we do not know about this RCF business. We are not allowed to know. We are kept in the background. We are not allowed to work on the committee or to work for our forests. We are not allowed. When we are allowed, our community relationship with RCF will grow strong. It will grow as strong as our gardens. As strong as our children. As strong as our bilum.

During Nanasuanna's speech, there was total silence in the tent. Even the babies sitting with their mothers outside the tent seemed to sense the importance of the moment, because their ubiquitous crying stopped. After her speech, Nanasuanna had tears running down her face. As I looked around, I realized that this was a pivotal moment for women's roles in conservation. If Nanasuanna's speech was not addressed, it would mean that the project would go on as usual, with men running it and women sitting on the sidelines. If her speech was addressed, it would mean that women might have a larger role to play in the conservation project, thus making it more equitable. After a few moments, Lohala, an old man not related to Nanasuanna or her husband, spoke. He said that he and his wife had spoken many times about the fact that women did not have a very large role in the conservation business and that they both thought it was wrong. After he broke the silence, many men made similar speeches. Everyone clapped at the end of that session, and it was agreed that women would come to play a much larger role in the future. When I arrived in 2004, Nimi was on the Wildlife Management Committee.

In June 2003, I was given the following list of "things we need for Maimafu to become developed," by a group of young men from Maimafu who were living in Goroka and who identified themselves as representatives of "The Association of Six Tribes (Mengino, Abigarima, Motai, Haoninamo, Kuseri, and Kusa), the Maimafu village NGO":[77]

1.   We Need Help To Export Organic Coffee. Due to increasing airfreight and the dropping Kina, life has become miserable. Coffee exporters in Goroka use our organic coffee to blend their coffee. This is unfair.

2.   Sub district settlement/village development should include:

    a. Village housing scheme, including layout of town, tin roofs for houses, and a saw mill to build new permanent homes

    b. School, primary and high school, housing for teachers, money for students who complete grade 10 to go to college

    c. Health post, health workers, fund for treatment in GKA [Goroka] base hospital (no less than K10,000 — to be managed by NGO chairman)

    d. Law and order, including a police station in Maimafu

    e. Commerce office, including a full time development officer to help village folk

    f. Bank, mini bank to serve the people of the village. The money will operate on one account in a commercial bank (to be managed by village NGO)

    g. Mini hydroelectric power station

This group of men told me that they had formed a village NGO and that they no longer needed the services of the RCF, that they were "through with conservation." Their NGO would be structured with "a chairman, a board of directors, an executive committee, and the community." The chairman would be "elected by the villagers" and he would appoint the board of directors from each clan. This set of directors, and the chairman, would have to live in Goroka in order to manage the village NGO and the funds that are sure to flow to it from the grants that they receive from "international donors." So, it seems that some of the people from Maimafu have learned a bit about bureaucracy from the NGOs with which they have been acquainted over the past three decades. And they understand that in order to access the sorts of power that have money to give for development projects, they must have a kind of institutional structure like that of an NGO. With this, villagers have decided that since the RCF and other outsiders have not fulfilled their side of the agreement in a series of contracts that villagers see as exchange related, they will stop entering into these agreements with outsiders and bring development themselves. But with all these local critiques of development and development interventions, the BCN chose to blame the residents of the CMWMA for the failures of the project:

> Our greatest challenge in the development of the Crater Mountain Wildlife Management Area continues to be the community's low level of literacy and experience with the modern cash economy as well as the historical presence of inter-clan conflict and suspicion of one another. The average level of formal education is grade one, most residents have never traveled beyond the boundaries of the WMA and have only recently begun to personally manage small sums of cash. Fear of traditional sorcery and loyalty to clan affiliations underlies social behavior.[78]

CHAPTER 4

Conservation Histories

All stories that recount history are complex, messy, and intensely politi-cal. They ebb and flow over time within oral traditions and in people's minds. Such stories move and change according to those who are doing the remembering and why they are telling the story. When people recount a history, they choose what to tell and how to tell it, including and excluding information based on their preferences and intentions (Braudel 1980:27). During the inter-views I conducted concerning the history of the Crater Mountain Wildlife Management Area (CMWMA), people chose the events and connections they wished to convey to me. Similarly, in now presenting the narrative reconstruc-tions I collected about the project, I am choosing what I wish to convey to the reader. I also present data that I collected from published reports, grant pro-posals, and conservation organization documents. In laying out multiple ver-sions of the project's history, I attempt to incorporate a greater range of events as well as multiply positioned voices within a long span of time.

In this chapter, I tell the history of the Crater Mountain project through the voices of a few of the people who lived it and wrote about it, and show that individual accounts of the history have been given in ways that meet particular needs or reflect certain interests. Elsewhere (West 2000), I have located the history of the Crater Mountain project, and the interactions among its diverse participants, within the colonial history of New Guinea. In what follows I do not recount that history, since others have recounted it more fully than is possible here (Connolly and Anderson 1987; Gordon 1951; Howlett 1967; Schieffelin and Crittenden 1991a; Souter 1964).

Within the published history of the CMWMA, there is a recounting of history that centers on specific events, such as the first U.S. Peace Corps volunteers (USPCV) in Maimafu, the first field coordinator, and the moment of project origin. The published versions of the project's history are presented from the perspective of expatriate researchers and elite national biologists working for the Research and Conservation Foundation of Papua New Guinea (RCF), the Wildlife Conservation Society (WCS), and the Biodiversity Conservation Network (BCN). This history recounts antecedent events as planned and necessary steps leading to the project's current form (A. Johnson 1997; Pearl 1994). Although project publications and reports purport to expose considerable time depth for the project, they recount a history of events that is both fractured and incomplete (Johnson 1997:397–399; Pearl 1994:198–201). This official and published history does not include the voices or perspectives of people from the villages within the CMWMA.[1]

In reproducing the project's history here, I do not dispute Ranajit Guha's argument that productions of history are "orientalisms" and that they tell as much about their producers as they do about the people, places, and times being produced (1988). Nor do I disagree with Gayatri Chakravorty Spivak's argument that once a group of people is constituted as a "they" by Western social science, their voice is fundamentally altered (1988:). I also keep in mind that even with the "repatriation of history" or the "restoration" of "colonized subjectivity, experience and agency" to history, the history is still being written by the "West" (Rosalina. O'Hanlon 1988:190–195). With all of these things in mind, I attempt to tell the story of the Crater Mountain project by accessing as many multiply positioned voices and accounts as possible. In what follows, I also attempt to refrain from producing and reconstructing a history that implies that all individuals in Maimafu or all conservation practitioners had the same experiences of history or that they all speak with the same voice (Spivak 1988). In the history that I reconstruct, I attempt to elaborate multiple subject positions without assuming one version of history takes precedence over another.

Many of the anthropologists who have worked in Papua New Guinea (PNG) have shown that the people with whom they work, no matter how seemingly isolated and remote their villages are, have had rich histories of relationships with others (see Barth 1987; Biersack 1995b; Gewertz and Errington 1991; Morren 1986; R. Wagner 1972, 1978).[2] Historically, Gimi have had social-, political-, and trade-related interactions with the Pawaia and Daribi to the south, the Chimbu to the west, and Fore to their east.[3] In this chapter, I document the history of the conservation-related actions on Gimi lands and not the social relations between different ethnolinguistic groups over time. This is not because I do not think that those interrelations are equally important in terms of

Gimi notions of history, exchange, and social relations; it is simply because of the kinds of questions I am asking about history in this chapter.

The colonial history of Papua New Guinea set up the conditions that allowed local people to begin to imagine other possible worlds and lives that have come to be called development. Gimi incorporated the outsiders that they met through colonial patrols across their territory and through their own movements, via the Highlands Labor Scheme (a colonial project in which young men from the Highlands were recruited to work on coastal plantations), into their worldview, and their worldview changed because of these incorporations. The ideas and assumptions into which the new events were incorporated gained new meanings through the contact with the historical events that they assimilate (Sahlins 1981). All events are used to both reinterpret the past and to make predictions about the future. In addition, the altered cultural categories that arise from these incorporations go on to shape the ways that future events are understood (ibid.). These historic events also created a social landscape whereby outsiders could come to imagine PNG and in turn represent the island and its inhabitants to a world audience that was primed for an image of the last and ultimate "other."[4]

In a discussion of the nature of the late colonial experience in Papua New Guinea, and the experience of those involved in certain "patrols," Edward Schieffelin (1991a:1) asks several intriguing questions: "What is the nature of the experience of initial contact between peoples of utterly different worlds, and how do factors of social structure, cultural perception, and historical contingency affect it? How, in turn, does this experience affect the subsequent perceptions, relations, and actions of the people involved?" By asking these questions, Schieffelin is making explicit the link between these colonial encounters and changes in the way the participants understood the past and came to imagine the future. The contact that came with these patrols changed the cultural categories of the people involved in them. It set the stage for and began the social, economic, cultural, and political processes that have become known as development. They were also the "last major discoveries of peoples previously unknown to the outside world" (ibid.:2), which contributed to the fascination that New Guinea has continued to hold in the Western imagination, and to the proliferation of anthropological writing about the island. These final "discoveries" fixed the place and its "nature" and "culture" squarely in the Western consciousness as the last primitive, as the ultimate other.

Throughout the 1920s and 1930s, patrols were made into the remote areas of Highlands New Guinea, and by 1935 the only area of Papua not to have been "explored" was the region between the Strickland and the Purari Rivers (Hays 1992b:43). The Strickland-Purari patrol, organized by the Papuan colonial administration in 1935 and led by Jack Hides and James O'Malley, found the area to be populated by thousands of people who had yet to come into contact with expatriates (Schieffelin and Crittenden 1991a). Expatriate members of some of these early encounters went on to write accounts of their trips to New Guinea. These narratives caught the public eye and worked to create an image of romantic adventure and of New Guinea as a last frontier (Schieffelin and Crittenden 1991c:51). Indeed these journeys were fantastic; by finding the population they did in the Strickland-Purari area, Hides and O'Malley changed perceptions of the Highlands overnight, just as Mick Leahy had done in the Mandated Territory (Schieffelin and Crittenden 1991d:233). By the end of the first third of the twentieth century, the majority of colonial "exploration" was over. The world was still beset by colonial domination, but "imperialist nostalgia" had already begun to set in (Rosaldo 1989). The movement into the Highlands of New Guinea "exercised a powerful grip on the imagination of the reading public. It was almost the last place on earth where one could still go where no white man had gone before" (Schieffelin and Crittenden 1991d:233). The place in the world imagination that these early narratives carved out is still fertile ground when it comes to perceptions and imaginings of New Guinea.

PUBLISHED ACCOUNTS

One of the groups of people that moves in and out of the CMWMA is a set of conservation-related actors who work with and for nongovernmental organizations (NGOs). Many of these people have attempted to write the history of the Crater Mountain project. Mary Pearl begins her account of the Crater Mountain project with the "Crater Mountain peoples' exposure to the outside world in 1958," the year that Australia became the dominant colonial power in New Guinea (Pearl 1994:198).[5] She writes, "Australian patrols that reached the Crater area in 1957–1958 were part of a broad-based Highlands pacification program that began around 1948" and that these patrols were "charged with persuading the Gimis [*sic*] and Pawaians [*sic*] to stop fighting and practicing cannibalism also discouraging them from hunting birds of paradise" (ibid.).[6]

She continues, "a local taboo against killing one species, the Raggiana bird of paradise, already existed," and she then explains that "local people" explained these restrictions in terms of religion: "Since they believe the souls of their dead reside in some birds of paradise species, they assumed that the Australians, whom they perceived as returning ghosts, wanted to ensure the safety of their route to the land of the dead" (ibid.).[7] Pearl then argues that this created a connection at first contact between "outsiders" and "development" with conservation ideals (ibid.:199). Pearl's account of this contact is in line with patrol reports, which recount the patrol officers attempts to "teach" the local people that birds of paradise should not be killed, and with stories I collected from old men about the early patrols.

It is important to highlight this historic connection between outsiders and birds of paradise: it tied outsiders to a precedent of telling local people how to behave with regard to nature without the outsiders' having any indication that changes taking place elsewhere were indeed taking place in the so-called Crater Mountain area and without having any real understanding of Gimi notions of their natural environment. Gillison (1993:66–67), in her analysis of the Australian colonial administration's attempt to make "sanitation a main priority," discusses Gimi memories of early patrols into their territory. She describes people's memories of Kiaps (colonial officials) admonishing Gimi for eating their dead and for shooting birds. These birds were at the time disappearing in other sites in the Highlands, but there was no indication that they were disappearing from lands held in tenure by Gimi. Indeed, Gillison (ibid.:26) recounts that the men she worked with in the early 1970s had memories in which men from other places where birds were disappearing came to Gimi lands because the birds were so plentiful there. O'Hanlon (1990), who has written extensively about the trade in bird of paradise skins, argues that the boom in world coffee prices in the 1970s along with the growth of the industry in PNG would have almost certainly led to a decline in the number of birds killed for profit.

Pearl, using Gillison's 1993 *Between Culture and Fantasy: A New Guinea Highlands Mythology* as her primary source, fails to capture the cosmological or epistemological significance of what happened when men with white skin came to Gimi and told them to cease historic warfare practices, funerary and cannibalistic rites, and hunting practices. It is worth citing Gillison's reading of this situation in order to expose the trauma associated with this moment and to demonstrate the traditional significance of birds of paradise among Gimi. With regard to joining together prohibitions on fighting, eating the dead, and killing birds, Gillison writes about the deep meaning that this had for Gimi:

> Both White men and Birds of Paradise were believed to "house" the *kore*, spirits of dead relations. By eating the dead and killing birds, Gimi surmised, they had been keeping the *kore* inside Gimi territory so they could not "fly" to Australia. Unwittingly, they had restricted the movement of ancestral spirit, "closed the road" along which black ghosts and white men traveled, impeding the return to their Gimi birthplace. (Gillison 1993:67)

Gillison reports that even with this spiritual upheaval, there was a critique of the Australian interest in curtailing these practices. She argues that some Gimi saw it as stemming "from a covert self-interest, a wish to protect their own freedom of movement, that coincided with the Gimi desire for an afterlife" (1993:69). Here we see the beginnings of the local critique of expatriates that has grown up over the course of the production of a "nature" on Gimi lands that needs to be conserved.

A. Johnson (1997) also recounts the history of the CMWMA, but her portrayal begins with the "biological significance" of the area (ibid.:394). With this, she indicates that it was this biological significance that first drew conservation practitioners to the area, and that this is the primary reason that the project has emerged. Indeed, the area that has become the WMA spans a wide topographic range and wide range of forest types. It was not, however, this range or the biological diversity encompassed by it that drew conservation-related actors to the area. Gillian Gillison went to work with Gimi peoples in the 1970s because of the paucity of ethnographic data on their way of life, and David Gillison became interested in their forests because of his wife's work, not, initially, because of the range of ecological diversity there.

Conservation scientists first came to work near Crater Mountain in 1987, when Debra Wright and Andrew Mack, University of Miami graduate students, came to conduct field-based studies there. Wright and Mack, whom A. Johnson discusses in her paper (1997:398), wanted to work where there were a lot of cassowaries, as Mack planned to conduct his Ph.D. work on them.[8] With the help of Malcolm Smith, a helicopter company owner and pilot who had flown above much of the forest to the north and south of Crater Mountain, Mack and

Wright determined that the area to the south of Crater Mountain would be a good site for their studies.

In 1987 they set out to hike from Haia, a village that is now part of the WMA, to the forests in the Purari river basin. As the story goes — as it has been recounted to me by several people — the terrain was treacherous, and while Wright and Mack were extraordinarily good in the bush, during what was thought to be the middle of the hike, Wright fell ill with malaria. The hiking party stopped at the site of what is now the Sera Research Station, one of the research centerpieces of the CMWMA. The WMA came to encompass lands held by Pawaia peoples and Gimi peoples because of the connections forged between Wright and Mack and Pawaia, and between D. Gillison and Gimi. Write, Mack, and D. Gillison were interested in conservation in PNG and concerned about the economic development potential of the people with whom they had worked.

The WMA is an artifact of social relations and historic circumstances that have little to do with the "biological significance" of the area at all. To indicate otherwise actually takes away from the importance of serendipity in conservation. The CMWMA came into being because D. Gillison cared about the forests and people near Gillian Gillison's field site, and because Wright and Mack cared about the forests held by Pawaia peoples and the people from Haia village, who had come to be their friends and research assistants.

ETHNOGRAPHIC ACCOUNTS

In this section, I provide ethnographic accounts of the history of the Crater Mountain integrated conservation and development (ICAD) project using lengthy transcripts from interviews and conservation organization documents. I use these narratives to demonstrate the complexity of the multiple understandings of the history of the Crater Mountain project and to provide the context for my analysis.

D. Gillison recounted the following story when I asked him in September 1997 how and why the Crater Mountain project was begun:[9]

> I started photographing ritual theater when we first went there, and the thing that kept happening was that the guys would say, "You are not going to understand theater unless you understand the forest and what's in it." And so that's

when I started going into the forest with them. A lot of the rituals that are associated with initiation are derived from animal behavior. So some of the guys said, "We get the ideas from the animals," but some said "No, they get the ideas from us," so I started looking at the animal behavior, particularly birds of paradise. They were very important to them, and so I started watching them, and they are some of the most extraordinary things in the world.

There is nothing like it, absolutely the top of the evolutionary tree, I mean, birds of paradise and bower birds are to avian what humans are to mammals. And so I fell in love with the birds and I started trying to learn how to photograph them. And gradually, bit by bit, I transferred my interests from theater and human beings to animals.

And then I would come back there during the academic summer, and when it's summer here it's display season in New Guinea, or rather parts of New Guinea, where I was working at the time. And just before I left to come home after one season, I found with these guys a quite extraordinary lek of birds of paradise — they were Princess Stephanie birds of paradise, and you see them all the time, I mean people wear them all the time; they have very long black tails.[10] People wear them in on their heads. They are a really beautiful bird.

I went away and came back the following year, and I had made a deal with them, and this was the most extraordinary lek I had ever seen. It was 1977 or 1978, and it had taken me forever to get near them. I said, "Guys — " Well, I had paid about three different teams to find birds for me. One group found them: there were forty displaying males in the lek, which is a large lek; it was so incredible. Anyway these guys, I said; well, I knew that this was an extraordinary find for them too. This was money to these guys. They could get forty kina a piece for the males, so I said, "Look, I will rent the birds from you," to keep them alive until I could come back. So we made the deal, and I talked to the big-man. So I said, "When I come back, I will pay *x* amount of kina. So we made a deal.

At that point, I only had two days until I had to leave, but they built me a platform to watch them and they were so tame, they were just flying around; the males were chasing the females. But all I had was this great big telephoto lens, and I couldn't focus on them.

Well, I got back the following year, and I said, "This is what I want to photograph." They weren't there. It turned out that after lots of arguing, I mean it looked like the lek had just gone away. But then guys from an enemy village came over and said, "You are looking for your birds aren't you? Well they killed them all." So I asked what happened.

And then I knew they hadn't gone away. I was angry; we had had an agreement. I was really upset: they were lying, and they had killed them. So I started packing and said that I was leaving, I was going away. I was mad. I was really laying it on. I got all my cargo out, and these guys were watching. I had thought I could really trust them.

So the next morning, I was getting ready to go and the group came up to me and said, "are you really leaving?" and I said "Yeah." So they told me the truth about what had happened.

This kid, this kid called——, who was a lovely kid, I knew him. He used to hang out with me in the bush years ago, and he had died. And he died while I was away. And he was so important that they had had a lot of death dues to pay. They had to buy head [giving them adequate compensation for the death] and pay a lot. They had to pay off all the mothers' brothers. They had to pay so much money, they had to kill the birds to get the money. "We thought about you," they said, "but we had to get the money."

Then they said, "Well look, we want to make this up to you. We don't want you to go, so we will give you some land." So we went up into the mountains, and they said, "Here, this is for you. This is your land." I mean, it was ridiculous. I mean, they said that all of this as far as I could see was mine.

But then they said, "But we are making a deal with you. If we give you this, you have to find us an income. If we give you this and keep these birds, then you have to find us an income."

So I didn't know what I was doing, but then I said, "Sure."

David's description of why the conservation project began includes some important points. First, it shows David's love for the birds of paradise. He was, and is, fascinated by these birds. Their beauty has inspired his career as a photographer and his life as a conservation activist. While he initially traveled to Papua New Guinea to photograph people, he became so interested in the birds that he altered his primary photographic focus. Much conservation seems to stem from this kind of individual attraction to a particular species. This sort of separation of one of the constitutive parts of a natural system from that system, and its subsequent treatment as a kind of ecofetish, is a key component in both the commodification of nature and in reconfiguring the environment in ways that extract it from the social relations of exchange with Gimi. In this instance, birds of paradise were disaggregated from the complex anthropogenic nature in which they can be found. This is not to say that D. Gillison stopped talking to or working with people during his many trips to PNG. The point is that once a particular species, or type of species, becomes the focal point for conservation interventions, both the anthropogenic origins of the system in which it exists and the people involved in the complex interactions between nature and culture begin to recede into the background.[11]

D. Gillison's narrative history also shows that his actions of paying men to insure the safety of birds connected conservation and cash within the area as early as 1977 or 1978. Prior to this, it is possible that men hunted the birds and sold them for plumage, but according to my ethnographic data, the birds were probably not a major source of income among Gimi. In addition, anthropologist Leonard Glick says that he did not encounter Gimi selling skins for profit in the 1960s when he conducted his fieldwork. While birds of paradise were occasionally hunted for plumage to be used in local ceremonial practices, men from Maimafu argue that plumes were never sold to outsiders. There is no way to verify if men from Ubaigubi sold birds of paradise for plumage often, or if the account offered by D. Gillison is an example of people using them as a source of emergency income.

The historic narrative also shows how outsiders are incorporated into social life among the Gimi through gifts and exchange. Due to the long-standing work of G. Gillison and to D. Gillison's numerous visits to the area over the course of several years, the Gillisons had become a part of the community. For D. Gillison to threaten that he would leave and never return meant that people thought that they had to do something to compensate him.[12] They performed the ultimate compensation for that time: they "gave" him land. In D. Gillison's published work, he extends the above account to discuss the ways in which he, and other expatriates, attempted to begin an ecotourism business on this land (D. Gillison 2002). This lodge was allowed by Gimi, allowed in that it was built on their land, because it was seen as part of an exchange relationship in which Gillison and other expatriates would get to use the land in exchange for the cash, tourists, and the social relations of development and "development" that were perceived as promised.

D. Gillison's story about the history of the Crater Mountain project can be juxtaposed with local accounts of the same history. Mattanaba, an old man from Maimafu, told the following story when I asked him in July 1998 about the origins of the project:

Before, all of us here, we did not know about conservation. We did not know what kind of work it is. Here, we just knew the work from the past. The first time I went to Ubaigubi, they did not know conservation either. They just knew the work from the past and the traditions from the past. We would go to the men's house, a thing that is a tradition from the past where only men went, and we would sit down and share food and talk about things.

One day I went to Ubaigubi and after visiting with my sister, I went to the men's house. This was during the time that David Gillison and his wife were there in Ubaigubi. Now his wife, she did work like yours. She wanted to know old stories and such. But David, he spent time in the men's house. He would stay in the men's house and listen and stay up all night if we went on with our stories.

Now, during this time I saw that men in Ubaigubi were getting money from David. He paid them for work and for taking him to see birds. I saw this and I thought that it was good work.

One day I saw David Gillison and heard him asking some men to take him to "Crater Mountain." Now I did not know what he was talking about, so I asked him, "When you call that name out, what are you calling 'Crater Mountain'; what mountain is that?"

He said, "This bush down below, if you go on top very high, this is the mountain that I am calling Crater Mountain." He said this.

I got up and said, "This, this is my mountain. It belongs to me. It is not a mountain that belongs to Ubaigubi or Herowana or Haia. It is mine. It belonged to my father and his father before him. They named it the name of a bird that lives there. They called it Bopoyana [rufous woodcock]. Bopoyana. Bopoyana."

David Gillison got up, and he went to get a book. He went and got it and came back, and it had bird pictures in it. He said to me, "You look at this bird book, and you find this Bopoyana and you show it to me."

I looked through it, and there was Bopoyana. So I showed him. Then I told him all about the bird. I told him that at 6 p.m. Bopoyana gets up from his bed, and he cries to his brothers. Then he goes around to see others and gets food. Then at 5 a.m. he gets up, he looks around his house, and he does the same. This is his custom.

Then David Gillison said "all right." He said, "Sometime when I get a helicopter, I will come and get you and we will go look at the birds on the mountain."

I went back home and waited for him. Then one day a man came to Maimafu in a helicopter and he knew my name. He said, "Hey, you! David Gillison says you are to show me to the top of Bopoyana."

So, I took him to the top. This was a Papua New Guinea man. He was not a white man. We looked for the birds, but we did not see them. We slept at the head of the water, and we looked and looked. But we did not see the birds.

When we got back to Maimafu, he didn't pay me. I had gone on a long walk with him. I had shown him the top of the mountain. He said paying me was not the work he was doing. This was the first time I heard the name of RCF. He said that he worked for RCF.

The next time I saw people who wanted to look at birds was when I went to the camp. A white man was building a big house for tourists. We had a big meeting. David Gillison got up, and he said that conservation was a way to make money. That it would bring tourists, who had money, and that it would mean that we would have jobs. He made a big speech. Then he told us that if we wanted to make money, we had to sign our names to this paper on conservation.

I was the only man there from Maimafu.

After we signed our names, we were supposed to tell him all of the land that belonged to us. So I told him. I told him that if you go to the head of the river He where the clear water is and you go on top from there where there are many tree kangaroos, that is where my land starts. Then if you go to the river Nimi and you go down, down, down and you go to the place where Kayaguna has a little house, that is where my land starts. Then you go to the waterfall, and you see the place where the Raggiana birds of paradise "sing sing," that belongs to me too. Then I said that the harpy eagle lives on my land near the waterfall. And that water fowl live on my land that holds the round waters [lakes].

After I told him this, so did others. He said that we would make money and that he would get the Peace Corps to come to our villages. He said that they would bring development. He said he would send the boss of the Peace Corps to Maimafu, and he did. She came and told us that the Peace Corps would bring development and asked us if we wanted them to come. Everyone said yes!

Next Jamie came to Maimafu. Jamie talked the talk of conservation, and he said that we would make plenty of money if we joined with RCF. He had us sign a paper and tell him what land we hold.

Next Jonathon came. He stayed with me. There was a full moon when he came. He came to study the harpy eagle. He came and then he left. He left some cargo, but there was no money.

All this time I had been telling people in Maimafu that we had joined up with RCF to make money. But this was not happening. Men started getting angry with me. They said, "Hey, we think that you have made it so we have sold our land away to RCF. What do we have to show for it?"

I got up and said, "I am not a smart man. I do not have too much intelligence. But, I know that this conservation is good work. It is a good project. We will get money. The people who come here will give us money for our work. David Gillison said that this would happen. Scientists will come. Tourists will come. The work will come up. We cannot complain. We have to be patient. We are not there yet, but work will come up. We cannot complain because if we do RCF will leave, and we will not have any work until another company comes."

And I continued. I said, "Now Jamie told us that RCF would help us with the school. He said that RCF would make the teachers come. And Jamie told us that RCF could help with the medicine. He told us that the doctors would come. RCF will help us work this road to better education and health. RCF will also help us old people get some education. We can learn to start businesses. They will help us. RCF will show us the good road to follow. They will help us. They will help us get things we need from Goroka. They will help us get a road to Maimafu. They will help us maintain the airstrip."

I also told them that in the past when another man went to your bush, there was a fight. You had to make a trap for him and catch him and then fight him. But now RCF will make sure that other men do not hunt in our bush. They will keep other men from hunting there. They will help with this.

When I was done, when I was finished talking, everyone knew that RCF was the best way to go. Everyone understood.

Mattanaba's story shows his conception of the history of conservation on his land. Unlike D. Gillison's story recounted above, it is a very personal narrative that revolves around social relationships of a promissory nature. He sees the history as one in which, over and over again he is promised things, in exchange for his labor and his land, which never eventuate. In his mind he was promised payment and it was not given; he was promised that the Peace Corps volunteers would bring "development," and they did not. He was promised that the RCF would make the school work, bring medicine to his village, help build a road to Maimafu, help maintain the airstrip, and in general perform the role that the government is supposed to perform; and the organization, in his eyes, has not done any of this. Mattanaba feels like he has given all he has to give: his time, his presence — as he is a big-man who holds sway with others in the community — his labor, and his land, and that he has received nothing worth noting in return.

The story also shows the salience of land claims and the early land disputes associated with conservation. The very land that D. Gillison was "given" by men from Ubaigubi, in Mattanaba's mind and knowledge of history, belonged to Mattanaba's clan. His story also shows the early frustrations with misunderstandings about payment. Mattanaba expected to be paid for his time, and in his recounting of the history, he paints D. Gillison as someone not to be trusted when it comes to payment, even though D. Gillison did pay him, and the RCF has extensive records of Gillison's payments. From the beginning, outsiders associated with conservation, while valorized for their knowledge and money, were seen as duplicitous with regard to payment for services rendered. One of the issues here is that for Mattanaba, nothing that D. Gillison does will ever be enough.

Mattanaba's story then goes on to chronicle the actions taken on the part of outsiders to create a conservation project. Tourism and research as tourism were introduced and inextricably tied to local desires for development and for cash incomes. Particular researchers and their projects are recounted and are remembered as part of local attempts to work with D. Gillison. Finally, the NGO RCF is tied to this history. There is no separation in Mattanaba's mind between the current actions of the RCF, or anyone else who wishes to do conservation on Gimi lands, and the past history of conservation efforts in the area.

Mattanaba's origin story is also a locally accepted time line for the Crater Mountain project. He includes the "true" origin of the project and then the events that he sees as most important. But Mattanaba's story is something more. It is a story that weaves his life into the time line of conservation. Conservation, and interactions with the agents of conservation, has become part of the way that Mattanaba makes himself. He sees himself as the "father of conservation" in his village. He derives status from his associations with conservation and with D. Gillison. Mattanaba told me one day that he had "worked his life for the conservation project."

Yet, not all local constructions are the same. In contrast to the long and detailed time lines and origin stories provided by D. Gillison and Mattanaba, other members of the Maimafu community have a different notion of the project origin and history. A woman named Kumpalahoyi, when asked the same question that elicited the above responses from D. Gillison and Mattanaba, said in June 1998:

> RCF came a while ago. They made promises to the men about the forest. Something about birds and not hunting them. It was a big joke because they were talking about birds of paradise, and men don't hunt those anyway.
>
> My husband told me that it was all nonsense. He said that some of the men just wanted to work for David Gillison and that the whole thing would go away. But, he was wrong! After a while they all started talking about how RCF was going to bring lots of money to Maimafu. The men said that RCF was now the government and that they would bring money and services and development.
>
> Now look. RCF is here, and they bring other outsiders to Maimafu but they do not bring goods, or services, or development!

Kumpalahoyi's story is like the stories that most women tell about conservation. They do not feel that they are participants in it; nor do they feel like they have derived many benefits from it. Kumpalahoyi voices frustration with the RCF but also a kind of sense of humor about the origins of the project. She shows us that not everyone, as the RCF would have us believe, was consulted about participation in the project. She also calls into question the participatory nature of the project from its inception.

INSTITUTIONAL ACCOUNTS

In contrast to the accounts above, institutional accounts and time lines highlight the building of the institutions of conservation. The following "time line" was given to me in 1996 by a conservation practitioner when I asked the individual to answer the same question I had asked D. Gillison and Mattanaba. This person gave a reason of being "too busy" for not answering the question but offered to "write something up" for me, which took the form of a time line. Presented below, is an example of using history to show institution building and, when compared with the two histories recounted in appendices B and C, of using history to garner funds from agencies.

1962 — Leonard Glick, an American medical anthropologist and physician, arrives with his wife and one-year-old baby in Hegeturu, ten kilometers from Ubaigubi. Glick leaves in 1964.

1973–1975 — David and Gillian Gillison build a house in Ubaigubi and become the first of what is to be a continuous tradition of visiting researchers and fieldworkers in the Crater area.

1977 — D. Gillison returns to Ubaigubi to continue photographing Gimi ritual and documenting sources of ritual imagery in nature.

1979 — D. Gillison in Ubaigubi and Herowana to continue work on ritual theater and sources of imagery in nature. D. Gillison approached by group of Gimi landowners (Ubaigubi, Maiva, and Herowana villages) and asked for help in establishing possible conservation sites. Landowners in Ubaigubi elect the first WMA committee in Crater. D. Gillison approaches a Goroka businessman and resident, for help in finding ways for the Gimi to preserve their habitat. This businessman visits New York and with D. Gillison makes a presentation to WCS asking for support for an ecotourist facility that he wants to build.

1980 — D. Gillison in Ubaigubi, Herowana, Maimafu, and Kuasa area. Crater landowner committee expands WMA management area and concept. Committee asks Gillison to communicate their interests to the Department of Environment and Conservation in Port Moresby and also to assure WCS in New York of their continued interest. Dr. Don Bruning, curator of Ornithology, Bronx Zoo/WCS, visits Crater and observes Raggiana bird of paradise displays from one of Gillison's treetop hides. Bruning and D. Gillison continue discussions with landowners. D. Gillison begins preliminary negotiations for land set-asides for what will become Crater's first ecotourist facility, the Augumahatai Wildlife Lodge near Ubaigubi. Craig McConaghy, assistant district commissioner, the Lufa Area, concludes formal negotiations between the Goroka businessman and landowners from Ubaigubi. Villagers begin clearing the Augumahatai site.

1981 — Construction of the Augumahatai Wildlife Lodge. Dr. Archie Carr, WCS Asia director, visits Crater with Don Bruning.

1982 — Informal beginnings of the Crater Mountain ICAD project with the first attempts to establish a national protected area while addressing the socioeconomic aspirations of the local landowners through the development of environmentally sensitive enterprises. D. Gillison returns to Crater. Don Bruning returns to Crater with Dr. Arthur Risser of the San Diego Zoo.

1982 — D. Gillison begins construction of Rutunabi House at Ubaigubi using WCS and personal funds. Rutunabi House (the Zoo House) becomes a residence for visiting scientists. Augumahatai Lodge becomes major, if only temporary, income sources for the villagers of Ubaigubi. William Peckover, ornithologist and nature photographer, makes the first of many subsequent research trips to Crater.

1982–1983 — Bruning, D. Gillison, Peckover, and Risser, with the support of a majority of the Crater landowning big-men, begin moves to permanently gazette Crater Mountain Area as a national Wildlife Management Area.

1983–1984 — WCS/NYZS [New York Zoological Society] funds (sixteen months) Bill and Kate Bray, first lodge managers for the Augumahatai Wildlife Lodge. The Brays prepare the lodge for the first tour, arranged by Don Bruning, WCS.

1984 — The first Founder Board convened. First independent biologists arrive in Crater. A small but growing stream of national and expatriate biologists, small business, and development advisers begin visiting the proposed WMA.

1986 — WCS is instrumental in establishing the national nongovernmental organization which is called the Research and Conservation Foundation of PNG (RCF), which is the lead agency in the Crater Mountain project.

1987 — On the advice of Don Bruning, biologist Andy Mack arrives in the WMA on a reconnaissance expedition. Mack lives and works at the Zoo House in Rutunabi.

1988–1989 — Mack returns with biologist Debra Wright and begins construction of the Crater Mountain Biological Research Station (CMBRS) at [the river] Sera near Haia. Wright and Mack receive funding support from WCS, and other U.S. research organizations. D. Gillison appointed Conservation Fellow by WCS.

1989 — WCS funds a small group of landholders from Ubaigubi, Herowana, and Maimafu, who become paid wardens for the nascent WMA.

1990 — The RCF receive its first outside funding grant from the MacArthur Foundation. (Grant prepared by Dr. Mary Pearl of WCS, with [D.] Gillison's assistance.) Seldon (Jamie) James, WCS Conservation Fellow, arrives in Crater for a two-year stay.

1990 — Steve and Kristi Booth arrive as the first USPC volunteers at Ubaigubi.

1990 — Handicraft business established in the community of Ubaigubi under the Booths' guidance.

1991 — James and D. Gillison prepare Biodiversity Conservation Network USAID [United States Agency for International Development], planning grant.

1991 — Mack and Wright begin the construction of the Crater Mountain Biological Research Station (CMBRS) at Herowana.

1991 — Gideon Kakubin, becomes chairman of the board of RCF.

1991 — RCF's first general manager, Karol Kisokau (former secretary Department of Environment and Conservation), hired.

1991 — Arlyne Johnson, RCF's first scientific director, appointed. Arlyne Johnson prepares BCN implementation grant.

1992 — Handicraft business established in the community of Herowana.

1992 — The first resident field-worker, John Ericho, arrives to conduct ongoing on-site technical and management training in WMA development. He holds regular meetings with the newly formed Management Committees to develop the laws and enforcement procedures.

1993 — The Herowana Committee hosts the first Annual WMA Meeting and from then on meets regularly with resident field-worker.

1994 — WCS representatives, along with RCF operatives, conclude ten years of often frustrating negotiations by finally establishing the Crater Mountain Wildlife Management Area. (We suspect that without the timely support of Paul Barker of the Prime Ministers Department, and others in the government, the 3,000-square-kilometer reserve would not, even now, exist.) As a result of the gazettal, landowners set aside sections in the WMA as hunting-free reserves.

1994 — Ubaigubi women elect their own representatives to the local Wildlife

Management group. Through Samantha Gillison (David's daughter) they seek funds in an attempt to create a sewing group.

1995 — After serving as a residence for visiting scientists for approximately thirteen years, John Ericho, now RCF acting manager, and D. Gillison, acting for WCS as a Conservation Fellow, hand over "Rutunabi" house to the people of Ubaigubi to be used as a income-producing guesthouse.

1995–1996 — The first national resident field-workers placed in the WMA communities of Maimafu, Herowana, and Haia.

1996 — RCF education program commenced. Dr. Mark Solon becomes chair of RCF.

This linear history of events can be compared with the narrative reproduction of the project's history as recounted in the joint RCF–WCS BCN Implementation Grant Proposal (1995):

> In 1979, Big Men in Ubaigubi expressed their concern over declining fauna to the first researchers working in the Crater Mountain area, David and Gillian Gillison. The decline was attributed to uncontrolled collection of plumage and furs for sale as ornamentation and food.
>
> In an attempt to provide an alternative form of development which would encourage conservation, a private capital-intensive ecotourism enterprise was initiated in Ubaigubi in the 1980s. The New York Zoological Society (NYZS) provided technical support in the development of the eco-enterprise. With a bank loan, a lodge was built, helicopter access established, and natural and cultural history tours organized. Residents in Ubaigubi served as enterprise employees as laborers, cooks and guides.
>
> In the late 1980s the enterprise closed due to financial constraints generated by the transport costs (there is no airstrip in Ubaigubi) and market constraints. The lodge was turned over to community management. Transfer of management skills nor market connections had been achieved in the short duration of the lodge's existence and the structure was soon dissembled for individual use.
>
> The enterprise was replaced by a broader community-based conservation initiative based in Heroana [*sic*] and supported by the newly-formed Research and Conservation Foundation of PNG of which David Gillison and then Secretary of

the Department of Environment and Conservation, Karol Kisokau, were founding members. NYZS and The Wildlife Conservation Society (WCS) provided technical and sponsorship assistance in establishment of the new national non-governmental organization, RCF.

Reflecting on the Ubaigubi experience, involved agencies and CMWMA community leaders have learned some valuable lessons. Ubaigubi maintains that they want to "watch and learn" from the community-based initiatives of the current ecotourism activities in Heroana. Heroana leaders say they want to try ecotourism but want to consult with Ubaigubi on how to build the community commitment needed for success which was not achieved in the first attempt.

The FSP (Foundation of the People of the South Pacific) began to work in collaboration with RCF in Crater Mountain in 1990 by sponsoring Peace Corps volunteers in the village of Ubaigubi. RCF placed the first volunteers in Heroana in 1992. Volunteers were sponsored in response to community requests for assistance with health improvement, literacy instruction, and development of alternative income generation.

In 1989 in Haia, researchers Andy Mack and Deb Wright, with support from WCS, among others, constructed a biological research station at the Wara Sera site and conducted four years of research during which time many Pawaiians [*sic*] were employed as field assistants, guides, and porters. The overwhelming positive reception of the Pawaiians to the economic development derived from the Wara Sera Research Station gave rise to the concept of research as an economic enterprise.

To provide further support for this concept and in response to requests for eco-enterprise development by Heroanans, [*sic*] another research station was constructed in the village of Heroana by RCF with support from the MacArthur Foundation in 1992.

In that same year, WCS, with support from the Ortenburg Foundation, sponsored the first Crater Mountain Field Coordinator, Seldon James. He became responsible for coordination of conservation and enterprise development activities scheduled in the WMA as well as general environmental awareness. James worked with communities to organize the first landowner committees, representatives of each land-owning clans to provide community-based directives to project development.

In 1993, three collaborating agencies, RCF, WCS, and FSP[,] and Crater Mountain landowners were awarded the Biodiversity Conservation Network Planning

Grant to develop the Crater Mountain ICAD project, with an emphasis on establishing direct linkages between enterprise development and biodiversity conservation.

Under the initiatives of the grant, a workshop with representatives of all communities in the WMA and governmental and non-governmental agencies was held to define the goals of the Crater Mountain ICAD project. On October 14, 1994, WCS working with RCF and Crater landowners were successful in achieving official national gazettal of the Crater Mountain Wildlife Management Area.

In addition to published accounts of history and local peoples' personalized narratives about the history of the Crater Mountain project, there are other narratives concerning the project's historic origins that are reproduced by NGOs in grant proposals and organizational publications. These are geared toward the agencies that will be assessing them for funding. They are slightly altered with every proposal, depending on what aspect of the Crater Mountain project and its history the NGO wishes to highlight.

The grant proposal written by RCF employees in 1995 for the acquisition of funds from the BCN focuses on biodiversity and threats to biodiversity. In this grant proposal, the history of the project is recounted so that it indicates that the project has from the beginning been about tying conservation to development. The mandate for BCN and the Biodiversity Support Program (BSP) was the tying of conservation efforts to economic development to test the hypothesis that if local people used forest products to gain cash incomes, they would work to conserve these resources. This version of the project history makes it seem as if this was the clear goal of the Crater Mountain project from its very beginnings.

In a more recent grant proposal, written to access funding for "institutional support" for the RCF from the Dutch development organization the Interchurch Organization for Development Co-operation (ICCO), the origins are produced in a different light. In this proposal, the Crater Mountain project's history was recounted in a way that highlights institutional issues and a supposed primary commitment to socioeconomic development (appendix B).

The multiple versions of the history of the Crater Mountain project highlight three things. First, there is a general perception that David Gillison and his efforts to conserve birds of paradise began the Crater Mountain project. Second, local perceptions of the project are personal, are remembered in terms of promises made about the future by outsiders and the RCF, and are tied to Gimi ideas about exchange. Third, differently positioned individuals provide different accounts of the history based on their particular interest in recounting the history.

The history of the Crater Mountain project is infinitely malleable. This is important because local people are often portrayed by conservation practitioners as manipulative and dishonest when it comes to land claims and the history of their interactions with the RCF. The above data indicate that everyone associated with the project uses history to meet her or his needs. Here I am talking about both the institutions and individuals associated with the conservation project and the local people involved in the project. Both conservation practitioners and activists and Gimi recount history in a way that serves their purposes. In many ways, this is where external actors and Gimi have the most in common. For Gimi, there is a particular understanding of what happened in the past, depending on whom you are talking to and on what you want to happen in the future. This is not so different from the RCF and its portrayal of history in funding proposals. Nor is it different from David Gillison's passionate discussion of history with Gimi and conservation on their lands.

CHAPTER 5

A Land of Pure Possibility

In the early mornings, the clouds rise like steam from a teakettle out of deep fissures between the tropical mountains. The rain from the previous evening drips from the kunai grass covering the roofs of the houses. A horn signals the beginning of a prayer meeting at Foketai — there is a traveling Seventh-Day Adventist (SDA) missionary spending a week there, and he holds prayers every morning and afternoon. A man from Motai shouts through the morning mountain mist that a man from Okapa, who has recently married a young woman from Motai, is going to walk to his new land holdings near Mengino. At Kuseri a woman wails, and her sorrow travels in the cacophony of bird songs down the mountain and through the valley out toward Chimbu Province. Her son is sick with malaria, and he has had a very hard night. At Beabatai, a bell rings signaling one hour until the beginning of the school day. It calls all the children whose parents could afford to pay this year's school fees. A tall man from Daru, one of the teachers at the community school, rings the bell. He will leave the village in a few months, and the school will once again shut down for over half of the school year.

It is June 2001, and I am sitting on the floor eating a sweet potato listening to the sounds of the village. I've spent the night at Harabo's house, and I'm mesmerized by the sunlight coming in through the woven bamboo slats of his walls as it illuminates the smoke from the cooking fire. It's like lasers, the light cutting through the smoke. The sweet potato is hot and delicious, and as I bite into it, I burn the top of my mouth and I feel the blister begin. I've got a bit of a cold from the previous night: we had stayed out late, spending much of the evening at Kabi's house telling stories and talking about this year's coffee crop. My lungs are thick with the smoke from the cooking fire because I am not accustom to spending the night in a house with a fire in it. The cooking fire is built in a wooden pit in the floor, and it is lined with dried bark and a layer of rocks. The house I live in when I am in the village does not have a cooking fire in it. Apropos of part of our conversation last night, about how expatriates drink coffee and Papua New Guineans don't and thus rarely have it to offer to guests, I would very much like a cup of strong black coffee to knock off the morning chill.

Harabo has a nice house, but it is small. He, his wife, and his two children live in a one-room structure that also houses their harvested coffee crop — held in bags that will be carried to the airstrip to be sold to coffee buyers — a pile of sweet potatoes, bananas, and other garden foods, along with all of their possessions. They have a few plates and cups, an empty oil tin, cooking oil and rice, numerous net string bags, a backpack, four pots and pans, a wire grate that serves as a grill over their cooking fire, and their clothing. Harabo also has a pair of shoes, which he wears on Saturday when he serves as a lay minister in his church. On the wall behind the door, there are two photographs that have been inserted into cracks in the bamboo wall, so that the people in them are staring out at you. One photograph is of Harabo with the director of the Research and Conservation Foundation of Papua New Guinea (RCF) at a conservation-related meeting held the year before. The other is of me, my grandmother, and my mother on Christmas in 1996, the year before my initial fieldwork. I kept this picture in my house in 1997 and 1998 and when I left Maimafu after my first year of fieldwork, Harabo asked me if he could have it so that he would not forget our friendship and the fact that I had become his sister.

When I was a child, specific images of New Guinea became fixed in my imagination, but as I try to think about those images now, I cannot recall them. When I try to remember them, the images that flow into my mind are of that morning at Harabo's house, or of the day, a year later that my husband and I, along with Harabo and all the other people in Maimafu who think of me as their sibling or child, prepared for our wedding feast. On the morning of the feast, we sat under a temporary kitchen shelter with a grass roof, and we peeled sweet potatoes, bananas, and pumpkin. We stuffed greens and pitpit into bamboo tubes for steaming. We dug huge earthen ovens and filled them with garden food and "lamb flaps" (mutton scraps) that my strict-vegetarian husband disgustedly, but good-humoredly, bought for the feast. We all made speeches about how, when I was a child, the food from the gardens in Maimafu nourished me.[1] We listened to Nimi talk about how he carried me up and down mountains on his shoulders. We discussed how I came to be an adult because of the social relations that made me — the food that was given, the long talks and walks and conversations, the things that I gave people, and many other sorts of exchanges. And we talked about the day that "my father" marked my bride price.

The images that come to me now when I think of Papua New Guinea (PNG) are of the people I have known and worked with over the past several years. They are images of things that really happened, but they are filtered through a complex web of information, emotions, and ideas. And, in a very Lacanian sense, they are beyond language; they are a bodily experience that once I put into language, as I must do even when I begin to think about them, become something else entirely. My writing about them and thinking about them leaves a kind of ethnographic imprint on them (Crapanzano 1980). Before I went to Papua New Guinea, the images I had of it as a place, and of the people that live there, were visual, textual, and discursive. They were images of an imaginary "other." Now, some of the images I have of PNG are visual, but many of them are sensorial in other ways. Some of the images are auditory, such as hearing in my mind, every time the telephone answering machine picks up a call, Fefa's voice as it laughingly calls out across the mountains that he is calling his son on "bush telephone." Some are gustatory, such as tasting hemoglobin when I fall down while running, and immediately being on the slopes of Crater Mountain holding onto Fefa's hand as he pulls me to safety. Some are olfactory, such as catching a whiff of smoke from the fireplace at a bar in New York City, and being back in Harabo's house.

In this chapter I explore the imaginations of people from Maimafu, looking for ideologies and images concerning "what white people are like,"[2] and how people from Maimafu see the actors associated with the conservation-as-development project. I also explore the imaginations of expatriates as they manifest particular ideologies concerning and images of "what the Gimi are like" and "why conservation at Crater Mountain is important."

While this might appear to be an unorthodox way to analyze the consequences of conservation-as-development interventions, in this chapter I foreground the actions of conservation-as-development — to be discussed in the following chapter — in the imaginations and exchanges of conservation and development. I examine what discourse, ideologies, and images do and how they, in addition to meaningful human action, are constitutive of reality (Brosius 1999a:277).[3] I agree with Brosius when he argues that environmentally focused discourses "in their constitutiveness define various forms of agency, administer certain silences, and prescribe various forms of intervention" (ibid.:277–278). And I want to extend this to examine the role of the imagination and certain imaginaries in the constituting of reality as they are related to the production of space (Lefebvre 1991:43).

In this book I take the imagination to be a process (Crapanzano 2004:1) that can contribute to a product and wish to distinguish between the *imagination* and the *imaginary*.[4] The imaginary is a set of collective ideas and aspirations that are tied to intentionality or intentional action (Anderson 1983; Appadurai 1996; Taylor 2002). They hold shared hegemonic ideologies and representations that have become like common sense and are transported and reproduced by media, stories, visual images, and the like (Appadurai 1996:145; see Taylor 2002). Agents with power strive toward fulfilling them or creating them, making them come true. It is collectivity and consciousness that are the distinguishing characteristics between imaginaries and the imagination. States, organizations, and social groups work toward the fulfillment of their shared image of the future, a future that exists in the imaginary.

The working toward a collective action is what Arjun Appadurai (1996:7) means when he discusses the imagination as a "staging ground for action." Here, however, I think that Appadurai conflates the imagination and the imaginary. He is focused on collective action and argues that the imagination is now the property of collectivities and "communities of sentiment" (ibid.:8). My argument however, following Crapanzano (2004), is that the imagination is an individual process that may or may not lead to individual or collective actions that produce a product of some sort, and that may or may not contribute to the social imaginary (Crapanzano 2004:6). The imaginary, the collective vision of a group that may well have been generated by the imagination at some point, is a historical artifact that merges the individual processes of imagining with the image-making ability of politics and history. An imaginary can be acted on without face-to-face contact between the people who have come to share it (Anderson 1983). Space, place, nature, and culture can be produced from this imaginary contingent upon individual action as it is directed by the desires of a collectivity or by the desires of a few with extreme power.

First Michael Taussig (1987), and more recently Hugh Raffles (2002),

Nancy Leys Stepan (2001), and Candace Slater (2002) have shown how individual imaginations of the environment and society work in combination with political economies and historical trajectories to produce imaginaries of the Amazon that come to be taken as real and that direct and filter the production of space. Bruce Braun (2002) has done the same with the rain forest on the West Coast of Canada. Each of these authors, although not necessarily relying on specific discussions of the imagination or imaginaries, works to demonstrate the movement between individual actors' imaginings of the environment and of society and the physical, psychological, and material productions of natural and cultural spaces.

My examination of the imagination in this chapter is focused on the level of the individual, although that scale has not been the prime site for this sort of analysis within anthropology (Crapanzano 2004:1). I am particularly interested in the ways that Gimi and their interlocutors — the people with whom they are in a dialogue over the meaning and value of their forests — imagine each other and the forest, the past and the future. I'm also interested in the kinds of imaginaries at play in the creation and implementation of conservation-as-development projects. "Development" is in itself intimately tied to the imagination (Sachs 1995:4).

With the title of this chapter, I invoke Crapanzano's use of the trope of "the hinterland" as a way of coming to understand the imagination (2004:15). Through the use of the trope, he shows the spatial dimension of the imagination, and this fits nicely with Henri Lefebvre's (1991:33) articulation of the role of the social in the production of space. Part of Lefebvre's dialectical formulation of the production of space rests on the imagination, but according to Harvey (1990:219) Lefebvre's formulation is left too vague. The idea of the imagination as spatialized by Crapanzano brings together Lefebvre's tripartite, productive practices of space: spatial practice, representations of space, and representational spaces (Lefebvre 1991:38–39).

PRODUCING OUTSIDERS I: WHAT "WHITE PEOPLE ARE LIKE"

The imaginations of people from Maimafu with regard to what expatriates are like and what life in America and Australia is like come most directly from media (in the form of the radio and newspaper), the movement of individuals from the community to other places, and the expatriate visitors that they encounter in their village. Many households have battery-operated radios, and the majority of news in Maimafu is from Pidgin radio broadcasts. People listen to the news, to "human interest" stories, and to music. During the time that I lived in Maimafu in 1997–1998, I recorded thirty-three incidents in which individuals made special trips to my house to ask about something that they had heard on the radio.[5] These questions ranged from "What does Beastie Boy mean?" to "What is the relationship between the International Monetary Fund and the United States?" In addition, news about major world events such as the collapse of the World Trade Center in 2001 comes to people via radio broadcasts. After the World Trade Center disaster, the residents of Maimafu assumed that my husband and I were dead. They heard on the radio that up to 6,000 people might have died, a number later drastically reduced, and they could not image that that many people had died in New York, where we live, and that we could have been safe. My research assistant was in mourning when an SDA missionary landed his plane on a Friday after the events of September 11, and he served as the minister for the Saturday services in the church near the airstrip. During the sermon, he talked about the event and then told everyone there that my husband and I were alive and well and that he had talked to us by electronic mail. The media of first the radio, and then the Internet, allowed them to be connected to me and me to be connected to them.

The stories told by men who have traveled widely and then returned to Maimafu are another source of images of whiteness and images of the rest of the world. This travel may include either trips to the coast to work on plantations or extended visits to relatives living in cities. These people bring back their impressions of what white people are like and of what development is like. One man, who has spent much time outside of the village, takes great pride in his ability to explain to his friends and family what whites are like. He derives a certain amount of status from possessing this knowledge, and he advises village leaders on matters having to do with their interactions with whites. He said, when I talked to him in January 1998, that whites are

> Basically okay. But, not always. It depends. Americans seem to be better than Australians. The whites in Goroka, which are mostly Australian, are racist. They treat black men like they are our bosses even when we don't work for them. They act like we don't belong in the places they go. They look at you funny or like you are stealing when they see you in the Brian Bell [department store] or the Haus

Cargo [warehouse trade store]. They don't trust black men, but here is the joke: I don't trust them either! So when the mining company came and I saw that the white man with the government mining man was Australian, I knew to tell my father and other men to be careful.

That narrative is in stark contrast to the following one collected from the same man during the national elections four years later, in 2002:

I think that the main problem with the government today is that black men run it. That is why I am voting for Mal Smith [an Australian-born man running in the election]. He is a white man, and he will not steal from us. Having him as governor of the Eastern Highlands will be better than having a black man again. It will be like having the Australians back.

Over the years that I have worked in Maimafu, there has been a shift in the local portrayal of "what white people are like." During my first fieldwork there, the general community sentiment was that expatriates were not to be trusted. They were seen as sneaky, bossy, and overly critical of local ways of doing things. In addition, and this will be discussed at the end of this chapter and at length in the concluding chapter of the book, expatriates are seen as not fulfilling their end of the agreement in relations that Gimi assume to be exchange-based relationships.

But with regard to the national elections, in 2002 I was constantly struck by the seemingly complete turnaround in local discussions about whites. Almost everyone I interviewed in 2002, not only in Maimafu but also across the Gimi-speaking region (as I spent all of June that year walking throughout the region with political candidates during the national election campaign period), articulated a deep distrust for "black men" who were running for political office. Many of them recalled the days of Australian colonial rule with a misty-eyed nostalgia. Young people, who would not have been born during the colonial period, were less likely to express this sentiment, but older people expressed it freely and often.

The other source of ideas about outsiders and the outside world comes from people who come to visit Maimafu. Biologists, tourists, missionaries, aid workers, government consultants, anthropologists, geologists, helicopter pilots, and others have all visited Maimafu. The interactions that these individuals have

14. Man and *very* large python.

with people and the stories that people tell about these interactions add to local images of the other.

Rick, while sitting on a rock next to the river and watching me wash my clothes, told me that he liked me because I never got upset when he joked with me. I stopped washing my clothing, looked over at him, and said, "You joke with me? What, I am outraged. I thought that every single word that comes out of your mouth is the truth from God's mouth to my ears." He, his wife, and his brother, broke out laughing. This was because Rick is a notorious joker and prankster. One morning a few weeks earlier, I awoke at dawn to Rick knocking on my door. At the time I did not know it was Rick who was knocking, since all I heard were loud repetitive blows on my door and lots of giggles. I dressed, went to the door, opened it, and found myself face to face with a six-foot-long python. Rick was holding it in front of the door as if it was the one doing the loud knocking. When I opened the door, Rick, standing off to the side, said, in a voice that was supposed to be the snake's, "Listen Paige, I have already eaten one of Nasi's chickens this morning, and now I am hungry for a researcher. You all come here to do your research, and now I think that it is time for me to eat one of you."[6]

Rick's identification of me as someone who was able to joke with local people, was the highest compliment that he could have paid me. This is because outsiders from America, Australia, and Europe are seen as humorless or unable to understand jokes. Nimi, a man who often joked with me about my bride price, said, in May 1998,

> We joked with that woman about her bride price. I asked her how much her husband had to pay for her. We know that is a tradition from here and not a tradition from your place. She got very upset and started telling us about the ways that white people get married. She made it seem like what we do is wrong like the white way is the better way. I was joking with her!

The language barrier between the researchers who come to Maimafu and the local people most likely adds to this perception of humorlessness. In addition, it takes a while to understand the differences in humor between Americans and people from Maimafu. It was only after many months living there that I began to "get" people's senses of humor, and it is only now, after a number of years of research, that I can actually make jokes myself. From reading Gillian Gillison's work, I understood, from the beginning of my fieldwork, that humor is an important part of local social life, but it was difficult, at first, to discern what was serious and what was play.

When I suggested to a group of men from Maimafu, during a focus group, that perhaps they just did not understand outsiders' senses of humor, they assured me that this was not the case. Rather, they argued, whites just did not understand humor and that, with few exceptions, "all whites are serious all the time." This generalization is based on a few interactions and probably rooted in linguistic differences and barriers. One of the outsiders that was seen as having a sense of humor was a biologist working for the Wildlife Conservation Society (WCS) and living at the Sera Research Station. Many people in Maimafu had met him during the WCS biological surveys and, in addition, while working at the Sera Research Station, he often talked on the RCF-run radio. People would gather outside the RCF office every morning to listen to these radio messages and broadcasts. This biologist's Pidgin was excellent, and people thought that he was hilarious. When I asked my friends about this man, they said that he was an exception to the rule that, in general, "white skins" are humorless.

Another general stereotype about expatriates in Maimafu is that we are all clumsy. I did little to dispel this stereotype. The landscape around Maimafu is rugged and difficult; and the forest is dense and often, to my eyes and body, impassable. People from Maimafu can traverse this landscape with no problem, but it is much more difficult for outsiders. One large source of jokes about expatriates comes from our falling down all the time. A man told me in 1998:

> Now this woman, she fell every two minutes. It was like walking to the waterfall with a baby. It was like leading a newborn! I thought I should carry her! Her legs are like a baby's; they shake and tremble and then she falls. I would look forward after just a second of looking away, and there she would be laid out on the ground like a big white baby!

In 2003, while conducting research on local hunting practices, I was told that people were thrilled when they realized that my students, all from PNG, would be carrying out much of the fieldwork that involved climbing up mountains to obtain GPS (Global Positioning System) points for certain animal-kill sites. When I protested that I was "good in the bush," Harabo relayed an exhaustive list of every single time I had ever fallen down while walking with him. He then proceeded to do a dead-on imitation of me walking up a steep slope.

Another pervasive image of what whites are like concerns tinned fish and garden food. Expatriates are seen as not liking to eat garden food and as loving tinned fish. People asked me on numerous occasions what the food "was like" where I came from; and when I told them that most of the things that I eat at home are from gardens, but that I have to buy them at a market since I do not have my own garden, they were incredulous. Whites have become inextricably tied to "cargo" and material goods. We are seen as having unlimited capital and an almost unlimited desire for store-bought foods and other commodities. This image is derived from the number of possessions that most whites, myself included, bring when they come to stay in Maimafu. People there have few material possessions and almost no access to store-bought foods. When they see the things that we bring in on planes with us, they connect that with wealth. The connection between expatriates and the material culture of modernity is also connected to the permanence of our cargo. The things that we bring with us to Maimafu are not, for lack of a better term, as biodegradable, as all of the material culture from Maimafu. Tin roofs, plastic bottles, rubber boots, the plastic bags that rice comes in — all of these things last forever, or seem to.[7]

PRODUCING OUTSIDERS II: KEYS TO KNOWLEDGE

Mr. Kayaguna, a man respected by the entire community, said to me one day, in a conversation about why he was so insistent about development coming from whites, that "white people have knowledge, and I know nothing." This is a man who is, by rural Papua New Guinea standards, highly educated. He has also brought significant "development" to his village. Not only has he worked with SDA missionaries to get the tools for the villagers to build their airstrip; he has also worked to get money to pay people to build the main trail that runs throughout the village. Moreover, he runs his own coffee business, and he sent three of his children to school. Yet in 1998, he argued that he knew "nothing" and that the only way that "development can come to Maimafu" was if white people brought it. By 2003, he had decided to bring development to Maimafu himself through gold mining, yet he still assumed that it would be social relations with whites, and money from whites, that would bring this economic opportunity to his people.

Dabi, who owns her own sewing machine, was the first woman from Maimafu to go to the house of the new Peace Corps volunteers in 1998. She went bearing gifts: a pumpkin, some greens, an egg, and some peanuts. After her visit, the female volunteer came to visit me. She asked me why Dabi wanted her to teach a sewing class to women in Maimafu, since Dabi knows how to sew, owns her own machine, and often sends money with the SDA pilot for fabric to be purchased in Goroka. I had never discussed this with Dabi before, so I went to visit her and asked her. Dabi said,

> This white woman from the Peace Corps, she knows how to sew. She must teach us. I can sew a little, but not like a white woman would know how. I am not smart enough to teach other women. I do not know enough. Paula must teach us with her knowledge that she has gotten from the Peace Corps. They teach their volunteers how to bring development to villages!

People in Maimafu, in general, see their recently acquired knowledge as second best when it comes to knowledge held by whites. This is not to say that they see their other forms of knowledge as second best. They see their "traditional" knowledge — knowledge about gardening, the forest, hunting, the past, and other local practices — as far superior to any knowledge that whites might have about these subjects. They do not, however, tie having this kind of knowledge to being able to "get" development. My friend Naba told me, "To get what white people have, development, you have to know how to think like a white person. That is what we do not know how to do here, and that is why we do not have development."

In addition to being seen as the holders of knowledge about development and how to get it, whites are also seen, for the most part, as being rich. Again, this image is tied to the amount of "stuff" that we bring into Maimafu with us. One day in 1998 a group of village men approached me and asked me if I had paid Eteni, a man who helped me with my house, 30,000 kina. I was astounded. I tried to explain that since I was a graduate student at the time, in a year of work I did not make 30,000 kina, so I certainly did not give Eteni that much money. The rumor had gotten started because of some controversy about who was to get the rent that I paid for my house. While I attempted again and again to explain that I did not have that kind of money, people brought it up for the entire time I was in Maimafu. I do not believe that everyone finally understood and believed me. I was still seen as rich.

Expatriates are often suspected as having made their riches from Papua New Guinean resources. An Australian-born white man who is now a citizen of PNG, Mal Smith is the owner of Pacific Helicopters, the current governor of the Eastern Highlands Province, and a wealthy and very well-known man (he was about thirty-five years old). The following story is about how he made his fortune (January 1998).

> Once a long time ago, there were monkeys here in our forests. They were like the ones in the WCS magazines.[8] They lived in the forest and they ate plenty of good food. They, like the tree kangaroos, lived in the trees. There were many of them. We know they were here because if you go to a cave near Herowana you can see their footprints in the dirt. They are set in the floor of the cave forever. They are set there to show that the monkeys lived here.

One day Mal Smith came in his helicopter to see the monkeys. He heard about them when he was still a young man, and he wanted to see the riches of our monkeys. He saw them and he liked them, so he stole them. He stole every single one of them. He put them in his helicopter and took them away and sold them. That is how he first became a rich man.

This story is, of course, fantastic. There have never been nonhuman primates in New Guinea.[9] But it illustrates the image of whites as people who come to the forests of Papua New Guinea, see what they like, and take it to make a profit.

This image is also reflected in local misunderstandings of the grant-getting process. One day a group of men heard a story on the radio about the RCF's receipt of a large grant from Japan. The men came to my house and asked if I knew that the RCF had received 300,000 kina from the Japanese government. I told them that I had not. It was explained to me that the RCF must be making money off the forests around Crater Mountain and not giving any of that money to the people of Maimafu. One man said, "We knew that this would happen." This grant story was the source of much concern in the village and was discussed frequently during my stay. People asked me constantly about the grant money and what it was to be used for. They asked if I thought that the money should go to them and not to the RCF. I always said that I did not know the specifics of what the grant money was for or how much it was. I also always said that I thought that they should talk to the RCF about whether they should get any of the money or not.

The "Japanese" grant situation illustrates that Maimafu villagers think that whites are out to make money off of their forests and also that conservation scientists look for someone to blame for their own failings. When the RCF received the grant and the media picked up the story, there was no formal attempt on the part of the RCF to dispel rumors about the use of the name Crater Mountain by the nongovernmental organization (NGO) to become "rich." The village "resident biologist," already overworked, was expected to explain the grant-getting process to people. He attempted to clarify the story for the people of Maimafu, but his efforts were hampered when the RCF "office" in Goroka told him that he was not allowed to discuss the grant money in detail with the residents of the village. Specifically, he was prohibited from telling people what would be done with the money. It was set to be spent on "improvements" at the

Sera Research Station, and the biologist told the residents anyway despite the prohibition. After his explanation, the residents of Maimafu still believed that the money rightly belonged to them and was being stolen by the RCF.

During the 1998 RCF annual meetings residents brought the grant-money issue up, and it was quickly dismissed with little discussion. Afterward, the conservation scientists talked about how "locals" were not capable of understanding the grant-getting process. They did not address the local concerns or the moral questions about money generated by locally held forests not going to the people who hold them. Marcus said to me, "They tell us that if we do not hurt our bush, money and development will come to us. We do like they say. Then when money comes from the Japanese, we do not get any of it. I do not understand that."[10]

There is also the idea that outsiders come to the village and Gimi forests to get knowledge and then take it away. I was often asked about what I was going to do with the knowledge that I was collecting, and people often discussed their belief that white researchers take the data they gather while in Maimafu, and in the forests held by people from Maimafu, and then go back to their homes and write books that they sell for large amounts of money. Gimi often ask these sorts of questions about tourists, and tourists provide insight into both the practices of conservation-as-development and the images of the other that come with it, as tourism is often intercultural interaction.

CONSERVATION NARRATIVES

Narratives are "governed by tropes and genres — metaphor, metonymy, synecdoche, irony, allegory, and so on — which produce and regulate history, ideology, empirical knowledge" (Said 1989:221). They are sites where politics, history, interpretation, and tradition "converge" (ibid.). Said argues that "Jean-François Lyotard's thesis is that the two great narratives of emancipation and enlightenment have lost their legitimizing power and are now replaced by smaller local narratives based for their legitimacy on performativity, that is, on the user's ability to manipulate the codes in order to get things done" (ibid.: 222). The narratives employed by conservation-related actors to describe people from Maimafu and from other rural villages, the local environment inside the Crater Mountain Wildlife Management Area (CMWMA), and the "threats" that local people pose to their ancestral lands work to produce a kind of conservation reality on which further projects and interventions are premised.[11] I, like Errington and Gewertz, see narratives as "critically important" aspects of social life that "organize desire and compel action by providing statements or images of" things to be desired, attained, or avoided, and that "anchor people in their pasts, situate them in their presents, and — of even more importance — project them into their futures" (Errington and Gewertz 2004:3–4).

Conservation scientists, activists, and practitioners who work in Papua New Guinea make the choice to work there for various reasons. They have complex personal and psychological histories, symptoms of which are evident in the explanations of their choice to work in "New Guinea" that they offer. One young male biology student said, when we spoke in December 1997,

> New Guinea. I mean you know. It's fu———ing out there. I was like, 'Where is the most far out place to go?' I graduated and couldn't see myself going straight to graduate school, so I looked around and saw this ad to come here and work at the Sera Research Station. I was like, cool. I can work and figure out if I want to do this biology thing and hang out in like the most remote place on earth.

When I questioned him about where his image of New Guinea as "far out," "out there," and "the most remote place on earth," came from, he said,

> Damn, that's a good question. I guess partially it came from this Introduction to Anthropology class that I took my freshman year. I mean I guess I knew something about the biology stuff from classes, but nope, it was the anthropology class. You know, I mean you really must know. All that stuff about tribes and fights and shit. That's wild. But no, also, I mean after I saw the ad I looked at the web and there is a ton of stuff. There are all these Web pages about environmental stuff and tours too.

The importance of media is clear in this man's discussion of why he came to New Guinea (Appadurai 1996:33). The young man accessed the Internet and "researched" his options on the Web, where he found numerous Web pages devoted to PNG, its environment, its people, and travel. With this he was provided with "large and complex repertories of images, narratives, and ethnoscapes . . . in which the world of commodities and the world of news and politics are profoundly mixed" (ibid.:35). Papua New Guinea was filtered through the Internet. The information this man gathered was partially factual, partially designed to "sell" the country as a tourism destination, and partially news related. All of it fed his imagination.

The young man also mentions the academic discipline of anthropology. Taking a class in anthropology contributed to, or perhaps even created, his early imagination of New Guinea.[12] Said (1978:149) has discussed the power of various academic disciplines in creating or producing the Orient, and anthropologists have been concerned with the ways that their writing of ethnography produces "otherness" (see Clifford and Marcus 1986).[13] In Appadurai's oft-used framework for the analysis of global cultural flows, he fails to address academic disciplines as one avenue for these flows, as they are not sufficiently "electronic" for him (Appadurai 1996). And yet, the academic disciplines of anthropology, ecology, and biology often plant the image of New Guinea — both visual images through photographs in textbooks, and discursive images through lectures and course readings — in the minds of people who eventually visit the island.

The young biologist also mentioned his biology courses. In addition to the images first engendered by anthropology, he remembers hearing about the biodiversity of New Guinea in his more "scientific" classes. Another biologist, a graduate student working on his Ph.D. in PNG, attributes choosing to go to Papua New Guinea to his academic training in "island biogeography," the ability to secure funding for a project in Papua New Guinea because it is "unknown to science," and meeting two biologists who had previously worked in New Guinea.

This older biologist reported to me that after having worked in Latin America during his early years as a graduate student, he met two more advanced student biologists who had worked in the Crater Mountain area. He said jokingly that they "won him over to the dark side," and he altered his plans and proposed to work in New Guinea. When I asked him why, he said that it was because of their stories about the rich and "unknown-to-science" biodiversity in their site. Again, this trope of the biological frontier emerges as a prime mover for the imagination of what New Guinea is like. In the 1800s Wallace imagined the island as having such a storehouse of unstudied plants and animals that he was driven to despair by his inability to move easily around the island (1880:492).

In today's world, there are groups of individuals who are moving throughout the world rapidly. They may be "tourists, immigrants, refugees, exiles, guest workers, and others," and as they move they take their ideas and imaginations with them (Appadurai 1996:33).[14] Along the way the individuals that make up these groups come into contact with other individuals, and their stories and ideas flow into the imaginations of others.

PRODUCING THE GIMI I: CO-OPTING ANTHROPOLOGICAL TERMS

The Crater Mountain Wildlife Management Area covers two language groups, Gimi and Pawaians [*sic*]. The Gimi population is bigger than the Pawaian with the Pawaians population numbering somewhere in excess of 600, while we calculate that the Gimi living within or about the northern borders of Crater probably reach four times that number. The Gimi villages of Crater are traditional Highland "Bigman" societies. Each clan has one or more "Bigmen" (chiefs) who maintain their position through their skill as politicians or fight leaders. The Gimi are subsistence farmers who follow shifting agriculture or swidden farming patterns.

The criteria for maintaining status as a Bigman in present day Crater Society is evolving constantly, the Gimi sections of Crater in particular are in the process of rapid social change. In the past Bigmen would have achieved their power through political skills or their ability to lead as a warrior. To this list one must now add the role of the businessman, parliamentarian, or government bureaucrat. (RCF/WCS 13:1995).

In most publications about the Crater Mountain project, the same images of Gimi speakers are produced in each chapter (BSP 1996, 1997, 1998; A. Johnson 1997; Pearl 1994; RCF/WCS 1995). Gimi-speaking peoples who live in three distinct villages and speak three dialects of the western dialect of Gimi are, in the space of approximately two paragraphs in each publication, described as bigman societies, shifting or swidden agriculturists, and people whose subsistence practices threaten their ancestral forests. Population estimates for Gimi speakers living in the CMWMA are also given. The constant reproduction of these factors is significant.

In each of these publications, thousands of individuals are described in a few paragraphs. The paragraphs dedicated to cultural background information are insignificant compared to other sections such as site background; project goals, objectives, activities, and outputs; baseline geographic information; biological significance of the area; endangered and threatened species; economically and culturally valuable species; and threats to biodiversity. The people who hold the land that is being discussed as highly biologically diverse, under threat, and in need of conservation are discussed only after descriptions of plants and animals. The people and their cultural practices are clearly of secondary importance.

While the designation "big-man society" is useful in anthropological explanations, its deployment as a shorthand way of describing all of the social relations within a society is problematic. Anthropologists have argued that this type of sociopolitical organization is often an elaborated version of the village headman system. Big-men have social and political power because of their generosity, fitness, bravery, eloquence, wealth, ability to navigate government bureaucracies, long-distance travels, and so on. Big-men also have that role because of their support in villages other than their village of residence. This system ties people regionally and creates connections among villages. Furthermore, big-men societies are almost always associated with complex systems of horticulture and exchange. Finally, big-men are not "chiefs," as chiefs are political leaders in chiefdoms, which are a completely different form of sociopolitical organization.

People in Maimafu do indeed exhibit some of the cultural characteristics associated with big-man societies in the anthropological literature. The problem with the NGO publications is that they never describe those characteristics. The same is the case with the references to agricultural practices. Saying that "the Gimi" are "shifting or swidden agriculturists" does not supply any information about how people garden, what they grow, or how they choose land for new gardens. It does not cast light on the social relations involved in horticultural practices. Nor does it exhibit any knowledge about the differences, much discussed in the anthropological literature, between agriculture and horticulture. My data suggest that people living in Maimafu village are horticulturists who predominately cut tertiary and secondary growth when preparing new gardens. The lack of attention paid by environmental conservationists to local horticultural practices is troubling. Much of their rhetoric concerning local people as threats to the environment is based on how people use their land and population. Both of these issues are intimately tied to subsistence practices. There are marked differences between horticulture, agriculture, and swidden agriculture, and these differences are significant for conservation planning.

The NGO focus on land use and population is important for many reasons. Conservation activists and practitioners working on this project often argue that local population growth puts too much pressure on local biological diversity and that population control measures should be put into place in the villages. This focus on population is part of a wider tendency to create images of local people as threats to the environment. The focus on land use and tenure is part of the same tendency. The NGO preoccupation with land ownership and tenure is understandable in that understanding land tenure is a key to conservation-related actions in the country. However, in NGO publications and in conversations with conservation practitioners, land relations are boiled down to questions of who owns the land? This simplification of genealogical and historic land-use practices demonstrates, again, the lack of understanding of local sociality and local cultural configurations.

In using these anthropologically generated terms for social and subsistence practices in a way that does not rely on the anthropological literature about Gimi peoples, conservationists are limiting the ability of those reading their publications to understand life in the rural villages involved in the Crater Mountain project. They are also limiting their own ability to understand local environmental uses. I would like to say that these anthropological terms are employed in order to describe succinctly the people involved in the project, but that is not the case. None of the expatriates who designed the integrated conservation and development project (ICAD) demonstrated any complex knowledge about local political systems, local gardening practices, or local property relations, the very subjects that speak directly to local uses of the environment.[15] Rather, the conservation practitioners who initially designed and managed the ICAD at Crater Mountain used anecdotal information provided by others and assumed from their previous fieldwork experiences, not good social scientific data and explanations, as their primary source for understanding local social and subsistence practices. In addition, the Papua New Guinean staff of the RCF were expected to understand and translate Gimi social life for others on the project. All of these project staff were from urban centers, and none of them had any experience in the social sciences. They were expected to understand Gimi peoples sociality simply because they were Papua New Guinean also. While some of the long-term "field staff" for the RCF did have a good grasp of local social events and politics, their suggestions were often overruled by expatriate project staff.

PRODUCING THE GIMI II:

THE DESCENT OF THE TRUE PRIMITIVE

"Gimi culture, before decontrol in the early 1960s, was a rich and exotic fusion of ritual, myth, and bush knowledge built on the experiences of countless generations living in Crater forests. As was often the case elsewhere, administrators and missionaries working in the northern regions of the Gimi language area have been the perpetrators of massive cultural change. Many Gimi now believe that it is sinful to participate in or to be allied with the traditional rites of initiation and marriage. Gimi Christians consider the theater associated with these rites to border on evil. The culture that existed before Western penetration of Crater fathered a land philosophy of unexpected power and beauty. In the last ten years, most ritual culture has disappeared (RCF/WCS 1995:14)."

One hot afternoon during my fieldwork in 1998, I had a conversation with a conservation activist visiting Maimafu. While walking along a mountain trail past bamboo houses and vegetable gardens, he said, "The Gimi in Maimafu are so acculturated that it's like they are not even real Gimi." We had been discussing the role of the SDA Church in the community, and he wanted to know what effects I thought it had on local hunting practices. His sentiment that the people living in Maimafu are somehow less Gimi than other people because of their current daily social practices and beliefs is important. The idea that indigenous peoples are fixed sets of communities that somehow loose their authenticity when they stop practicing particular sets of behaviors indicates a lack of understanding of the history of change over time in human societies. It puts "natives" into a precarious position, in which when they fail to fulfill the expectations for them located in a Western imaginary fixed on the primitive, they are deemed inauthentic (Braun 2002:33).[16]

Almost all of the tourists, and many of the conservation activists, who have visited Maimafu during my time there have voiced disappointment when they found out that there are few local ritual practices tied to mythology, no initiation rituals, and little traditional dress.[17] The "loss" of these imagined markers of indigenousness was seen as tragic. One tourist, disappointed when he realized that everyone in Maimafu wore secondhand clothing from Australia, voiced his opinion by saying "I guess I just thought that it would be more like those Discovery Channel shows and National Geographic." His comments reflect a media-saturated image of what indigenous New Guineans are supposed to look and act like. New Guinea and its inhabitants are produced as exotic and colorful. The television invites the viewer to gaze upon people who are visually other. The tourist and the conservation activist mark the images and actions created by a Eurocentric imaginary as indicators of authentic indigenousness. Maimafu's village guesthouse has a book that all tourists to the village are asked to sign. A few of the comments from the book (entry dates following each) illustrate the imaginations of the tourists, and they articulate ideas and images of "other":

Really nice place and people. Great fresh local foods. Great Christmas in the bush away from Western Rubbish. Wish I had more time. I love PNG DON'T LET IT BECOME ANOTHER COMMERCIAL CONSUMER COUNTRY! It has problems, but it can be paradise. BAN COCA COLA! (26 December 2000)

Absolutely Brilliant! I've had the most amazing time from Herowana to Haia. Would love to come back to one of the villages and read "THE CELESTINE PROPHECY," and listen to Pink Floyd on a Walkman and just relax my brain in the future. (24 January 2001)

A spectacular setting and a great guesthouse. People friendly and villages very hobbit like. Loved my stay. (5 October 2001)

Beautiful place — Crater Mountain feels like the top of the world. Hope to return one day soon! I hope a small few don't spoil this paradise for the majority that call it home. (27 October 2002)

This is the most beautiful stretch of RAINFOREST I've ever seen. Untouched and pristine. (20 February 2003)

On an occasion, while voicing frustration with the property disputes in Maimafu, a conservation practitioner said, "It's not like they do anything else in the traditional way; why do they have to be so damn picky about this?" His remark was answered by a conservation biologist with the following remark: "They just do it because they can. They do it because they want to screw up other people's chances of getting something they aren't going to get." Some activists and practitioners see the residents of Maimafu as employing traditional cultural structures and practices only when they are to their advantage. Of course, a person's act of picking and choosing which customs to evoke at a particular time has been documented widely in Melanesia and is a kind of cultural practice in itself.

Much anthropological work has highlighted the production of tradition in Melanesia (Feinberg 1995; Hobsbawm and Ranger 1983; Jolly and Thomas 1992; Keesing and Tonkinson 1982; Lindstrom and White 1995; Linnekin 1992; White and Lindstrom 1993). Popular productions of culture constitute a valid area of inquiry for anthropologists (Lindstrom and White 1995:201). They are examples of local people working to make sense of modernization through existing cultural categories and that work, in turn, altering the categories through which development is processed. These productions of culture are contingent and political. They are sometimes the active attempt by local people to make political statements or to gain access to arenas of power (Lindstrom and White 1995). They highlight the fact that "concepts of (native) tradition and (European) modernity surround most fieldwork transactions," and they allow us to see the working out of the tensions between modernity and the traditional (ibid.:204). Jocelyn Linnekin (1992) reviews much of this literature and problematizes the role of anthropologists in the "deconstruction" of local cultural forms. She highlights the political dilemmas associated with talking about cultural construction in the Pacific, questions the motives and desires of those who are "theorizing" the construction of culture, and calls for anthropologists to be careful when talking about authenticity. The choice on the part of the conservation practitioners to see one kind of tradition as essential to Gimi-ness and another as a choice about behavior is tied to the anthropologically debunked notion of people without history (Wolf 1982).

Gimi-speaking peoples are seen as more "Gimi-like" if they practice the traditions associated with them in the imaginations of Westerners. They are seen as less Gimi-like if they do not. This form of essentializing creates a set of assumptions in which people in Maimafu and their cultural practices are seen as having less value than other people and other cultural practices. This imagination of an essential Giminess causes conservation practitioners and activists to question social and subsistence rights of people living in Maimafu because such rights do not fit into this imaginary of New Guinea as primitive. This lack of essential traditional practices is used as one argument for wresting the control of land from people. While the "Gimi" of the past had "a land philosophy of unexpected power and beauty" (RCF/WCS 1995:14), the people in Maimafu, because of their "acculturation," are seen as threats to the land. Their behaviors, which are not seen as sufficiently traditional, are seen as problems and threats to biodiversity. A discourse has emerged in which it is argued that if local people alter their traditional practices and beliefs, then they are not really authentic and therefore forfeit their rights to stewardship over their ancestral lands (Povinelli 2002).

Taussig (1987:27), in a discussion about the inscription of colonial ideas on the bodies of native South Americans, argues that "perhaps, as in the manner strenuously theorized by Michael Foucault in his work on discipline, what was paramount here was the inscription of a mythology in the Indian body, an engraving of civilization locked in struggle with wildness whose model was taken from the colonists' fantasies about Indian cannibalism." Just as the body of the Indian became a site for the collapsing of violence, ideology, power, knowledge, economy, force, and discourse (ibid.:29), the bodies of villagers from Maimafu have become sites for the collapsing of a set of images of the primitive and New Guinea. These images, while described using the language of anthropology, are not based in any understanding of the anthropological literature. These narratives become a reality, and they become the filters through which future actions and practices are carried out. Thus, image and imagination lead to an imaginary in which Gimi who do not fit the initial image are seen as not deserving of their rights to land.

RHETORICAL DEVICES OF NGOS I: PATERNITY AND CARGO

The people here, in Maimafu, Herowana, Ubaigubi, and Haia, are simple. They are uneducated. They do not know things about the environment like we do. They do not understand what they have here. They do not understand the value of their land. They are very simple people. We come here to teach them. We come here because we have the knowledge about how they can make their way in the world.

Let me tell you a story. In Pidgin we call it a *tokpiksa* [talk picture]. I like to use these examples with villagers because they are easy for them to understand.

Suppose that I was your father and you were my son. I would take you and help you learn all that you need to know to make your way in the world. I would teach you how to hunt. I would teach you about being a man in our village. We would talk about the world, and I would show you the way. I would not let you hunt alone at first. I would not let you stand up and speak to the other men at first. I would help you along the way. I would make you strong with my knowledge, and then I would let you be your own man.

RCF is the father and Maimafu, Herowana, Ubaigubi, and Haia are our sons. But remember that the father looks after his children until they are independent. RCF has been finding food for its children. Scientists are part of that food. Tourists are part of that food. Now we must look for more food. But the villages, they are children still. They are not ready to go out and get their own food.

The above discussion, from an RCF employee in August 1997, of kinship obligations is not only an attempt to locate people from Maimafu on a plane of the "underdeveloped"; it is also a strategic use of local knowledge. The speaker, a man from PNG, understands well what it means to locate people in a fictive kin relation in which they have obligations to a "father." They must listen to their father, show him respect, stand behind him in conflict, and give him what he asks of them. A father gives rise to his children through the things that he gives them — his clan's life force, food, shelter, school fees, and the like. To invoke this image is a powerful discursive trick on the part of the RCF employee. He draws on the Gimi belief that they come into being because of the transactive relations with others, and the power of the father and men. Yet he, and other RCF employees, fail to conduct themselves as if they are the other half of the relations of exchange that he invokes. He says that the RCF will look out for the people of Maimafu until they are independent and that then they will "get their own food." Here we see him playing with Gimi belief in the generative nature of social relationships as a metaphor for conservation on the one hand, and attempting to use a kind of Western set of paternal relations on the other. In addition, the imaginary people in the narrative are all male, so although the exchange of women and women's labor are significant parts of the obligations between men, they are invisible in the tokpiksa.

When many conservationist practitioners talk about the people living in the CMWMA, they do so in a trope of their parental relationship to them. Local people are discursively produced as too childish in their understandings of conservation and as "not ready yet" for access to development. The use of the metaphors of kinship is tied to a pervasive image of the people who live in these rural villages as simple and childlike. Over the course of my fieldwork, I have documented this image of the parent-and-child relationship used when people from Maimafu fought over property relations, argued with conservation biologists, tried to communicate with a mining company, attempted to gain employment in the RCF office, and made demands about their development needs. It is often used whenever people try to gain power in their relationship with NGOs. These discursive productions are a form of infantilizing paternalism in which indigenous people are seen as climbing an educational ladder toward "the modern" and toward the social relations of production and consumption that are inherent in post-Fordist capitalism.

The other metaphor used often by RCF employees and conservation practitioners is that of a "cargo cult mentality." At one August 1998 meeting between NGO employees and residents of the CMWMA, a young man stood up and made the following statement:

> What we do not see here is the true hand mark of RCF. We see that you are here; we see that you are getting things from us; but what we do not see are the things that we need. We do not see medicine. We do not see a water supply. We do not see goods that we need. We do not see a source of meat for our children. Now let me make a talk picture for you. All of these things that you say that you have given us are little things.

This speech, about the lack of return that people in Maimafu feel on their investments in conservation in terms of services and the social relations that will allow them to access development, was met with the following comment from the RCF employee running the discussion: "You people are just hungry for cargo. You have a cargo mentality where you think we should give you things and that you should not have to work for them."

The initial commentary by the young man from Maimafu is a well-put-together critique of the RCF. He is showing that people are willing to work hard for what they get and that they understand that when they work hard they deserve some return. He is saying that the people from Maimafu do not feel that they are currently getting the return that they were promised. The RCF employee, instead of addressing these issues, immediately draws upon the trope of cargo. With this, he implies that people from Maimafu do not want to work but rather that they think that they deserve material wealth magically and mysteriously, to come to them.

So-called cargo cults or millenarian movements can be seen as early examples of local attempts to understand and, perhaps, take part in the articulations between modernity, capitalism, and development. These sociopolitical religious and economic movements are one of the most creative articulations between the traditional and the modern (Gewertz and Errington 1991:32; see also Kaplan 1995; Lattas 1992). And anthropologists have theorized them as some of the first local pushes for development (Whitehouse 1995), as well as locally generated critical analyses of colonialism and globalization (Lindstrom 1993). The language of cargo cults can be traced to early debates and conversations between expatriates over the lives and futures of people living on the island of New Guinea (Lindstrom 1993). But it is in anthropology that they take on a life of their own, and by this I mean that it is with anthropological writings about them that they become things or objects of study (Wolf 1982). Early anthropologists such as F. E. Williams and Margaret Mead described so-called cargo cults in their analyses of external influences on village life and the role of these influences in cultural change (Mead 1956, cited in Worsley 1968). And since then, other anthropologists have discussed them widely. The term refers to millenarian movements in Melanesia during early colonization and after World War II in which local leaders, who argued that a time when all of the material culture of whites would come to locals was on its way, emerged as charismatic cult figures (Foster 2002:177 n. 1).[18]

The anthropological literature on these movements shows that they were moments in which Melanesians tried to work out the relationship between labor, material culture, religion, and the agents of the colonial world. The cargo cults were political and religious, secular and spiritual, and a creative reworking of modernity (Pred and Watts 1992). By this I mean that Melanesians tried to make sense of their changing worlds by fusing traditional understandings of exchange and labor with newer understandings of what was happening with the coming of whites (Gewertz and Errington 1991:chap. 1; Foster 2002: chap. 2). One of the things that makes these movements so interesting is that they were in almost every sense very early development projects, and in fact they were the first participatory development projects. But since they were instigated and controlled by local people, the colonial government felt threatened by them (Mead 1956:208, cited in Worsley 1968). They were conduits for capital and the creation of relationships that might allow for goods and services that were belittled by the colonial government precisely because they were generated

15. Boys with "hunted" lizards.

from the periphery and not the center. They were sociopolitical movements with specific historical backgrounds that show, when analyzed well, the intersection of capitalism, religion, politics, and desire (Kaplan 1995). They allowed Melanesians to work out feelings of insecurity and fear in the face of massive social change, brought about by interfaces with modernity, and to understand the economic changes that were taking place all around them, and they were also ways that local groups asserted independence or resistance (Worsley 1968: 221). They were never just about objects; rather they were about social relations and attempts to understand new forms of relationships that came with intercultural interactions.

Dismissing the development needs of Maimafu village by referring to local desires as a cargo mentality is an exercise in power. The local critiques of the RCF have little to do with commodity goods and much to do with local attempts to gain access to services and cash-earning possibilities. To say that the young man's speech was about cargo is to employ a convenient trope without addressing his criticisms.

RHETORICAL DEVICES OF NGOS II:
THREATS TO THE ENVIRONMENT

"Land-use impacts on biodiversity include sago plantings, sweet potato garden plots, and the cutting of wood for fuel or local timber use. Hunting for subsistence and commercial purposes has already extirpated some species of game in certain regions of the WMA. Cuscus and tree kangaroo populations are seriously depleted. Cassowary populations are still strong, but the high rate of removal of cassowary chicks suggests a significant population crash might occur in a few years with the death of the existing adult populations (Andrew Mack, personal communication, 1995). An increasing human population in the region will continue to have an escalating impact throughout the area" (Johnson 1997:369).

One afternoon my research assistants, Esta and Nara, and I were sitting in the front yard of my house when Nara said, "Do you have anything written by RCF about Maimafu?" I went into the house and returned with the monograph cited above (Johnson 1997). Nara began to read, while Esta and I continued planning our upcoming trip to a mountain lake. After about an hour, Nara said, "Why do they never translate this kind of thing into Pidgin so that my father can read it? Or into our language?" I said that I did not know but that it might be fun to translate parts of it into Unavisa Gimi. We set out to do a translation experiment. Nara translated a few paragraphs into Unavisa Gimi and then gave them to Esta, and she translated them back into English. "Land-use impacts on biodiversity include sago plantings, sweet potato garden plots, and the cutting of wood for fuel or local timber use," when translated into Unavisa Gimi and then back into English, becomes "The villagers use the forest. They have gardens with sago and sweet potatoes. They cut trees for firewood and trees to build houses."[19]

The tone of the original monograph is one of indignation that local people use the forest.[20] The paragraph is under the section heading "Threats to Biodiversity." When the paragraph was translated into Unavisa Gimi and then back into English, that tone disappeared. The connotation of threats to the environment was gone. While there is the ability to express threat in Unavisa Gimi, and people often do — there can be a threat of an impending fight or a person can threaten a mischievous cassowary — a person cannot threaten the forest. When we discussed the differences in the translations, both translators said, "it did not

16. Girl helping with garden work.

make sense" to talk about interactions with the forest in terms of threats, because those interactions are necessary uses of the forest and land.

The paragraph from the Johnson chapter is an excellent example of the way that conservation practitioners portray residents of Maimafu and their subsistence behaviors as threats to the environment. In all of these portrayals, there is the overarching image of human impact as unnatural and damaging. While the image of threats is prevalent in all published material, there are little other than anecdotal data to back up these claims. To my knowledge, and confirmed by conversations with the scientific director of the RCF and with WCS biologists, when the Crater Mountain project began, there had been no baseline study done to document the level of biodiversity on lands held by people of Maimafu; nor has any baseline data been collected about local land, animal, and forest use. I do not, under any circumstances, mean to say that people in Maimafu, or elsewhere in the CMWMA, are not possibly using the forest in unsustainable ways. Indeed, my research on hunting practices in 2003 indicates that given the reproductive rates of certain species, people are "overhunting" some species. My argument is that the a priori assumption that people are using their environments in ways that are unsustainable leads to certain conservation-related policies and practices that might not have a conservation benefit at all.

In the early pages of the 1995 proposal given to the BCN to secure funding for the ICAD project, the NGO discusses human "threats" and "impacts" extensively. The proposal goes on, however, in pages 50–72 to propose a list of questions to be answered with the "monitoring component" of their project. These questions, to be asked and answered after the policies of conservation and development have already been implemented, include the collection of basic baseline data about human interactions with the environment, population, land use, hunting, other socially relevant behaviors, and studies of biological diversity in the area. The people are portrayed as a threat to the forests before there are any data to indicate any sort of impact on their environment.

There are even predictions made about what will happen in the future based on anecdotal evidence, since no systematically collected data about any of these issues existed at the time that this proposal was written:

The growing number of residents concentrated around villages in the CMWMA will have a significant impact on wildlife populations in the near future. Before residents began congregating around the airstrip and the government sponsored facilities (aide post, school, DPI station), they roamed through the forest in small bands. Now that they are concentrated for long periods of time in the village, some sections of their forests are perhaps not hunted as heavily. Men from Heroana [*sic*], however, have been known to trespass on Pawaiian [*sic*] land and harvest wildlife using shotguns. This would further suggest that the land around Heroana is experiencing a shortage of game. Most grown men remember fondly early hunting trips with their fathers when they would return to the village from the forest with plenty of game. Today, when one sees village children eating meat, it is most likely wild rat. (RCF/WCS 1995:12)

People living in Maimafu, Herowana, and Ubaigubi are sedentary and have never "roamed through the forest in small bands," unless this refers to small male hunting parties. Since the context of the sentence is that of settlement patterns, I assume it does not. Sedentary life does not mean that parts of the landscape that are held in tenure are not hunted simply because they are far away from villages. Indeed, in much of PNG, people have access rights to hunting grounds that are far from their village, and in order to access these places, they must cross the land of other clans or villages (Morren 1986). In the preceding quotation, there is a correlation implied between the anecdotal evidence about men from Herowana "trespassing" on land held in tenure by people from Haia and the level of biodiversity or number of species on land held in tenure by people from Herowana. There is no evidence to back up this correlation, and there are many other possible explanations.

In addition, the quotation carries with it a sort of social analysis and explanation based on locally generated scripts. The author has clearly spoken with people from Haia, the village within the CMWMA where Pawaia peoples reside, and been told that Gimi speakers from Herowana trespass on their lands. This is perhaps the most prevalent form of complaint about land-related issues in the Highlands of PNG. Men are constantly discussing the trespasses that have taken place on their lands. While these trespasses may sometimes have occurred, it is more often the case that these stories are similar to Rudyard Kipling's *Just So Stories* stories in that they teach a lesson. The other local explanation embedded in the conservation narrative is that of the loss of hunted animals around villages and the richness found around them in the past. While game numbers are indeed lower around villages, this would have always been the case. Human habitations are not good habitats for many of the tree-kangaroo, cuscus, wallaby, and ringtail populations that people prize as game. They are, however, prime locations for rats and bandicoots. Men also tend to idealize the past when it comes to hunting. In every instance during my fieldwork, when I have asked someone if there was more game in the past, they have said yes. While this may be the case in some instances, to rely on men's "Just So" stories as data on which to base a conservation intervention is problematic.

The grant proposal continues in the same vein:

Overhunting has already extirpated some game species in some regions of the WMA. Cuscus and tree kangaroo populations are seriously depleted. Cassowary populations are still strong, but the high rate of removal of cassowary chicks suggests a significant population crash might occur in a few years with the death of the existing adult populations. Overall, the threats to biodiversity are real and of major consequence, but they have not reached the critical point yet. With the implementation of improved land-use and extraction practices, biodiversity could be conserved in a substantially pristine condition. Delay of implementation of such practices will create a situation requiring efforts to bring about a recovery of biodiversity, a much more difficult and undesirable situation. (RCF/WCS 1995:12)[21]

Again, there was no nonanecdotal data on populations of tree kangaroo or cuscus around Maimafu at the time that this proposal was written. There is good evidence that human hunting strategies have changed enough over the past several years to make them unsustainable in many of the world's tropical forests (Robinson and Bodmer 1999). But until quite recently, no one was studying hunting in Crater Mountain.

The language used to describe what can happen if the RCF and WCS are granted this money — "biodiversity could be conserved in a substantially pristine condition" — indicates a true lack of understanding of land-use patterns in the area and of the concept of landscape in general (Willis, Gillson, and Brncic 2004:402). The biodiversity that exists in and around Maimafu is the by-product of human habitation and use.[22] The people of Maimafu, through the subsistence patterns that the NGO wishes to curtail, produced the landscape in which they live. So there is, therefore, no "pristine condition" to preserve. The problematic nature, then, of protecting biodiversity from the very people whose tenure, hunting, gardening, and settlement actions produced the landscape is apparent. Indeed, if conservation in these terms were to "succeed," the practitioners would end up with a very different landscape than the one that they set out to conserve.

In these portrayals of people as threats, some of the actions attributed to the inhabitants of Maimafu, Herowana, and Ubaigubi are factually incorrect:

It is still unclear how much biodiversity is lost following slash-and-burn and regrowth. It is abundantly clear, however, that the growing numbers of people will increase the impact on biodiversity due to excessive cutting for fuelwood and construction materials and damaged water quality by poor land-use near streams and poor sanitation. This impact will be compounded by a larger labor force looking to increase their incomes with larger coffee gardens. (RCF/WCS 1995:12)

None of these people practice slash-and-burn agriculture. They do not burn the forest. They clear secondary and tertiary growth with bush knives, weed garden plots by hand, and burn piles of brush.

This production of people as a threat is pervasive in both the literature and ethnographic interviews with conservation practitioners. It is tied to the idea that people from rural villages do not know how to manage their forests. I was constantly told that villagers needed to learn the skills to set up "successful land-use management plans." Not only was it never made clear to me what these skills might be; it was also never indicated to me, by people from Maimafu, that they want to manage the land that they hold the rights to in any way other than the way that they do now. This is not to say that people do not want some sort of "police force" to keep others off their land; they do. Men argue that violations of traditional tenure rules are not punished harshly enough these days. But no one indicated to me that they wanted to change their own behavior in any way.

According to the NGO, people are a sustained threat to their environment. They are not seen as the producers of the environment. As I have shown elsewhere in this book, the cultural practices in Maimafu have added to the biological diversity in the area. The absence of pigs in Maimafu, due to adherence to SDA taboos against the consumption of pork, and thus the lack of pig disturbance in the surrounding forests, has added to the biological diversity. In addition, land discursively produced as "remote" and without "human disturbance" is land that has been used for hunting and other subsistence practices for many years. While on hunting trips men plant trees, alter landscapes, plant gardens, and conduct other environmental management techniques that produced the landscape that we see today.

The forests of Papua New Guinea are relatively unstudied compared to forests in other tropical countries. They are highly biologically diverse and are seen as relatively intact by biological researchers (Sekhran and Miller 1994). Papua New Guinea has thus become the frontier for biological research and biological conservation. The biological diversity of PNG is also discursively produced as having benefits (Beehler 1994:37). There appears to be an ethical mandate of sorts among conservation practitioners to protect this diversity, and conservationists tend to speak of the worldwide implications of the loss of this diversity. The conservation biologists, practitioners, and activists I worked with see themselves as studying and protecting this biological diversity for the good of humanity. They see what they do as a moral imperative that perhaps transcends local rights. This seems to be the case with many conservationists, and it is directly tied to their own personal experiences and the culture of late modernity in the "West" (Taylor 2002). This ethical mandate to conserve biodiversity is also reflected in the language of the BCN. In one of their reports they state:

> Biodiversity represents the very foundation of human existence. Yet by our heedless actions we are eroding this biological capital at an alarming rate. Even today, despite the destruction that we have inflicted on the environment and its natural bounty, its resilience is taken for granted. But the more we learn of the workings of the natural world, the clearer it becomes that there is a limit to the disruption that the environment can endure.
>
> Beside the profound ethical and aesthetic implications, it is clear that the loss of biodiversity has serious economic and social costs. The genes, species, ecosystems and human knowledge which are being lost represent a living library of options available for adapting to local and global change. Biodiversity is part of our daily lives and livelihood and constitutes the resources upon which families, communities, nations and future generations depend. (BSP 1999:3)

The people living within the boundaries of the CMWMA are characterized by NGOs as both ignorant of and threatening to their environments. By using anthropologically based terminology to discuss indigenous or local peoples, NGOs give the illusion of attending to those local social practices and social relations that affect biological diversity. Yet, as I have shown in this chapter, in the case of the Crater Mountain project, conservation activists and practitioners employ these terms without understanding their meaning, a knowledge of the extensive ethnographic literature on Gimi speakers, or a set of basic sociocultural practices. There is no acknowledgment on the part of the NGOs that the current inhabitants of Maimafu village and their ancestors created, through their cultural relations with nature, the environment that the NGOs wish to insulate from human impact.

It is troubling that there is such a full-scale failure to acknowledge the local production of the environment given the recent growth of literature on "local knowledge" or "indigenous knowledge" in conservation and development circles. Paul Sillitoe (1998a and 1998b), who has written extensively about local knowledge both theoretically and ethnographically in the PNG context, argues that

> Local knowledge in development contexts may relate to any knowledge held collectively by a population, informing interpretation of the world. It may en-

compass any domain in development, particularly that pertaining to natural resource management. . . . It is conditioned by socio-cultural tradition, being culturally relative understanding inculcated into individuals from birth, structuring how they interface with their environments. (1998a:204).

Elsewhere (Ellis and West 2004), Ellis and I have argued that accepted definitions of local or indigenous knowledge must be taken further with respect to local history, biology, and economics and that they cannot simply focus on biological knowledge. Yet, even with this critique of the indigenous knowledge literature, I take seriously the anthropological fact that people know things about their environments. I do not argue that local people are somehow "ecologically noble savages" (Redford 1991) but rather that the current social practices of people in Maimafu, as they are both related to and separate from the environment, have emerged over time and have given local people unique ways in which to cognize their environment. I also argue that this unique cognition, which is historically contingent, should be taken into account by anyone who wishes to understand environmental change over time in the Crater Mountain area. The constant discursive production of Gimi-speaking peoples as threats to their environment elides this local knowledge, silences local environmental history, and disregards what some would argue is the lifeblood of anthropology: the analysis of local social and environmental relations.

In the introduction to this chapter, I cited Brosius's argument that environmentally focused discourses "define various forms of agency, administer certain silences, and prescribe various forms of intervention" (Brosius 1999a:277–278). Through the discursive analysis of the co-opting of anthropological terms by conservation biologists, the production of residents of Maimafu as indigenous people "fallen from grace," the use of the tropes of paternity and cargo, and the constant production of local people as threats to their natural environments, I have demonstrated what Brosius argues. These discursive productions define agency, administer silences, and prescribe interventions. They create a conservation reality based on an imagined primitive and a misuse of anthropological ideas.

Conservationists often either ignore the rich body of ethnographic data available about Gimi speakers or misinterpret and misrepresent these data. They co-opt anthropological terms as a shorthand and thus misrepresent Gimi. But in this misrepresentation, they make Gimi legible as "the Gimi" in ways that are important. This misuse pushes me as an anthropologist to do certain kinds of research in response, such as the discursive analysis contained in this chapter. The conservationists associated with the Crater Mountain project have noble intentions, but their effectiveness in providing development options and in understanding the human uses of biological diversity are hampered by the lack of attention they pay to anthropological data.

CHAPTER 6

The Practices of Conservation-as-Development

This chapter is concerned with two kinds of objects or things: New Guinea harpy eagles (*Harpyopsis novaeguineae* in scientific nomenclature; *lugilipagili* in Unavisa Gimi; *luipa* in Tok Pisin) and New Guinea net string bags (*ko* in Unavisa Gimi; bilum in Tok Pisin). These two kinds of things, birds and bags, are valuable and their value depends on the sorts of judgments people make about them (Appadurai 1986). In the past harpy eagles had value because they were a part of an arsenal of stories that Gimi told each other in order to teach and entertain. Bilum had value because they are both handy and necessary for carrying things (babies, sweet potatoes, and various possessions, for instance) and because they are made and given by women. Today, birds and bags can still have this sort of value. People still tell stories about the harpy eagle and use and give bilum. But the kinds of judgments that people make about birds and bags, which bestow this sort of value on them, are changing. Over the course of the conservation-as-development project at Crater Mountain, harpy eagles and bilum have come to have other kinds of value in that they have become commodities. Their transformation into commodities is significant because it illustrates the process by which conservation-as-development is working to change the local social institutions that bestow value on objects and the people that produce them.

Commodification is the process by which things are drained of the social significance premised on the human judgments mentioned above, infused with monetary value, and inserted into a social and economic system premised on hierarchies of value. People often forget their place in the workings of this system, and in the construction of these hierarchies. As such, the system and the hierarchies become naturalized, and social relations come to mirror and reflect the workings of capitalism. For Marx, a commodity is a physical or "sensuous" thing that satisfies human needs and that is exchanged for something else (Marx

1990 [1867]:125, 163). Its physicality is connected to its use value; and its relationship to other things, as determined by people, is connected to its exchange value (ibid.:148). Just because a thing has a use value does not mean that it is a commodity. It is only when someone produces use values, through his or her labor, which will be exchanged with someone else, that the commodity possibility comes into being (ibid.:131). So a commodity is made up of use value, exchange value, natural material, and labor.

In a market-based system, things or commodities can only be exchanged by way of a universal equivalent form, money. As an equivalent form, money causes us to forget that the exchange value of the commodity is the embodied form of human labor (Marx 1990 [1867]:150, 158). Exchange value, as expressed by money, also is always distinguished and abstracted from use value (ibid.:127). The thing that makes commodities equivalent to each other is the amount of labor that went into their production, but the money form obscures this relationship. A process of abstraction takes place in which labor, and the social relations of labor, are forgotten and the commodity comes to be seen as having value in and of itself and in relation to money. With this, commodities become fetishes (ibid.:165), and the producers of things become laborers who are forgotten. People become alienated from the things that they make and from the people for whom they make them; thus social connections break down, and social communities such as the ones that Gimi had until recently begin to dissolve. Indeed, money itself becomes the community (Marx 1973, cited in Harvey 1996:120).

Environmental conservation interventions based on neoliberal economic models move both the environment and social relationships into the realm of commodities. Using ethnographic examples, this chapter examines changes in social relations, disruptions in political institutions, and the creation of in situ biodiversity-based commodities, as these transformations are associated with attempts to conserve biological diversity through the further integration of rural places into commodity-based economic systems of market exchange. Appadurai (1986) has argued that by focusing on the social life of objects, we can clearly see that politics create the link between the exchange of objects and their value. Here I wish to focus on the politics by which two kinds of things, birds and bags, have been turned into commodities in order to show changes in the ways that value is created.

The examples that follow will demonstrate some of the social transformations resulting from conservation interventions that have as their central organizing principle the idea that markets will work to conserve and develop rural places. The first example, that of an income-generation project based on the scientific study of New Guinea harpy eagles, shows how oral histories regarding land rights have been reified and codified, how social relations between men and among clans have been disrupted, and how the semiotic meaning of the eagles is being transformed. The second example, women's production of net string bags as part of a "handicraft" business, demonstrates how women's rights to and control over the products of their labor has been decreased, how social relations between men and women has been affected, and how women now produce both for the market and for social transaction, thereby adding to the amount of labor women are expected to perform.

For Marx, production was literally the transformation of nature into culture (Smith 1990:16–28). Prior to their integration into commodity-based systems of production, most people in Papua New Guinea (PNG) transformed what we think of as *nature* into what we think of as *culture*, symbolically, materially, and ideologically.[1] As discussed in chapter 2, the residents of Maimafu have a long history of social interactions with the market economy. Since the 1970s, they have transformed the environment into commodities through coffee production, and since the late 1960s some people have sold their labor for cash. My argument here with regard to conservation and commodities is not that conservation, as the BCN Biodiversity Conservation Network (BCN) and the Research and Conservation Foundation of Papua New Guinea (RCF) conceived it, was the first moment of the commodification of the environment. Rather, it is that today in Maimafu, participation in conservation-as-development has worked to disengage people and their social institutions from the environment in a way that may well lead to environmental destruction instead of environmental conservation. This is because when systems of valuing objects and people change, as they have, the ways in which people's surroundings are valued also changes. Both examples in this chapter show the link between the creation of commodities and changes in the way that the environment is valued.

The consequences of the actions to be discussed are not intended consequences. Intentions, actions, and beliefs combine to produce praxis, or "productive meaningful action" (Bernstein 1971; Bourdieu 1977, 1990; Sahlins 1976; Werlen 1993; Vazquez 1977). There is no such thing as blind praxis, "no praxis without a conscious subject or author with respect to whom that praxis can be seen as an end or result of activity" (Vazquez 1977:259). This is not to say that all praxis results in an outcome that was intended by the actors. Michel Foucault teaches us that action and intention often produce unintended consequences. Once an act is performed, it takes on a life tied to its actor but also combined with other actions and forces. It becomes a part of reality and has the power to do things that the actor never intended; indeed, often "people know what they do, they frequently know why they do what they do, but what they don't know is what what they do does" (Foucault, cited in Dreyfus and Rabinow 1982:187; Ortner 1984:146). This is my argument with regard to some of the actors associated with the income generation projects in Maimafu. In particular, the United States Peace Corps (USPC) volunteers who initiated them.

In the 1995 grant proposal written to earn funding from the BCN, the conservation practitioners working for the Wildlife Conservation Society (WCS) and the RCF wrote the following with regard to the Crater Mountain project's "goals, objectives, activities, and outputs":

> The primary goal of this project is to test the hypothesis that the establishment of economic enterprises which rely on the viability of site biodiversity and provide direct socioeconomic and environmental benefits to landholder communities will result in conservation of site biodiversity.
>
> To achieve this goal the following objectives will be pursued and associated activities conducted to realize each objective:
>
> Objective 1. Establish locally owned and operated enterprises based on the research and eco-tourism potential of the WMA with a viable infrastructure to service research and eco-tourism development.
>
> Objective 2. Develop the local environmental and economic knowledge base required to successfully manage eco-enterprises and associated natural resources.
>
> Objective 3. Develop biological and socioeconomic monitoring systems to allow for sustainable use and evolutionary management of the WMA.
>
> Objective 4. Integrate results of enterprise, biological and socio-cultural components to assist landowners in evolving a working land use management plan which provides for biodiversity conservation and enterprise sustainability.
>
> Objective 5. Utilize Papua New Guineans as teachers, trainers, and consultants in order to strengthen the national ethic, technical capability, and self reliance in the conservation of natural resources. (RCF/WCS 1995:45)

Each of the income generation projects I discuss in this chapter are tied directly to objective 1, and were intended, by the RCF, to serve as one form of development for the residents of Maimafu.

In the 1995 grant proposal for BCN funding, under "CMWMA [Crater Mountain Wildlife Management Area] Technical Assistance Activities for Skill Development," "activity eleven" is stated as follows:

> While the major objective of the project is to link conservation with economic opportunity, it is also very important to remember that there are people living in the CMWMA who have daily concerns about their health, the health services that families require, the education of their children, and communication with urban centers where more services are available.
>
> To recognize and meet these concerns, Peace Corps Volunteers will remain in three communities in the CMWMA, Ubaigubi, Herowana and Maimafu (Maimafu placement is expected to take place in September, 1995). In 1996, expatriate volunteers at Ubaigubi will be replaced by national volunteers from the NVS, the National Volunteer Service.
>
> The presence of volunteers represent the need for addressing the basic human needs of residents of the CMWMA. In particular, there is a critical need for the development of the health services available to the community. The USPC and NVS have been requested to maintain volunteers who have strong backgrounds in health care and nutrition. It is the role of these volunteers to coordinate the development of the health and education services existing in the community with national and international resources. Also, by working with elementary school teachers, the volunteers can help to improve the quality of the health materials that are used in classrooms.
>
> In this role, the volunteers will be asked to work with CMWMA residents and the Enterprise Coordinator on improvement of sanitation and hygiene for visitor services. They will also assist Community Health Workers with the organization of a basic first aid course and review of evacuation procedures for guides and research assistants working with visitors in the CMWMA. (RCF/WCS 1995:46–47)

In Maimafu there have been three sets of USPC volunteers, and they have been directly connected to the income generation projects that are the heart of the development side of conservation-as-development. The first set of volun-

17. U.S. Peace Corps volunteer.

teers left the village after the male volunteer had a reaction to Larium, a drug used as a prophylaxis for malaria.[2] These volunteers were devastated by having to leave the country, and they have maintained ties with the village through letters, through several post-USPC visits, and through a foundation established by one of their families to help residents pay for secondary schooling. People in Maimafu have fond memories of these volunteers.

The second set of volunteers, who came to replace the first set, came from another USPC site in the country near the end of their service. They were well liked by the community and stayed in the village almost a year. These volunteers worked with residents of Maimafu during the first days of the BCN-funded integrated conservation-and-development (ICAD) project. They helped to establish the "handicraft" business that will be discussed later in the chapter.

The third set of volunteers, who arrived during my fieldwork in 1998, left after four months in the village. They left because of philosophical differences between themselves and both the USPC and RCF, and because of safety concerns.[3] Their major philosophical difference with the USPC was that it forbade them from working with Maimafu's residents in terms of health care or the community school. While they were allowed to run workshops for residents on health-care-related issues, such as sanitation and birthing in the village, they were not allowed to work directly with the provincial health care officials to procure medical supplies for the village aid post or to provide medical care for residents themselves. While they were allowed to teach *tok ples* (local language) preschool, they were not allowed to take the place of government-paid teachers in the community school, even when, as was the case during their stay in Maimafu, there were not teachers in the community school.

THE HARPY IS A STRONG MAN

One of the three ways that the RCF has attempted to "increase the average annual per capita income of clans" in Maimafu has been through "research business" initiatives (A. Johnson 1997:397). With these interventions, the non-governmental organization (NGO) attempts to serve as a broker by marketing the area as a "research hot-spot." It brings biological researchers into the area and arranges for the "local people" to serve as guides, carriers, and research assistants. People from Maimafu are paid "sleep fees, ground fees, and gate fees" by the researchers for the use of their land and forests. Besides the increase in local income, this initiative is designed to meet the second project "goal" of "increasing the level and range of understanding and skills of community residents" (ibid.), by increasing their understanding of conservation and producing skilled labor for scientific research projects.

In 1997, the Maimafu "research business" generated a total village income of 495.94 kina, which meant an average of 3.09 kina per village resident. The sum was unusually high that year because the WCS and Conservation International held a biological training course in Maimafu in October, and much of the income came from that course. During my 1997–1998 fieldwork, eleven researchers (including myself) came to work in Maimafu. The research project which best illustrates the unintended social and ecological consequences of the ICAD project, and that best shows the process by which neoliberal approaches to conservation commodify the environment, is the New Guinea Harpy Eagle Project.

The "Harpy Eagle Project" started many years ago, even before the formal establishment of the CMWMA. As described by Mattanaba, a man of approximately forty-five years, in July 1998:[4]

I went to Ubaigubi and met David Gillison when I was a young man. He went to the forests to look at birds and walked everywhere with the men from Ubaigubi. He has been all over to see birds and take their pictures. So, I went to see this white man. Then, one day, some years later, I heard that he wanted men to come and tell him if they knew where a harpy eagle nest was. He wanted me to tell him if they had one on their land. I heard that he would pay for the nest, so I went. Then, after he hired me to look out for the bird, I heard his talk about conservation. I heard what he said. He said that our ground was our wealth and that we could look after it, and white people would come and pay us to see the birds and the forests. I thought this was good. I heard his talk and then carried it back to Maimafu. I worked hard to convince men here that it was a good idea to join up with Ubaigubi and Herowana and David. I am the father of conservation here; I started when I was a young man, and now my hair is gray and my last child has been born. I brought all this to my place.

When Mattanaba was a young man, he left Maimafu and worked on a coastal plantation near Lae. There, he says, he saw what money could do, and when he came back to Maimafu to get married and plant a coffee garden, he "already knew what development was." When he went to Ubaigubi and heard David Gillison talk about the benefits that people could obtain if they agreed to look after their forests, he decided that conservation was the road to realize his vision of development. When Mattanaba "heard David's talk," he also heard a series of promises being made to him. These included promises about cash income, access to job opportunities, and access to white visitors and tourists. Mattanaba decided to carry this message, and these promises, back to Maimafu with him and to "talk the talk of conservation" with his brothers and cousins.

Mattanaba's memory of the beginnings of the Harpy Eagle Project is slightly different from the history remembered by David Gillison in the summer of 1997:

In 1978, I found a guy going through Ubaigubi on his way to town with a harpy chick and the parent's plumes. I decided then to add the bird to the list of things worth trying to protect in Crater. Later, around 1980, in RCF's early—very early—days, I got word that there was a harpy in Maimafu. I went out and met Mattanaba. He, and others there who supported him, said the bird was his, and so I arranged for some of the MacArthur money to go to him.[5] We paid him for four or five years to act as our Maimafu harpy watcher. I also arranged for the

RCF secretary to pay people in Ubaigubi and Herowana. Mattanaba's job, like that of the others, was to report on sightings, spread the word that "live Eagles are like coffee," i.e., money etc., and let us know what was happening in general. I didn't have much faith in Mattanaba, but he was a landowner with a bird on his ground. What we wanted was to start feeding the idea that conservation was not altruism — it was also an investment — into a rumor pool.

I remember those days that we were like mad missionaries tracking around Crater hocking the bird for all its worth. Eventually, we had an understanding with someone in every village that if they spotted a harpy, and if it started to nest, then they were to contact us, and we would then try to find a researcher to come study it. Many false starts.

The New Guinea harpy eagle was the beginning of the relationship between conservation science, conservation-as-development, and local politics in Maimafu. In addition to the new cultural salience that it has gained, now that foreigners want to study it, the bird is also imbued with cultural importance from the past. One female informant of approximately fifty years, Lamana, told me the following story in March 1998:

Once, in the past, a young new mother took her baby, her firstborn child, to the garden with her. She was hungry for sweet potatoes, and there was no one around her house to go with her. So she went alone. Her husband was out hunting with his father and his brothers, so he was not there. So she went alone. She walked to the garden, and she was nervous that a sorcerer would get her, so she walked quickly. And she got there safely. When she got to her garden, she hung the new baby up in its bilum from a tree branch, and started digging sweet potatoes. She sang to her child while she dug the potatoes. Then she sang to the potatoes. All morning, she sang and she dug, and she sang and she dug. Then, all afternoon, she sang and she dug, and she sang and she dug. Then, when the sun was getting cool, all at once she saw a shadow on the ground, and heard her new baby cry, and turned to see the harpy eagle's feet coming down out of the sky and snatching the baby out of its bilum. She screamed, but it was too late. The bird flew away with her baby.

The story of the bird and the baby once taught young women not to go to gardens by themselves. The story also echoes other mythical stories in which the firstborn child is especially prone to befall some sort of tragic death because of the actions of one or both of the parents (Gillison 1993:227). The bird's strength and its ability as a hunter were recognized in the past, and are often the first characteristics brought up when it is discussed today. It is still widely recognized and feared as a "thief" who will come close to the hamlets and steal chickens, kittens, and puppies. The birds had a particular set of meanings attached to them, and they had a particular kind of value. By this I mean that they were valued because of their symbolic importance and their supposed strength and hunting ability.

People now have a host of new ways of valuing the eagles and new stories about *lugilipagili* and the scientists who have come to study it. As explained in July 1998 by Kadaguna, a man approximately forty years old:

> That one came, Jonathan. He was fine near the houses, but he was not a man who was good in the bush. He was slow and fell down too much [*much laughter and imitation of someone falling down*]. We couldn't take him to see lugilipagili nests, because he would have hurt himself [*laughter*]. That is true. Jonathan, he fell, and then got angry with me because he fell down, so I stopped going with him. But he told us that if we found another nest, plenty of his white friends would come and want to see it. He said that if we found one, he would send people, and we would be rich.

The bird and its nests have come to be seen as valuable because of the research money that they might generate, and thus they have become highly commodified objects — a point to which I shall return in the this chapter's concluding section. In addition, the Harpy Eagle Project has become a social site where individual conflict and institutional disharmony are being played out.

When Mattanaba sent word back to David Gillison that the bird on his land was beginning to build a nest, the first researcher came to study the bird. David had some difficulty in finding the researcher and the money to pay for his trip, as he told me in 1999:

> Finally, one day when I was in Ubaigubi, I got a message from Mattanaba, saying that his bird was building a nest. When I got back to the U.S., we went crazy trying to get a researcher, or researchers, out to do work on the bird. At one stage, I had the famous condor man from U.S. Fish and Wildlife ready to go. I

spent time with him, trying to seduce him into the idea, and for a while it seemed to work. But at the last moment, he didn't get the sort of package he wanted, so no go. We went to others. Many people were really keen and helpful. . . . But nothing came of it. In 1982, I went out to push Crater and its prospects as a great place to do research and to support conservation. One of the people in the audience helped us get Jonathan as a volunteer.

When the researcher finally came, Mattanaba, regarding himself as both the "father of conservation" and as the one whom D. Gillison had chosen to "look out for" the harpy eagle, "adopted" the young man. He told Jonathan to call him father, and he explained that he and his wife and family would take care of Jonathan while he was in Maimafu. He even gave him a name in the local language.

Mattanaba and the researcher spent days looking for the birds close to the village, and Mattanaba organized groups of young men from his family into "hunting parties" in order to visit outlying lands in the search for nests. One day, when Mattanaba and the researcher were taking a walk to a nearby waterfall, they saw a harpy eagle. They followed it and found its new nest, which Mattanaba said was on his ground. The researcher was thus able to return to the United States with a report that there were indeed New Guinea harpy eagles nesting on land "owned" by people living in Maimafu. Before he left, he told a large group of men that this would mean lots of money for Mattanaba and Maimafu.

The WCS or RCF did not employ this young researcher, and he was new to working in the field of conservation science. He had no previous experience with ICAD projects and no formal training in terms of community relations and conservation. He made outrageously inappropriate promises to the people of Maimafu regarding how much money would come with the protection of harpy eagles and told people that "Whites will come to your village as tourists to see these birds." He is an example of how one person can alter the trajectory of a conservation-related intervention or a conservation science study that must have the support of local people for its success.

Back to the story of the eagle and its study: Now that a researcher had found a harpy eagle, money had to be raised for the continued study of the bird. David says, "After that, the years went by; we plugged on through false start after false start." While further funding for the Harpy Eagle Project was being secured in the United States, the RCF staff, not wanting to disappoint the local people or lose their cooperation in finding other nests, continued to tell them that if they protected the harpy nests, money and researchers would come to the village. But people in the village were getting nervous. They kept hearing that money would come because of the bird, but then it never did. And they kept seeing that Mattanaba had derived status and benefits from his association with the project. This was particularly contentious because there was a contest over the ownership of the land on which the harpy eagle nest had been found. Mattanaba argued that it was his own land, but a young man of about thirty years named Paul argued that it was his. One day, in a fit of rage and frustration, Paul took an axe and cut down the tree that contained the nest. Having recounted this incident, Paul told me in August 1998: "I am a young man, and my belly gets hot and full of anger. Now I regret cutting the tree down, but I was angry with Mattanaba for not sharing what he got from Jonathan. It is my land, so he should have shared with me."

The claims concerning this particular piece of ground are complex, and they illustrate issues in property relations that are often overlooked when conservationists attempt to establish the "ownership" of particular tracts of land.

There are a number of stories of the property relations involved in this case. Members of one family, who were not directly involved in the conflict between Mattanaba and Paul, put the story as follows when I discussed it with them in 1998:

In the distant past, the ground near the waterfall, the place where the harpy nest was found was Aerafena ground.[6] Then one day, a girl child from Aerafena got married to a man who was Kegegaina. They had a son, and as he grew into a man, her [Aerafena] family told him that when he could find *kama* and *kile* [two species of tree kangaroo] on the ground near the waterfall, then the ground would be his.

He was a strong hunter, and soon he found kama and kile. He killed them and brought them back to his mother's brothers, and then he held the ground. He grew older and married, and had a daughter. His daughter grew up, and one day married a man from Folisa. His daughter then had a son. This son grew into a fine strong hunter, and his grandfather [the Kegegaina man who had got the ground from his Aerafena grandfather] said to him, "When you can find kama and kile on the ground near the waterfall, the ground will be yours." He found them, and the ground passed to him, to Folisa.

Today, Folisa still holds that land. But now, Aerafena men say that they want the ground back. In the past, we always recognized the ground claims from the past, but now the Aerafena say that since RCF has come, and since [the RCF people] have their own customs, they will not recognize that the ground is Folisa anymore. They say that it is Aerafena, and that's all there is to it.

Another family said:

It has been ground that we hunt on for a long time. That is it. That is the truth. It was land on which our grandfathers shared hunting rights with other men. It was a good place for kama and kile. But now we are all SDA, and we do not eat kama and kile. But anyway, it was never ground that belonged to other men. They hunted on it; that's all. It was always Aerafena land.

Paul's family said:

The ground near the waterfall, where the nest was, belongs to Amamiaya men. They hunted on it in the past. Everyone says that the ground was Aerafena in the distant past, and that is true. But that was before Aerafena and Amamiaya were different. In the distant past, they were the same, and the man who first found kama and kile on that ground was the grandfather of Amamiaya, so the ground is rightfully Amamiaya land.

Mattanaba said:

The ground is my ground. Sara is my sister. She is married to a man who is Amamiaya. Paul is their son. Paul married a Kalikalipa girl, a girl from my line. So it is my land.

A person with no claim to the land said:

When Mattanaba went to Ubaigubi, he heard the talk of the photographer. He heard that the photographer would pay 100 kina a month for anyone who found a harpy eagle nest on their ground and then agreed to look after it and make sure that no other man killed it. Mattanaba came home and found a nest on Amamiaya ground, and went back and told the photographer that it was on his ground. So after that, he started getting money to look after the nest. But the ground was not his. It was Amamiaya ground. All the Amamiaya men were angry about him getting money for something on their ground.

Then Jonathan came, and he walked to the nest and said, "Yes, this is the bird we want to watch." So Mattanaba got the money from the photographer, and he got to walk with Jonathan, and Jonathan gave him lots of things and money. He called Jonathan "my son," and Jonathan gave him plenty of things when he left Maimafu. Mattanaba never asked the Amamiaya if they wanted half the money or half of the things that Jonathan gave him. He just kept it all to himself.

All the Amamiaya men got madder and madder at Mattanaba. It was their ground. When RCF told everyone that Jonathan's boss was going to come back and work here and do research, everyone got even madder still at Mattanaba. The ground is not his, but he was going to get even more money and more things from scientists. But then, Paul went and cut the tree down. He is a young man and gets angry easily. So he just went and cut it down because it was his right and it was his ground. And that was that.

An RCF employee misunderstood and compounded the already existing problem, when talking about a tree that was thought to contain a newly identified harpy eagle nest: "If we could just find out who owns that land which [the tree] is on, we could pay them to watch out for it. They could keep Paul from cutting the tree down again."

Instead of acknowledging the sociohistorical nature of property relations land tenure in PNG, the employee quoted above relied on a simplistic understanding. Examinations of property rights and land tenure have an extremely long history in anthropology (see McCay and Acheson 1990).[7] And anthropologists have tended to examine them in terms of the social relations between people as they are related to and embodied in land (Oles 1999:38). In Melanesia, the relationship between social life and land "is particularly rich and important" (Knauft 1999:222), and it has been examined as such. Particular attention has been paid to social life and land as they articulate with environmental concerns (see Crocombe and Hide 1971; Jacka 2003; Morren 1986, Rappaport 1984; R. Wagner 1972). This relationship between social life and land as it is tied to questions of identity, group affiliation, changes in the landscape, changes in external sites of power, commodification of resources, and "development" in general has also been examined (Knauft 1999:223; see also J. A. Bennett 1995; Filer 1990; Hyndman 1994).[8]

In Maimafu, local representations of property relations can never be taken simply as true statements about the world. Robert Ira Blinkoff (2000:11) uses the word *portrayals* to describe such representations among the Sokamin and argues, "Layers upon layers of portrayals exist. Privilege one layer and you mask or delegitimize another. Try to blend layers and you lose complexity." Generalizations about property relations are therefore problematic. Property relations and practices in Maimafu, as is the case elsewhere in Melanesia, are dynamic, and they vary along historical, social, economic, and political dimensions. Land tenure is also intimately tied to the genealogical system in the village.

In Maimafu, rights to, and relationships with, different kinds of land are held at multiple levels within the community, and decisions about land usage are rarely made entirely by individuals. While individual choices are sanctioned or not sanctioned by the community, these choices are made in accordance with various kinds of valid claims to land. Claims are made on the basis of kinship or lineality, previous use or the history of use, the history of social relations, and exchange or gift relations, and mythological relations. They are also based on current social, political, economic, and individual and group interests (see Gillison 1993; West 2000). Claims made on these diverse grounds are all possibly valid, and different claims made using different justifications made by different groups or individuals about the same tract of land are common. In addition, these justifications have changed over time.

Changes in Maimafu people's social relations with the landscape most likely resulted from a variety of events: the process of "pacification" or the end of "traditional warfare," the missionization and changes in hunting practices following the adoption of SDA beliefs, and the introduction of coffee. Also contributing were changes in settlement patterns associated with construction of the Maimafu airstrip, the influx of money into the community, and the local involvement of the RCF and its conservation agenda. All of these events altered the way in which land was valued, and valuation is one of the keys to making claims.

People make claims when something is at stake. Claims always reflect some kind of interest or value, and the value of things and places changes over time. The land with the tree that cradles the harpy eagle nest may or may not have had an articulated value before the nest was found. The stories show that it was valued historically as "good" hunting ground for tree kangaroos. That evaluation may have lapsed as some people gave up eating foods that are prohibited by the SDA dietary rules. But when the nest was found, the land once again had immediate value, and past claims were revived. This is not to say that land is not held by particular family groups and used by particular individuals; it is, and knowledge about these use rights is complex. The point is that conflicting claims are part and parcel of traditional land tenure systems and the rules and practices of tenure are manifested and illuminated in conflict.

Mattanaba's claims and his version of the local property relations are valid, as are Paul's and those of all the other families. There are cultural mechanisms by which these claims would have been worked out in the past. And this may have included violent conflict and the fission of groups. Now, individuals turn to the RCF to decide which land claim is "really" valid. This puts the RCF in a difficult position. There is no way that everyone will be happy with decisions made. This hurts the RCF's ability to work in the village, and it causes a profound sense of social disruption. In addition, turning to the RCF, as to a sort of governing body with its own special power, forces people to tailor their land claims to fit the perceived desires of this organization. It also means that some voices are silenced. Men who participate in the RCF-sponsored Management Committee have more power in RCF-related claims, relations, and decisions than men who do not.

Mattanaba is Paul's maternal uncle, a familial relationship that is socially important, and one that means that the two men have many other ties. This dispute caused the two men to fight each other with bush knives, and disrupted relations between their respective lineages. This was especially disruptive because they are both part of one larger primary descent group. Finally, this type of dispute is not good for conservation. As Sara, who is Mattanaba's sister and Paul's mother, said: "This fight, it is not good. It makes trouble in my life. If I saw the bird, I would shoot it myself."[9]

The other salient point with regard to property claims in Maimafu is that they are the living memory of social relations within and between groups and individuals. To disregard this historical nature is to effectively erase the unwritten history of the place and the people. In Maimafu, this means discounting the importance of six generations of oral tradition. Any sort of codification of property relations erases this history.

The interventions carried out within the parameters of the New Guinea

Harpy Eagle Project have also worked to turn the birds into commodities. In the past, these animals had a cultural salience that was tied to local myth and legend; they now have social importance because of the money that is imagined might flow from them. Now, their salience is tied to cash and conservation and the power that is derived from cash and association with the conservation project.

DO YOU KNOW HOW MUCH WORK IT IS TO MAKE A BILUM?

The following ethnographic example, in addition to being an example of the process of commodification, is given in order to demonstrate the ways in which social events often having little to do with conservation per se are seen locally as being tied to the RCF Crater Mountain project. In this instance, I show that major changes in women's labor requirements and a regional increase in the monetary amount of bride price payments, which are not themselves a consequence of the Crater Mountain WMA or of the RCF's efforts, are nevertheless combining with local changes brought about by the income generation projects to create a set of material circumstances in which local women are generally unhappy with the ICAD project. This example also shows that women in Maimafu feel that they have been "left behind" by the ICAD project, and that their needs have not been addressed by the RCF. Finally, it shows the ways in which conservation-as-development's premise, that commodities based on in situ biological diversity will lead to income generation for local people, is fundamentally flawed because there is little market for the products that are produced and because the market that does exist is nearly impossible for the residents of Maimafu to access in a way that is highly beneficial to them. Nami, a woman of about forty years, spoke to me about this in August 1998:

> Let me tell you how much time it takes. No, let me show you. Tomorrow you will come with me. All day I work. All day. I get up and go to the garden. I come home and cook for my family. Then I go to the other garden, the one further away. Then, on the way home, I get the trees for the bilum or the plants to make dye. All the while my young children are with me. Where is my husband all day? He is at the RCF office, playing cards and talking conservation. After I get home, I cook again, and then I start stripping the bark from the wood. The next morning, I put the

wood on the roof to dry; and when I come home from the garden, I strip it again and make it into bilum string. I turn and I turn. Do you see [the marks on] my leg from turning string? Do you see it? Then I make the bilum, and my husband takes it to the RCF office, and if I am lucky, someone buys it. I do not want to make them anymore; it is too much work, but my husband says that it is good money, and he is right, but it is too much work. You will see tomorrow.

Another of the income generation projects that the RCF has sponsored in Maimafu is a village handicraft or artifact business in the form of a store. This project as mentioned earlier in the chapter was started by USPC volunteers as a way for individuals in Maimafu to "capture the benefits" of the increased global consumer market for "rainforest products" (BSP 1996). The RCF was to market these goods nationally and internationally, and they were also to be sold locally to tourists and researchers out of the RCF village office. People in Maimafu made 3,897.60 kina from the handicraft business between 1 February 1997 and 31 December 1997, which meant an average of 4.87 kina per village resident. Of the 328 items sold, 178 were bilum (the net string bags made of natural fibers and dyes that are called bilum in Tok Pisin), while 139 were spears, and 11 were other items. Men make spears, axes, baskets, bows, and necklaces. Women make the bilum.

Women in Maimafu make beautiful "traditional" bilum. They are tightly looped, with deep rich natural hues rubbed meticulously into the fiber. Bilum production is a source of pride for women, and making them is a sign that a young girl is becoming a woman and learning to do women's work. The act of making a bilum for someone, and then giving it to that person, is an important part of women's gift giving and exchange. In many cases, a bilum is the one household item that truly belongs to a woman or young girl. Although women use pots and pans, bush knives, and other items of material culture, most of these items belong to either their husband or their father. The bilum is a form of material culture that is used every single day by every woman, and even by many of the men, and making them is very labor intensive (Mackenzie 1990).

The bilum, however, is also often a labor of love. The Gimi word for bilum as mentioned above, is *ko*, and *ko* is also the word for uterus. A tree kangaroo has an *ahme ko*, or "breast bilum," in which you might find pouch young, and a woman has a *ko* in which a baby rests in utero before it is born. When a young woman has her first child, her mother often makes her a bilum in which to carry

18. Woman making net string bag.

the baby. This is a profound act of giving, in which the mother reproduces her own ko, in which her daughter rested until she was born, for her grandchild.[10] These bags are also intimately related to women's roles as gardeners and as the nurturers of sweet potatoes, the staple crop among Gimi (Gillison 1993:chap. 6). They are in many ways the most important local symbol of women's labor.

Today, most women in Maimafu prefer to use "store wool," purchased in Goroka, to make their bags, if they can obtain it. Not only do they like the bright colors, but more important, a bilum made with store wool takes much less time and labor than one made with traditional fibers. The traditional material is obtained from the inside of young branches of tulip trees (*Gnetum* sp.). Women go to patches of secondary growth, find the young trees, cut the branches, and carry them back to their homes. They then strip the bark from the branches and lay them on the ground or on the roofs of their houses to dry. When the branches are dry, the women separate the fibrous insides into strands and "turn" the strands into coarse string. This turning process involves rolling the fibers back and forth on the length of skin right above the knee. Once the fiber is turned into string, the woman begins making the bag. She uses a long metal needle to apply the technique of looping the threads through a series of knots. If she decides to use natural dyes to color the string, then she must go and gather these materials as well. Women in Maimafu use plants that make blue, pink, yellow, and occasionally orange dyes. Once the plants are gathered, the woman chews them up as she needs them, and dyes the string by rubbing the masticated plant material into the fiber while holding it between her toes. The patterns are not random, and women know exactly how much of the string to dye to get the desired designs.

The amount of time that it takes to make a traditional bilum varies depending on a woman's other time commitments. Since women work all day doing other things, a lot of bilum making takes place in the evenings. But when women are sitting and talking, waiting for a plane to land at the airstrip, waiting for food to cook, or participating in any other work or activity that leaves their hands free for a minute or more, they are normally working on a bilum. It is constant and repetitive work, and women complain endlessly about having to make these "traditional" bilum bags for sale at the RCF artifact shop.

As I have already mentioned, the act of giving a bilum is an important part of women's exchange relationships (see Mackenzie 1990, 1991; Stewart 1996; M. Strathern 1981). One day, close to the time when my research was set to end in September 1998, Barbara came to my house. I had seen her working on an intricately crafted traditional bilum for about three weeks, and had commented to her that it was especially nice. We had spent quite a bit of time together recently talking about bilum production, because she was one of a core group of old women who had decided that since I was about to be married when I returned to the United States, I had to learn how to make a bilum. When the old women decided that I had to learn this skill, Barbara, a female of approximately forty-five years and their spokesperson, said:

> Now we know your work is like a man's work — that you write your book and that you do not have a garden and that your work is listening to stories, but you must know this. You cannot go to a marriage being an empty woman, a woman who brings nothing with her. You have to have some skills. Making a bilum is good, and you can go home and teach your mother and your grandmother how to make them. But you have to learn and learn now.

19. Woman making net string bag.

With this lesson, I began my bilum-making tutorial. It was not an easy skill to learn. And it was with this new directive from the old women that I began to talk about bilum production frequently.

When Barbara came to my house that day, she asked to see my bilum, a piece of work that had taken on a life of its own. As I would sit down to converse with the village women, I would also pull out my bilum and work on it. Almost instantly, it would get snatched out of my hand with much laughter and some-one would add a string of the color with which she was currently working. On the day when she came to my house, Barbara examined the bilum and then looked at me. She said, "You have worked hard. This is for you," and handed me the bilum that I had so admired. I said *Da* (Thank you), squeezed her hand; put my sweet potato, notebook, pens, and sunscreen into my new bilum; and walked outside with Barbara.

Barbara's husband's house was right next door to the house I lived in during my initial fieldwork in Maimafu. She and I had developed a friendship and the beginnings of an exchange relationship. Every morning, she would bring me a sweet potato, and I always shared my evening food with her, and gave her small items such as a potato peeler, some needles and thread, a dress, and razors. She and her husband had three sons and one daughter. Their daughter was married, as was one of their sons. One son was a teenager, who was going to school, while the third son, Mark, was a widower with four young children.

Mark was living right next to his parents, and his mother had taken over full responsibility for raising his children. Mark's wife died in the month following the birth of their fifth child. She was then in her late twenties, and some village stories say that she died from poisoning. Her husband agreed with this, saying that someone poisoned his young wife because people were jealous of the fact that he was on the RCF Management Committee. I was in the village when she died, and I heard many stories about how much blood she lost when her final child was born. I also heard one woman say that she had gone back to work too soon after the birth.[11]

In addition to cooking and cleaning for her extended family, Barbara was working in her husband's coffee gardens. She also cleaned and processed the beans by hand during coffee season, and she helped her sons with their own coffee gardens. Barbara had recently planted a peanut garden in the hope that she could transport the peanuts to Goroka and sell them in the town market. She had made more than twenty bilum bags for the RCF artifact shop, and she used her bilum income to help pay for her youngest son's school fees; for her family's "head payment" obligations;[12] and to buy cooking oil, rice, and noodles from Goroka.

Barbara had also begun to help her newly married daughter with some of her wifely duties. Barbara said that her daughter's husband was expecting his wife to do "all the work" because he had been obliged to pay 1,000 kina in bride price for her. Women say that in the past, when bride price was lower, men would make a bigger contribution to the family's daily labor. But now, since bride price was never less than 1,000 kina, men were expecting their wives to "make up" for the amount of money that had been spent on them. I heard this argument repeatedly during the year in which I lived in Maimafu. Mark's wife's relatives secretly say that she died because she worked too hard.

On the night after Barbara had given me the bilum, I heard yelling coming from her house. This was strange because it was neither Barbara nor her husband who was making the noise, but their son Mark. The next morning, I got up and, as I did every morning, went next door to say good morning to Barbara. She was not home. I went back to my own house, got dressed, and started my day's work. When I got back that night, Barbara was still not home. After dinner, I went down to John's house to catch up on the day's gossip, and was surprised to find out that I was part of it.

The fact that Barbara had given me the bilum had made her son furious. He had gone to her and yelled at her that she had broken one of the Management Committee laws, and that she had to come and make me pay her for the bilum. He and some of the other members of the Management Committee had met to discuss the issue, and they had decided that she was in the wrong. He had insisted that she come immediately and wake me up in order to get the money, saying that it was "illegal to give a bilum to a researcher." She had refused. She said that it was her bilum and that she would give it to anyone she liked. He countered, saying that it was not hers but was "owned" by the RCF Management Committee. Finally, her husband sided with his son, telling Barbara that she had to come and ask me for the money. The next morning, they woke up to find that she had taken Mark's four children and gone to stay at her daughter's house.

Barbara's story highlights some of the key issues about the role of women in this conservation and development project, and in the community more broadly. Throughout the period of my research, the growing demand for women's labor in recent years has been a constant topic of conversation. Young women and older women alike complained about this increase during private interviews and women's focus groups. Older women and particularly vocal women, usually women from other places who had married into Maimafu, also complained about this trend in mixed company and in more public focus groups. Patricia, a woman about ten years younger than Barbara, said in September 1998:

> This has to stop. I will not see my daughter married here, here in Maimafu, if things do not change. But it is hard now. When I married my husband, he paid 200 kina plus pigs and other things for me. That was right. Now, when my son wants to marry, we will have to pay so much. I will have to work, make traditional bilum bags, grow a peanut garden, and work harder in our coffee garden, very hard, to make money. So will his uncles. Everyone will. So when she, my daughter-in-law, comes, my son and his uncles will say that she will have to work at everything. I see how hard it is for new married women now. I see them die from working too soon after having a baby. But what is there to do?

These words echo the frustration that women were currently feeling. Patricia was married to her husband in about 1974, and her bride price comprised some cash, a number of pigs, kina shells, and a few other items.[13] Since then, bride price had increased throughout the Gimi-speaking region to its current level of 1,000 kina.[14] The obligation to pay this amount of money was certainly putting pressure on the groom's extended family. But the amount of work now expected of young married women was extraordinary. On top of their household work, garden work, cooking and cleaning, child rearing, and other duties, all women were now expected to make bilum bags for sale in the artifact shop.

Learning to make these traditional bags is a way of maintaining a link to local traditional knowledge, and a way of participating in both the historic forms of exchange relations and the commodity-based economy. It is an act that embodies the juxtaposition of the modern and the traditional. It is also an act that commodifies a product of women's labor in a way that typically fetishizes the object and erases the process of production and the social relations contained in the product (Marx 1990 [1867]:165). The bilum becomes a commodity, and the social nature of its production is lost. The extensive process of gathering the wood, drying it, turning it, and then weaving it into a bilum, the changing of "the forms of the materials of nature in such a way as to make them useful" (Marx 1990 [1867]:163), is erased by this process of commodification.

In the past, in the social network of exchange in which these net string bags moved around as social objects, and not as commodities, the women who produced and exchanged them came into social contact with each other (Mackenzie 1991). The social relations between people and their work, and the material relations between people and things, were clear. The values in these bags were both use values and values for exchange, but not exchange value as it is determined by an equivalent form. Knowledge of the individual labor that went into making the bags, and their currency in a social system based on exchange, made up their values. Now, the value in the bilum made for market is purely exchange value, and the value of women's labor is being lost in this new system of commodity production. As women's labor is increasingly linked to cash exchanges through the payment of higher bride prices, the value of women's labor is being commodified at the same time that it is being socially erased. The connections which women now make between high bride price, high labor expectations, the general devaluation of their labor, and the demands of bilum production for the handicraft business are making them hostile to the practice of "conservation."

My argument here is not that bilum are always commodities or that *bilum as commodities* and *bilum as objects of exchange* cannot exist at the same time in Maimafu. My argument is that the process by which these objects become commodities in some instances is one that changes the way women's labor is valued in all instances. That women's labor is now valued in terms of commodity exchange even when it is labor that has little or nothing to do with the production of commodities.

While this situation is not the "fault" of the RCF by any stretch of the imagination, women who feel frustrated and unconsulted about their "development desires" voice their frustrations through criticism of the RCF (West 1999:3). The majority of the women with whom I worked in 1997, 1998, and 2001 saw no benefit coming to them from the Crater Mountain project.[15] While they acknowledged the cash income that they received from bilum production, they did not regard this as an adequate reward for the amount of labor that they were putting into their product. The project interventions, which led to the hand-icraft business in Maimafu, were undertaken with no knowledge of the existing stresses on women's labor, and no in-depth analysis of what an added burden of labor might mean for women's health and rights or for the conservation project itself. Two Peace Corps volunteers started this venture during a stay in Maimafu that was arranged by the RCF after some women suggested that they would like to have a bilum business similar to the one that had already been set up in Herowana village. The business thus began as a response to wishes expressed by a few local women, but it was also undertaken without adequate social data on women's labor. These data would be quite difficult for the RCF's resident field coordinator to collect, because he was male and was already burdened with his official duties.

Aside from the additional stress on village women, and the confusion about the value of their labor, this intervention without social understanding has detracted from the general goals of the project. Women from Maimafu say that conservation has to do with the bush, so it is "men's business" or "something that belongs to men." They do not see any positive link between conservation and their own lives. What they see, for the most part, is that conservation adds to their existing hardship and creates conflict in the community.

The commodification of the bilum, and the new control that men are trying to exercise over the exchange of these products, as illustrated by Barbara's husband's demand that I pay for the bilum she had given me, alters both past and present social relations within the community. It undermines women's autonomy and puts their actions into a new realm of exchange, where their value is less than it was in the past. Finally, it upsets their notions of what exchange relations, and thus social relations, should be like. When Barbara resurfaced after the fight with her son and husband, she came to see me. I offered to pay her for the bilum she had given me, hoping to mollify the angry men in her family, but she refused to accept any money for it and said: "You came here and we became family. When I came to live with my husband, his mother gave me a bilum. Now I give you what I choose to give you. It is what I want, and I do not know why Mark and other men do not see that."

In March 2004 a colleague who works in PNG sent me an e-mail asking me if I had seen the Web page for New Guinea Craft (www.newguineacraft.com).[16] I had not seen it. On the page there are bilum, priced between forty-five and ninety-five Australian dollars, from several of the villages around Crater Mountain. New Guinea Craft is a recently begun business located in Canberra, Australia, and owned by a couple who were volunteers in PNG.[17] The company attempts to work with people in remote areas of PNG to create markets for their crafts. They currently market bilum, baskets, and pottery in Australia and are attempting to find markets for the crafts in other parts of the world. Their Web site has the following statement regarding artifacts and local culture:

> The village people in PNG need new markets for their craft. They have a capacity to produce a lot more craft than is presently needed by the tourist and artifact markets. Our network of village weavers and crafts people will mean many more local PNG village people will benefit. It will also mean that these traditional cultural values and abilities will be passed on to the younger generation. New Guinea Craft through its efforts to encourage village level economic development in PNG will give the customers of New Guinea Craft a small insight into the rich diversity of the PNG culture through their beautiful hand-crafted PNG art and craft products.

The owner of New Guinea Craft needs to charge three times the amount he pays for the bilum in order to meet his overhead and to make a small profit. The

20. Teenage girls at a party for the arrival of a visiting conservation biologist.

only way he can continue to help people in PNG create markets for their crafts and bring those crafts to market is by making a profit. It has to be worth his time and effort. The person in Lae, PNG, from whom he buys the bilum pays about 15 kina per item and turns them around to the owners of New Guinea Craft for 40 kina. If New Guinea Craft sells the bilum to a museum shop or store that trades in "native crafts," the shop usually marks the items up another 100 percent. With this, the bilum become too expensive for the general consumer market in this sort of item.

New Guinea Craft is currently trying to find a way to get the bilum directly from the RCF or from a middle person in Jayapura, a town on the Indonesian side of the border that runs down the center of the island of New Guinea, who can deal in higher volume and who has a lower overhead that his current contact in Lae. As it is the company's goal to help people living in rural areas in PNG make a profit and maintain parts of their material culture that they find valuable, they want to work directly with "weavers" at Crater Mountain. But there is a problem with this:

The problem with Crater Mountain people is that the weavers look at the prices a few bilum sell to the odd tourist who comes through the area, and therefore they demand this tourist price for their product. If they are to have a thriving village industry, they need to sell to me for between 15 kina and 20 kina per bilum. At this price, I can sell to art gallery shops for US$12 to US$17, and then they can put on their markup and the bilum would end up costing US$24 to US$34, which would probably work. The other problem I have is that bilum are an unknown product, which is why most of my customers are already familiar with the product. If I sell at exhibition or market, people who don't know about them will buy them because they can feel and see — when I do go to a market, many people rave about the bilum. However, in order to make our business viable, I need to sell more online to people who don't know about them.

Interestingly, the person that New Guinea Craft currently works with as their supplier in Lae gets the bilum from a person from one of the Gimi villages in the CMWMA. This Gimi man brings them to Lae, about 100 at a time, and sells them there for 15 kina each. The owners of New Guinea Crafts are currently trying to expand their market, and one of their strategies has been to contact anthropologists, as they are seen as a potential market for the crafts.

CONSERVATION COMMODITIES AND THE CREATION OF VALUE

I said in the introduction to this chapter that in a market-based system, things or commodities can only be exchanged by way of a universal equivalent form, money. In Maimafu today we see a mixed system, one in which things as commodities and things as noncommodity gifts exist in tandem. Harpy eagles and bilum are now, in some instances, commodities, and the social relations that surround them are changing because of this. The ethnographic examples in this chapter illustrate the way in which "income generation" projects have affected village people's lives, often in unintended ways.[18] I have shown why these consequences took the forms they did and that these forms are tied to the social history of place, nature, politics, and economics. The first ethnographic example, the Harpy Eagle Project, which is a "research as a business" initiative, involves mostly men.[19] It has affected men's relations with other men and between extended family groups, land claims and property relations, the ways that history is used to claim use rights to land, and general social relations in the village. The harpy eagle case demonstrates how conservation interventions can enhance already existing inequalities between men.

The second ethnographic example, the traditional bilum project, a "handicraft business," mainly involves women.[20] The bilum project has added more stress to the already overburdened lives of village women, altered women's gift-giving and exchange systems, commodified the products of women's labor, and compounded the already existing confusion about the worth of women's labor. It has created tension within families, especially between husbands and wives, and also disrupted village social relations. The bilum case demonstrates how conservation interventions can aggravate existing inequalities between men and women.

These two examples demonstrate how local social relations among men and between women and men have been altered by the commodification of string bags and harpy eagles. In both cases the relations between people, work, and the products of their labor are lost. For men, the fundamental effect of this is a change in their social identification with place and the environment. For women, it is a loss in their social identification with the products of their labor and, by extension, the loss of some of the power they traditionally hold in the community.

Although there was some knowledge of the local social context on the part of those working in the villages of Haia and Ubaigubi, two of the other villages in the CMWMA, there was no baseline social data collected prior to the implementation of these projects in Maimafu. I have shown that a more complete understanding of genealogical information, property relations, women's labor, and local history on the part of the project managers may have mediated the negative outcomes and would have made these projects more successful in local social and economic terms.

Both the eagles and the bilum have become objects that can move through a commodity phase in their biographies (Appadurai 1991). Although they are not always commodified, there is now always the potential for them to be valued in ways that are tied to the market and to the hierarchy of value into which they have been placed by actors from outside of Maimafu. In the past, the eagle was valued because of its role in stories and myths, and because it was a bird. As was discussed in chapter 4, men's life forces often, when they leave their bodies upon death, spend time in the bodies of birds. While there is not any evidence from my work or other ethnographies of Gimi peoples that these life forces sought out harpy eagles, there is still the association between men, value, and birds. Bilum were valued in the past because of their role in exchange, their connection to women as nurturers and the providers of care for babies and sweet potatoes, and as the material embodiment of women's labor. They were intimately connected to the bodies of women thorough their symbolism as ko.

When birds and bilum become commodities, they are drained of their social meaning, given value because of their relation to other commodities, and located within a system of meaning and value in which their worth is measured by money. They come to seem as if they contain value like a spirit or a soul, as if they have value and are not *made valuable* by history and society. Even though they are the same articles, they are socially, ideologically, and imaginatively different (Taussig 1980:25). A harpy eagle, as a physical thing or a sensuous thing, to use Marx's term, is valuable to science because it is rare, unknown, and, when compared to other raptors, gigantic. The eagles, as conservation commodities, contain the whole history of biological classification, of exploration and discovery of new species, of Sam the cartoon eagle from 1970s American television, of the symbolism of eagles from elsewhere, and of all the social relations between and among the people who have studied eagles. In many ways, they also contain the whole history of conservation in PNG. They come to embody what is seemingly important about biological diversity in the country: the rarity, the uniqueness, and the "little known to science" aspects of nature there. The value of the eagle is not in and of the eagle, though its commodification might make it seem so — it is a value produced by a set of social relations of production in science and in the imaginations of scientists. And what of the labor and value that went into the eagle that is forgotten as it becomes a commodity? That labor is the labor of scientific practice (Latour 1987:7), and the nature of the bird is its relation to all the processes of the forest that it influences and that influence it.

The bilum becomes a commodity, and it too seems to have value in and of itself. It seems to have value because it is something to be bought and sold and consumed. But as a commodity, its value is imagined to be derived from its location in relation to other commodities. Barbara disappears from her bilum when they appear on the New Guinea Craft Web page. In my mind's eye I see her, walking up and down a mountain to harvest the saplings that she used to make the string, drying them on the roof of her house, stripping and turning the bark, dying the string using ginger from her garden, laughing and joking by the fire at night as she weaves the bag. All of this, all of her labor and her love, vanishes from the bilum-as-commodity. It is infused with new value and meaning. It becomes "primitive" art—the mark of "the other"—and with this, comes to embody the sorts of imaginaries of PNG that live in the minds of expatriates and collectors. And it is put into relations with other bags. It can be compared to a Hermès bag or a backpack, and its value can be determined accordingly.

As commodities, birds and bilum are put into relation with money as the universal equivalent form; indeed, this is what causes us to forget about the labor that went into them. Money is a "representation of socially necessary labor time and price is 'the money name of value'" (Harvey 1996:152). But money is "slippery" and "unreliable" in its role as representation (ibid.), and it forces abstraction from use value. The usefulness of things, birds and bags, is slowly forgotten, and an illusion of use value takes the real use-value's place (Haug 1986:95).

Modern consumers, like the ones who buy bilum on the New Guinea Craft Web page, no longer buy use value, but rather they buy the appearance of use values (Haug 1986). The consumers today have desires that are so shaped by capitalism that they don't see use value at all:

> Out of a complex of needs a segment is cut which is possibly "satisfiable" with commodities. The commodities are developed whose appearance and symbolism fit the selected need like a key in a lock. The targeted buyer is then confronted with articles in which unsatisfied areas of the consumer's being seem to find perfect expression and satisfaction. The instinctual response to these things is employed to turn human beings into buyers. If they cannot help but reach automatically for the goods, it is because the promise and thus the illusion of a life superior to their own, with which the agents of capital have made these things, has been stolen from them, the people who have become their buyers. Now they give up their life and strength in labour, in exchange for an illusory use of their life. (Haug 1986:96)

Here we see that the "big lie" or "illusion" of consumption is that it is classless — that it is the great equalizer—that it is the one place where everyone can be equal. It is also the case, with commodities like bilum, that the consumer comes to imagine that a bit of the "native" that they imagine as residing within the commodity rubs off on him or her. But this is, of course, only the case if there is actually a consumer ready to buy the bilum.

As is clear with the example of New Guinea Craft, the BCN sought to create systems of production for rain forest products based on in situ biological diversity without confirming that there was actually a market for the products. There appears to be little international market for bilum, and in PNG, every woman can make her own bilum.

And how does the commodification of birds and bilum come to be articulated with the intended goal of the conservation of biological diversity? The value that comes to be located in the body of the eagle, the whole history of biology, for us is not tied to the money form; it is a kind of value that is imagined as intrinsic to the eagle. Yet for the residents of Maimafu, that value is now forever conflated with monetary value. If one believes that the imaginary of values inhering in nature is crucial for a conservation ethic (see Leopold 1968), then this seems to preclude the likelihood that conservation ideologies will ever take hold in Maimafu (Dove 1993:23).

Michael Dove has argued that stating of the "problem" of deforestation as something that can be "solved," by "helping" forest-dwelling peoples curtail their destructive practices and employ forest-based systems of commodity production, is an espousal of a kind of rhetoric that "helps to structure perceptions of tropical deforestation as a problem of the poor forest-dwellers" (Dove 1993: 17). He also argues that the thesis that nontimber forest products can be developed to help forest people meet their cash and development needs — which the BCN stated as its "core hypothesis" — is "at odds with the historical development of such products" and that evidence shows that these sorts of interventions are usually carried out at the expense of forest people (ibid.). If there were markets for these products, wealthy and powerful people located at the "core" would certainly have already found a way to get them out of the "periphery" (Dove 1993). And if there are not already markets — if the products are found to have enough value to make their extraction really a possibility for bringing significant cash income or development — the state, or other powerful actors, would create and manage new markets at the expense of the people who live where these products naturally occur.

CHAPTER 7

Exchanging Conservation for Development

I began the first chapter of this book with a quotation from an invitation sent to wealthy New Yorkers in 1985, inviting them to come to a party and meet Gillian and David Gillison while learning about the Gimi, New Guinea, and birds of paradise. The invitation invokes the imagination regarding birds of paradise and people: "As they watch this splendid creature, the Gimi envisions the spirit of his ancestor; the scientist one of the last of a spectacular species" (*New Yorker* 1985:36). The scientist is portrayed as imagining the future, one in which there may well be no more birds of paradise. A scientific future that is linear—if viable breeding populations of the birds are not protected today, then tomorrow there will be no birds. The human actions of "conservation" are the only way to protect these birds. The Gimi man is portrayed as imagining the past, one that is tied to his ancestors and his ancestral forests. But what is not captured in this invitation is the fact that Gimi past is not linear—what one does today and tomorrow affects the past; how one participates or does not participate in exchange relationships with other people and with the forests remakes the matter that is both his own body and the bodies of his ancestors.

There is an inversion of this representation of Gimi and Scientist in the real day-to-day workings of conservation-as-development. Scientists want to hold on to the past—an imagined past of biological diversity that is A. R. Wallace's country of cassowaries, tree kangaroos, and birds of paradise, which is untouched by "civilized" hands and that has more "strange and new and beautiful natural objects" than any other place in the world (1880:494, 504). This imagined New Guinea of the past is what Crapanzano has called "the beyond," a thing that is made by our dreams, ideas, and desires but that can never be reached (2003:14). While Gimi are constantly striving for the future—an imagined future of development that is either the hybrid modern-village that older people dream about, a place with health care, schools, and services; or the new-village that younger people dream about, a place that is urban. These imagined villages of the future are also made by dreams, ideas, and desires.

Scientists associated with conservation-as-development also want the imagined Gimi of the past. They envision a Gimi person who has a "land philosophy of unexpected power and beauty" and who possessed a "culture" that was "a rich and exotic fusion of ritual, myth, and bush knowledge" (RCF/WCS 1995: 14). But the existence of the Crater Mountain Wildlife Management Area (CMWMA) and its conservation-as-development interventions works to make Gimi persons in ways that are radically different from either this imagined Gimi or the real Gimi of the past. Gimi personhood resides at the confluences of social relationships that encompass bodies of knowledge, practices, and specific social capacities that can only be expressed in reference to other people (Gillison 1993; M. Strathern 1988). Scientists, by pulling Gimi into social relationships with them through the actions of conservation-as-development, have been one side of the transactions that have made new kinds of Gimi personhood and new forms of Gimi social life.

Maimafu Gimi want imaginary interlocutors. They want scientists, activists, conservation practitioners, Peace Corps volunteers, anthropologists, and others who make, participate in, and are made by the sorts of social relationships that Maimafu Gimi are used to. They want outsiders to be in and of the world in the same way that they are — constantly making and remaking personhood through social relations of exchange. Both sets of actors strive for an "other" that is imaginary and a future that is the beyond.

I invoke "the beyond" here because Crapanzano's reading of it speaks specifically to conservation-as-development at Crater Mountain and conservation and development in general. What is accessible to us, or what we take to be accessible, the things "we actually perceive, experience, touch, and feel," as the present, is "always determined by" the imagined presence of that beyond (Crapanzano 2003:17). All that we experience is made and remade by the imagined — the imagined past and the imagined future. Conservation-related actors and Gimi are literally experiencing the present in fundamentally different ways through their imaginations of the past and the future. But once the beyond is "imagined, dreamt, projected, calculated, prophesied — so constructed," we begin to destroy it (ibid.:15).

In order to achieve conservation, as scientists and activists imagine it, there has to be a kind of slowing of the modern and the movement of surplus capital into out-of-the-way places and then a stasis of sorts. In order to achieve development, as Gimi imagine it, there has to be a speeding up of the modern and the movement of capital into Maimafu. From the beginning of the conservation-as-development project at Crater Mountain, conservation was explained to villagers in terms of slowing and stasis — regulating overhunting, setting aside areas of their forests — and in terms of governmentality — creating conservation-related bureaucracy, writing laws. Gimi in turn demonstrated, through their participation in what they thought were exchange-based relationships and transactions with outsiders, that their understanding of development was movement and progress toward a future in which they had the necessary social relationships to help them access the goods and services they want and need. There is an inherent contradiction here. In order to achieve conservation as conservation practitioners see it, one cannot have development as Gimi see it; the two imaginaries of the future are completely different. One is about keeping an imaginary past and one is about striving for an imaginary future, and they both determine how people experience what is actually accessible to them: the present. Because of this contradiction, the fundamental experience of conservation-as-development for Gimi, is one of nonreciprocation. They imagine the future as one in which social relations with conservation actors will allow them access to development. Given that, they experience the present in terms of not being given the chance to form those relationships and of not being reciprocated fairly.

As "the beyond," both the imaginary past of stasis and the imaginary future of rapid modernization and change are seemingly right on the horizon for the people involved in the CMWMA. For Gimi, if they can just create the social relationships with conservation professionals that will give them access to development, then the future will come to pass. Most of their readings of and reactions to present-day situations and events are meant to create these relations. When these relations do not come to pass, the beyond is destroyed — as it has to be (Crapanzano 2003:17). But when it is destroyed, horizons and possible futures fall away, and Gimi are left with despair. For conservation professionals, if they can just convince Gimi — and the Pawaia peoples, about whom I have not written (Ellis 2002) — to use and value the forests around Crater Mountain in ways that the conservation professionals see as "sustainable," they will have achieved conservation, and the future will be stable. Most of their readings of and reactions to the present are assessing Gimi in these terms. And, because of the aforementioned differences in the ways the two groups understand what conservation is, Gimi are not "conservation minded" in the ways that conservation professionals need them to be. So the conservation professionals see their imagined horizon slipping father and father away, ultimately to be destroyed, and they are filled with a sense of despair.

Finally, the invitation discussed above illustrates the differences in how Gimi and the people associated with the CMWMA see and understand what I have called "the environment" throughout this book. Gimi, like others in Papua New Guinea (PNG), do not see the environment as a "vista," "backdrop," or as biological diversity (Leach 2003:195). What I have called the environment throughout this book exists for Gimi in their engagement with it. It is valuable and meaningful to them because they have a social relationship with it—one that is incredibly active. It generates Gimi, and Gimi generate it—through their life force and exchange as manifest in procreation, hunting, and initiation—and there are times in which person and forest are one, the moment a man becomes a bird of paradise during initiation, for instance. Conservation-related actors see the environment in a radically different way. They see it as existing apart from Gimi and indeed as being threatened by Gimi practices and social life, but imagine it as existing "in" Gimi in the form of "human nature" (N. Smith 1990:3).

MAKING SELF AND OTHER

In the fall of 2004 I spent some time in Maimafu with a twenty-one-year-old student from the United States named Thomas. He came to visit me for a month and was incorporated into social life in Maimafu as my son.[1] In addition to forcing me to learn about some of the sacrifices of motherhood, like giving up the best sweet potato and being blamed for perceived shortcomings in your offspring, Thomas's visit also afforded me the opportunity to see my friends and informants explain their "customs" to an outsider who was thought to be interested in social life because of his connection to me, but was understood to know nothing about it because of his youth and inexperience in the country.

One afternoon my friend Harabo and my "father" Kabi were at my house when the conversation turned to giving and getting in Maimafu. As we were talking, Kabi began rummaging around in a net string bag that he carries with him at all times. It is a tightly woven one that his wife made for him many years ago, its colors faded and its corners patched, that holds all of his most important possessions. As Kabi talked, he unpacked the bag, deliberately laying its contents on the table. There was tobacco, a razor, keys, some newspaper strips (for cigarette rolling), some plants for medical and other purposes, a kitchen knife (which he uses to make the fine detail on spears), and a file for sharpening knives. Kabi told Thomas, with Harabo and me translating, about the file, which I had given him in 1998 right before I left Maimafu after my first year of fieldwork there. It was the file I used to sharpen my pocketknife and my bush knife, and I had brought it from the United States with me. Kabi said, "My daughter [meaning me] is in the file, and the file is in her. When I use it I think of her, always. She is there with me, but it is not my memory of her. We, she and I, are there talking, laughing, eating Ahmanane [cassowary] as I sharpen my knife." He then went on to say, "I use the sharpened knife to make spears, and I want to give you [Thomas] one of them. I will give you a spear, and then when you go away and you see it in your house I will be there with you, and your mother [meaning me] will be there with you because of the file." Kabi was explaining to Thomas that the file is the material manifestation of Kabi's and my relationship and that we are made through that relationship and others.

Harabo, during our discussion, made the argument that conservation-as-development actors enter into relationships with villagers that they see as barter relationships — a thing for a thing, be it labor for money or be it not hunting in exchange for "income generation projects" — while many villagers enter into these relationships thinking that there will be long-term social relations in which things are given and received and in which people are made. Maimafu Gimi want to become and be made in ways that they see as developed, and the relations that they enter into with conservation-as-development actors are thought to be one way of becoming so.

I am not arguing, by either asking Harabo and Kabi questions about exchange or by recounting this interaction, that people in Maimafu use the terms, or understand social life in the terms, that anthropologists do. Our idioms for making sense of social life in Melanesia are not used by the people that we write about. But, I do think that some people in Maimafu think about social practices and their meanings and that their analysis of social life can help us understand some things. Harabo is about thirty-five years old. He is of a generation whose parents were competent Gimi (meaning that they knew what one had to know to be socially appropriate Gimi at all times) and whose children will not be competent Gimi in the same way as one's parents were (Gewertz and Errington 2002).[2] In other words, what it means to be Gimi has changed, radically, over the course of Harabo's lifetime. Because of this, he has a sort of insight into Gimi social life that others might not.

After our talk with Thomas and Kabi, Harabo and I went outside and talked a bit more about exchange, social reproduction, barter, and conservation-as-development. Harabo was one of the initial members of the Maimafu Management Committee, or the group of adult male "leaders" identified by the conservation organization as the people who should serve as the intermediary between themselves and the residents of Maimafu. Since the early 1990s, Harabo has been "working for conservation." He has attended countless meetings both of the Maimafu Management Committee (Management Committee Meetings) and of larger groups of men associated with the conservation-as-development project (Research and Conservation Foundation [RCF] annual meetings). He has helped build the village guesthouse, worked to provide food and other things for RCF employees who have lived in Maimafu over the years, visited with conservation biologists and tourists who have come to Maimafu, and served as a mediator between the RCF and villagers in times of dispute, as well as performing other tasks that he sees as the work of conservation. These are in addition to the things that he has received a wage for — taking tourists on bush walks and working for biologists who need local field assistants to carry things or to build bush camps, for example. The nonwaged activities that he has participated in were done in the spirit of exchange — not barter. They were not done to get something in return immediately but rather as a way of building a long-term relationship with the RCF and its agents. Harabo feels strongly, more strongly according to him than he feels just about anything else, that the RCF and its agents have not reciprocated. Harabo did not receive a wage for the "work" of conservation — so it was not valued by conservation practitioners as waged labor — but neither did he enter into the kinds of social relationships of reciprocity that he feels he deserves.

The residents of Maimafu expect something in return for their work for and their cooperation with conservation-as-development and its agents, and they are indignant that they have not gotten it. Development was to be the return for participation, and villagers see development as much more than cash and the conservation-as-development organizations and their agents as more than barter partners. It is not a quid pro quo relationship; it is one of social reproduction in which villagers assumed that they were entering into relations that would give them allies in their efforts to access and negotiate the world outside of Maimafu, a world of wealth, medicine, education, technology, and knowledge. But conservation-as-development actors assumed that their relationships with villagers were quid pro quo relationships. In fact, they assumed that by helping villagers learn to sell their labor and commodities based on in situ biological diversity, that they had fulfilled their side of the deal. Yet villagers did not imagine that the social relations they had entered into ended there at all. In addition, the people of Maimafu fully expected to become "developed" persons through their social interactions with the agents of conservation-as-development. And their idea of developed persons is people that can access the goods and services of development without help from outsiders.

From the beginning of contact with outsiders, Papua New Guinean and expatriate alike, Gimi saw them as a way to access goods, services, and new kinds of social relationships. They also saw them as a way to imagine their future and a future of a certain kind of material good. Traditional bits of material culture — houses, the net string bags made by women, stone axes, spears, and shields — all made from things found in the forests, are impermanent; they can easily go back to the forest through disintegration and decay. They mirror older Gimi views of self and forest, and the movement of matter from use by people to storage in the reserves of the ancestral forests. Today's material culture — things bought and sold in Goroka and elsewhere and brought to Maimafu — all made from nonforest materials are enduring, and they seem to last forever (Ingold 2000:181). Old things, things from the past, are seen as markers of the lack of development people feel, and new material culture bits are seen as markers for what it means to be developed. This is evidenced by a comment made to me in June 2003 by Eato, a man of about forty-five to fifty, about the history of interactions between outsiders and residents of Maimafu:

> The first time I saw a white man, I was a boy. I remember his shoes. I saw them, and I thought that they must be made of the skin of black men. I remember my father talking about them, about how the white men came from the north, from the Goroka side, but how all of the other things from other places, kina shells, bush knives, *laplaps* [a cloth, sarong-like wrap], hatchets, they had all come from the south, towards Haia.[3]

CRITIQUING CONSERVATION-AS-DEVELOPMENT

One day before the RCF annual meeting in 1998 — the meeting that culminated in the fight between Kelego and Lasini that I described in chapter 1 of this book — a group of men approached me and asked me to type up a list of questions for them and print it for them so that it would look "professional" when they gave it to the RCF. I was also asked to translate the questions into English and give it to the "boss of the Wildlife Conservation Society [WCS]" when I returned to the United States.[4] These two lists of questions can be found in appendices C and D in full. These questions encompass the local critique of conservation-as-development and bring together all of the arguments I've made about conservation-as-development in this book. In what follows I will discuss each question.

The first three questions (1 through 3 in appendix C and 6, 7, and 9 in appendix D) are "What does the name Management Committee mean?" "What is an NGO?" and "Why did you give us this uniform; does it have some sort of meaning behind it?" These questions are concerned with how people have and have not been made through the transactions of conservation-as-development that have given rise to the CMWMA. And they are an opening reminder that Gimi ways of making people are not static. Gimi ideas of time are not linear history, in which events happen and then are assumed to exist historically in the past. Rather, people live in continuing transactions with people, and their identity through those relationships fluctuates based on those relationships, which then have to be constantly reformed and remade. Even though people have been told what a nongovernmental organization (NGO) is and what the Management Committee is, that relationship between them as Management Committee and the RCF as an NGO does not have meaning unless it is rearticulated. The uniforms are a material manifestation of that relationship.

One of the other questions (9 in appendix C and 8 in appendix D), is also about the creation of persons through transactional relationships, as these relationships are generated because of the CMWMA:

> When people come and work here and then go and get a big name for themselves by using what they learned here, what do we get out of it?

And the question in Melanesian Pidgin:

21. Author with Wildlife Management Committee (in their uniforms).

Ol lain long RCF na saentist kam insait long bus bilong mipela na kisim bikpela nem bilong ol, ol mekim wanem wok insait long Kreta maunten na kisim dispela nem? John Ericho, kisim "dupiti generol menesa."

[Everyone from the RCF and the scientists who come into our forests make big names for themselves; what kind of work are they doing at Crater Mountain that allows them to make names for themselves professionally? (For example,) John Ericho has become the "deputy general manager."]

Outsiders, scientists, U.S. Peace Corps volunteers, anthropologists, and others come to Maimafu and "work" or "conduct research." After they leave, villagers hear stories about their professional success, how someone has been given a title (deputy general manager or professor, for example), and they create stories in which the data gathered in Maimafu has been used to make people rich. Gimi then wonder why others are gaining prestige and material gain through the interactions they have with the residents of Maimafu and their forests and why the converse is not the case. Why are others "getting development" from their social relations with Gimi, while Gimi are not? Why are others creating economic, social, and cultural capital through their participation in the spatial production that is Crater Mountain?

The preceding pair of questions also express Gimi's desire to be compensated in some way for the success that outsiders have gained from working in and around Maimafu. They and their forests gave rise to these successes, so they deserve some benefit in return. For example, when I returned to PNG in 2001 after having been away since November 1998, writing my Ph.D. dissertation and then receiving my Ph.D., I was now "Dr. Paige West." To the people of Maimafu, that "success" and title belongs as much to them as it does to me. In some ways this is almost a physical manifestation of their ideas about exchange and personhood. I became more than I was in the past: Before I had been a student, a social role that is seen as fairly powerless, but on the way to power. Now I was a professor, a teacher, and a "doctor," all social roles that are extremely powerful. I had attained that status because of the hard work of my Gimi friends, through their telling me stories, through their teaching me their language, through their feeding me and looking after me — through our social transactions — I had become more than I was before. They, certainly, had a right to claim that my becoming was only possible because of them.

The previous pair of questions were about the value of persons. The following (question 4 in appendix C and question 5 in appendix D) are about the value of knowledge:

> Many scientists come here, and they get our knowledge. They listen to our stories, and they use us to find the plants and animals they are looking for. They take this away from our place and write reports about things. We want to see these reports. Where are these reports?

And the Melanesian Pidgin version:

> Inap mipela kisim olgeta riopt na stadi ol saentist na narapela wokman mekim long bus bilong mipela? *Saentist na ol narapela wokman save kam long ples long RCF na kam raun long bus na mekim sampela stadi tasol taim ol igo bek, ino gat ripot isave kam long ol komuniti long harim na save.

People in Maimafu feel that they contribute to the scientific research that goes on in and around their village in ways that are not fully acknowledged or compensated. The question is also about the value of knowledge. People know that their forests are valuable in terms of the knowledge taken by others from it. They want to understand this, and they want to access the value of it in these ways. A young man told me, after translating this question, that if he could just understand what sorts of things outsiders wrote about, then perhaps he could write reports, make money from them, and make a name for himself. If he did this, he would gain power and prestige and thus put himself in a position to both "get development" and "bring development" to Maimafu.

The previous questions also speak to the villagewide feeling that somehow Gimi are being left out of the knowledge loop. In Maimafu and elsewhere in PNG, people are careful with their deployment of information and knowledge. They understand that knowledge is powerful and that one can gain both material and social benefit from holding onto it. People often hear a bit of information and hoard it, sharing it only with the members of their patriclan. Because of this, people assume that there is knowledge kept from them by researchers and that if they "get the reports" written by the researchers, they will have access to this knowledge.

The next pair of questions, the introduction to the letter and question 5 in appendix C, and question 1 in appendix D, discuss payment, but are about the differences in the ways that conservation professions and Gimi understand the work of conservation:

> We have worked for RCF on this Management Committee for eight years now. We have worked hard. We have done what was asked of us. We have told people not to kill animals in the forest. We have told people not to cut down trees. We have worked on the guesthouse, and we have worked on other things. We have never gotten paid for this work. Why doesn't RCF pay us since we work for them? RCF says that they don't have the money to pay us; why then does the RCF office staff in Goroka get paid?

The residents of Maimafu do not see the work that they do for the RCF as the "work of conservation." The first part of the question enumerates the kinds of things that villagers feel like they were asked to do in exchange for "development." These things were regulating hunting and land use through the Management Committee Laws and serving on the Management Committee. The second part alludes to all the things people feel they have done "for RCF." These are things that they see as labor for which they should receive a wage. These are building and maintaining the village guesthouse, working with the "artifact business," and giving time and money to RCF activities that they do not see as part of the exchange relations of conservation. By turning some work into waged labor—for example, carrying bags and other cargo for scientists; selling net bags to people; protecting certain species that occur in certain places, such as the harpy eagle—the conservation organization has created a system of evaluation in which people are beginning to wonder why some labor gets a wage and some labor is meant to be compensated in other ways. It does not make sense to people that sometimes they "work" for the RCF and get paid, and sometimes they "work" for the RCF and do not.

This question also brings up the conflation of the RCF with Crater Mountain and Maimafu village. For villagers, the RCF and "Maimafu villagers" are in the CMWMA in the same ways. By this I mean that they see the WMA as a joint production created by the social relationships and generative actions of themselves and RCF employees. For them, the RCF exists in and for Crater Mountain; it is not a separate entity. Crater Mountain as a spatial production has coincided, according to the people of Maimafu, with the RCF as an organization. Both of these "things" are, for the people of Maimafu, generated out of their productive capacity. They produce the forests at Crater Mountain, and their forests (and hence they) produce the institutions that they work with.

The following question (number 8 in appendix C and number 3 in appendix D), begins in a similar way to the previous question, but it ends with an analysis of the relationship between "Crater Mountain" (as spatial production and discursive production), the RCF, and conservation funding:

> We were told by RCF that if we looked out for our forest and we worked to keep people from hunting and from cutting trees, then money and development would come into our village. We were told that we would get money and that we would get development. So we, the Management Committee, started working. We talked to all the old men, all the men who are the fathers of the land. We told them that if they quit hunting and looked out for their ground, that development and money would come inside our place. They believed us, and they did it. Then we all waited. Now we have heard that lots of money has come inside of the Crater Mountain Wildlife Management Area. We heard about this 129,000 kina

that the Japanese sent to us. But we have not seen this money, and we have not seen development. This puts us in a bad place with the people that we convinced to see things our way. All of the old men, the fathers of the ground, have heard about this money coming to RCF, but they have not seen it. Where is this money?

People from Maimafu hear about grants that the RCF and WCS have gotten all the time. They hear about them through village gossip — people who have been to Goroka to visit the RCF offices — and through the media. People often see copies of the two national newspapers, and the RCF often issues press releases when they receive a major grant. When people from Maimafu see that the RCF or WCS has gotten money, they do not understand why that money is not distributed to them. They make the argument that the WCS, RCF, and CMWMA exist because of their hard work and that they should derive benefit from the grants received "using their name." By "their name," people mean the name Crater Mountain. This sentiment is also expressed in the following: "We are like a fence around a garden. We have worked to keep people out and to keep things right, and now there are things growing inside. Who is eating the food in our garden? Us or RCF? What are we getting out of this relationship?" (see question 10 in appendix C and question 10 in appendix D).

The next set of questions is about what the people of Maimafu feel, in addition to pay, that they should be receiving from their participation in conservation-as-development. They ask for material things but are really challenges to the RCF to enter into socially appropriate relations with Gimi: "When we work for RCF or for a scientist associated with RCF or for a tourist, what happens if we get hurt or we get killed? Will RCF pay compensation to our families?" (see question 6 in appendix C and question 2 in appendix D) and "We are no longer hunting in our forests because RCF said if we didn't hunt, people would come and give us money to study and look at the animals. Where are we supposed to get meat now? Our children have to have meat in order to grow, and old people have to have it in order to not get sick. We don't have money to buy it, and we don't have any businesses to raise it. Where are we supposed to get it now?" (see question 7 in appendix C and question 4 in appendix D). When there is trouble in Maimafu, and elsewhere in Papua New Guinea, for people to feel whole again afterward, compensation must be paid. By invoking the notion of compensation, villagers are both challenging the RCF to behave in a more Gimi-like fashion and attempting to expand the range of participatory activities that they can engage in as a part of conservation-and-development (Filer 1997). By bringing up compensation, they are also expressing political concerns about the nature of the project (Kirsch 2001).

When one person has food in Maimafu and another does not, the food is shared. Even the smallest bit of cassowary meat will be split in half if someone in a group will go without. By bringing up the lack of meat in Maimafu, the question challenges the RCF to share its food, literally and figuratively: literally in that people see the prohibitions on hunting as contributing to the lack of protein in their diet, and figuratively in that development is often talked about in metaphors of food and consumption. In terms of the literal aspect, people in Maimafu are lacking in protein, but it has nothing to do with prohibitions on hunting. People hunt when they want to, and they derive the majority of their protein intake from hunted animals. Their deficiencies are due to the SDA prohibitions against having pigs, yet they will not confront the church about this.

And finally, both lists end with questions (question 11 in both appendices C and D) about the production of space:

Whom does "Crater Mountain" belong to? Is it ours or is it yours? With your answer, who is the boss?

And the slightly different:

Kreta Maunten em bilong husat? Bilong yu or bilong mi? Em bilong me so mi kisim bek sapos nogat gutpela aekim long ol askim bilong mi.

[Whom does Crater Mountain belong to? Does it belong to you or to us? It belongs to us, so if you don't answer all of these questions for us, we will take it back.]

These questions are a nuanced response to and critique of the production of space that is the CMWMA. In *The Production of Space*, Lefebvre explains that space is socially produced and not a static field in which human action transpires (1991:26). In his explanation he posits that physical space, mental space, and social space are all coproduced, that they all "underpin" and "presuppose" each other (ibid.:14). In elaborating he discusses *spatial practice*, or everyday mean-ingful actions, saying that "the spatial practice of a society secretes that society's space" (ibid.:38); *representations of space*, or "conceptualized space, the space of scientists, planners, urbanists, technocratic subdividers, and social engineers," or the space that is dominant in any society (ibid.:38–39); and *representational spaces*, or "space as directly lived through its associated images and symbols," the spaces with which the imagination seeks to "change and appropriate" dominant space (ibid.:39).

The last two questions (contained in question 11) are about the politics of the production of space at Crater Mountain and surrounding the CMWMA. They are meant to challenge the RCF in their thinking about space. Residents of Maimafu almost think in Lefebvre's terms; they understand that the CMWMA exists only in the social transactions and relations between people and between people and the environment. Here they express the tension that they feel be-cause of the ways in which conservation-as-development pulls on Lefebvre's triad of categories that are dialectically related in the social production of space. Gimi are, through their daily social lives in and of the forests, what Lefebvre called *spatial practice*, "secreting" the space that is the CMWMA (Lefebvre 1991: 38). But at the same time, the agents of conservation-as-development are pro-ducing the *representations of space* that are dominant in the day-to-day workings of the CMWMA at its level of governmentality and bureaucracy. Both Gimi and conservation practitioners are living the space of the CMWMA as *representational space*, hence through images and symbols, but these images and symbols are different for the two groups, so the two groups are literally living different spaces within the same spatial production. Finally, they are imagining radically different changes and appropriations to that spatial production.

As a social product, and not a static field, space is always being made and remade, but the CMWMA is a spatial product at the confluence of two different modes of production. For Lefebvre, "Each mode of production has its own particular space, the shift from one mode to another must entail the production of a new space" (Lefebvre 1991:46). The CMWMA is a space produced of two radically different modes of production and thus a space that is constantly pulling and pushing its producers by bringing them together and ripping them apart.

BACK TO THE FIGHT

"God West, you look terrible."

"Thanks Tymisties. Do you sweet-talk all the girls like that or just me?"

The banter between myself and a conservation biologist echoed through the forest on the bright early morning before the fight. We, after our playful verbal exchange, talked about the day we met almost a year before. He told me that he was amazed that I had "made it" living in Maimafu for a year. I told him that I appreciated his vote of confidence and that when I wrote the "trashy novel" I was planning about the whole experience of working with biologists, I would be sure to make him a star character.

This exchange took place after Henano, my "mother," shared her sweet potato with me. It was before the fight in which Kelego, Henano's husband, and Lasini, another resident of Maimafu, argued over who "owned" the conservation project and who had derived the majority of benefits, economic and social, from the influx of conservation professionals and others onto their ancestral lands. It was about five hours before Henano, in an attempt to pull Lasini off of her husband, was hit in the head with a sharp bush knife.

In addition to the comfort offered to me that morning by Henano, through the giving of food and the recounting of our shared jokes about women's labor, this verbal exchange with the biologist comforted me. Over the past year I had built a social and research relationship with this man, talking with him over the shortwave radio, seeing him in Goroka during field breaks, visiting the Sera Research Station, where he was working. He was the biologist who asked me to explain the fight to him succinctly.

In 1971 anthropologist Napoleon Chagnon and filmmaker Timothy Asch, made the classic anthropological documentary *The Ax Fight*, which they released in 1975. In it, they document a fight among a group of Yanomamo, and interspersed among the bits of footage is Chagnon's explanation of "why" the men are fighting.[5] The film, and Chagnon's work in general (Chagnon 1995), argues that warfare is a fundamental feature of social life and that violence is a male strategy for reproductive fitness. For Chagnon, kinship, alliance, and village fission and fusion are all tied to the biological push to reproduce, and humans are programmed for violence. The film also explores questions of inter-

22. Author and Harabo reenact *The Ax Fight*, a film by Napoleon Chagnon, after describing the ending of her book to Harabo.

pretation and translation on the part of anthropologists. While Chagnon's goal with his reading of the ax fight is a positivist explanation, he is looking for answers about human nature that can be generalized from the Yanomamo to all people. I spent the past seven years looking for explanations for one fight between Kelego and Lasini and trying to trace out the causal chains that led up to it and the layers of meaning that encompass it (Vayda 1983, 1995; see also Griffin 1993).

The fight was about the imbalances, both perceived and real, that have come into being because of the conservation-as-development project. Social life in Maimafu is, in part, geared toward attempts to achieve a sort of balance. But it is an imagined balance that can never be realized. While exchange theory in anthropology has often made the assumption that "things balance out over time" (Knauft 2002:38), and while Gimi try desperately to make them balance, there is always a feeling that someone has gotten more than they have given or more than they deserve when compared to what others have given and received. Indeed, for individual actors and groups, any system that anthropologists think about as exchange-based and reciprocal often "covers up or effaces the fact that some individuals or groups gain or lose significantly, and sometimes dispropor-tionately, relative to others" (ibid.:38).

The initial fight between Lasini and Kelego happened away from the central meeting area. We only knew that there was trouble when we heard the crying and screaming and wailing coming toward us. We were sitting there in a seem-ingly endless expanse of green: in the dream of an environmentalist—rolling green mountains as far as the eye can see—but then, for the biologists, nature was interrupted by culture. While the men and all of the visitors, except for two, were fixated on the fight, the women of Maimafu went to work on Henano's injuries. The others overlooked her at first. Her pain was not exciting and the fight was.

After the fight, and after the compensation negotiation began, the "problem" of Henano's injury came up. Her skull was split open by the impact of the bush knife, and she was in danger of dying from the wound. Her husband did not have the money to send her to the hospital in Goroka, and the mission planes refused to offer free airfare to anyone who is injured in a "tribal fight." The hospital in Goroka has a similar rule: no one injured in a fight will be given free medical care. So what were all of these rich white people and wealthy Papua New Guineans to do about this dying woman whose injury was the result of a fight perceived to be "about" their conservation project? They, of course, had a meeting.

People were of two minds. One argument was "It was not the RCF's fault," so the RCF should not pay for her airfare, as it would encourage a dependency on the organization by local people. This was supplemented with the argument that Henano's extended family could "come up with" the money if they "really wanted to." The other argument was, in the face of life or death, "Who cares about all that?" The language of compassion and responsibility supplemented this argument.

In the end, an expatriate who owns a charter airplane service was contacted on the radio, and he flew into Maimafu to collect Henano and her son, Luke. Luke accompanied her to Goroka because he speaks Melanesian Pidgin fluently and understands some English. The conservation organization chose to pay for neither her airfare nor her hospital fees; all of the expatriates agreed, and most of the Papua New Guineans working with the NGOs agreed, that if the RCF paid for her ticket and medical care, it would "set a precedent," which would be "dangerous." Robert Bino, the RCF resident scientist who made Maimafu his home for three years, paid both her airfare and fees.[6] This is precisely the sort of social relationship that people from Maimafu want from the agents of conservation-as-development. Robert was one of the only people working with the RCF to understand this sort of social obligation and to reciprocate in socially appropriate ways. Robert is from Rabaul, did not grow up in a village setting, and often found the social practices and "customs" of the people in Maimafu to be confounding and challenging. Over the course of his time there, he was the village coordinator for three years. He came to understand the expectations people had for him and for conservation-as-development, and he came to participate in social transactions the ways in which the residents of Maimafu expected him to.

Henano recovered partially from her injury and returned to the village a few days before I was to leave. While the doctors in Goroka advised that she stay in the hospital, she and her son did not have the money to buy food, so they had to return to the village. I went to visit her when I heard that she had returned. When she saw me approaching her house, she, holding the large dirty bandage on her head, walked down the steps and then toward me. We met in her yard, surrounded by chickens, her grandchildren, two mean cassowaries, her sons, gardens, and the mountains that I have imagined since I was a child. She said, tears running down her face, "Oh daughter, I was so worried that you had gone," and I said, "Oh mother, I was so worried that you had gone." Now when I go to Maimafu and I see Henano, we reminisce about Kelego, who died a few years ago. We also talk about the whereabouts of one of the expatriate advisors to the RCF — Henano's son had named his daughter after her. We laugh about the fight. It all seems so long ago.

In the early morning of the day that I was to leave Maimafu in 1998, about three months after the fight, Esta and Nara, my two research assistants, came to my door. I was not expecting them. We had planned to meet at Wayoarabirai and walk together to the *mumu* (feast) that the men on the Maimafu Management Committee had planned for later in the day. When I opened my door, I was shocked to see the two of them together. But there they were, standing at my door at 5:00 a.m. Esta said, in Unavisa Gimi and using my real name, "*Paige,* you must come with us now."

That morning we walked to the top of Tulai, up the ridge from my house at Motai, and began saying good-bye. I walked down every ridge that comprises Maimafu village and went to every home. I hugged people, often falling to my knees in the embrace of the women, wept openly and loudly, thanked people for allowing me to live with them, and accepted a small gift at every home. Some women gave me a *bilum* (a profound act, given the controversy over Barbara's gift of one to me earlier in the year), some gave me peanuts, and a few gave me unfinished bilum fiber as a symbol that I would not forget how to be a good village woman and "turn" the fiber into string. After the gift from the women, each man would hug me and press a small piece of paper containing money into my hand. Every single household gave me money.

I discovered later that the night before, after I had gone to bed, the old men and women talked late into the night about the journey that I was going to make in order to get back to my other home and my other family. I can imagine it now. Long stories about crossing the ocean from men who worked on plantations in Rabal. Concerned faces peering at the filthy ripped map that we used to discuss world issues in our many conversations about the rest of the planet. Laughter over memories of my using a jug, two rugby balls, a little boy named Esimbo, and myself running in circles to try and explain the alignment of the planets after a solar eclipse that we had seen in August.

They all agreed, late in the evening, that mine was indeed a long trip. They worried that I would not be able to find food. Some of the women suggested that they send *kaukau*, *kumu*, and *pitpit* — the three local foods that I love the most — with me in a sturdy bilum. The men explained that the big planes are not like mission planes and that commercial pilots do not allow people to bring food on the long journeys. After some discussion, they decided to take up a collection for me. They were afraid that I would go hungry if they did not.

These acts on the part of the people of Maimafu were meant to ensure that I would be okay, that I would have enough to eat during my travels. They were also meant to ensure that I would come back to Maimafu. So many of the people, expatriate and Papua New Guinean, who come through Maimafu because of the CMWMA visit the village once and then never return. These acts of giving upon my leaving were meant to cement my social ties and obligations to the residents of Maimafu, to make me bound to return and to brings gifts when I did. Now, when I do return to Maimafu, and I am lucky to have been able to do so frequently over the past seven years, the obligations I have are thick, as are the obligations that reach me at home in New York. I receive letters, e-mails, and the occasional telephone call, from people from Maimafu who find themselves in Goroka or Port Moresby in need of school fees, money, help finding a doctor, a new wristwatch, help opening a bank account, and countless other bits of development. It is my social obligation to help them if I can.

As we arrived in Maimafu in June 2003, Kabi limped, holding a crutch under his arm as he approached our plane. Even while landing, I had been scanning the rapidly gathering crowd for his face. And there he was: my father, my protector, and my friend. But he was not well. A few weeks before, while climbing a tree to gather *femomo*,[7] he had punctured the bottom of his foot on a short broken branch. The wound had become infected, as there were no antibiotics or antibiotic ointment in the village health center, and he was barely able to walk. After we unpacked and got the students settled — I had four postgraduate students from the University of PNG with me in Maimafu — my husband and I went down to see Kabi and take him some antibiotics. It was a simple thing really: some little pills that cost less than five U.S. dollars in a pharmacy in Goroka cured Kabi's infection in a matter of days. Another simple thing, a cheap pair of shoes, would prevent this from happening again. But shoes are hard to come by in Maimafu.

I spent much of my time that summer with Kabi, talking about hunting and Gimi names for animals. It was the summer that he explained how men became birds and ancestors during initiation: for a split second the matter that makes up a man, birds, and forests, comes together with the matter that was his ancestors and that would be his offspring, and they are all one. One afternoon that summer, I asked Kabi about his clan's flutes. I had read all of Gillison's work on the Gimi flute myths (Gillison 1993:4–5), and much of the other anthropological literature on them, but I had not asked many older Gimi men about these flutes.[8] I had talked to a lot of women and young men about them, but for some reason I felt uncomfortable talking to the old men about them. When I asked Kabi that day, he told me some stories that resonate with Gillian Gillison's work, and then he showed me what it looked like to become a bird. He stood up and mimicked the display behavior of the bird of paradise associated with his clan's flute. That day Kabi taught me that men became the birds during initiation, that for a few moments men and birds were one.

In Aristotle's famous example in which things become commodities, he shows us how a shoe becomes a thing that has exchange value that is "qualita-

23. Kabi.

tively identical with any other commodity," no matter how different the two things are in terms of use value, form, or symbolic value (Taussig 1980:25). This "socially necessary fiction" is what underlies capitalist relations and what makes them appear natural (Taussig 1980:26; N. Smith 1990). With this, and with the social relations that come into being in order to measure out these equivalencies and create the hierarchies of value upon which the system is based, "communality and mutuality give way to personal self-interest, and commodities, not persons dominate social being. The exchange ratio of commodities mediates and determines the activities of people," and the social relations among people come to be seen as the social relations among things (Harvey 1990:99–103; Marx 1990 [1867]:163–177; Taussig 1980:26). The consequence of all of this is that things, as commodities, come to be seen as having value in and of themselves, not as the products of human labor or the social relations of that labor.

The notion of scarcity is built into this system of evaluation. And to talk about anything through the language of scarcity is to bring it into a commoditized psychic landscape. If an object or thing is seen as less readily available, it will be put into equivalence with objects or things of great value. This notion of scarcity shoots through all of the scientist's and activist's discussions of birds of paradise that I've presented in this book. With regard to the birds, there are not many of them. They are found only in certain places, many of them only on the island of New Guinea, and they are valuable and precious for this reason. From the beginning of written records concerning New Guinea, these birds have been some of the most important curios and commodities that have brought people from other places to the island. They had great monetary value for early collectors and great value for science for early naturalists. Today they are symbolically valuable to Papua New Guinea; indeed the Raggiana bird of paradise is the symbol of the nation-state, in that it embodies the imagined reality of the island: beautiful, exotic, remote, untouched, and unstudied, and on the edge of extinction by the modern (Gewertz and Errington 1991:28). They are economically valuable in that they bring tourists and scientists to the country. They have become, even when their skins are not being bought and sold, a kind of hyperreal commodity (Baudrillard 1975, 1988): they are a sign, and object, and image firmly lodged in the imaginations of many, engendering a particular imaginary of people and place. The birds themselves have become "hollowed out things" that work to draw in meanings seemingly not connected to them at all (Taussig 2000:254).

But not every encounter with birds of paradise or the forests in which they live is evaluated in this way or tied to this system yet. One day I asked my father, "Kabi, how do you know the forest?" And he said, "Negesu naho, negesu nowe, negesu nasigi, negesu nasa, negesu nabahau, negesu naliu, negesu naba, negesu nadapu" (My eyes, my ears, my nose, my mouth, my teeth, my skin, my father, my bones).

Appendix A:
Locally Generated History of Maimafu

The History of Maimafu and the Lufa District of Papua New Guinea by Mr. Kaya-guna Kelego as Given to Paige West on This Day of Her Research for Her Book on Maimafu Village

1933	First Seventh-Day Adventist (SDA) missionaries in the Eastern Highlands
1948	James Leahy starts the first coffee plantation in the Eastern Highlands
1949	First Lutheran missionary in the Lufa District (in Kisaveroka)
1951	First patrol by a white man on our land
1952	First Lutheran mission built at Lufa
1952	New Tribes Mission built at Kami
1953	Faith Mission built by Master Ben at Gona
1954	Australian patrol post moved to Lufa
1955	First colonial appointed luluais [village chief, appointed by colonial government] and tultuls [assistant village chief] in Lufa District
1960	Large settlement moved to old Motai from Abigarima.
1960	First governmental representation from Maimafu (Molekey)
1961	First Kiap comes to Maimafu
1962	Master Ben comes to Maimafu
1962	Total eclipse of the sun
1962	First missionaries into Maimafu (SDA — Mr. Kassa), 1962–1977
1962	Large settlement moved to new Motai from old Motai
1963	Last public male initiation in Maimafu
1964	First coffee seeds to Maimafu
1964	Landslide in Maimafu
1966	First man from Maimafu (Kayaguna) goes to school, 1966–1970

1970	Kayaguna Kelego serves as a missionary for SDA, 1970–1974
1972	David Gillison goes to Ubaigubi
1974	Kayaguna Kelego marries Dabi
1975	Political independence from Australia for Papua New Guinea
1975	Nara Kayaguna is born [his son]
1977	"Road" in Maimafu built [large trail connecting ridges]
1980	Community hospital construction begins in Maimafu
1980	Kayaguna Kelego and wife, Dabi, carry coffee to Ubaigubi
1982	Maimafu community begins work on the airstrip
1982	Mattanaba talks to David Gillison, and he says that conservation will be development
1982	Kayaguna Kelego runs for Lufa Open Seat and looses
1983	First RCF meeting at Ubaigubi
1984	Community hospital opens in Maimafu
1984	Everyone in Maimafu agrees to stop raising pigs in the village
1987	Kayaguna Kelego runs for provincial government and looses
1989	Sera Research Station on Haia and Herowana ground is built
1989	Mal Smith builds tourist hotel in Ubaigubi
1990	First U.S. Peace Corps couple go to Ubaigubi
1991	Kayaguna Kelego elected a provincial member to parliament
1992	Airstrip opened and first airplane lands in Maimafu
1992	Community school built in Maimafu
1993	Jamie James comes to Maimafu to talk the talk of conservation
1993	BHP comes to Maimafu to talk about a mine
1995	RCF passes the law that we can no longer hunt
1995	Robert Bino comes to work for RCF and live in Maimafu
1996	—— [the first researcher] comes to Maimafu to see harpy eagles
1996	The Tree Kangaroo people [a team of scientists studying tree kangaroos] come to Maimafu
1996	—— and —— come to Maimafu to work for the Peace Corps and leave soon
1996	BHP goes to Quasa and starts a camp
1997	The UPNG [University of Papua New Guinea] students come to Maimafu [for the WCS training course]
1997	Tene Pone (Paige West) comes to Maimafu to live
1997	—— and —— come back to Maimafu to see tree kangaroos

1997	—— and —— come to Maimafu to see harpy eagles
1997	Three German men come to Maimafu as tourists
1997	Michael comes to Maimafu as a tourist
1997	People in Maimafu begin work on village guesthouse
1998	—— comes to Maimafu to study plants
1998	The government comes in a helicopter to talk about the mine
1998	The tree kangaroo people come back to Maimafu
1998	—— and —— come to Maimafu to work for the Peace Corps
1998	RCF has annual meeting in Maimafu

Appendix B: Proposal to the ICCO

The Crater Mountain Integrated Conservation and Development (ICAD) initiative informally began in 1982 with the first attempts to establish a national protected area while addressing the socioeconomic aspirations of the local landowners through the development of environmentally sensitive enterprises.

Since its initiation, the primary goals of the project have been the long-term conservation of biodiversity in the Crater Mountain area and the process of attempting to integrate conservation and development components to achieve the product of a functional national Wildlife Management Area as described under the national legislation.

The Wildlife Conservation Society (WCS), an international nongovernmental conservation organization within the New York Zoological Society, was the first conservation agency to sponsor researchers and fieldworkers in the project area, as early as 1975. WCS was also instrumental in the establishment of the national nongovernmental organization, The Research and Conservation Foundation of Papua New Guinea (RCF), in 1986, which today serves as the lead agency in the Crater Mountain project. Over the years, numerous national and international governmental and nongovernmental agencies have provided financial and technical assistance to RCF and WCS in the implementation of the project.

The effort to establish a national Wildlife Management Area had very informal beginnings which developed from contact between expatriate scientists and the landowners in the area.

It is important to note that for over a decade, it was through these personal relationships that steps for gazettal of the WMA and establishment of fledgling eco-enterprises of research and eco-tourism developed. It was not until 1993, with the achievement of formal gazettal of the Gimi and Pawaiian [sic] lands as a national Wildlife Management Area, that the ongoing activities took on the official title of a "project" with the following documented objectives (RCF / WCS 1995):

> To increase the average annual per capita income of clans (landowning groups) from the establishment of locally owned research and eco-tourism enterprises in the WMA

> To increase the level and range of understanding and skills of community residents who work in the research and eco-tourism enterprises in the WMA

> To increase the number of decisions and actions which integrate the results of enterprise, biological, and socioeconomic monitoring programs in a WMA management plan

> To increase national involvement and human resource exchange within the WMA as teachers, trainers, and consultants work toward conserving natural resources in the WMA

The first two objectives had been informally in place since the first discussions with the Gimi tribe in the 1970s.

The last two objectives evolved in the 1990s with the realization that the establishment of environmentally sound and sustainable businesses was not possible without a process for assessment and for increased national involvement at all levels.

Today, the emphasis of conservation efforts in the Crater Mountain area is on building the capacity of local communities and their organizations to assume the principal role of managing the operations in the Wildlife Management Area. As such, the project is an ambitious effort to engage an extremely high level of community participation in management of the conservation and development components of the Wildlife Management Area.

Expatriate scientists were among some of the first outsiders to spend extended periods of time with WMA communities. Their concern for the unique biodiversity and cultures of the area was the impetus for their ongoing informal dialogue with Crater communities about mechanisms of establishing and operating the Wildlife Management Area and the associated eco-enterprises.

Length of stay and impact of field researchers have varied over the last two decades: some have stayed only months, while others have developed long-term friendships with members of Crater communities, some returning for intermittent periods of up to twenty years. Characteristics that have been common to most field researchers have been a respect for the cultures of the WMA and an obvious admiration and enthusiasm for the WMA's unique natural resources. Most have been diligent workers who have enthusiastically lived and labored in their fieldwork alongside residents of the WMA who were their assistants, guides, and companions.

A significant example of these relationships is Australian photographer, David Gillison, who has worked with the Gimi tribes since 1973.

In the early years of his work, he returned for consecutive seasons to his field site near Ubaigubi village, where his original interest in the recording of the ritual theatre of the Gimi led him to the forest with Gimi men to document the displays of the birds of paradise from which the they said that the cultural theatre had evolved (Gillison 1983). These interactions solidified a strong mutual respect and commitment between David and community members which gave rise to the first informal discussions with Gimi villages about the status of these unique birds and the mutual concern for their decline as well as associated Gimi traditions.

A similar relationship between community and scientist evolved in the south half of the WMA, where biologists Andy Mack and Deb Wright came to work on Pawaiian land near Haia in 1987. In the process of building a research station and conducting five years of fieldwork, they would inevitably engage in ongoing dialogue with Pawaiian community members about the uniqueness of Crater's natural resources and the options of land use which the Pawaiians were considering.

Along with Gillison, Mack, and Wright came numerous field assistants over the years, who later came back to do further studies of their own. In this way, a unique "family" of scientists has evolved to live and work with the Gimi and Pawaiian on various studies of natural resources in their forests.

Beginning in 1984, the project began to place resident and intermittent fieldworkers as trainers in the WMA. They were both expatriate and national and from a variety of disciplines, including biologists, teachers, small business, and rural community development backgrounds.

The focus of their work has been on providing technical assistance to village counterparts in business, community development, and WMA management. Initially, expatriates played a central role in field implementation. As of 1995, all are in volunteer and advisory positions only, with national staff or community counterparts directly responsible for field implementation. As with the scientists, most resident fieldworkers who have stayed for periods of two years or more have formed close friendships with Crater communities.

Business trainers in the position of tourism lodge managers were first present in Ubaigubi from 1983 to 1986. In 1990, the project began to utilize United States Peace Corps (USPC) Rural Community Development volunteers as field trainers. The USPC program requires that the village provide bush material housing for the volunteer in return for the technical assistance which they receive.

The volunteer is initiated with the development philosophy that his or her role is to train and support village counterparts and not to lead and do work for the community that it does not want to do for itself. Since 1990, seven USPC couples have served in WMA communities, and volunteers are still working with the project in three of the five WMA villages.

In 1993, the WCS placed the first resident field coordinators and scientists on the project staff in the WMA. While the USPC volunteers continued to work with small business and community service committees, the field coordinators were assigned to strengthen and assist the clan leaders who sat on the newly formed WMA management committees. The coordinators also live in village housing and spend much time in community meetings as well as on the trails of the WMA.

As the first field coordinator, Jamie James became known and admired by the communities for his capacity to briskly patrol the rugged country between all five WMA villages. James was followed by two national biologists, John Ericho and Robert Bino, who have been equally well received and respected as mentors to Crater communities.

In 1986, The Research & Conservation Foundation was incorporated. Administratively, the functions and responsibilities were carried out on an ad hoc basis by the Honorary Secretary to the RCF Board of Directors, Anne Love. On October 14th, 1991, the Board recruited the current General Manager as the first foundation employee, to define the policy, mission statements, organizational structure, duty statements, and other administrative protocols.

In early 1992, WCS sponsored Dr. Eleanor Brown, who worked for a short period of time to assist with the institutional strengthening of RCF. Kisokau continued on with the assistance of the former board chairman, Gideon Ka-

kabin, a few board members (Iamo Ila, William Peckover, and, in particular, Anne Love, Honorary Secretary to RCF Board).

In 1993, Kisokau was the only employee of the Foundation. He wrote a draft policy paper on the mission statements, organizational structure, duty statements, and other administrative protocols for the RCF.

In 1994, RCF contracted Ms. Arlyne Hedemark Johnson to a position of Scientific Program Director. She was responsible for developing project proposals to seek financial support for institutional strengthening and serves as the chief technical adviser to the ICAD project in the Crater Mountain Wildlife Management Area. The total staff strength for the year 1994 was two in the Port Moresby office and three individuals in the field.

In 1995, RCF recruited Kathy Panap to provide day-to-day support services. At Crater Mountain, WCS sponsored two (2) national biologists (John Ericho and Robert Bino), and RCF continue to work with the two USPC volunteers. Overall staff strength this year was seven.

In 1996, with the approval of BCN and MacArthur Foundation project proposals, additional staff were recruited to carry out specific tasks and assist in the increasing workload. Under MacArthur Foundation an education director position was funded, and RCF recruited Ms. Doreen Iga (BA). With BCN support, we recruited Andrew Alembo (BEC; bachelors degree in economics and accounting) as administration and finance director; Stanley Kundal (Dip. Bus. & Accounting) as senior enterprise coordinator; and Nick Mangen and Andrew Kutapae as field enterprise officers.

Recently, John Ericho has assumed the role of the Senior Project Officer, and Peter Minimulu has taken his place as a field research coordinator. Ms. Cathy Hair joins our staff as the WCS project scientist to advise in the development of the Crater project monitoring and evaluation protocol. We have added four more USPC volunteers in two WMA villages.

Today, staff strength totals 18. This includes 11 Crater Mountain staff in the field, 3 Crater project management staff in Port Moresby, 1 education officer and 3 administrative secretariat staff.

[RCF, ICCO grant proposal 1997].

Appendix C: Letter to the RCF

Dear RCF,

July 18, 1998

Mipela ol Crater Mountain Wildlife Management Area Management Committee bilong Maimafu makem Honenabo, Kuseri, Uya, Lioni na Ugubi group laik
tekim yupela lo kam na holim CMWMA mitin long hauslain bilong mipela. Mipela
hamamas lo yupela kam. Mipela bin kam lo hia nau long haus bilong Tene Pone
lo toktol lo sampela askim we mipela I laik askim long dispela mitin. Mipela bin
askim Tene Pone lo putim dispela ol askim lo computer bilong em na mekim ol
kopi bilong em bilong yupela. Tenk yu lo ridim na bekim ol dispela askim:

1. Wanem minin bilong "menesment komiti?"
2. NGO em wanem samtin?
3. Long wanem yupela ol RCF givim dispela unifom, igat sampela samtin
   bihain?
4. Inap mipela kisim olgeta riopt na stadi ol saentist na narapela wokman
   mekim long bus bilong mipela?
   • Saentist na ol narapela wokman save kam long ples long RCF na kam
     raun long bus na mekim sampela stadi tasol taim ol igo bek, ino gat ripot
     isave kam long ol komuniti long harim na save.
5. Pei bilong ol komiti. Inap mipela kisim pei?
   • Pei ino save go antap
   • Nogat moni I kam long ol komiti tru RCF ol yet save wok na kisim
     moni.
   • Mipela hatwok long lukautim bus na stopim ol man long bagarapim
     bus na nogat helpim ikam long RCF. Ol lain bilong opis I kisim moni na
     mipela komiti nogat. Sapos RCF nogat moni, wanem has mipela nogat?

6.   Nogat kompenseisen nau, RCF bai givim kompenseisen o nogat?

   • Sapose wanpela man igo wantaim wanpela saentist long bus na kisim hevi olsem wara karim ol igo o pundaun bai RCF mas kompenseit.

7.   Bai mipela kisim ol abus we?

   • Olgeta bus I tambu long kisim abus so igat sampela rot bilong kominiti bai kisim helpim o nogat?

8.   Sampela moni ikam insait long Kreta maunten long dispela Kreta maunten nem. Dispela moni go we?

   • Risets grent moni kam long ol komiti

   • Man long ples ol less long dispela moni bai misyus nambaut ol I laik em mas kam stret long komiti

   • Dispela risets grent mas mipela laik bai kam stret long komiti so mipela ken yusim long wokim sampela wok olsem wara saplai na haidro.

   • Mipela bin harim ol I tok bai kam long papa graun na ol mas yusim gut. Tasol mipela ino save lukim dispela moni. Ol harim olsem ol mas lukautim bus na abus na ol komiti bihainim, tasol ol harim tasol na ol no save lukim dispela moni so RCF mas tok klia long mipela long dispela. Ol laim long RCF mas tokim klia mipela we dispela mani wok long go.

9.   Ol lain long RCF na saentist kam insait long bus bilong mipela na kisim bikpela nem bilong ol, ol mekim wanem wok insait long Kreta maunten na kisim dispela nem?

   • John Ericho kisim "dupiti generol menesa"

10. Menesment komiti I olsem banis bilong gaden na wanem kain kaikai I kamap mipela ino save husat save kaikai?

11. Kreta Maunten em bilong husat? Bilong yu or bilong mi? Em bilong me so mi kisim bek sapos nogat gutpela aekim long ol askim bilong mi.

Appendix D: Central Questions for the "Boss of wcs" from Residents of Maimafu Village

1. We have worked for RCF on this Management Committee for eight years now. We have worked hard. We have done what was asked of us. We have told people not to kill animals in the forest. We have told people not to cut down trees. We have worked on the guesthouse, and we have worked on other things. We have never gotten paid for this work. Why doesn't RCF pay us since we work for them? RCF says that they don't have the money to pay us; why then does the RCF office staff in Goroka get paid?

2. When we work for RCF or for a scientist associated with RCF or for a tourist, what happens if we get hurt or we get killed? Will RCF pay compensation to our families?

3. We were told by RCF that if we looked out for our forest and we worked to keep people from hunting and from cutting trees, then money and development would come into our village. We were told that we would get money and that we would get development. So we, the Management Committee, started working. We talked to all the old men, all the men who are the fathers of the land. We told them that if they quit hunting and looked out for their ground, that development and money would come inside our place. They believed us, and they did it. Then we all waited. Now we have heard that lots of money has come inside of the Crater Mountain Wildlife Management Area. We heard about this 129,000 kina that the Japanese sent to us. But we have not seen this money, and we have not seen development. This puts us in a bad place with the people that we convinced to see things our way. All of the old men, the fathers of the ground, have heard about this money coming to RCF, but they have not seen it. Where is this money?

4. We are no longer hunting in our forests because RCF said if we didn't hunt, people would come and give us money to study and look at the animals. Where are we supposed to get meat now? Our children have to have meat in

order to grow, and old people have to have it in order to not get sick. We don't have money to buy it, and we don't have any businesses to raise it. Where are we supposed to get it now?

5. Many scientists come here, and they get our knowledge. They listen to our stories, and they use us to find the plants and animals they are looking for. They take this away from our place and write reports about things. We want to see these reports. Where are these reports?

6. What does it mean to say we are the Management Committee?

7. What is an NGO?

8. When people come and work here and then go and get a big name for themselves by using what they learned here, what do we get out of it?

9. Why did you give us this uniform. Is it bilas [decoration], or is there meaning behind it?

10. We are like a fence around a garden. We have worked to keep people out and to keep things right, and now there are things growing inside. Who is eating the food in our garden? Us or RCF? What are we getting out of this relationship?

11. Whom does "Crater Mountain" belong to? Is it ours or is it yours? With your answer, who is the boss?

Notes

Preface

1. In March 2005, through a joint venture with Macmin, Triple Plate Junction, a British mining company, began a major series of exploration drills in the area.

2. *Biodiversity* is both a scientific concept and a socially constructed political slogan (Haila 1998:165; see also Takacs 1996). For the designers of the Crater Mountain Integrated Conservation and Development Project, biodiversity was a measurable quantity of plants and animals that could be monitored over time to test the hypothesis that if people are given access to markets which depend on biodiversity, they will work to conserve biodiversity.

3. Throughout this book I write about conservation scientists, planners, practitioners, and activists. Often in the anthropological literature on environmental conservation, the terms *conservationist* and *environmentalist* are used to demarcate certain groups of people working within the global environmental movement. The use of these terms collapses into one category a series of differently positioned actors with different agendas. I take *conservation scientists* to be people conducting scientific research that it is hoped will be of benefit to conservation practices, *conservation planners* and *conservation practitioners* to be people working for conservation organizations that have the waged labor positions involving design and implementation of conservation projects, and *conservation activists* to be people working for conservation in terms of politics, but not necessarily employed by a conservation organization. There are times when these categories overlap, but in general, I try to discuss this when it is the case.

4. *Gimi* is both the name used to describe an ethnolinguistic group and the name used to describe their language. Following Dorothy Hodgson's (2001) examination of the social creation of "the Maasai," I take invocations of "the Gimi" to be tied to historically constituted images and imaginaries concerning the people who speak the Gimi language. Throughout this book when I refer to the Gimi, I am referring to these images and imaginaries and not to Gimi peoples. In referring to Gimi peoples I will simply say Gimi.

5. All of the citations for Gillison in this book are for the work of Gillian Gillison unless otherwise indicated. While David Gillison has published a book concerned with his experiences in Papua New Guinea (2002), it is predominantly a book of photographs.

6. See Arun Agrawal (1996), Arturo Escobar (1995), James Ferguson (1994), and Anna Lowenhaupt Tsing (1993) for examples of this later approach in anthropology.

7. Even with this critique, anthropology is still "predicated on the fact of otherness and difference, on the lively, informative thrust supplied to it by what is strange or foreign" (Said 1989:213).

8. I have been trained in entirety in a postcritique of ethnographic authority discipline of anthropology. I began graduate school in 1991 and never had a relationship with the idea of writing ethnography that was not fraught with, yet made fascinating by, questions about authority, text production, power, and representation. I never thought that I would be attempting to understand or describe "a physically and symbolically enclosed world" (Marcus 1998:109). I also had no idea about the real complexities that would be involved in managing my relationships with participants in a research project where differences between participants' access to power were so profound.

1. *New Guinea–New York*

1. An international border bisects New Guinea, the third-largest island in the world. The western half of the island is part of Indonesia and known to Indonesians as Irian Jaya or Papua. It is known to many in the global human rights community as West Papua. The eastern half of the island is the nation-state of Papua New Guinea. The island has a long and rich colonial history, and this border is tied to that history (Brookfield and Hart 1971; Gordon 1951; Howlett 1967; Hughes 1977). In this book when I say "New Guinea," I am referring to the island as a whole, and when I say "Papua New Guinea," I am referring to only the eastern half of the island, the independent nation-state of Papua New Guinea (PNG).

2. Longtime expatriates in the country say that it draws "missionaries, mercenaries, and misfits." Matt Loney, a former British Voluntary Services Overseas (VSO) volunteer, used the phrase for the title of his recent travel memoir (Loney 2001). In the book Loney uses images of cannibalism and savagery to spin a tale in which he appears as a modern-day explorer. He even goes as far as to attempt to find an Amazon-like tribe of warrior women in the deep forests of Papua New Guinea. His is an excellent example of contemporary travel literature that relies on precolonial and colonial images of New Guinea and its natives in order to titillate modern readers.

3. See Hugh Raffles, *In Amazonia: A Natural History* (2002), Nancy Leys Stepan's *Picturing Tropical Nature* (2001), and Candace Slater's *Entangled Edens: Visions of the Amazon* (2002), for extraordinarily detailed examinations of Wallace's role in the production of the European imaginary of tropicality and in the material production of the Amazon.

4. See James A. Boon (1990:2–27).

5. See Taussig (2000:269) for a reading of Walter Benjamin's (1978:335) notion of

the flash of recognition in which the signifier and its signified are mimetically connected as the flash is tied to second nature or produced nature.

6. This point has been made by many ethnographers of Papua New Guinea (Gewertz and Errington 1991; Knauft 1999; Lederman 1998; LiPuma 2000).

7. See David Harvey (1990) for a history of the rise of flexible forms of capital accumulation and their relation to Fordism. See Neil Smith (1990) for an analysis of the role of capitalism in the production of a nature seemingly far from capital.

8. All of the spellings in Gimi in this book are spellings given by field assistants who are literate in Melanesian Pidgin and English, and who are native Gimi speakers. Bopo-yana is a spelling that is also used by Gimi speakers.

9. See the following three patrol reports for discussions of the first patrols through Gimi territory: Carey (1950); Young-Whitforde (1950); Eisenhauer (1950).

10. Please see note 3 in the preface.

11. The WCS is an international conservation organization that is tied to the New York Zoological Society and the Bronx Zoo. Its predecessor was Wildlife Conservation International (WCI; formerly a division of the New York Zoological Society), the organization mentioned in the *New Yorker* article discussed at the beginning of this chapter.

12. Throughout this book I will consistently use these acronyms, but for clarity, the first time that an organization or name from the abbreviation list is mentioned in each chapter, I will provide its full name.

13. These ridgetops span a topographic range of 1,500 to 1,700 meters.

14. In terms of early processes used to make people and places anthropologically "legible," Gimi peoples were as of yet "unplaced" in 1954 (Read 1954:20). Indeed, they were also unnamed—Kenneth Read (ibid.), in his survey of the "Cultures of the Central Highlands," after discussing the Kainantu sub-area states that left unplaced are "a large population living to the south of Mount Michael," but he goes on to argue that these cultures are "not likely to differ very greatly from [those of the Kainantu sub-area]."

15. D. Carleton Gajdusek (1968:55) indicates as much in his journal, and people from Wayoarabirai confirm this.

16. Gimi do make "Maimafu" and other "villages" places and conflate the places with themselves as a "people" when interacting with outsiders. For instance, people will say, "Mi-pela ol lain Maimafu" (We are all people from Maimafu) when interacting with expatriates. Leonard Glick reports similar ways of making place and people in the early 1960s (1966:4).

17. English is the national language of Papua New Guinea and is used in government, education, business, and commerce. Melanesian Pidgin is a Creole language that began as a lingua franca, sometime in the nineteenth century, on Pacific Island plantations. In colonial times, it was a language of contact, trade, and labor. While living and working in Maimafu village, I have conducted my research in Melanesian Pidgin and on occasion in Unavisa Gimi, but I am not completely fluent in Unavisa Gimi. During my fieldwork I employed research assistants, and when needed they worked as translators.

My census data indicate that in Maimafu 75 percent of the adult males between the ages of twenty and forty-five report that they speak Pidgin fluently, and that 50 percent of the adult males over forty-five report that they speak Pidgin fluently. Ninety percent of the young men in Maimafu between the ages of fifteen and twenty report that they speak Pidgin fluently, and all males under forty-five understand some Pidgin and have basic speaking communication skills.

The data for women are less easy to interpret. During my census research, men answered most of the language questions at each household. When I asked if their wives spoke Pidgin, most responded, "She hears it but does not speak it." When I asked if their mothers spoke Pidgin, most responded, "No." When I asked if their daughters spoke Pidgin, most responded, "Yes, but she is too shy to speak it." My experience during participant observation leads me to believe that about 50 percent of the women in Maimafu speak Pidgin, but that a higher percentage understand it. I do not know if "shyness" or inability leads women not to speak Pidgin in front of outsiders. Few of the women over forty speak fluent Pidgin. Most Pidgin-speaking women between the ages of twenty and forty refused to speak Pidgin in front of men or other large groups of women. Generally, women under twenty spoke Pidgin in same-sex groups and in front of male kin, but not in front of nonrelated males. All of the women and children who have lived on the coast speak Pidgin fluently.

18. In his 1957 synthesis report, Wurm termed "the south-eastern and southern potions of the Eastern Highlands Districts, south and west of the Kratke Range and the Purari as far to the south as the Papuan border, with the exception of the Fore area," as "linguistically unknown" (33).

19. In the Gimi language, when one refers to the language spoken, the local language, or *tok ples* in Melanesian Pidgin, one says either *agesu kaina* or *ikika kaina*. Gillison (1993:26) translates *ikika* as "one" and *kaina* as "speech" or "talk." Glick (1967:372) also translates *kaina* as "speech." I translate *agesu* as *age* (he, she, it) + *su* ("possessive"). So *agesu kaina* is "the language of the person who is speaking it right now." Although the distinction might seem less than important, I think it is a marker of Gimi understandings that language, and other cultural forms, change over time. So *kaina* is a language, any language, *ikika kaina* is a shared language, and *agesu kaina* is the living form of a shared language that is being spoken at this very moment. A note on possessive forms, though: *su* is the possessive only when one is saying "I," "we," and "he, she, it"; *ne* is the possessive for "you"; and *si* is the possessive for "they."

20. The Gimi language is classified as Trans–New Guinea phylum (so non-Austronesian), central and western part, East New Guinea Highlands stock, East-Central family, Fore subfamily (Wurm 1977:468; Wurm 1961, 1962), has two dialects (eastern and western), and six subdialects (Hogai, Labogai, Hagavisa, Liborei-Karo, Unavisa, and Herowana) (DeLoach and Troolin 1998:8). Gimi is closely related linguistically to Fore —with the two languages sharing about 46 percent of their basic vocabulary (Wurm

1960:20) as well as to Gende, Saine, Gahuku, and Bena Bena (also in the east-central family) (Wurm 1977:469; Wurm 1961, 1962). Gimi is interesting to linguists because it is "intermediate" between language families (Wurm 1961:11). It shares a high percentage of vocabulary with the languages of the Gende-Siane-Gahuka-Kamano-Fore family but has some structural features (its verbal system and the way possession is expressed) similar to the Gadsup-Auyana-Awa-Tairora family, while some (its pronominal system and the way verbs indicate their objects) structural features are like the former family (ibid.). The Gimi languages are spoken in the Unavi and Labogai census divisions of the Okapa and Lufa Districts in the Eastern Highlands Province (DeLoach and Troolin 1998; Ryan 1972). West Gimi is spoken "between Mount Michael and the East Gimi dialect on the east, the Tua River on the west and northwest, and Crater Mountain on the south," with the language area covering 700 square kilometers (DeLoach and Troolin 1998:7).

21. It is also located at the border between what have become known within anthropology as the "Central Highlands" and the "Highlands fringe" culture areas (Hays 1993; Hyndman and Morren 1990).

22. When I hear the different subdialects, I do not hear a difference unless a native speaker points out the different vocabulary to me.

23. Pawaia is another of these legibility-making techniques. It is a "generic name used to refer to people who speak the same language in the area from the Purari River up to the edge of the highlands at Karimui" (Ellis 2002:21). The language spoken there is Tßehōe (Ellis 2002:23).

24. Lamb flaps are the fatty bits of mutton that are not considered edible in Australia and New Zealand. After the salable pieces of meat are packaged and sent to market these pieces are packaged and sent to Papua New Guinea.

25. In this book I use past, present, and future tenses. Using the ethnographic present is problematic in that it creates a sense of timelessness in which cultural differences are fixed and in that it removes ethnography from history in a way that exoticizes ethnographic subjects (Tsing 1993:xiv). Using the past tense also engenders representational problems. It allows readers to dismiss the lives of people in marginal or rural places as "passing out of the present into the past," and it suggests that people and their social institutions are history rather than that they have history (ibid.). Therefore, I use multiple tenses in order to illustrate different understandings and experiences of the past, the present, and the future and in order to show that in daily life there is a constant slippage between the past, the present, and the future in both discourses and in actions.

26. I do not mean to mirror or invoke "Yali's question" from the work of Jared Diamond. The questions posed to me by people from Maimafu about race and power are in fact antithetical to Diamond's posing of "Yali's question." Diamond assumes a particular linear version of history (Errington and Gewertz 2004) that is refuted by the questions asked of me by these people. Their questions assume that power relations are central

to social domination, while Diamond's work does not take questions of power into account (ibid.:7–14).

27. See Roy Rappaport (1984) for an extensive discussion of the role of this plant in the marking of boundaries in PNG.

28. See Aletta Biersack (1999) for an excellent and concise description of political ecology within anthropology.

29. In addition, these interventions form theoretically productive, as well as practically important, venues for considering the interface between local and global communities and processes (see Biersack 1999; Blaikie and Brookfield 1987; Brosius 1999a; Escobar 1999; Stott and Sullivan 2000), race and gender (Rocheleau, Thomas-Slayter, and Wangari 1996), colonialism and the environment (Peet and Watts 2004; Neumann 1995; Hodgson 2001), and environmental justice (Johnston 1994).

30. Theoretical treatments of conservation include the analysis of the commodification of nature (Blum 1993; Hecht, Anderson, and May 1988; Schroeder 1995), environmental justice (Hecht and Cockburn 1990, Neumann 1995), and environmentalism (Milton 1993, 1996).

2. *Making Crater Mountain*

1. Thanks to Morgan Sellers for this image.

2. See Eric Kline Silverman (1998) for an analysis of the ways in which Melanesians produce cartographic space through cosmology and social understandings of land and sea.

3. See David Bickford (2004); John Ericho (1998); John Ericho, Robert Bino, and Arlyne Johnson (1999); Paul Igag (2002); Paul Igag and Steve Murphy (2002); Arlyne Johnson (2000); Andrew L. Mack (1990, 1994, 1995a, 1995 b, 1995c, 1997, 1998a, 1998b, 1999); Andrew L. Mack and Gretchen Druliner (2003); Andrew L. Mack et al. (1999); Andrew L. Mack and J. Jones (2003); Andrew L. Mack and Debra D. Wright (1996, 1998); Mack et al. (1998); J. Ross Sinclair (2000); Wayne Takeuchi (1999); Mark Watson and Smith Asoyama (2001); George D. Weiblen (1998); Debra D. Wright (1997, 1998); Debra Wright et al. (1997); and Debra D. Wright et al. (1995).

4. See West (1994) for an analysis of wilderness as a social product.

5. Margaret Rodman (1992) argues that places come into being through discourses and rhetorics and shows that as these ways of talking and knowing change, places also change. Eric Hirsch and Michael O'Hanlon (1995) argue for analyses of place and space that use the concept of landscape and conceptualize it as a sociocultural process.

6. Oates fails to consider the fact that the intrinsic value of nature protected early on in the conservation movement was a dehumanized nature. Nature was intrinsically valuable, and humans were not seen as a part of that nature.

7. ICDPs are part of a larger "people-oriented" set of strategies for conservation that

include community-based conservation (CBC), community-based natural resources management (CBNRM), and comanagement. Steven Brechin et al. (2002:44) argue that "while these strategies vary in important ways, they seek to increase the development options of resource-dependent rural communities as a means of increasing nature protection." In two papers (Brechin et al. 2002; Wilshusen et al 2002), Brechin, Peter Wilshusen, Crystal Fortwangler, and Patrick West review the history of CBC efforts and the protectionist paradigm being set forth by some who have criticized CBC efforts.

8. In this initial review, eight of the protected areas (both national parks and multiple-use areas) were in Africa, five in Asia, and five in Latin American (Wells, Brandon 1992:11).

9. The emergence of ICDPs coincided with the emergence of the debate over the "ecologically noble savage" (Redford 1990).

10. Perhaps most important, the purveyors of ICAD projects failed to discuss or analyze a concern that should have been central to their thought: there is a "tendency toward a reduction in species diversity in many commodity based systems" (Schroeder 1995:327; Shiva 1992).

11. See Brechin et al. (2002) for an excellent summary and review of the 1990s literature on CBC.

12. See Wilshusen et al. (2002) for a brilliant rebuttal to the arguments offered by these authors.

13. See Colin Filer (2000), Ron Martin (2000), John Wagner (1999, 2002), and Flip Van Helden (1998, 2001b), for recent analyses of ICAD projects in Papua New Guinea.

14. The need to bypass the state is often justified in PNG through arguments about the "weakness" of and impending failure of the state. Robert Foster (2002:esp. 3–7) examines the discourses of "failure" and "weakness" with regard to the state in PNG.

15. In all of the BCN-related publications—books, journal articles, and Web-based documents—there is not one externally funded anthropological analysis of a BCN-funded project cited. This is striking given that the organization's stated goal was to examine projects and determine their successes and failures. All of their published assessments of its funded projects are based on data collected by people employed by the BCN or by one of its partner institutions.

16. A group of American-, Asian-, and Pacific-based businesses, NGOs, and government institutions, US-AEP "enhances environmental protection and promotes sustainable development in Asia and the Pacific by mobilizing U.S. environmental technology, expertise, and financial resources" (BSP 1997:120) and is funded by the USAID under its "Trade Promotion Coordinating Committee."

17. The chaos variable is subject to the following "initial subhypothesis" : "if chaos increases, then conservation decreases," and it is to be measured through "incidents of tidal waves, volcanoes, droughts, political, and economic turmoil" (Salafsky et al. 2001: 1589). Apparently if one uses a chi-square statistic, this variable has the following ob-

served association: "many projects beset with natural and human-caused disasters" yield "anecdotal evidence" that "indicates that disasters can bring a team together" (ibid.).

18. These so-called variables are also enumerated in all of the BCN reports and Web publications.

19. See Mack (1995c) and Wright (1998) for their Ph.D. dissertations. See Mack (1990, 1995a, 1995b, 1997, 1998a, 1998b), Mack and Druliner (2003), Mack and Jones (2003), Mack and Wright (1996), and Wright et al. (1997) for other publications related to their work on land held by Pawaia peoples.

20. Wright and Mack are now the country codirectors of the WCS PNG. They have an unfaltering commitment to both conservation and the creation of social and economic opportunities for Papua New Guineans. Since the late 1990s, but really taking shape fully in 2000, they have run biological training courses for students from the University of Papua New Guinea.

21. See Robbins (2003) for a discussion of recognition, self, and exchange in PNG that shows how social relations with expatriates, in particular, does and does not lead to rural villagers creating whole selves that are fully human.

3. *Articulations, Histories, Development*

1. Kuseri is the accepted spelling today for the hamlet that Gajdusek (1968:54) identified as Kuserebe.

2. In the past, Gimi men lived together in large men's houses which contained as many as twenty people or as few as three. Along the paths around these houses were the homes of women, children, and men below initiation age (Glick 1967a:372).

3. Kiap is the term used for Australian colonial patrol officers.

4. Like Jerry Jacka (2003:21 n. 6), when I use the word *development* in relation to Gimi narratives, understandings, and ideologies, I am translating several different phrases in Melanesian Pidgin. These include *develapmen, gutpela sindaun, kisim sevises, sevises,* and *senis.* When Gimi discuss development in their own language they use those Melanesian Pidgin phrases.

5. Natu was about fifty-six years old in 2004. On 5 February 1962, there was a total eclipse of the sun in New Guinea. People remember this event. I used this date as a marker when interviewing and talking about historic events. I asked, "When that happened, were you the same size as —— son, —— son, or —— son?" (In this case, Natu would have pointed out a young man of about fifteen years.) I then added the appropriate number of years to whatever age the person who was pointed out reported. While this is not a flawless method, I found that it gave me a general idea about when people in Maimafu think that things happened historically. Natu remembers that he was between fourteen and sixteen in 1962 during the eclipse.

6. In Unavisa Gimi the terms are *na auara* and *nara*, which name both male first cousins, and elder and younger brothers, respectively, and sometimes wives of these men.

7. *Dendrolagus goodfellowi* and *Dendrolagus dorianus* respectively.

8. Foster frames the importance of understanding change in Melanesia with a discussion of custom:

> The gloss of "custom" is a paradox, a claim about historical continuity expressed in a creolized form that bespeaks historical change. It is a paradox that raises a familiar question about the relationship between continuity and change, structure and process: how do things stay the same as they change, and change as they stay the same. This is a question of social reproduction and social transformation, of how people continuously produce their social relations amidst circumstances that they cannot always anticipate but must nevertheless engage. It is a question, moreover, that has received increasing attention with the conceptual shift toward "a time oriented anthropology," an anthropology preoccupied with events, processes, and history. (Foster 1995:2)

9. Fredrik Barth (1987) demonstrates a deep history of cultural hybridity among rural peoples in New Guinea with regard to cosmology, ritual, and religious practices. Jacka (2003) also demonstrates these hybrid forms with relation to religion, environment, and economy.

10. Current and historic social articulations are different in Papua New Guinea than elsewhere in the world, and cultural practices that are seen as traditional have maintained much of their local salience (Knauft 1999). Such cultural differences, as well as the vast numbers of different ethnolinguistic groups in Papua New Guinea, have drawn anthropological researchers to the island in great numbers, as it has been seen as a "natural laboratory" for the study of cultural variation and for the testing of anthropological theories (Knauft 1999:196). One of the reasons for this maintenance of traditional cultural practices in the face of rapid change elsewhere is the relative lack of long-term or permanent settlers on the island during the colonial period. This failure to settle Papua New Guinea rapidly resulted in a relative absence of land alienation (ibid.:189): today in Papua New Guinea, at least 97 percent of the land is still held by local landholders. This situation is complicated by the state's desire to lure multinational companies to the country, but local people still have substantial control over the ways their land gets used. This maintenance of local boundaries and land rights has contributed to the maintenance of local traditions and practices (ibid.). Much of the ethnography of Melanesia is rich in the description of local culture. In addition, the ethnography from the region, and particularly from PNG, counters some of the documentary "thinness" of the current post-structural and postmodern ethnography that has been heavily influenced by cultural studies (Knauft 1999; Lederman 1998).

Many anthropologists, however, consider Melanesia as a "culture area" that is out of date, while others associate it with "tribal" ethnography (Knauft 1996) and with the idea of the "primitive" (Lederman 1998:436). As anthropologists have fought to keep our discipline out of the academic "savage slot" (Lederman 1998; Trouillot 1991) in the face of growing academic interests in globalization, transnationalism, and other postmodern forms, Melanesia, and PNG in particular, have come to be seen as the most anthropological of the anthropological. And many anthropologists wish to distance the discipline from the area because of its association with the topics (e.g., cannibalism, kinship, and exchange) that are stigmatized because they are seen as "canonical" and "conservative" (Lederman 1998:436).

11. For an analysis of traditional mythology among Gimi speakers, see Gillison (1993).

12. Bihu is both the name of a mythical snake and the name given to several python species.

13. There was, however, a white American missionary in the area before local conversions to Christianity. "Master Ben," or Ben Wertz, and his mission will be discussed later in this chapter. Today, all of the pilots working for mission-related air services are expatriates, but all of the SDA missionaries living in Maimafu are Papua New Guinean. As of December 2004, there were two SDA missionaries living in Maimafu.

14. Ronald Berndt (1954:190) argues that among Fore, reactions to very early sightings of the first plane and contacts followed the following trajectory: "beginnings in precise forms of aim-directed behavior, which were a response to fear of the unknown or unpredictable, followed by curiosity, and were later a response to the gradual infiltration into the region by rumors. This led to a development of an ideology on an indigenous basis, to cope with such a situation. And this in turn caused a fluctuation of anticipation and disillusionment, of tension and the release of tension, centered on expectations involving spirits of the dead and what they represented; it involved action which was both precautionary and propitiatory."

15. Today, the site where Gillison carried out most of her work, Ubaigubi, is considered by both Gimi from Maimafu and outsiders to be more "traditional" than Maimafu.

16. Gimi dig large pits, fill them with stones, heat the stones, and place food into these earthen ovens to cook.

17. Over the past few years (2001 to 2004), I have collected numerous accounts of male initiation that mirror Gillison's account (1993). Bana's story was collected in a large group setting, and most of my recent accounts have been collected one-on-one or in very small groups. I think that in 1998 people were still unsure of my purpose in Maimafu and were a bit uncomfortable talking to me about rituals and myths that had been "outlawed" by the missions.

18. There was an SDA mission station in Kainantu, to the northeast of Gimi lands, as early as 1951 (C. Berndt 1953:112).

19. *Bus Kanaka* is a very derogatory term used to describe someone from the rural areas in New Guinea.

20. The RCF does not tell people not to hunt "at all." Rather, the organization has attempted to create a "wildlife management plan" that allows for some hunting with "traditional" hunting implements. Any discussion about hunting on the part of the RCF is perceived as a call to not hunt at all by people in Maimafu.

21. Kastom has been discussed widely in the literature in Melanesianist anthropology. It has been seen as a set of politicized discourses (Lindstrom and White 1993) connected to colonization (Keesing 1982) and commodification (Foster 1995), and discussed in terms of missionization and Christianity (Tonkinson 1993), among other things. It is often invoked in highly political ways (Keesing 1982) and has been seen as a politicized "invention of tradition" (Hobsbawm and Ranger 1983). Ellis (2002:47) has discussed the understanding of kastom among conservation practitioners working with the CMWMA.

22. I had had numerous conversations with Kabi, a man with whom I am quite close, about his father before I found his father's name in the patrol reports or in Gajdusek's journals. It was rather stirring to come upon the name while sitting in front of a microfiche reader at the archive in Port Moresby. Kabi is one of the people who has "adopted" me, and seeing Karubo's name was the first time that I felt the real bonds that are forged by fictive kin. I felt a connection to this man — to his history and his family's present. In 2003 when I gave Kabi and Philip, one of Kabi's sons, a copy of Gajdusek's journal entries for Maimafu, Philip translated for his father the mention of his grandfather — Kabi speaks Pidgin but not English, and I had translated the English into Pidgin for Philip. Kabi sat silently for a while and then told me that I had brought my grandfather home to where he belonged.

On several occasions in 1998, expatriates associated with the conservation project made comments about the use by Maimafu Gimi of fictive kin terms to categorize me. One woman in particular delighted in pointing out that "they just do it to try and get close to you so that they can ask you for things." I am reminded of Glick's (1967a:381) argument that "the Gimi approach kinship terms as cultural objects that can be manipulated to say different things on different occasions and to serve purposes more subtle than those for which they are overtly intended." Given that Glick worked with Gimi who were interacting with other Gimi, it seems that they use these cultural objects in power relations with both each other and with outsiders.

23. I attribute some of my own safety and research success in Maimafu village to Kabi. The day I arrived in the village, and while I was standing next to the plane unloading my "cargo," he announced that he had dreamed that I was going to come to the village to live and work. In his dream I was a tree kangaroo and possibly held within my tree-kangaroo-self the life force of his deceased daughter.

24. Thanks to Robin Hide for suggesting to me that this narrative may describe the Highlands dysentery epidemic of 1943–44.

25. This story was recounted to me by a Lawana, a woman who at the time was approximately fifty years old.

26. Given the importance of the moon in traditional Gimi stories with regard to conception (Gillison 1993:206, 215, 118), menstruation (ibid.:11, 184), and sorcery (ibid.:330), and the relationship between the sun and the moon in this myth (ibid.:329), the eclipse would have most certainly had profound effects on the people living in Maimafu in terms of their beliefs.

27. This was the SDA Church's strategy throughout the Highlands from early on in their work there (C. Berndt 1953:121).

28. Robbins draws on the work of John L. Comaroff and Jean Comaroff (1992, 1997) here.

29. See Dorothy Hodgson (2001) for an examination of the role of the Catholic Church in the creation of ideologies of development and the delivery of services seen by locals as "development."

30. This section is based on interviews with SDA Church officials in PNG, lay ministers in Maimafu, and the data presented on the SDA Web page: http://www.adventist.org/beliefs/index.html.

31. This belief that there will be people left on earth during this time period goes against official SDA church doctrine — the official belief is that there will be no life on earth during this time period.

32. I have been referred to the following for documentation of this future: Cor. 6:2, 3; Jer. 4:23–26; Pet. 3:13; Rev. 20:1, 21:1–7, 22:1–5.

33. Gajdusek (1968:54) mentions, however, that Kuserebe (Kuseri) was already impressively "landscaped" in 1962, with poinsettia shrubs and pigs that were "under control."

34. Although the vote to rid the village of pigs took place in 1982, people say that the actual slaughter of the last pig did not take place until an important wedding ceremony in 1984. I have no verifiable data concerning when the last pig was killed. A helicopter pilot living in Goroka thinks that he saw pigs in Maimafu, near the site of the current airstrip, as late as 1990.

35. Please see appendix A, "Locally Generated History of Maimafu." This appendix is a translated version of a time line that Mr. Kayaguna gave to me. He compiled this time line after an interview, in which I questioned him about the sequence of events in the history of Maimafu. He used his own records, from school and church, notes he took from a book that he had seen one day in Goroka, and his own memory of events. The title of the time line, "The History of Maimafu and the Lufa District of Papua New Guinea by Mr. Kayaguna Kelego as given to Tene Pone on this day of her research for her book on Maimafu Village," is the title that it was given by Mr. Kayaguna.

36. Glick (1968a:201) spells this as *aona*, and translates it as "soul," "power," "vital spirit," and "familiar spirit," arguing that each of these translations highlights some feature of the concept.

37. G. Gillison has written extensively about dreams in her 1993 book. In this section, I cite Gillison, but everything mentioned has also been confirmed by my own ethnographic work. I used Gillison's work as a guide in asking questions about dreams.

38. See Gillison (1993, 1994) for lengthy discussions of Gimi cannibalism. It is not my purpose here to examine historic instances of the consumption of human flesh or stories about these practices. Gillison has covered these extensively in her work. It is important to mark, however, that each of the interviews that I conducted in which cannibalism was discussed and in all of my casual conversations about it, people told me that only women and children ever consumed human flesh. This is a claim that Gillison has repeatedly made (see 1993:75, 120, 231).

39. Gillison reports that both the man and woman have to have the same dream for a child to be conceived. In my discussions about childbirth, with women only as it was not appropriate for me to discuss childbirth with men, women did not mention this.

40. Gillison (1980:163) argues that the auna of a woman's father is present in her unborn child—which she carries inside her even when not pregnant—and that it must be driven out of her by the auna of her husband's clan.

41. Marilyn Strathern (1988) draws extensively on Gillison's work with Gimi to make arguments about gender, gifts, and societal integration.

42. Each Gimi clan has a flute, and that flute has the name of a bird because for clan members the flute literally is the bird, not because it sounds like it. The myths of the flutes are intimately tied to historic relations between the genders. See Gillison (1980, 1993) for lengthy discussions of the connection between birds and flutes.

43. In Gillison (1993:224–228) *neki maha* is translated as "mad ground." In Sam McBride and Nancy McBride (1973:4), it is spelled *neki maa* and translated as "crazy ground."

44. Horara is alive today. He is about twenty years old, badly deformed from his childhood injuries, and mute. He is not deaf, and he seems to be able to follow instructions and participates in garden and coffee-related work, as well as going to church. He lives with his eldest brother. Upon the death of his parents, Horara's sister-in-law took pity on him and decided that he should come to live with them. She says, "God would want me to keep him safe. He was attacked by Satan when he was just a baby; now we must keep him for God."

45. This story was also recorded by Gillison (1993:159–164). The version in her 1993 book contains much more detail than the version I recorded. Her version is a combination of two stories from the over thirty that she recorded (ibid.:159), while mine is a direct translation of the only one of these stories that I collected.

46. I took Gillison's 1993 book with me to Maimafu and spent hours with people looking at it and talking about it. Some of the stories that she recounts are so perfect that old men said to me that they had forgotten the details of these stories, which they heard in childhood, until they heard the versions that Gillison tells.

47. See Dianne Rocheleau and Laurie Ross (1995) for an ethnographic analysis of this production of scale in terms of forest use.

48. I collected this story in 1997 from the oldest woman in Maimafu. Her name is Kobe, and she insisted that I use her real name in my work. Upon my explanation that I was going to give her a pseudonym she said, "But then people won't know who told you this story." In my dissertation I used a pseudonym with this story after all, but upon my return to Maimafu in 2002 with a copy of the dissertation, she wanted to know where the stories I had collected from her were. She got very angry when I told her that I had masked her identity, and she made me promise to use her real name from then on.

49. See Gillison (1991) for an analysis of the relationship between the flute myth and Gimi exchange principles and Gillison (1993) for extensive analysis of historic marriage rituals among Gimi. See Gillison (1994) for a psychoanalytic analysis of the unconscious meanings of Gimi marriage and sister exchange.

50. *Tambu* is the Melanesian Pidgin word for "taboo." When my husband is in Maimafu, people do not speak his name but refer to him as Tambu. There are cultural sanctions against speaking the name of the man who marries into your family. He has been to Maimafu three times: in 1998 for three months, in 2001 for one month, and in 2003 for three months.

51. None of my research was geared toward a systematic and thorough medical anthropological study of women's health issues. I did, however, observe a number of factors that could be contributing to this high incidence of mortality among pregnant women; they are in the chapter text that follows.

52. Gona is known throughout the Gimi speaking region as the village with the best health care. The health center there is run by Barbara Howell through the Faith Mission. The Faith Mission has numerous centers throughout the region. Since I began working in Papua New Guinea in 1997, the mission has built several additional small aid posts in villages near Gona. In 2002 I toured the Faith Mission's aid post in Quasa and was stunned by its efficiency and the training of its staff.

53. The value of the kina has fluctuated quite a bit over the past few years. During 1997, it was worth roughly 0.50 U.S. dollars, but by 1998 it was worth roughly 0.33 U.S. dollars.

54. *Meri* is the Melanesian Pidgin word for woman. It is paired with the English word *discount*.

55. Frederick Errington and Deborah Gewertz (1987a: 113) argue that among the Chambri, "although education is not a substitute for initiation, it is perceived to be as necessary as initiation for the transformation of a child into an active and competent exchanger." This young woman's father had this view—he saw his investment in her education as a way of getting a return in the future, not only through her bride price, but also through her expected monetary contributions to her younger siblings' education and the like.

56. Historic forms of marriage among Gimi centered on "sister exchange" (Gillison 1993:15, 58, 156, 255–261); today, this is not the norm in Maimafu. While children are pressured by their parents to make marriages that are productive alliances for their family, the desired norm of a "double marriage"—in which the father of one bride becomes the father-in-law of the other, and hence the father of one son becomes the father-in-law of the other—is no longer regularly practiced. In addition, "marriage season" now coincides directly with the coffee-growing season, with high marriage time being in November and December, at the end of coffee season when people are flush with cash.

57. In the past, the mother of the bride might have contributed pigs that she raised to the bride price (Gillison 1993:52).

58. Thanks to Craig McConaghy (personal communication, 2004) for this information.

59. *Didiman* is the Melanesian Pidgin term for a man working for the PNG department of agriculture.

60. Indeed, land tenure studies are some of the most important contributions by Melanesianist anthropology to both the wider field of cultural anthropology and the subdiscipline of environmental anthropology. Others, most recently Bryan Oles (1999) and John Wagner (2002), have reviewed the literature on land tenure in the Pacific.

61. Gimi peoples have long-standing trade relations with people in the Pio-Tura region (Gajdusek 1968:68).

62. In the ethnography of Melanesia, the analysis of the social force of development has a long history, and variable outcomes of local-global processes in the context of so-called development are well documented. This ethnography shows that development and change are experienced in different ways in different places depending on the history of cultural contact, local traditions, and existing cultural categories, as well as the local political-economic circumstances. The literature often uses an approach to the analysis of cultural change that allows for attention to both structures and process. By this I mean, the *structures* of local cultures and how everyday cultural practices shape and are shaped by historical and social processes, and the *processes* of historical change and modernization, and how modernity is shaped by local conditions and cultural understandings (Carrier and Carrier 1991:9–23).

It is almost impossible to write about Melanesia without taking both structure and process into account. George Morren, in a discussion of change among the Miyanmin, illustrates:

> In our science, every ethnographer must grapple with both the ethnographic present and present reality. [Lewis] Henry Morgan and [Robert] Lowie alike believed that their subjects stood for something enduring, ancient or primitive; and I too, wonder about the essentials of Miyanmin-ness signaled by the use of such words as "traditional" and "precontact." With only a synchronic database at our disposal, this has been

a convenient axiom because we will only see what we will see within a narrow slice of time. The reality is that all of our research has been carried out in a maelstrom of change, change so rapid that it reinforced our illusions of primordial stability. Ultimately our confusion is reflected in attitudes toward modernization, which are conflicting at best and tempered both by romanticism and by the historic sensitivity that, although inevitable, little good can come of it [such attitudes]. (1986:291)

The relationship between structure, process, and custom (culture) is central to any examination of change in Melanesia. This set of relationships between events, processes, customs, and history is precisely what Escobar is talking about when he discusses the anthropology of modernity (1999). It is simply an anthropology that takes seriously the contingent nature of events. By contingent nature, I mean the fact that actions and events are influenced by a range of processes: social and economic, cultural and political, material and historic. These processes are tied to events on local, regional, and global scales. This view of actions and events as contingent is particularly important if one takes seriously Karl Marx's argument about the universalizing tendency of capital but if one also sees the evidence of local articulations with capital as more creative and diverse than Marx anticipated (Pred and Watts 1992; Taussig 1980, 1987).

Foster argues that two different analytical approaches with regard to Melanesian studies have emerged over the past decade (Foster 1995:3): one that highlights "fundamental differences between Melanesian and Western presuppositions about social reality" and one that "highlights similarities between Melanesian and Western social realities" (ibid.). The "New Melanesian Ethnography" and the "New Melanesian History" are the labels Foster gives these analytical approaches (ibid.). The former "constructs an opposition between Us and Them in order to criticize a mode of anthropological inquiry unselfconsciously predicated upon Our presuppositions," while the latter "deconstructs dichotomies between Us and Them in order to criticize a mode of anthropological inquiry that emphasizes (even essentializes) the otherness of the Other and de-emphasizes the contingent effects of time (history) and power (colonial and capitalist domination)" (ibid.).

Foster goes on to argue that there need not be a choice made between these two approaches when writing ethnographically about Melanesia (1995:3). Social life in Melanesia is such that local cultural articulations are different from other places in the world, and their description (rich and thick) has become the hallmark of Melanesian ethnography (Knauft 1996). But it is also the case that these cultural articulations and practices have a rich history of change influenced by regional relations, colonization, disease-related mortality, natural disaster, World War II, local conversion to Christianity, mining and logging ventures, and other historic events. The use of both of these analytical approaches enriches our understandings of actions and events and the processes in which they are embedded (Foster 1995).

Two of the most prolific ethnographers of modernization, development, and tradition or custom in PNG are Debra Gewertz and Fredrick Errington (Errington and Gewertz 1987a, 1987b, 1993a, 1995, 1996; Gewertz and Errington 1991, 1993, 1995, 1996). Gewertz and Errington offer an explicit treatment of development in Papua New Guinea among the Chambri (Gewertz and Errington 1991). They convey the encounter between the Chambri as a cultural group and as individuals — through the transformative nature of tourism — with the global system (Gewertz and Errington 1991:3). Their recent work focuses on modernity as the mediator between the local and the global and on Chambri definitions of what it means to be modern or developed (Errington and Gewertz 1996; Gewertz and Errington 1996). For Gewertz and Errington, modernity is directly tied to the ways the Chambri imagine themselves and their future, and modernity has altered the Chambri's process of self-creation (Gewertz and Errington 1996:485). But the Chambri have also retained certain traditional ideas about what it means to be Chambri (ibid.:489). They have actively woven together experiences with modernity and how they see themselves as modern citizens, with how they see themselves in relation to traditional cultural forms (ibid.).

In work specifically on the role of tradition in the local engagement with development via capitalism, Errington and Gewertz (1996:114) argue that Papua New Guineans invoke "culture in dealing with a fluidity of identity and a shift in the locus of important resources in a late-20th-century, postcolonial 'modernity' — a modernity progressively affected by transnational capitalism and by state power." They also show that transnational commodity producers are incorporating the traditional into their marketing campaigns and that these incorporations are transforming the relationship between people and tradition (ibid.:119). They show a creative appropriation by local people of the social forms produced by companies and, with this, demonstrate that local people are active in reworking local cultural identity to include ideas about development and modernization (ibid.:123). Other ethnographers have also show a link between the construction of identity and local development (Brison 1995; Gorle 1995; Leavitt 1995; Pomponio 1992).

In an analysis of development in Papua New Guinea and the ways in which local understandings of material changes are incorporated into local culture, Michael Smith shows the moral dilemmas that villagers face because of their desires for the material goods associated with development and the commodification of social relations that development has engendered (Smith 1994:198). By demonstrating local images of the future, he shows what the Kragur villagers think it means to be modern (ibid.:11). He concludes that people's "efforts to understand the roots of European prosperity may be leading them to redefine good social relations in a manner more compatible with life in a capitalist political economy" (ibid.:233). He also concludes that with this attempt at understanding, the Kragur have also played an active role in shaping the political economy on their island. They have reworked the capitalist system to fit into their cultural categories, and altered their cultural categories to fit the capitalist system (ibid.: 233–234).

63. Development is, along with being grounded in this Saidian quandary of "us and them," firmly rooted in modernity, and it rests upon the valorization of what Dorothy Hodgson (1997) has described as the oppositional categories of modernity. These "oppositional categories" are directly linked to the representations that Said exposes. Therefore, development not only changes power relations, that are of course social relations, in terms of economics and politics, but development also changes power relations in terms of images of self and other. In other words, development marks and creates difference (Hodgson 2001).

64. Jacka makes a similar argument with regard to the structuring of conceptualizations of development among the eastern Ipili and the Enga (2003:24).

65. One of the main reasons that teachers refuse to go to rural schools in Papua New Guinea is because it is so difficult for them to take breaks and see their families.

66. The initial colonial interest in New Guinea began as part of the rivalry between the British, Dutch, and Portuguese over the Indonesian islands, with the first Dutch settlement on the island in 1828 (Gordon 1951:30). Between 1884 and 1885, both Britain and Germany laid claim to eastern New Guinea. British New Guinea (1884–1906) was made up of the southeastern half of the island, including the islands at the southern tip; German New Guinea (1884–1914) was made up to the northeastern half of the island, including the islands off the northeastern coast (Griffen, Nelson, and Firth 1979). In 1901, the new parliament of the Commonwealth of Australia requested that they be given the administrative duties associated with New Guinea (Gordon 1951). In 1906, the British parliament debated the Papua Bill, which gave the colony the new name of the Territory of Papua and transferred the authority for management over to Australia.

67. The British colonial period in Australia began in about 1788 with the dispatch of criminals by King George to the continent. On 1 January 1901 Australia was granted independence from Britain.

68. This sentiment is also shared by conservation scientists currently working in PNG. One of the scientists with whom I work says, "Basically I think it [the Fauna Act] is just a meaningless piece of paper. . . . A real problem is that DEC [the Department of Environment and Conservation] does very little to enforce the Fauna Act. There is no effective protection of any species in PNG, full stop" (personal communication, 2004).

69. This sense of New Guinea as a natural laboratory comes directly from anthropology. Bruce Knauft (1999) writes a social history of this concept in his work on Melanesia as a culture area.

70. Jamie James, personal communication 4 October 2002.

71. Van Helden writes about this project in several places (1998, 2001a, 2001b). In July of 2002, Van Helden, Ellis (see Ellis 2002), and I spent three days together at the Society for Conservation Biology's annual conference in Canterbury, England. Although Ellis and I had known each other since 1996, this was the first time that I had met Van

Helden. Our conversations about the Bismarck-Ramu ICDP and the Crater Mountain ICDP were extraordinary. The projects were extremely similar, as were the local critiques of the projects. In an eerie fashion, the three of us could finish each other's sentences with our own analyses of the conservation interventions. J. Wagner (2002) also worked in an area in PNG with an ICDP, and although he was not present at our meeting in 2002, his work also resonates with similar critiques and analyses.

72. For the most troubling production of "Crater People" and collapsing of place and culture, see D. Gillison (2002).

73. The linguistic convention of calling a married woman "wife of" her husband is tied to the taboos against speaking names of members who are nonfamily. The director of the RCF spoke in Melanesian Pidgin and said, "Meri bilong Nelson, yu laik tok long sampela samting?"

74. I tape-recorded the entire annual meeting in 2001. Parts of it are difficult to hear, but Nanasuanna was standing close to me, so this is a direct translation.

75. In Pidgin backbone is *bun bilong baksait*, but she used the English word *backbone* here.

76. The repetition here is because the first time she said, "We know how to make a *bilum*" was in Melanesian Pidgin and the second was in Unavisa Gimi. Making a bilum, as I have already mentioned, is a profoundly feminine task. "Layge nahabado sumake ko" is literally "our fingers' bilum."

77. The list is reproduced below exactly as I received it.

78. See http://bcnet.org/bsp/bcn/learning/crater15.htm.

4. *Conservation Histories*

1. An exception is Ellis (2002:148–208), who has written a version of this history focused on the Pawaia peoples' understandings and experiences of the CMWMA.

2. Indeed, although Papua New Guinea is often seen as existing within the "savage slot" (Lederman 1998) in anthropology, most contemporary anthropologists working in PNG write about the intercultural contacts they observe that people are taking part in. The dynamic nature of culture in Oceania was the topic of a panel at the American Anthropological Association annual meeting as early as 1982 (Dan Jorgensen, personal communication, 2003). So although the wider discipline has imagined the anthropology of Papua New Guinea as replicating the discipline's troubled atheoretical past (Knauft 1999), the fiction of "peoples without history" (Wolf 1982) has had less hold on Melanesianist anthropology that other subfields of anthropology.

3. For ethnographic accounts of these ethnolinguistic groups, see David M. Ellis (2002); Robin Hide (1984); Hide et al. (1995); Roy Wagner (1967, 1969, 1970, 1972, 1978, 1991a, 1991b, 1996, 1998, 2001); Shirley Lindenbaum (1969, 1979, 1981, 2002); Robert Glasse and Lindenbaum (1967); and Ronald Berndt (1954, 1962, 1964, 1971).

4. For a contemporary example of this representation, see Kent Flannery (1999).

5. This is the first instance in printed material where the two distinct ethnic groups which live in what is now the CMWMA are conflated into "Crater Peoples."

6. The first patrols into "the Crater area" were not in 1957 and 1958. As discussed in chapter 1, the "three-pronged" patrol was carried out starting in 1950 on the orders of George Greathead; their purpose was to "contact" the last people living south of Mount Michael and north of Karimui who had not yet been contacted.

7. Gimi believe that the soul or life force (Gillison 1980) of a man returns to the forest when he dies. This force does not, however, "reside" in a bird of paradise. While the force may take refuge in certain species for a short period of time, they eventually go back into clan grounds and become part of the matter from which all life flows. This representation of Gimi cosmology is both erroneous and deeply troubling. The conflation of Gimi belief that their clan forests are the repositories for matter that is not at play elsewhere and some notion of "conservation" is a backward reading of Gimi cosmology. The point is that Gimi believe that nothing ever ends, that all matter is here for all time and that through the process of exchange it simply changes form over time (Gillison 1980, 1993). This, as mentioned earlier, makes Gimi notions of matter and form antithetical to conservation notions of loss.

8. Two species of cassowary can be found within the CMWMA: the northern cassowary (*Casuarius unappendiculatus*) and the dwarf cassowary (*Casuarius bennetti*).

9. D. Gillison has published a similar account of the history of the WMA in his recent book (2002). I conducted this interview with him before the publication of that book.

10. A lek is a display area where many males of a species gather to perform mating displays in order to attract females. Birds of paradise spend substantial time and effort on these displays, and given their extraordinary plumage these displays can be spectacular. I appreciate Andy Mack's help with this description (Andrew Mack, personal communication, 2003).

11. For an excellent recent scientific discussion of the anthropogenic nature of biodiversity, see Pinedo-Vasquez et al. (2002). For an excellent anthropological account of the anthropogenic nature of rivers and forests, see Raffles (2002).

12. In July 2002 I lost my temper with a man from Maimafu. He had been stealing matches from me every day. When I lost my temper with him I said, "This sort of behavior makes me want to leave Maimafu and never come back." In the heat of the moment, that was indeed how I felt. It is hard to work there, and little things such as constantly having your matches stolen wear on you. When I screamed this at the man, he immediately started to cry. He told me that my leaving would be the worst thing in the world. He said that my returning to Maimafu year after year made me a part of the community and that if I left and never came back, there would be a "hole in the world." Part of his response was based on the fact that he could tell that I was very angry with him, and he wanted to get himself out of my line of angry words. But part of it was based on

Gimi notion that personhood is made up of social connections and obligations between people, and if someone dies or "leaves forever," an empty space in both people and social life appears.

5. *A Land of Pure Possibility*

The title of this chapter is taken from Crapanzano's *Imaginative Horizons* (2004:16).

1. This is, of course, metaphorical, since I first visited Maimafu in 1997.

2. *White people* is an uncomfortable term. I use it because it is the term used by people in Maimafu when they refer to expatriates. In Gimi they say, *Ago Bana* or *Ago Badaha* ("white man" or "white woman"), and in Melanesian Pidgin they say, *Ol wait lain* or *wait man na meri* ("the white people" or "white men and women").

3. See Lamont Lindstrom (1990) for the most complete analysis of the role of discourse in the making and unmaking of Melanesian selves and lifeways.

4. Jamon Halvaksz deserves my gratitude for pushing me to think through these terms and their usage in anthropology. His dissertation (2005) addresses these issues extensively.

5. This does not include the hundreds of times that these sorts of questions came up during other conversations.

6. The sexualized nature of this is not lost on me; nor would it have been lost on Rick. It was not, however, apparent to younger people who did not grow up with the older cosmological and mythological stories told to them (see Gillison 1993:143).

7. This difference between the permanence of expatriate-related material culture and impermanence of local material culture was pointed out to me by several of the participants in the 2004 Association of Social Anthropology in Oceania panel "Mining in the Pacific."

8. People have seen copies of the WCS's conservation magazine (*Wildlife Conservation*) both at the RCF office in Maimafu and at the Sera Research Station. This story was told to me in Maimafu, but I have heard that it is also told in Herowana and Haia.

9. Today there are monkeys, which have been imported as pets into West Papua by Indonesian settlers, on the island.

10. In 1999 at the RCF annual meeting, the topic was again brought up. I did not attend these meetings, but afterward numerous RCF and WCS employees contacted me via e-mail and blamed me for the controversy about the Japanese grant. They said that people from Maimafu said that I said that they should be given the money directly and that the RCF should not make money off their bush and then keep it all for themselves. Instead of addressing this topic at the meetings with landowners, the employees flooded me with e-mail about my behavior "ruining" conservation efforts in Maimafu. In September 1999 I received a letter from the general manager of the RCF. The letter states that the members of the Maimafu Management Committee approached him and the project director and

informed them that I had told them that the RCF was withholding money received from the Japanese government that should rightly belong to the landowners. It was claimed that I had said landowners should rightfully be receiving fortnightly paychecks from the RCF for their labor. The letter then goes on to state that the RCF's relationship with people from Maimafu "declined" after my arrival, so it must be that I "really did say those things to the villagers." Interestingly, this letter arrived about a month after I had sent a chapter of my dissertation that critiqued the RCF to the RCF general manager and his staff for their comments.

11. See Ellis (2002) for an analysis of these produced images with regard to Pawaia people.

12. While I think that the politics of representation is well addressed within anthropology, the politics of teaching, as it creates images and ideologies about other places, is only now beginning to be addressed. For some analysis of this, see Akhil Gupta and James Ferguson (1999). Some essays in this volume explore the ways that anthropology textbooks and classes define such terms as *local*, *field*, *fieldwork*, *other*, *we*, and *they*.

13. The literature on the politics of ethnographic writing is extensive. The 1986 book by James Clifford and George Marcus was perhaps the first real collection of anthropological meditations on this topic.

14. In his work on "ethnoscapes" Appadurai slips between reading their ideas as imaginations and as imaginaries. He focuses on the collectivities of tourists, immigrants, refugees, and others, yet the individual interactions between people in which one discusses or envisions one's image of place, space, nature, or culture for and with another seem to be lacking.

15. The exception to this, from my point of view, is David Gillison. Having worked among Gimi since 1972, he surely understands many local sociocultural articulations. The only conclusion I can come to when reading the documents cited in this section is that he was not consulted during their production. I am particularly troubled by the images created of Gimi in these reports and proposals because of his knowledge and because of G. Gillison's many publications about Gimi social and ecological life. Indeed, her 1993 book is a veritable roadmap to Gimi culture.

16. Anthropologists have written widely in criticism of this location of indigenous people as authentic voices of the past, which they cite as even taking place within certain schools of anthropology, often debunking myths of "true primitives" and of seemingly isolated groups being a "window to our evolutionary past." Anthropologists have also written about the created exoticness of indigenous peoples by outsiders (see Kahn 2000).

17. See West and James Carrier (2004) for a lengthy discussion of the tourism business in Maimafu.

18. See Lindstrom (1993) for a history of the term and its importance in anthropology. See Foster (2002:chap. 2) for an analysis of the term as it is related to the commodity fetish and the strangeness of money as the universal equivalent form.

19. "Namatai sa waname ya ahloha. Namatai sa waname su mehe gehe. Kau bai gehe. Namatai sa waname ohku ahloahtine namaya hoah." Translated by Esta and Nara, 12 January 1998.

20. There is a rich history of external analyses of how people in Papua New Guinea use their forests for shifting cultivation and the building of homes. One of the first government reports on the land-use practices of local people (Womersley and McAdam 1957: 36) reads almost exactly like the Johnson 1997 paper with regard to the description of "problematic" uses of the environment by local people.

21. Note that although the language in this quotation is almost exactly like the language in the quotation that I used to open this section, the quotations are from different publications.

22. Indeed, some recent studies have shown that the human habitation and alteration of the forests in the Pacific in general and Melanesia specifically are some of the most complex and ancient forms of this activity in the world (Bayliss-Smith et al. 2003; Denham et al. 2003).

6. *Conservation-as-Development*

1. See Gillison (1980) and M. Strathern (1980) for extended discussions of nature and culture in Highlands Papua New Guinea. Both argue that the nature/culture distinction is an artifact of Western analysis and not a reflection of how people in PNG see the relationship between social selves and the environment. Philippe Descola argues that the dichotomy has been used strategically in anthropology, especially by Claude Lévi-Strauss, as a tool for understanding social relations with nature and for understanding mythological relations as they allow humans to transcend the animal and become cultural beings (1996:84).

2. The USPC requires that all of its volunteers living in malarial areas take Larium during service.

3. The USPC no longer sends volunteers to PNG, because of security issues.

4. All quotations are from transcribed interview tapes. Interviews were conducted in a mix of Melanesian Pidgin and Unavisa Gimi. All tapes were transcribed while in the field with the help of a native speaker of Unavisa Gimi who is fluent in Melanesian Pidgin and English.

5. The MacArthur Foundation in the United States is a major source of funding for conservation projects.

6. Aerafena, Kegegaina, Folisa, Amamiaya, and Kalikalipa are all pseudonyms for extended family names.

7. For excellent recent summaries of land tenure studies in pacific anthropology in relation to place, see Bryan Oles (1999), and in relation to common property theory, see John Wagner (2003).

8. The literature on property and land in Melanesia and the Pacific is extensive. Indeed, most anthropologists who write ethnographically about the area include detailed descriptions of people's social relations with land. It is not my desire to review that literature here but simply to make the point that this literature is out there and easily accessible to people working on conservation-related projects in PNG. Anyone who has spent any time in Papua New Guinea knows that land and land ownership are two of the most discussed issues in the country. Everyone there has some sort of familial tie to some bit of land, and traditionally personhood and identity have, in part, been tied to familial social relations over and with land. Much of the conflict in the Eastern Highlands today is related to land disputes (Westermark 1997).

9. See Michael Dove (1993) for a discussion of Steinbeck's "The Pearl" (1945), a story in which a poor man finds a giant and valuable pearl that brings only unhappiness and violence to him and his family, causing him, in the end, to destroy the thing of great value (1993:23). Dove argues that an apt analogy to the conservation of tropical forests can be made here: "If indigenous people are deprived of rights to all but the least and meanest of forest resources, they may well follow the example of (the pearl diver) and destroy that which was theirs by right but the enjoyment of which was denied them" (ibid.).

10. I am indebted to Kobe for explaining this to me. In the summer of 2003 while discussing another research topic, she told me what making a bilum means to her. Although I had my tape recorder close at hand, I did not record our conversation. There was something sacred about it, something that seemed beyond research to me. She told me that I had to hurry up and have a child so that she could make it a bilum before she dies. And then she told me that many years ago she had made a bilum for my mother, although she did not know it at the time, and that the reason I had come to work in Maimafu was because I was trying to find that bilum. Kobe knows quite a bit about my personal history, and that day she also told me that perhaps the reason my mother, who was very young when I was born and who had a rather difficult time as a single mother in Georgia in the 1970s, floundered early on as a parent was because she did not have the bilum.

11. Mark's wife's death was most likely due to a postpartum hemorrhage brought on by low iron levels and general health problems due to multiple births at a very young age (Dr. Tani Sangvi, personal communication, 1999). Her poor health was due to numerous factors, and her death is mentioned here to demonstrate the precarious health situation of women in Maimafu. These health issues are, of course, not the fault of the RCF, but rather the result of numerous historical changes in women's labor roles, changes in the local diet following conversion to the SDA Church, and changes in the locally understood "value" of women.

12. The Tok Pisin term *het pe* (head payment) refers to customary transfers of wealth associated with various rites of passage.

13. Cash then would have been Australian currency. The man to whom she is married worked on the coast before their marriage, so he would have had access to cash.

14. During July 2000 a young woman from Maimafu was married with a bride price of almost 3,000 kina. She is known locally as an exceptionally "hard worker," and this was the highest bride price ever paid in its entirety in one payment. My research assistant had the highest bride price ever marked in the area — 6,000 kina. It took her husband's family three coffee seasons to pay the price.

15. In 2002 most women did see the village water supply and the funds to support local schooling as significant development impacts engendered by the work of the RCF.

16. Thanks to John Wagner for alerting me to this Web page.

17. The data presented here regarding New Guinea Craft were collected through an e-mail conversation with one of the owners of the company. He graciously agreed to answer my questions on short notice and to allow me to write about his business.

18. The income generation projects implemented by the RCF had slightly increased the average per capita income of some individuals in the village, but they had hardly made any impact on the average per capita income of the village as a whole. In 1997, while 3,897.60 kina was earned through the artifact production business, 2,475.94 kina through the research business, and 102.30 kina through the tourism business, the total earnings from conservation-related enterprises were still negligible when compared to village income from coffee production. The average per capita income from coffee production during the 1997–1998 growing season was 79.82 kina, while the average per capita income from all conservation-related enterprises in 1997 was only 8.09 kina. These figures must be seen within the context of the real costs incurred by individuals living in the village. At the time of my initial fieldwork, a single-dose treatment of quinine for a bout of malaria cost 12 kina; a flight from Maimafu to Goroka cost approximately 31 kina each way; and school fees for one year at an SDA high school cost approximately 1,200 kina.

19. From interviews in 1998 with men between the ages of twenty-three and forty-five, I found that almost 80 percent of the men who participated in the RCF projects expressed a positive opinion about them. In fact, they wanted more opportunities to increase their cash incomes. Males below the age of twenty-three generally had little contact with either the RCF or the income generation projects, except in a few instances when they had worked as carriers for visiting scientists. As a group, they also wanted increased opportunities for cash income, but they made an explicit connection between cash income and education: 75 percent of these younger males wanted to "go to school" and then obtain employment outside of Maimafu. Men over the age of forty-five also had little involvement in the research or tourism projects. Some older men produced spears and baskets for the handicraft shop, and these men expressed satisfaction with the cash income they were earning from this activity. The main point to be made about male perceptions of the ICAD project in 1998 is that men did see this increase in the flow of cash into the community as a phenomenon generated by the RCF, and therefore did not link it to the value of

conservation, because they did not associate the RCF directly with conservation. They saw these businesses as the products of their own labor, and not the labor of RCF personnel. In their own words, they did see the "hand mark" (*hanmak*) of the RCF in their lives because they felt that the RCF had not helped them in a way that promoted the social relationships they needed for self-sufficiency.

20. In 1998, women over the age of fourteen had a generally negative view of the income generation projects. While they acknowledged the increase in cash income, they thought that the extra strains on their labor and their time do not make this increase worthwhile. Almost all of the money generated by the sale of their bilum bags went to meet social obligations. After making their contributions to bride price and "head payments," women had little cash left to spare. Much of the cash that women had after these social obligations went to buy rice and other small trade-store goods for their families. Their only "disposable" income went to buy store wool to make bilum for themselves. In contrast to the majority of men in Maimafu, who saw the RCF as an organization that has little or no impact on their economic activities, women saw it as having a negative impact on both their social and economic lives. They saw an increase in the demands on their labor, unfulfilled promises about increases in health care and schooling opportunities, more fighting and conflict in the village, and greater opportunities for their husbands to excuse themselves from helping with daily subsistence activities.

7. *Conservation for Development*

1. Thanks to Thomas Pierce for helping me understand some things about being a mother and for letting me use his real name. Thomas was the recipient of a scholarship from Wofford College, which allowed him to travel the world for a year thinking about issues of community and development. While he was in Maimafu, he did not conduct research of any kind; he simply visited with people and talked to me about my research.

2. See Gewertz and Errington (1991) for a lengthy discussion of cultural competence and changes in "ways of being" in Papua New Guinea. While they are specifically interested in Chambri ways of being, and ways of being Chambri, their arguments fit with the Gimi context.

3. The "white man" to which Eato refers may well be Carleton Gajdusek. Gajdusek walked through Maimafu at the end of March in 1962 (Gajdusek 1968). Eato remembers that this white man was with lots of carriers from other places in Papua New Guinea and that he was "a man who seemed to like us." Eato, who would have been about ten years old at the time, also remembers that this white man came not long after the eclipse in February 1962.

4. The Melanesian Pidgin list of questions and the English list of questions differ slightly. The "translation" of the list took place with about twenty people making comments and helping me translate. Questions that are paired together in this section are

meant to be the same question but because of translation issues, they are at times a bit different.

5. Michael Dove helped me with understanding the importance of Chagnon's goals in examining that fight as opposed to my goals with examining the fight with which this book began.

6. This is Robert's real name, and I use it with his permission. His actions with regard to this event could have caused him to loose his job, but he did not care. He chooses to do "the right thing" and face the consequences.

7. *Femomo* is the root knot of a bromeliad that grows high in some trees; it is also one of the Gimi names for the long-beaked echidna.

8. See chapter 3 for a longer discussion of the flute myth and for references to relevant literature.

Bibliography

Abu-Lughod, Lila. 1993. *Writing women's worlds: Bedouin stories*. Berkeley: University of California Press.

Adger, W. Neil, Tor A. Benjaminsen, Katrina Brown, and Hanne Svarstad. 2001. Advancing a political ecology of global environmental discourses. *Development and Change* 32 (4): 681–715.

Agrawal, Arun. 1996. Poststructuralist approaches to development: Some critical reflections. *Development and Change* 21 (4): 464–477.

Allen, Bryant. 1990. The importance of being equal. In *Sepik heritage: Tradition and change in Papua New Guinea*, edited by Nancy Lutkehaus, Christina Kaufmann, William E. Mitchell, Douglas Newton, Lita Osmundsen, and Neinhard Schuster. Durham, N.C.: Carolina Academic Press.

Allison, Allen. 1993. Biodiversity and conservation of the fishes, amphibians, and reptiles of Papua New Guinea. In *Papua New Guinea conservation needs assessment report*. Vol. 2, *A biodiversity analysis for Papua New Guinea*, edited by Bruce M. Beehler. Washington, D.C.: Biodiversity Support Program.

Anderson, Benedict. 1983. Imagined communities: Reflections on the origin and spread of nationalism. London: Verso.

Appadurai, Arjun. 1988. Introduction: Place and voice in anthropological theory. *Cultural Anthropology* 3 (1): 16–20.

———. 1990. Disjuncture and difference in the global cultural economy. *Public Culture* 2:1–24.

———. 1991. Global ethnoscapes: Notes and queries for a transnational anthropology. In *Recapturing anthropology: Working in the present*, edited by Richard Fox. Santa Fe: School of American Research.

———. 1996. *Modernity at large: Cultural dimensions of globalization*. Minneapolis: University of Minnesota Press.

———. 1986. Introduction: Commodities and the politics of value. In *The social life of things. Commodities in cultural perspective,* edited by Arjun Appadurai. Cambridge: Cambridge University Press.

Bamford, Sandra. 1998. Humanised landscapes, embodied worlds: Land use and the construction of intergenerational sociality among the Kamea. In *Identity, nature and culture: Sociality and the environment in Melanesia,* edited by Sandra Bamford. Special Issue, *Social Analysis* 42 (3): 28–54.

Barth, Fredrik. 1956. Ecologic relationships of ethnic groups in Swat, North Pakistan. *American Anthropologist* 58:1079–1089.

———. 1987. *Cosmologies in the making: A generative approach to cultural variation in Inner New Guinea*. Cambridge Studies in Social Anthropology 64. Cambridge: Cambridge University Press.

Bates, Daniel, and Susan Lees. 1996. Introduction. In *Case studies in human ecology*, edited by Daniel Bates and Susan Lees. New York: Plenum Press.

Bates, Marston. 1953. Human ecology. In *Anthropology Today*, edited by Alfred Lois Kroeber. Chicago: University of Chicago Press.

Baudrillard, Jean. 1975. *The mirror of production*. St Louis, Mo.: Telos.

———. 1981. For a critique of the political economy of the sign. St. Louis, Mo.: Telos Press.

———. 1988. Simulacra and simulations. In *Jean Baudrillard: Selected writings,* edited by Mark Poster. Polity: Blackwell.

Bayliss-Smith, Tim, Edvard Hviding, and Tim Whitmore. 2003. Rainforest composition and histories of human disturbance in Solomon Islands. *Ambio* 32: 346–352.

Beehler, Bruce M. 1993. Biodiversity and conservation of warm-blooded vertebrates of Papua New Guinea. In *Papua New Guinea conservation needs assessment report*. Vol. 2, *A biodiversity analysis for Papua New Guinea*, edited by Bruce M. Beehler. Washington, D.C.: Biodiversity Support Program.

———. 1994. The global benefits of conservation in Papua New Guinea. In *Papua New Guinea country study on biological diversity* edited by Nikhil Sekhran, and S. Miller. A report to the United Nations Environment Program. Waigani: Papua New Guinea, Department of Environment and Conservation, Conservation Resource Centre; and Nairobi, Kenya: African Centre for Resources and Environment (ACRE).

Belcher, Capt. Sir Edward. 1843. *Narrative of a voyage round the world*. Vol. 2. London: Colbum.

Belsky, Jill M. 1999. Misrepresenting communities: The politics of community-based rural ecotourism in Gales Point Manatee, Belize. *Rural sociology* 64:641–666.

Benjamin, Walter. 1978. *Reflections: Essays, aphorisms, autobiographical writings*. Trans. Edmund Jephcott, ed. Peter Demetz. New York: Schocken Books.

Bennett, John William. 1976. Culture, ecology, and social policy. Chap. 2 in *The ecological transition: Cultural anthropology and human adaptation*. New York: Pergamon Press.

———. 1988. Anthropology and development: The ambiguous engagement. In *Production and autonomy: Anthropological studies and critiques of development*, edited by John Bennett and John Bowen. Durham, N.C.: University Press of America.

Bennett, Judith A. 1995. Forestry, public land, and the colonial legacy in Solomon Islands. *Contemporary Pacific* 7:243–275.

Bernard, H. Russel. 1995. *Research methods in anthropology, qualitative and quantitative approaches*. 2nd ed. Walnut Creek, Calif.: AltaMira Press.

Berndt, Catherine H. 1953. Socio-cultural change in the Eastern Central Highlands of New Guinea. *Southwestern journal of Anthropology* 9 (1): 112–138.

Berndt, Ronald M. 1954. Traction to contact in the Eastern Highlands of New Guinea. *Oceania* 24 (3): 190–274.

———. 1962. Excess and restraint: Social control among a New Guinea mountain people. Chicago: University of Chicago Press.

———. 1964. Warfare in the New Guinea Highlands. In special publication, edited by James B. Watson, *American Anthropologist* 66 (4) pt. 2:183–203.

———. 1971. Political structure in the Eastern Central Highlands of New Guinea. In *Politics in New Guinea*, edited by Ronald M. Berndt and Peter Lawrence. Nedlands: University of Western Australia Press.

Bernstein, Richard J. 1971. *Praxis and action*. Philadelphia: University of Pennsylvania Press.

Bickford, David. 1990. To catch a frog. *Wildlife Conservation* (May/June): 50–55.

———. 2004. Differential parental care behaviors of arboreal and terrestrial microhylid frogs from Papua New Guinea. *Behavioral Ecology and Sociobiology* 55:402–409.

Biersack, Aletta, ed. 1995a. *Papuan borderlands*. Ann Arbor: University of Michigan Press.

———, ed. 1995b. Introduction: The Huli, Duna, and Ipili peoples yesterday and today. In *Papuan borderlands*. Ann Arbor: University of Michigan Press.

———. 1999. Introduction: from the "new ecology" to the new ecologies. *American Anthropologist* 101:5–18.

Biodiversity Support Program (BSP). 1996. Biodiversity Conservation Network 1996 annual report: Stories from the field and lessons learned. Washington, D.C.: Biodiversity Support Program.

———. 1997. Biodiversity Conservation Network 1997 annual report: Getting down to business. Washington, D.C.: Biodiversity Support Program.

———. 1998. *Biodiversity Conservation Network 1998 annual report*. Washington, D.C.: Biodiversity Support Program.

———. 1999. Biodiversity Conservation Network 1999 annual report: Final report. Washington, D.C.: Biodiversity Support Program.

Blaikie, Piers, and Harold C. Brookfield, eds. 1987. *Land degradation and society*. London: Methuen.

Blinkoff, Robbie. 1999. Caretaking and companionship: Portraying property relations in Sokamin, Papua New Guinea. Paper presented for the Roskilde Training Seminar on Negotiating Property and Vindicating Land Claims, Denmark, October.

———. 2000. *Creating and maintaining access fields in Sokamin, Papua New Guinea*. Ph.D. dissertation, Graduate School of Arts and Sciences, Rutgers University.

Bibliography

Blum, Elissa. 1993. Making biodiversity conservation profitable: A case study of the Merck/INGio Agreement. *Environment* 35 (1): 25–35.

Bonner, Raymond. 1993. *At the hand of man: Perils and hope for Africa's wildlife*. New York: Vintage Books.

Boon, James A. 1990. Early Indonesian studies: Birds, words, and orangutans. Chap. 1 in *Affinities and extremes: Crisscrossing the bittersweet ethnology of East Indies history, Hindu-Balinese culture, and Indo-European allure*. Chicago: University of Chicago Press.

Borrini-Feyeraband, Grazia. 1996. *Collaborate management of protected areas: Tailoring the approach to the context*. Gland, Switzerland: International Union for the Conservation of Nature and Natural Resources (IUCN).

Bourdieu, Pierre. 1977. *Outline of a theory of practice*. Cambridge: Cambridge University Press.

——. 1986. The Forms of Capital. In *Handbook of theory and research for the sociology of education*, edited by John Richardson. New York: Greenwood Press.

——. 1990. *The logic of practice*. Stanford, Calif.: Stanford University Press.

Brandon, Katrina, and Michael Wells. 1992. Planning for people and parks: Design dilemmas. *World Development* 20 (4): 557–570.

Braudel, Fernand. 1980. *On history*. Trans. Sarah Matthews. Chicago: University of Chicago Press.

Braun, Bruce. 2002. *The intemperate rainforest: Nature, culture, and power on Canada's west coast*. Minneapolis: University of Minnesota Press.

Brechin, Steven R., Peter R. Wilshusen, Crystal L. Fortwangler, and Patrick C. West. 2002. Beyond the square wheel: Toward a more comprehensive understanding of biodiversity conservation as social and political process. *Society and Natural Resources* 15:17–40.

Brison, Karen J. 1992. *Just talk: Gossip, meetings, and power in a Papua New Guinea village*. Berkeley: University of California Press.

——. 1995. Changing constructions of masculinity in a Sepik society. *Ethnology* 34: 155–175.

Brookfield, Harold C. 1964. The ecology of Highland settlement: Some suggestions. Special publication, New Guinea: The Central Highlands. *American Anthropologist* 66 (4): 2.

Brookfield, Harold C., and Paula Brown. 1963. *Struggle for land: Agriculture and group territories among the Chimbu of the New Guinea Highlands*. Melbourne: Oxford University Press.

Brookfield, Harold C., and Doreen Hart. 1971. *Melanesia: A geographical interpretation of an island world*. London: Methuen and Company.

Brosius, J. Peter. 1995. Voices for the Borneo rainforest: Writing the history of an environmental campaign. Paper presented at conference, Environmental Discourses and Human Welfare in South and Southeast Asia, Hilo, Hawaii, 28–30 December.

———. 1999a. Analysis and Interventions: Anthropological engagements with environmentalism. *Current Anthropology* 40 (3): 277–309.

———. 1999b. Green dots, pink hearts: Displacing politics from the Malaysian rain forest. *American Anthropologist* 101 (1): 36–58.

———. N.d. Global conservation and the politics of scale. Paper presented at the Columbia University, Earth Institute Political Ecology Speakers Series. New York, March 2004.

Brosius, J. Peter., Anna L. Tsing, and Charles Zerner. 1998. Representing communities: Histories and politics of community-based natural resource management. *Society and Natural Resources* 11:157–168.

Brown, Michael, and B. Wyckoff-Baird. 1992. *Designing integrated conservation and development projects*. Washington, D.C.: Biodiversity Support Program.

Brown, Paula. 1970. Mingee-Money: Economic changes in the New Guinea Highlands. *Southwestern Journal of Anthropology* 26:242–260.

———. 1972. *The Chimbu: A study of change in the New Guinea Highlands*. Cambridge, Mass.: Schenkman.

———. 1995. *Beyond a mountain valley: The Simbu of Papua New Guinea*. Honolulu: University of Hawaii Press.

Brush, Steven. 1975. The concept of carrying capacity for systems of shifting cultivation. *American Anthropologist* 77:799–811.

———. 1992. Farmers' rights and genetic conservation in traditional farming systems. *World Development* 20 (11): 1617–1630.

———. 1993. Indigenous knowledge of biological resources and intellectual property rights: The role of anthropology. *American Anthropologist* 95 (3): 653–671.

Bryant, Raymond L. 2002. Non-governmental organizations and governmentality: "Consuming" biodiversity and indigenous people in the Philippines. *Political Studies* 50:268–292.

Bulmer, Ralph N. H. 1967a. Why is the Cassowary not a bird? A problem of zoological taxonomy among the Karam of the New Guinea Highlands. *Man* 2 (1): 5–25.

———. 1967b. Worms that croak and other mysteries of Karam natural history. *Mankind* 6 (12): 621–639.

Bulmer, S., and Ralph Bulmer. 1964. The prehistory of the Australian New Guinea Highlands. Pt. 2. *American Anthropologist* 66 (4): 39–76.

Burns, Peter 1999. *An introduction to tourism and anthropology*. New York: Routledge.

Campbell, C. T. 1964/1965. Yagaria Census division and part Labogai Census division. Lufa [District] 2:64/65. Unpublished report. Department of District and Native Affairs, Australian Administration.

Carey, Arthur T. 1950/1951. Report of patrol to the area south west of Henganofi and south of Mt. Michael–Bena Bena Sub-district: Central Highlands. Unpublished report. Department of District and Native Affairs, Australian Administration. No. 1

of 1950/1951, patrol dates: 4–22 July 1950. Microfilm: A7034, item 155 and 155A (reel 5).

Carey, Arthur T. 1951/1952a. Report of patrol to south of south-west Mt. Michael. Unpublished report. Goroka [town] 1:51/52. Department of District and Native Affairs, Australian Administration.

———. 1951/1952b Report of patrol to area south of Mt. Michael. Goroka [town] 3:51/52. Unpublished report. Department of District and Native Affairs, Australian Administration.

Carrier, Aschsah H., and James G. Carrier. 1991. *Structure and process in a Melanesian society: Ponam's progress in the twentieth century*. Chur, Switzerland: Harwood.

Carrier, James G., ed. 1992. *History and tradition in Melanesian anthropology*. Berkeley: University of California Press.

———. 1997. Introduction. In *Meanings of the market: The free market in Western culture* edited by James G. Carrier. Oxford: Berg.

———. 2003. Mind, gaze and engagement: Understanding the environment. *Journal of Material Culture* 8: 5–23.

Carrier, James G., and Daniel Miller. 1998. *Virtualism: A new political economy*. Oxford: Berg.

Caulfield, Mina Davis. 1969. Culture and imperialism: Proposing a new dialectic. In *Reinventing anthropology*, edited by Dell Hymes. New York: Pantheon.

Chagnon, Napoleon. 1995. *Yanomamo*. 5th ed. New York: Harcourt Brace Jovanovich.

Chagnon, Napoleon, and Timothy Asch. 1975. *The Ax Fight*. Timothy Asch Producer. Watertown, Mass.: Documentary Educational Resources (distributor).

Chapin, Mac 1990. The silent jungle: ecotourism among the Kuna Indians of Panama. *Cultural Survival Quarterly* 14: 42–45.

Clark, Jeffrey. 1993. Gold, sex, and pollution. *American Ethnologist* 20: 742–757.

Clarke, William. 1966. From extensive to intensive shifting cultivation: A succession from New Guinea. *Ethnology* 5: 347–359.

———. 1971. Place and people: An ecology of a New Guinean community. Berkeley: University of California Press.

———. 1973. The Dilemma of development. In *The Pacific in transition*, edited by Harold C. Brookfield. New York: St. Martin's Press.

Cleary, R. W. 1962/1963. "Labogai Census Division" Eastern Highlands District, Lufa [District] 4:62/63. Unpublished report. Department of District and Native Affairs, Australian Administration.

Clifford, James, and George E. Marcus, eds. 1986. *Writing culture: The poetics and politics of ethnography*. Berkeley: University of California Press.

Comaroff, John L., and Jean Comaroff. 1992. *Ethnography and the historical imagination*. Boulder: Westview Press.

———. 1997. *Of Revelation and revolution: The dialectics of modernity on a South African Frontier*, Volume II. Chicago: University of Chicago Press.

Conklin, Beth, and Laurie Graham. 1995. The shifting middle ground: Amazonian Indians and eco-politics. *American Anthropologist* 97 (4): 695–710.

Conklin, Harold. C. 1962. Lexicographical treatment of folk taxonomies. In *Problems in lexicography*, edited by Fred W. Householder and Sol Saporta. Indiana University Research Center in Anthropology, Folklore, and Linguistics, Publication 21. Bloomington: Indiana University Research Center in Anthropology, Folklore, and Linguistics.

———. 1964. Ethnogenealogical Method. In *Explorations in cultural anthropology*, edited by Ward H. Goodenough. New York: McGraw-Hill.

Connolly, Bob, and Robin Anderson. 1987. *First contact: New Guinea's Highlanders encounter the outside world*. New York: Penguin.

Cooper, William T. 1977. *The birds of paradise and the bower birds*. Boston: David R. Godine.

Crapanzano, Vincent. 1980. *Tuhami: Portrait of a Moroccan*. Chicago: University of Chicago Press.

———. 1992. Hermes' dilemma and Hamlet's desire: On the epistemology of interpretation. Cambridge, Mass.: Harvard University Press.

———. 2004. Imaginative horizons: An essay in literary-philosophical anthropology. Chicago: University of Chicago Press.

Crocombe, Ronald Gordon. 1968. That five year plan. *New Guinea and Australia* 3: 57–70.

Crocombe, Ronald Gordon, and Robin Hide. 1971. New Guinea: Unity in diversity. In *Land Tenure in the Pacific*, edited by Ronald Crocombe. Melbourne: Oxford University Press.

DeLoach, Ed., and David Troolin. 1988. Contact survey report of the Gimi language, western dialect. Unpublished report. Dallas: Summer Institute of Linguistics.

Denham, T. P., S. G. Haberle, C. Lentfer, R. Fullagar, J. Field, M. Therin, N. Porch, and B. Winsborough. 2003. Origins of Agriculture at Kuk Swamp in the Highlands of New Guinea. *Science*, 301, Issue 5630 (11 July): 189–193.

Descola, Philippe. 1986. Human-environmental relations: Orientalism, paternalism and communalism. In *Nature and society: Anthropological perspectives*, edited by Philippe Descola and Gísli Pálsson. London: Routledge.

Dirks, Nicholas B., Geoff Eley, and Sherry Ortner. 1994. Introduction to *Culture/power/history: A reader in contemporary social theory*, edited by Nicholas B. Dirks, Geoff Eley, and Sherry Ortner. Princeton: Princeton University Press.

Dirlik, Arif. 2001. Place based imagination: Globalism and the politics of place. In *Places and politics in an age of globalization*, edited by Roxann Prazniak and Arif Dirlik. Durham: Duke University Press.

Donne, R. W. S. 1965/1966. Report on Unave and Labogai census divisions. Lufa [District] 12:65/66. Unpublished report. Department of District and Native Affairs, Australian Administration.

Dove, Michael. 1993. A revisionist view of tropical deforestation and development. *Environmental Conservation* 20 (1): 17–25.

———. 1995. The theory of social forestry intervention: The state of the art in Asia. *Agroforestry Systems* 30 (3): 315–340.

———. 1996. Center, periphery, and biodiversity: A paradox of governance and a developmental challenge. In *Valuing local knowledge: Indigenous people and intellectual property rights*, edited by Stephen B. Brush and Doreen Stabinsky. Washington, D.C.: Island Press.

Dreyfus, Hubert L., and Paul Rabinow. 1982. *Michel Foucault: Beyond structuralism and hermeneutics.* Chicago: University of Chicago Press.

Dwyer, Peter D. 1983. Etolo hunting performance and energetics. *Human Ecology* 11: 145–173.

Dye, T. Wayne. 1990. Economic development at the grass roots. In *Sepik heritage: Tradition and change in Papua New Guinea*, edited by Nancy Lutkehaus, Christina Kaufmann, William E. Mitchell, Douglas Newton, Lita Osmundsen, and Meinhard Schuster. Durham, N.C.: Carolina Academic Press.

Eisenhauer, D. W. 1950/1951. Report of a patrol to that uncontrolled area south of Mount Michael. Bena Bena Sub-district: Central Highlands. Unpublished report. Department of District and Native Affairs, Australian Administration. No. 3 of 1950/1951, patrol dates: 3 July–12 August 1950. Microfilm: A7034, item 157 (reel 5).

Elkins, Paul. 1993. Making development sustainable. In *Global ecology*, edited by Wolfgang Sachs. London: Zed Books.

Ellis, David M. 2002. *Between custom and biodiversity: Local histories and market-based conservation in the Pio-Tura region of Papua New Guinea.* Ph.D. dissertation, Department of Anthropology, University of Kent, Canterbury.

Ellis, David M., and Paige West. 2004. Local history as "indigenous knowledge": Aeroplanes, conservation and development in Haia and Maimafu, Papua New Guinea. In *Investigating local knowledge: New directions, new approaches,* edited by A. Bicker, P. Sillitoe, and J. Pottier. London: Ashgate Publishing.

Ericho, John. 1998. Lessons from Crater Mountain ICAD project and some suggestions. In *The Motopure conference: ICAD practitioners' views from the field*, edited by Simon M. Saulei and Julie-Ann. Ellis. Waigani, Papua New Guinea: Department of Environment and Conservation.

Ericho, John, Robert Bino, and Arlyne Johnson. 1999. Testing the effectiveness of using a conceptual model to design projects and monitoring plans for the Crater Mountain Wildlife Management Area, Papua New Guinea. In *Measuring conservation impact: An interdisciplinary approach to project monitoring and evaluation,* edited by Kathy Saterson, Richard Margoluis, and Nick Salafsky. Washington, D.C.: Biodiversity Support Program.

Errington, Frederick K., and Deborah B. Gewertz. 1987a. *Cultural alternatives and a feminist anthropology*. Cambridge: Cambridge University Press.

———. 1987b. Of unfinished dialogues and paper pigs. *American Ethnologist* 1: 367–376.

———. 1993a. The triumph of capitalism in east New Britain? A contemporary Papua New Guinean rhetoric of motives. *Oceania* 64 (1): 1–17.

———. 1993b. The historical course of true love in the Sepik. In *Contemporary pacific societies*, edited by Victoria Lockwood, Thomas Harding, and Ben Wallace Englewood Cliffs, N.J.: Prentice Hall.

———. 1995. *Articulating change in the "Last Unknown."* Boulder: Westview Press.

———. 1996. The individuation of tradition in a Papua New Guinea modernity. *American Anthropologist* 98: 114–126.

———. 2001. On the generification of culture: From blow fish to Melanesian. *Journal of the Royal Anthropological Institute*, n.s. 7: 509–525.

———. 2004. *Yali's question: Sugar, culture, and history*. Chicago: University of Chicago Press.

Escobar, Arturo. 1995. *Encountering development: The making and unmaking of the third world*. Princeton: Princeton University Press.

———. 1998. Whose knowledge, whose nature? Biodiversity, conservation, and the political ecology of social movements. *Journal of Political Ecology* (5): 53–82.

———. 1999. After nature: Steps to an antiessentialist political ecology. *Current Anthropology* 40 (1): 1–30.

———. 2001. Culture sits in places: Reflections on globalism and subaltern strategies of location. *Political geography* 20:139–174.

Ethridge, Robbie. 2003. *Creek country: The Creek Indians and their world*. Chapel Hill: University of North Carolina Press.

Featherstone, Mike. 1990a. Global culture: An introduction. In *Global culture: Nationalism, globalization and modernity*, edited by Mike Featherstone. London: Sage Publications.

Featherstone, Mike, ed. 1990b. *Global culture: Nationalism, globalization and modernity*. London: Sage Publications.

Feinberg, Richard. 1995. Introduction: Politics of culture in the pacific islands. *Ethnology* 34 (2): 91–98.

Feld, Steven. 1996. Waterfalls of song: An acoustemology of place resounding in Bosavi, Papua New Guinea. In *Senses of Place*, edited by Steven Feld and Keith H. Basso. Santa Fe: School of American Research Press.

Feld, Steven, and Keith H. Basso, eds. 1996. *Senses of Place*. Santa Fe: School of American Research Press.

Ferguson, James. 1994. *The anti-politics machine: "Development," depoliticization, and bureaucratic power in Lesotho*. Minneapolis: University of Minnesota Press.

Ferguson, James, and Akhil Gupta 2002. Spatializing states: Toward an ethnography of neoliberal governmentality. *American Ethnologist* 29: 981–1002.

Fife, Wayne. 1995. Models for masculinity in colonial and postcolonial Papua New Guinea. *The Contemporary Pacific* 7: 277–302.

Filer, Colin. 1990. The Bougainville rebellion, the mining industry, and the process of social disintegration in Papua New Guinea. *Canberra Anthropology* 13 (1): 1–39.

———. 2000. How can Western conservationists talk to Melanesian landowners about indigenous knowledge. RMAP Working Papers, No. 27. Ed. Karen Fisher. Resource Management in Asia-Pacific Project, Division of Pacific and Asian History, Research School for Pacific and Asian Studies, Australian National University, Canberra.

———. 1997. Compensation, rent and power in Papua New Guinea. In *Compensation for resource development in Papua New Guinea*, edited by Susan Toft. Monograph no. 6. Port Moresby, Papua New Guinea, and Canberra, Australia: Law Reform Commission of Papua New Guinea.

Filer, Colin, and Nikhil Sekhran. 1998. Loggers, donors and resource owners. In *Policy that works for forests and people, Papua New Guinea country study*, edited by Colin Filer and Nikhil Sekhran. London: International Institute for Environment and Development in association with the National Research Institute of Papua New Guinea.

Finney, Ben. 1987. *Business development in the highlands of Papua New Guinea*. Honolulu, Hawaii: Pacific Islands Development Program, East-West Center.

Flannery, Kent. 1999. *Throwim' way leg: Tree-kangaroos, possums and penis gourds*. New York: Grove Press.

Foley, William A. 2000. The languages of New Guinea. *Annual Review of Anthropology* 29: 357–404.

Foran, S. P. 1964/1965a. Labogai census division patrol. Lufa [District] 3:64/65. Unpublished report. Department of District and Native Affairs, Australian Administration.

———. 1964/1965b. Labogai census division patrol. Lufa [District] 4:64/65. Unpublished report. Department of District and Native Affairs, Australian Administration.

———. 1967/1968. Unavi and Labogai census divisions. Lufa [District] 9:67/68. Unpublished report. Department of District and Native Affairs, Australian Administration.

Foster, Robert J., ed. 1995a. *Nation making: Emergent identities in postcolonial Melanesia*. New York: Cambridge University Press.

———. 1995b. *Social reproduction and history in Melanesia: Mortuary ritual, gift exchange, and custom in the Tanga islands*. Cambridge: Cambridge University Press.

———. 2002. *Materializing the nation: Commodities, consumption, and media in Papua New Guinea*. Bloomington: Indiana University Press.

Foucault, Michel. 1972. *The archaeology of knowledge and the discourse on language*, Translated by A. M. Sheridan Smith. New York: Pantheon.

———. 1977. *Discipline and punish: The birth of the prison*. New York: Vintage.

———. 1978. *The history of sexuality*. Vol. 1, *An introduction*. New York: Pantheon Books.

———. 1986. Of other spaces. *Diacritics* 16: 22–27.

Friedman, Jonathan. 1990. Being in the world: Globalization and localization. In *Global culture: Nationalism, globalization and modernity*, edited by Mike Featherstone. London: Sage Publications.

———. 1994. History and the politics of identity. Chap. 8 in Jonathan Friedman, *Cultural identity and global process*. London: Sage.

Gajdusek, D. Carleton. 1968. *New Guinea Journal, October 2, 1961 to August 4, 1962*. Vol. 2. Bethesda, Md.: National Institute of Neurological Diseases and Blindness.

Gajdusek, D. Carlton, and Michael Alpers. 1972. Genetic studies in relation to Kuru. 1. Cultural, historical and demographic background. *The American Journal of Human Genetics* 24 (supplement): 138.

Geertz, Clifford. 1973. *The interpretation of cultures*. New York: Cambridge University.

George, Kenneth M. 1995. Dark trembling: Ethnographic notes on secrecy and concealment in highland Sulawesi. *Anthropological Quarterly* 66(4): 230–239.

Gewertz, Deborah, and Frederick Errington. 1991. *Twisted histories, altered contexts: Representing the Chambri in a world system*. Cambridge: Cambridge University Press.

———. 1993. First contact with God. *Cultural Anthropology* 8: 297–305.

———. 1995. Why we return to Papua New Guinea. Paper presented at the 1995 meetings of the American Anthropological Association, during the session "Globalization and the Future of 'Culture Areas': Melanesian Anthropology in Transition," Washington, D.C., November 1995.

———. 1996. On PepsiCo and piety in a Papua New Guinea "modernity." *American Ethnologist* 23 (3): 476–493.

———. 2002. Margaret Mead and the death of Alexis Gewertz Shepard. *Amherst Magazine* (spring): 5–10. Amherst College: Amherst, Mass.

Giddens, Anthony. 1990. *The Consequences of modernity*. Stanford, Calif.: Stanford University Press.

Gillison, David 2002. *New Guinea ceremonies*. New York: Harry N. Abrams.

Gillison, Gillian. 1977. Fertility rites and sorcery in a New Guinea village. *National Geographic Magazine* 152, no. 1 (July): 124–146.

———. 1980. Images of nature in Gimi thought. In *Nature, culture and gender*, edited by Carol MacCormack and Marilyn Strathern. Cambridge: Cambridge University Press.

———. 1983a. Cannibalism among women in the Eastern Highlands of Papua New Guinea. In *The ethnography of cannibalism*, edited by Paula Brown and Donald Tuzin. Washington, D.C.: Society for Psychological Anthropology.

———. 1983b. Living theatre in New Guinea's Highlands. *National Geographic Magazine* 164, no. 2 (August): 147–169.

———. 1987. Incest and the atom of kinship: The role of the mother's brother in a New Guinea Highlands Society. *Ethos* 15: 166–202.

Gillison, Gillian. 1991. The flute myth and the law of equivalence: Origins of a principle of exchange. In *Big and great men: Personifications of power in Melanesia*, edited by Maurice Godelier and Marilyn Strathern. Cambridge: Cambridge University Press.

———. 1993. Between culture and fantasy: A New Guinea Highlands mythology. Chicago: University of Chicago Press.

———. 1994. Symbolic homosexuality and cultural theory: The unconscious meaning of sister exchange among the Gimi of Highlands New Guinea. In *Anthropology and Psychoanalysis: An encounter through culture*, edited by Suzette Heald and Ariane Deluz. London: Routledge.

Glasse, Robert M. 1969. Marriage in South Fore. In *Pigs, Pearlshells and women: Marriage in the New Guinea Highlands*, edited by Robert M. Glasse and Mervyn J. Meggitt. Englewood Cliffs, N.J.: Prentice-Hall.

Glasse, Robert M., and Shirley Lindenbaum. 1967. How New Guinea natives reacted to a total eclipse. *Trans-action* (December): 46–52. St. Louis: Washington University.

———. 1969a. Fore Age Mates. *Oceania* 39: 165–173.

———. 1969b. South Fore politics. *Anthropological Forum* 2:308–326.

Glick, Leonard B. 1963. *Foundations of a primitive medical system: The Gimi of the New Guinea Highlands*. Ph.D. dissertation, Graduate School of Arts and Sciences, University of Pennsylvania.

———. 1964. Categories and relations in Gimi natural science. *American Anthropologist* 66 (2): 273–280.

———. 1966. Personality categories in Gimi social organization. Paper read at the Annual Meeting of the American Anthropological Association. Pittsburgh, 20 November.

———. 1967a. The role of choice in Gimi kinship. *Southwestern Journal of Anthropology* 23: 371–382.

———. 1967b. Medicine as an ethnographic category: The Gimi of the New Guinea Highlands. *Ethnology* 6 (1): 31–56.

———. 1968a. Possession on the New Guinea Highlands: Comment. *Transcultural Psychiatric Research* 5 (3): 197–205.

———. 1968b. Gimi farces. *Oceania* 39 (1): 64–69.

Godelier, Maurice. 1982. *The making of great men: Male domination and power among the New Gu'mea Baruya*. Trans. Rupert Swyer. Cambridge: Cambridge University Press.

———. 1999. *The enigma of the gift*. Cambridge: Cambridge University Press.

Golub, Alex. 2005. *Making the Ipili feasible: Imagining global and local actors at the Porgera gold mine, Enga Province, Papua New Guinea*. Ph.D. dissertation, Graduate School of Arts and Sciences, Department of Anthropology, University of Chicago.

Gordon, Donald Craig. 1951. *The Australian frontier in New Guinea 1870–1885*. New York: Columbia University Press.

Gordon, Robert J., and Mervyn J. Meggitt. 1985. *Law and order in the New Guinea Highlands: Encounters with Enga*. Hanover, N.H.: University Press of New England.

Gorle, Gilian. 1995. The theme of social change in the literature of Papua New Guinea. *Pacific Studies* 18 (2): 139–149.

Griffen, James, Hank Nelson, and Stewart Firth. 1979. *Papua New Guinea: A political history*. Victoria, Australia: Heinemann Educational Australia.

Griffin, Larry J. 1993. Narrative, event-structure analysis, and causal interpretation in historical Sociology. *American Journal of Sociology* 98: 1094–1133.

Guha, Ranajit. 1988. On some aspects of the historiography of colonial India. In *Selected subaltern studies*, edited by Ranajit Guha and Gayatri Chakravorty Spivak. New York: Oxford University Press.

Gunder Frank, Andre. 2000. The development of underdevelopment. In *Imperialism: Theoretical directions*, edited by Ronald H. Chilcote. Amherst, N.Y.: Humanity Books.

Gupta, Akhil. 1992. Song of the nonaligned world: Transnational identities and the reinscription of space in late capitalism. *Cultural Anthropology* 7 (1): 63–79.

Gupta, Akhil, and James Ferguson. 1992. Beyond "culture": Space, identity, and the politics of difference. *Cultural Anthropology* 7 (1): 6–23.

———. 1999. Anthropological locations: Boundaries and grounds of a field science. Berkeley: University of California Press.

———. 2001. Culture, power, place: Ethnography at the end of an era. In *Culture, power, place: Explorations in critical anthropology*, edited by Gupta and Ferguson. Durham: Duke University Press.

Haila, Yrjö. 1998. Environmental governance and modern management paradigms in government and private industry. In *Co-operative environmental governance,* edited by Pieter Glasbergen. Dordrecht: Kluwer Academic Publishers.

———. 1999. Biodiversity and the divide between culture and nature. *Biodiversity and Conservation* 8: 165–181.

Hall, Stuart, David Held, Kenneth Thompson, and Don Hubert. 1996. *Modernity: An introduction to modern societies*. London: Blackwell Publishers.

Halvaksz, Jamon. 2005. *Re-imagining Biangai environments: Mining and conservation in the Wau Bulolo Valley, Papua New Guinea*. Ph.D. dissertation, University of Minnesota.

Haraway, Donna J. 1990. Primate visions: Gender, race, and nature in the world of modern science. New York: Routledge.

———. 1991. Simians, Cyborgs, and women: The reinvention of nature. New York: Routledge.

Hartwick, Elaine, and Richard Peet. 2003. Neoliberalism and nature: The case of the WTO. *Annals of the American Academy of Political and Social Science (AAPSS)* 590: 188–203.

Harvey, David. 1990. The condition of postmodernity: An inquiry into the origins of cultural change. Cambridge, Mass.: Basil Blackwell.

Bibliography

Harvey, David. 1996. *Justice, nature and the geography of difference*. Cambridge, Mass.: Basil Blackwell.

Haug, Wolfgang F. 1986. Critique of commodity aesthetics: Appearance, sexuality and advertising in capitalist society. Minneapolis: University of Minnesota Press.

Hays, Terence E. 1992a. Ethnographic presents: Pioneering anthropologists in the Papua New Guinea Highlands. Berkeley: University of California.

———. 1992b. A historical background to anthropology in the Papua New Guinea Highlands. In *Ethnographic presents: Pioneering anthropologists in the Papua New Guinea Highlands*, edited by Terence E. Hays. Berkeley: University of California.

———. 1993. "The New Guinea Highlands:" Region, culture area, or fuzzy set? *Current Anthropology* 34 (2): 141–163.

Hecht, Susanna, Anthony Anderson, and Peter May. 1988. The subsidy from nature: Shifting cultivation, successional palm forests and rural development. *Human Organization* 47 (1): 25–35.

Hecht, Susanna, and Alexander Cockburn. 1990. The fate of the forest: Developers, destroyers, and defenders of the Amazon. New York: HarperCollins.

Heidegger, Martin. 1971. *Poetry, language, thought,* translated by Albert Hofstadter. New York: Harper and Row.

Herdt, Gilbert H. 1981. *Guardians of the flutes*. New York: McGraw-Hill.

Hide, Robin L., ed. 1984. South Simbu: studies in demography, nutrition and subsistence. The Research Report of the Simbu Land Use Project, Volume VI. Boroko, Papua New Guinea: Institute of Applied Social and Economic Research.

Hide, Robin L., R. M. Bourke, B. J. Allen, D. Fritsch, R. Grau, P. Hobsbawn, and S. Lyon. 1995. Chimbu Province: Text summaries, maps, code lists and village identification. Agricultural Systems of Papua New Guinea Working Paper No. 12. Department of Human Geography, Australian National University, Canberra.

Hirsch, Eric, and O'Hanlon, Michael, eds. 1995. *The anthropology of Landscape*. Oxford: Clarendon Press.

Hoben, Allan. 1998. The role of development discourse in the construction of environmental policy in Africa. In *Concepts and metaphors: Ideologies, narratives and myths in development discourse,* edited by Henrik Secher Marcussen and Signe Arnfred. Occasional Paper No. 19, International Development Studies, Roskilde University, 122–145.

Hobsbawm, Eric, and Terrance Ranger, eds. 1983. *The invention of tradition*. Cambridge: Cambridge University Press.

Hodgson, Dorothy L. 1995. *The politics of gender, ethnicity and "development": Images, interventions and the reconfiguration of Maasai identities in Tanzania, 1916–1993*. Ph.D. dissertation, University of Michigan.

———. 1997. Embodying the contradictions of modernity: Gender and spirit possession among Maasai in Tanzania. In *Gendered encounters: Challenging cultural boundaries and social hierarchies in Africa,* edited by Maria Grosz-Ngate and Omari Kokole. New York: Routledge.

———. 1999. Critical interventions: The politics of studying "indigenous" development. In *Identities: Global studies in culture and power,* entitled "Unintended Consequences: On the Practice of Transnational Cultural Critique."

———. 2001. *Once intrepid warriors: Gender, ethnicity, and the cultural politics of Maasai development.* Bloomington: Indiana University Press.

Howlett, Diana R. 1967. *A geography of Papua and New Guinea.* Camden: Thomas Nelson and Sons.

Hughes, Ian. 1973. Stone-age trade in the New Guinea inland: Historical geography without history. In *The Pacific in transition: Geographical perspectives on adaptation and change,* edited by Harold Brookfield. London: Edward Arnold.

———. 1977. *New Guinea stone age trade: The geography and ecology of traffic in the interior.* Canberra: Department of Prehistory, Research School of Pacific Studies.

Hyndman, David. 1984a. Hunting and the classification of game animals among the Wopkaimin. *Oceania* 54: 289–309.

———. 1984b. Ethnobotany of Wopkaimin pandanus: A significant Papua New Guinea plant resource. *Economic Botany* 38 (3): 287–303.

———. 1994. Ancestral rain forests and the mountain of gold: Indigenous peoples and mining in New Guinea. Boulder: Westview Press.

Hyndman, David, and George E. B. Morren Jr. 1990. The Human ecology of the Mountain-Ok of central New Guinea: A regional and inter-regional approach. In *Children of Afek: Tradition and change among the Mountain-Ok of central New Guinea,* edited by Barry Craig and David Hyndman. Oceania Monograph 40. Sydney: University of Sydney.

Igag, Paul. 2002. *The conservation of large rainforest parrots: A study of the breeding biology of palm cockatoos, eclectus parrots and vulturine parrots.* Canberra: Australian National University.

Igag, Paul, and S. Murphy. 2002. Palm Cockatoo conservation in Papua New Guinea. *Psittascene* 51: 6–7.

Imbun, Benedict Y. 1995. Enga social life and identity in a Papua New Guinea mining town. *Oceania* 66 (1): 51–61.

Inglis, Amirah. 1975. *The white women's protection ordinance: Sexual anxiety and politics in Papua.* Sussex: Sussex University Press.

Ingold, Tim. 2000. *The perception of the environment: Essays on livelihood, dwelling and skill.* New York: Routledge.

Jacka, Jerry K. 2003. *God, gold, and the ground: Place-based political ecology in a New Guinea borderland.* Ph.D. dissertation, Department of Anthropology, University of Oregon.

James, Seldon. 1995. The Crater Mountain Wildlife Management Area: Recommendations for developing a natural resources management plan. Unpublished manuscript. Wildlife Conservation Society.

Johns, Robert J. 1993. Biodiversity and conservation of the native flora of Papua New Guinea. In *Papua New Guinea conservation needs assessment report*. Vol. 2, *A biodiversity analysis for Papua New Guinea*, edited by Bruce M. Beehler. Washington, D.C.: Biodiversity Support Program.

Johnson, Arlyne. 1997. Processes for effecting community participation in the establishment of protected areas: A case study of the Crater Mountain Wildlife Management Area. In *The political economy of forest management in Papua New Guinea*, edited by Colin Filer. NRI Monograph 32. Boroko, Papua New Guinea: National Research Institute.

———. 1998. Processes for effecting community participation in protected area establishment: A case study of the Crater Mountain Wildlife Management Area, Papua New Guinea. Pages 133–163 in The Motopure conference: ICAD practitioners' views from the field, edited by Simon M. Saulei and Julie-Ann Ellis. Waigani, Papua New Guinea: Department of Environment and Conservation.

———. 2000. *Monitoring and evaluation of an enterprise-based strategy for wildlife conservation in the Crater Mountain Wildlife Management Area* (Papua New Guinea). Ph.D. dissertation, University of Wisconsin, Madison.

Johnson, Arlyne, John Ericho, and Robert Bino. 2000. The Crater Mountain Integrated Conservation and Development Project: Testing and evaluating strategies for achieving biodiversity conservation in Papua New Guinea. In *Custom, conservation and development in Melanesia*, ed. by Colin Filer. Boroko: National Research Institute.

Johnson, Patricia L. 1993. Education and the "new" inequality in Papua New Guinea. *Anthropology and Education Quarterly* 24:183–204.

Johnston, Barbara Rose, ed. 1994. Who pays the price? The sociocultural context of environmental crisis. Washington, D.C.: Island Press.

Jolly, Margaret, and Nicholas Thomas, eds. 1992. The politics of tradition in the pacific. Special edition, *Oceania* 62 (4).

Jorgensen, Dan. 1996. Regional history and ethnic identity in the hub of New Guinea: The emergence of min. *Oceania* 66 (3): 211–229.

Jukes, Joseph B. 1847. Narrative of the surveying voyage of HMS *Fly* 1842–46, London. In *The Australian frontier in New Guinea 1870–1885*, edited by Donald Craig Gordon. New York: Columbia University Press.

Kahn, Miriam. 2000. Tahiti intertwined: Ancestral land, tourist postcard, and nuclear test site. *American Anthropologist* 102 (1): 7–26.

Kaplan, Martha. 1995. Neither cargo nor cult: Ritual politics and the colonial imagination in Fiji. Durham: Duke University Press.

Katz, Cindi. 1992. All the world is staged: Intellectuals and the projects of ethnography. *Environment and Planning D: Society and Space* 10: 495–510.

———. 1995. Major/minor: Theory, nature, and politics. *Annals of the Association of American Geographers* 85 (1): 164–168.

Kearney, Michael. 1995. The local and the global: The anthropology of globalization and transnationalism. *Annual Review of Anthropology* 24: 547–565.

Keesing, Roger. 1982. Kastom in Melanesia: An overview. In Reinventing traditional culture: the politics of Kastom in island Melanesia, edited by Roger Keesing and Robert Tonkinson. *Mankind* 13 (4): 297–301.

———. 1994. Colonial and counter-colonial discourse in Melanesia. *Critique of Anthropology* 14 (1): 41–58.

———. 1999. Theories of culture revisited. *Assessing cultural anthropology*. Ed. Robert Borofsky. New York: McGraw-Hill.

Keesing, Roger, and Robert Tonkinson, eds. 1982. Reinventing traditional culture: The politics of Kastom in island Melanesia. *Mankind* 13 (4): 297–301.

Kirsch, Stuart. 1993. Resisting the mine. Paper presented at the Annual Meeting of the American Anthropological Association. Washington, D.C., November 1993.

———. 1996. Acting globally: Eco-politics in Papua New Guinea. *The Journal of the International Institute* 3 (3): 14–15.

———. 2001. Property effects: Social networks and compensation claims in Melanesia. *Social Anthropology* 9 (2): 147–163.

Knauft, Bruce M. 1993. Like money you see in a dream: Petroleum and patrols in south New Guinea. *Oceania* 64:187–190.

———. 1999. *From primitive to postcolonial in Melanesia and anthropology*. Ann Arbor: University of Michigan Press.

———. 2002. *Exchanging the past: A rainforest world of before and after*. Chicago: University of Chicago Press.

Kottak, Conrad P. 1999. The new ecological anthropology. *American Anthropologist* 101 (1): 23–35.

Larson, Patricia, Mark Freudenberger, and Barbara Wyckoff-Baird. 1997. *Lessons from the field: A review of World Wildlife Fund's experience with integrated conservation and development projects 1985–1996*. Washington, D.C.: World Wildlife Fund.

Latour, Bruno. 1987. *Science in action, how to follow scientists and engineers through society*. Cambridge, Mass.: Harvard University Press.

Lattas, Andrew. 1992. Hysteria, anthropological disclosure and the concept of the unconscious: Cargo cults and the scientisation of race and colonial power. *Oceania* 16 (1): 1–13.

———. 1993. Sorcery and colonization. *Man* 28: 51–77.

Leach, James. 2003. *Creative Land: Place and Procreation on the Rai Coast of Papua New Guinea*. New York: Berghahn Books.

Leavitt, Stephen. 1995. Political domination and the absent oppressor: Images of Europeans in Bumbita Arapesh narratives. *Ethnology* 34 (3): 177–189.

Lederman, Rena. 1986. *What gifts engender: Social relations and politics in Mendi, Highland Papua New Guinea*. Cambridge: Cambridge University Press.

Lederman, Rena. 1998. Globalization and the future of culture areas: Melanesianist anthropology in transition. *Annual Review of Anthropology* 27: 427–450.

Lefebvre, Henri. 1991. *The production of space,* translated by Donald Nicholson-Smith. Oxford: Basil Blackwell.

Leff, Enrique. 1995. *Green production: Towards an environmental rationality.* New York: Guilford Press.

Leopold, Aldo. 1968. *A Sand County almanac and sketches here and there.* New York: Oxford University Press.

Lindenbaum, Shirley. 1969. Fore age mates. *Oceania* 29:165–173.

——. 1979. *Kuru sorcery.* Palo Alto, Calif.: Mayfield Publishing Company.

——. 1981. Images of the sorcerer in Papua New Guinea. *Social Analysis* 8: 119–129.

——. 2002. Fore narratives through time: How a bush spirit became a robber, was sent to jail, emerged as the symbol of the Eastern Highlands Province, and never left home. *Current Anthropology* 43 (supplement): 63–73.

Lindstrom, Lamont. 1990. *Knowledge and power in a South Pacific society.* Washington, D.C.: Smithsonian Institution Press.

——. 1993. *Cargo cult: Strange stories of desire from Melanesia and beyond.* Honolulu: University of Hawaii Press.

Lindstrom, Lamont, and Geoffrey M. White. 1990. *Island encounters.* Washington, D.C.: Smithsonian Institution Press.

——. 1993. Custom Today. *Anthropological Forum* 6 (4): 467–473.

——. 1995. Anthropology's new cargo: Future horizons. *Ethnology* 34: 201–209.

Linnekin, Jocelyn. 1992. On the theory and politics of cultural construction in the Pacific. *Oceania* 62 (4): 249–270.

LiPuma, Edward. 1988. *The gift of kinship: Structure and practice in Maring social organization.* Cambridge: Cambridge University Press.

——. 1994. Sorcery and evidence of change in Maring justice. *Ethnology* 33 (2): 147–163.

——. 2000. *Encompassing Others: The magic of modernity in Melanesia.* Ann Arbor: University of Michigan Press.

Loney, Matt. 2001. *Missionaries, mercenaries, and misfits.* London: Clinamen Press.

Lyotard, Jean-François. 1984. *The postmodern condition: A report on knowledge.* Trans. Geoff Bennington and Brian Massouri. Minneapolis: University of Minnesota Press.

Mack, Andrew L. 1990. Notes on the Dwarf Cassowary, Casuarius bennetti, in Papua New Guinea. *Muruk* 4: 49–52.

——. 1994. Notes on the nests and eggs of some birds at the Crater Mountain Research Station, Papua New Guinea. *Bulletin of the British Ornithologists' Club* 114: 176–181.

——. 1995a. Distance and non-randomness of seed dispersal by the dwarf cassowary Casuarius bennetti. *Ecography* 18: 286–295.

——. 1995b. Feathered foresters: Dwarf cassowaries sow the seeds of rainforest giants. *Living Bird* 14: 22–25.

——. 1995c. *Seed dispersal by the Dwarf Cassowary, Casuarius bennetti, in Papua New Guinea*. Ph.D. Dissertation, University of Miami, Coral Gables, Fla.

——. 1997. Spatial distribution, fruit production and seed removal of a rare, dioecious canopy tree species (Aglaia aff. flavida Merr. et Perr.) in Papua New Guinea. *Journal of Tropical Ecology* 13: 305–316.

——. 1998a. An advantage of large seed size: Tolerating rather than succumbing to seed predators. *Biotropica* 30: 604–608.

——. 1998b. The potential impact of small-scale physical disturbance on seedlings in a Papuan rainforest. *Biotropica* 30: 547–552.

——. 1999. The Vulturine Parrot (Psittrichas fulgidus) of New Guinea, a species in need of study. *Psitta Scene* 11 (4): 2–3.

Mack, Andrew L., and Gretchen Druliner. 2003. A non-intrusive method for measuring movements and seed dispersal in cassowaries. *Journal of Field Ornithology* 74: 193–196.

Mack, Andrew L., Kalan Ickes, J. Heinrich Jessen, Brian Kennedy, and J. Ross Sinclair. 1999. Ecology of Aglaia mackiana (Meliaceae) seedlings in a New Guinea rain forest. *Biotropica* 31:111–120.

Mack, Andrew L., and Josh Jones. 2003. Low-frequency vocalizations by cassowaries (*Casuarius* spp.). *Auk* 120:1062–1068.

Mack, Andrew L., and E. Scholes. 2003. Nesting activity of the Wallace's Fairy Wren Sipodotus wallacii. *Bulletin of the British Ornithologists' Club* 123:177–181.

Mack, Andrew L., and Debra D. Wright. 1993. The birds of Lake Teberu. *Muruk* 6:25–26.

——. 1996. Notes on the occurrence and feeding of birds at Crater Mountain Biological Research Station, Papua New Guinea. *Emu* 96: 89–101.

——. 1998. The Vulturine Parrot, Psittrichas fulgidus, a threatened New Guinea endemic: Notes on its biology and conservation. *Bird Conservation International* 8: 185–194.

Mack, Andrew, L., R. Yamuna, T. Donambe, and J. Pano. 1998. Effect of drought on birds at Maimafu, Eastern Highlands Province. *Science in New Guinea* 23: 125–131.

MacKenzie, Maureen Anne. 1990. The Telefol string bag: A cultural object with androgynous fours. In *Children of Afek: Tradition and change among the Mountain-Ok of central New Guinea*, edited by Barry Craig and David Hyndman. Sydney: University of Sydney.

——. 1991. Androgynous objects: String bags and gender in central New Guinea. Philadelphia: Harwood Academic Press.

Macmin Mining N. L. 1997. E.L.1115 Crater Mountain site report. Unpublished report.

——. 2000. "Macmin N. L. Current Projects Crater Mountain," http://www.macmin.com.au/Crater.html (accessed 9 February 2000).

Marcus, George E. 1995. Ethnography in/of the world system: The emergence of multisited ethnography. *Annual Review of Anthropology* 24: 95–117.

Marcus, George E. 1997. The uses of complicity in the changing mise-en-scène of anthropological fieldwork. *Representations* 59 (summer): 85–108.

———. 1998. Ethnography in/of the world system: The emergence of multi-sited ethnography (1995). In *Ethnography Through thick and thin*. Princeton: Princeton University Press.

Marcus, George E., and Michael M. J. Fischer. 1986. *Anthropology as cultural critique: An experimental moment in the human sciences*. Chicago: University of Chicago Press.

Margoluis, Richard, and Nick Salafsky. 1998. *Measures of success: Designing, managing, and monitoring conservation and development projects*. Washington, D.C.: Island Press.

Martin, Ron. 2000. Biodiversity conservation in Melanesia: addressing risk and uncertainty among stakeholders. RAMP Working Papers, no. 25. Ed. Karen Fisher. Resource Management in Asia-Pacific Program, Research School for Pacific and Asian Studies, Australian National University, Canberra.

Marx, Karl. 1973 [1939]. *Gundrisse*. New York: Vintage Books.

———. 1990 [1867]. *Capital*. Vol. 1. London: Penguin Classics.

Mauss, Marcel. [1925] 1990. *The gift: The form and reason for exchange in archaic societies*, translated by W. D. Halls. Foreword by Mary Douglas. London: Routledge.

May, Ronald James. 1990. Political and social change in the east Sepik. In *Sepik heritage: Tradition and change in Papua New Guinea*, edited by Nancy Lutkehaus, Christina Kaufmann, William E. Mitchell, Douglas Newton, Lita Osmundsen, and Neinhard Schuster. Durham, N.C.: Carolina Academic Press.

May, Ronald James, and Matthew Spriggs, eds. 1990. *The Bougainville Crisis*. Australia: Crawford House Press.

May, Robert M. 1978. The evolution of ecological systems. *Scientific American* 239 (3): 160–175.

McArthur, J. R. 1952/1953. Report of patrol to the area between Goroka and Mount Karimui. December 28 1952–February 11 1953. Department of District and Native Affairs, Australian Administration: unpublished report.

McBride, Sam, and Nancy McBride. 1973. Gimi anthropology essentials. Unpublished manuscript. Ukarumpa, Papua New Guinea: Summer Institute of Linguistics, Anthropology section.

McCay, Bonnie J. 1981. Optimal foragers or political actors?: Ecological analyses of a New Jersey fishery. *American Ethnologist* 8 (2): 356–382.

McCay, Bonnie J., and James M. Acheson, eds. 1990. *The question of the commons: The culture and ecology of communal resources*. Tucson: University of Arizona Press.

McCullers, Carson. 1998. *The member of the wedding (Play version)*. New York: W. W. Norton and Company.

McKellin, William H. 1991. Hegemony and the language of change: The pidginization of land tenure among the Managalase of Papua New Guinea. *Ethnology* 34 (4): 313–324.

McNeely, Jeffrey A., and David Pitt. 1985. Culture: A missing element in conservation and development. In *Culture and conservation: The human dimension in environmental planning*, edited by Jeffrey A. McNeely and David Pitt. Dover, N.H.: Croom Helm.

Meggitt, Mervyn J. 1965. *The lineage system of the Mae-Enga of New Guinea.* New York: Barnes and Noble.

———. 1971. The pattern of leadership among the Mae-Enga of New Guinea. In *Politics in New Guinea: Traditional and in the context of change, some anthropological perspectives.* Nedlands: University of Western Australia Press.

Merchant, Carolyn. 1989. *Ecological Revolutions: Nature, Gender, and Science in New England.* Chapel Hill: University of North Carolina Press.

Miller, Scott E., Robert Cowie, Dan Polhemus, and Lucis Eldredge. 1993. Biodiversity and conservation of the non-marine invertebrate fauna of Papua New Guinea. In *Papua New Guinea conservation needs assessment report.* Vol. 2, *A biodiversity analysis for Papua New Guinea*, edited by Bruce M. Beehler. Washington, D.C.: Biodiversity Support Program.

Milton, Kay, ed. 1993. *Environmentalism: The view from anthropology.* London: Routledge.

———, ed. 1996. *Environmentalism and cultural theory.* London: Routledge.

Moran, Emilio. 1979. *Human adaptability: An introduction to ecological anthropology.* North Scituate, Mass.: Duxbury Press.

———. 1990. Ecosystem ecology in biology and anthropology: A critical assessment. In *The ecosystem approach in anthropology: From concept to practice.* Ann Arbor: University of Michigan Press.

Morren, George E. B., Jr. 1977. From hunting to herding: Pigs and the control of energy in Montane New Guinea. In *Subsistence and survival: Rural ecology in the Pacific*, edited by Tim Bayliss-Smith and Richard G. Feachem. London: Academic Press.

———. 1980. Seasonality among the Miyanmin. *Mankind* 12: 1–12.

———. 1981. A small footnote to the "Big Walk." *Oceania* 52: 39–63.

———. 1986. The Miyanmin: Human ecology of a Papua New Guinea society. UMI *Studies in Cultural Anthropology, no. 9.* Ann Arbor: UMI Research Press.

———. 1995. The Miyanmin: Past, present, future indefinite. Report prepared for the Miyanmin People and Highland Gold, Pty., Ltd. Unpublished report. Port Moresby, Papua New Guinea.

Mosse, David. 2004. Is good policy unimplementable? Reflections on the ethnography of aid policy and practice. *Development and Change* 35 (4): 639–671.

The National 2002. October 4. Letters to the editor.

National Statistical Office. 1983. Provincial Data System, Rural Community Register Port Moresby (report). Papua New Guinea: Government Printing Office.

Neumann, Roderick. 1995. Local challenges to global agendas: Conservation, economic liberalization and the pastoralists' rights movement in Tanzania. *Antipode* 27 (4): 363–382.

New Yorker. 1985. Birds of paradise 61 (2): 35–38.

Oates, John. 1999. *Myth and reality in the rain forest: How conservation strategies are failing in West Africa.* Berkeley: University of California Press.

Ogan, Eugene, and Terence Wesley-Smith. 1992. Papua New Guinea: Changing relations of production. In *Social change in the Pacific Islands*, edited by Albert B. Robillard. London: Verso.

O'Hanlon, Michael. 1990. *Reading the Skin: adornment, display and society among the Wahgi.* British Museum Press, 1989; Australian edition, Crawford House Press, 1990.

———. 1993. *Paradise: Portraying the New Guinea Highlands.* London: British Museum Press.

———. 1995. Modernity and the "graphicalization" of meaning. *The Journal of the Royal Anthropological Institute* 1: 469–493.

O'Hanlon, Rosalind. 1988. Recovering the subject: Subaltern studies and histories of resistance in colonial south Asia. *Modern Asian Studies* 22 (1): 189–224.

Oles, Bryan Paul. 1999. *Keeping our roots strong: Place, migration, and corporate ownership of land on Mokel Atoll.* Ph.D. dissertation, Department of Anthropology, University of Pittsburgh.

Oliver, Douglas. 1991. *Black islanders: A personal perspective of Bougainville, 1937–1991.* Honolulu: University of Hawaii Press.

Orlove, Benjamin S. 1980. Ecological anthropology. *Annual Review of Anthropology* 9: 235–273.

Orlove, Benjamin S., and Stephen B. Brush. 1996. Anthropology and the conservation of biodiversity. *Annual Review of Anthropology* 25: 329–352.

Ortner, Sherry B. 1984. Theory in anthropology since the sixties. *Comparative Studies in Society and History* 26 (1): 126–165.

Papua New Guinea. 1966. Fauna (Protection and Control) Act of 1966.

———. 1975. Constitution of the Independent State of Papua New Guinea.

Pearl, Mary C. 1994. Local initiatives and the rewards for biodiversity conservation: Crater Mountain Wildlife Management Area, Papua New Guinea. In *Natural connections: Perspectives in community-based conservation*, edited by David Western, R. Michael Wright, and Shirley C Strum. Washington, D.C.: Island Press.

Peet, Richard, and Michael Watts. 2004. *Liberation ecologies: Environment, development, social movements* (2nd edition). London: Routledge.

Peluso, Nancy. 1992. *Rich forest poor people: Resource control and resistance in Java.* Berkeley: University of California Press.

———. 1993. Coercing conservation? The politics of state resource control. *Global Environmental Change* 3 (2): 435–519.

Peter, Hanns. 1990. Cultural changes in Gargar society. In *Sepik heritage: Tradition and change in Papua New Guinea*, edited by Nancy Lutkehaus, Christina Kaufmann,

William E. Mitchell, Douglas Newton, Lita Osmundsen, and Neinhard Schuster. Durham, N.C.: Carolina Academic Press.

Pigg, Stacy. 1992. Inventing social categories through place: Social representations and development in Nepal. *Comparative Studies in Society and History* 34 (3): 491–513.

———. 1993. Unintended consequences: The ideological impact of development in Nepal. *South Asia Bulletin* 13(1 and 2): 45–58.

Pinedo-Vasquez, Miguel, José Barletti Pasqualle, Dennis Del Castillo Torres, Kevin Coffey. 2002. A tradition of change: The dynamic relationship between biodiversity and society in sector Muyuy, Peru. *Environmental Science & Policy* 5: 43–53.

Polier, Nicole. 1994. A view from the "Cyanide Room" politics and culture in a mining township in Papua New Guinea. *Identities* 1 (1): 63–84.

———. 1996. Of mines and min: Modernity and its malcontents in Papua New Guinea. *Ethnology* 35 (1): 1–16.

Pomponio, Alice. 1992. *Seagulls don't fly into the bush: Cultural identity and development in Melanesia*. Belmont, Calif.: Wadsworth Publishing Company.

Posey, Daryl A. 1984. Ethnoecology as applied anthropology in Amazonian development. *Human Organization* 43: 95–107.

Povinelli, Elizabeth A. 2002. The cunning of recognition: Indigenous alterities and the making of Australian multiculturalism. Durham: Duke University Press.

Pratt, Mary Louise. 1991. *Imperial Eyes: Travel writing and transculturation*. New York: Routledge.

Pred, Allan, and Michael John Watts. 1992. *Reworking modernity: Capitalisms and symbolic discontent*. New Brunswick, N.J.: Rutgers University Press.

Rabinow, Paul, ed. 1984. *The Foucault Reader*. New York: Pantheon Books.

Raffles, Hugh. 2002. *In Amazonia: A natural history*. Princeton: Princeton University Press.

Rappaport, Roy A. 1984. *Pigs for the ancestors: Ritual in the ecology of a New Guinea People*. 2nd ed. New Haven: Yale University Press.

Read, Kenneth E. 1954. Cultures of the Central Highlands, New Guinea. *Southwestern Journal of Anthropology* 10 (1): 1–43.

Redford, Kent. 1991. The ecologically noble savage. *Cultural Survival Quarterly* 15 (1): 46–48.

Reed, Stephen W. 1943. *The making of modern New Guinea, with special reference to culture contact in the mandated territory*. Philadelphia: American Philosophical Society.

Research and Conservation Foundation of Papua New Guinea / Wildlife Conservation Society (RCF/WCS). 1995. Crater Mountain Wildlife Management Area: A model for testing the linkage of community-based enterprises with conservation of biodiversity. BCN Implementation Grant Proposal, RCF and WCS. RCF Library, Goroka, EHP, PNG.

RCF/WCS. 1997. A request to the Interchurch Organization for Development Co-operation for Institutional Support for Research and Conservation Foundation of Papua New Guinea. RCF Library, Goroka, EHP, PNG.

Ribot, Jesse C. 1999. Decentralization, participation and accountability in Sahelian forestry: Legal instruments of political-administrative control. *Africa* 69:23–65.

———. 2000. Rebellion, representation, and enfranchisement in the forest villages of Makacoulibantang, Eastern Senegal. In *People, plants, and justice: The politics of nature conservation*, edited by Charles Zerner. New York: Columbia University Press.

Robbins, Joel. 1995. Dispossessing the spirits. *Ethnology* 34: 211–224.

———. 2003. Properties of nature, properties of culture: Possession, recognition, and the substance of politics in a Papua New Guinea society. *Suomen Anthropologi* 1 (28): 9–28.

———. 2004. *Becoming sinners: Christianity and moral torment in a Papua New Guinea society*. Berkeley: University of California Press.

Robbins, Tom. 1990. *Even cowgirls get the blues*. New York: Bantam Books.

Robinson, John G., and Richard E. Bodmer. 1999. Towards wildlife management in tropical forests. *Journal of Wildlife Management* 63: 1–13.

Rocheleau, Dianne, and Laurie Ross. 1995. Trees as tools, trees as text: Struggles over resources in Zambrana-Chacuey, Dominican Republic. *Antipode* 27 (4): 407–428.

Rocheleau, Dianne, Barbara Thomas-Slayter, and Esther Wangari. 1996. Gender and Environment: A feminist political Ecology perspective. In *Feminist political ecology: Global issues and local experiences*. London: Routledge.

Rodman, Margaret. 1992. Empowering place. *American Anthropologist* 94: 690–656.

Roe, Emery. 1991. Development narratives, or making the best of blueprint development. *World Development* 19 (4): 287–300.

Rosaldo, Renato. 1989. Imperialist nostalgia. In *Culture and truth: The remaking of social analysis*. Boston: Beacon Press.

Rouse, Roger. 1995. Thinking through transnationalism: Notes on the culture politics of class relations in the contemporary United States. *Public Culture* 7: 353–402.

Rushdie, Salman. 1982. *Midnight's children*. New York: Avon.

Ryan, Peter. 1991. *Black bonanza: A landslide of gold*. Victoria, Australia: Highland House.

———, ed. 1972. *Encyclopedia of Papua and New Guinea*. Vols. 1–3. Melbourne: Melbourne University Press.

Sachs, Wolfgang, ed. 1993. *Global ecology: A new arena of political conflict*. London: Zed Press.

———, ed. 1995. *The development dictionary: A guide to knowledge as power*. London: Zed Press.

Sahlins, Marshall. 1963. Poor man, rich man, big-man, chief: Political types in Melanesia and Polynesia. *Comparative Studies in Society and History* 5: 285–303.

———. 1976. *Culture and practical reason*. Chicago: University of Chicago Press.

——. 1981. *Historical metaphors and mythical realities: Structure in the early history of the Sandwich Islands kingdom*. Association for the Study of Anthropology in Oceania, Special Publication No. I. Ann Arbor: University of Michigan Press.

Said, Edward, W. 1978. *Orientalism*. New York: Vintage Books.

——. 1989. Representing the colonized: Anthropology's interlocutors. *Critical Inquiry* 15: 205–225.

Salafsky, Nick, Hank Cauley, Ganesan Balachander, Bernd Cordes, John Parks, Cheryl Margoluis, Seema Bhatt, Chuck Encarnacion, Diane Russell, and Richard Margoluis. 2001. A systematic test of an enterprise strategy for community-based biodiversity conservation. *Conservation Biology* 15 (6): 1585–1595.

Salafsky, Nick, and Richard Margoluis. 1999. Threat reduction assessment: A practical and cost-effective approach to evaluating conservation and development projects. *Conservation Biology* 13: 830–841.

Salafsky, Nick, and Eva Wollenberg. 2000. Linking livelihoods and conservation: A conceptual framework and scale for assessing the integration of human needs and biodiversity. *World Development* 28 (8): 1421–1438.

Schieffelin, Edward L. 1991a. Introduction to *Like people you see in a dream: First contact in six Papua societies*. Stanford, Calif.: Stanford University Press.

——. 1991b. The great Papuan plateau. In *Like people you see in a dream: First contact in six Papua Societies*. Stanford, Calif.: Stanford University Press.

Schieffelin, Edward L., and Robert Crittenden. 1991a. *Like people you see in a dream: First contact in six Papua societies*. Stanford, Calif.: Stanford University Press.

——. 1991b. Colonial Papua and the tradition of exploration. In *Like people you see in a dream: First contact in six Papua societies*. Stanford, Calif.: Stanford University Press.

——. 1991c. The Strickland-Purari patrol: Starting out. In *Like people you see in a dream: First contact in six Papua societies*. Stanford, Calif.: Stanford University Press.

—— 1991d. Aftermath and reflections. In *Like people you see in a dream: First contact in six Papua societies*. Stanford, Calif.: Stanford University Press.

Schindlbeck, Markus. 1990. Tradition and change in Kwanga villages. In *Sepik heritage: Tradition and change in Papua New Guinea*, edited by Nancy Lutkehaus, Christina Kaufmann, William E. Mitchell, Douglas Newton, Lita Osmundsen, and Neinhard Schuster. Durham N.C.: Carolina Academic Press.

Schmid, Jurg. 1990. The response to tourism in Yensan. *Sepik heritage: Tradition and change in Papua New Guinea*, edited by Nancy Lutkehaus, Christina Kaufmann, William E. Mitchell, Douglas Newton, Lita Osmundsen, and Neinhard Schuster. Durham, N.C.: Carolina Academic Press.

Schor, Juliet B. 1999. The overspent American: Why we want what we don't need. New York: Harper Perennial.

Schroeder, Richard. 1993. Shady practice: Gender and the political ecology of resource stabilization in Gambian garden/orchards. *Economic Geography* 69 (4): 349–365.

Schroeder, Richard. 1995. Contradictions along the commodity road to environmental stabilization: Foresting Gambian gardens. *Antipode* 27 (4): 325–342.

———. 1999. Community, forestry and conditionality in the Gambia. *Africa* 69:1–22.

Scott, James. 1998. Seeing like a state: How certain schemes to improve the human condition have failed. New Haven: Yale University Press.

Sekhran, Nikhil, and Scott Miller. 1994. Introduction and summary. In *Papua New Guinea country study on biological diversity*, edited by Nikhil Sekhran and Scott Miller. A report to the United Nations Environment Program. Waigani, Papua New Guinea: Department of Environment and Conservation, Conservation Resource Centre; Nairobi, Kenya: African Centre for Resources and Environment (ACRE).

Shange, Ntozake. 1996. *Sassafras, cypress & indigo*. New York: Picador.

Sharp, Andrew. 1960. *The discovery of the pacific islands*. Oxford: Clarendon Press.

Shiva, Vandana. 1992. *The future of progress: Reflections on environment and development*. Bristol: International Society for Ecology and Culture.

Sillitoe, Paul. 1998a. The development of indigenous knowledge: A new applied anthropology. *Current Anthropology* 39 (2): 234–344.

———. 1998b. What, know natives? Local knowledge in development. *Social Anthropology* (6) 2:203–220.

Silverman, Eric Kline. 1998. Indigenous Mapping in Papua New Guinea. In *The history of cartography*. Vol. 2, bk. 3, *Cartography in the traditional African, American, Arctic, Australian and Pacific Societies*, David Woodward and G. Malcom Lewis eds. Chicago: University of Chicago Press.

Sinclair, J. Ross 2000. *The behaviour, ecology and conservation of three species of megapode in Papua New Guinea*. M.S. thesis. University of Otago, Otago, New Zealand.

Slater, Candace. 2002. *Entangled edens: Visions of the Amazon*. Berkley: University of California Press.

Smith, Michael French. 1994. Hard times of Kairiru Island: Poverty, development, and morality in a Papua New Guinea village. Honolulu: University of Hawaii Press.

Smith, Neil. 1990. Uneven development: Nature, capital and the production of space. Oxford: Basil Blackwell.

———. 1993. Homeless/Global: Scaling Places. In *Mapping the future*, edited by Jon Bird, Barry Curtis, Tim Putnam, and George Robertson. London: Routledge.

———. 1996a. The production of nature. In *Future natural*, edited by George Robertson and Melinda Marsh. London: Routledge.

———. 1996b. The new urban frontier: Gentrification and the revanchist city. New York: Routledge.

Souter, Gavin. 1964. *New Guinea: The last unknown*. London: Angus and Robertson.

Spivak, Gayatri Chakravorty. 1988. Subaltern studies: Deconstructing historiography. In *Selected subaltern studies*, edited by Ranajit Guha and Gayatri Chakravorty Spivak. New York: Oxford University Press.

Stepan, Nancy Leys. 2001. *Picturing Tropical Nature*. Ithaca: Cornell University Press.

Stewart, Pamela J. 1996. *Netbags: Cultural narratives from Papua New Guinea*. M.A. thesis, University of Chicago.

Stott, P., and Sian Sullivan. 2000. Introduction. In *Political ecology, science, myth and powers*, edited by P. Stott and S. Sullivan. London: Arnold.

Strathern, Andrew J. 1966. Despots and directors in the New Guinea Highlands. *Man* 1: 358–367.

———. 1971. Rope of Moka: Big-men and ceremonial exchange in Mount Hagen, New Guinea. Cambridge: Cambridge University Press.

Strathern, Marilyn. 1980. No nature, no culture: The Hagen case. In *Nature, culture and gender*, edited by Carolyn MacCormack and Marilyn Strathern. Cambridge: Cambridge University Press.

———. 1981. Culture in a net bag: The manufacture of a subdiscipline in anthropology. *Man* 16: 665–688.

———. 1988. *The gender of the gift*. Berkley: University of California Press.

Swadling. Pamela. 1996. *Plumes from paradise*. Boroko, National Capital District, Papua New Guinea: Papua New Guinea National Museum.

Takacs, David. 1996. *The idea of biodiversity: Philosophies of paradise*. Baltimore: Johns Hopkins University Press.

Takeuchi, Wayne. 1999. New plants from Crater Mt., Papua New Guinea, and an annotated checklist of the species. *SIDA* 18: 941–986.

Taussig, Michael. 1980. *The devil and commodity fetishism in South America*. Chapel Hill: University of North Carolina Press.

———. 1987. *Shamanism, colonialism and the wild man*. Chicago: University of Chicago Press.

———. 2000. The beach (a fantasy). *Critical Inquiry* 26: 251–277.

Taylor, Charles. 2002. Modern social imaginaries. *Public Culture* 14 (1): 91–124.

Terborgh, John. 1999. *Requiem for nature*. Washington, D.C.: Island Press.

Thomson, Herb. 1991. Economic theory and economic development in Papua New Guinea. *Journal of Contemporary Asia* 21 (1): 54–67.

Tonkinson, Robert. 1993. Understanding tradition — ten years on. *Anthropological Forum* 6: 597–606.

Trouillot, Michael Rolph.1991. Anthropology and the savage slot: The poetics and politics of otherness. In *Recapturing anthropology: Working in the present,* edited by Richard G. Fox. Santa Fe: School of American Research Press.

Tsing, Anna Lowenhaupt. 1993. In the realm of the Diamond Queen: Marginality in an out-of-the-way place. Princeton: Princeton University Press.

———. 1999. Notes on culture and natural resource management. Berkeley workshop on environmental politics, working papers, wp 99-4. Institute of international studies, University of California, Berkeley.

Tuzin, Donald. 1997. The Cassowary's revenge: The life and death of masculinity in a New Guinea Society. Chicago: University of Chicago Press.

Van Helden, Flip. 1998. *Between cash and conviction: The social context of the Bismarck-Ramu integrated conservation and development project*. NRI Monograph 33. Port Moresby: National Research Institute and the United Nations Development Programme.

——. 2001a. "Good business" and the collection of "wild lives": Community, conservation and conflict in the Highlands of Papua New Guinea. *The Asia Pacific Journal of Anthropology* 2 (2): 21–44.

——. 2001b. *Through the thicket: Disentangling the social dynamics of an integrated conservation and development project on mainland Papua New Guinea*. Ph.D. dissertation, Wageningen Universiteit, Netherlands.

Vayda, Andrew P. 1976. *War in ecological perspective*. New York: Plenum.

——. 1983. Progressive contextualization: Methods for research in human ecology. *Human Ecology* 11: 265–281.

——. 1986. Holism and individualism in ecological anthropology. *Reviews in Anthropology* 13 (4): 295–313.

——. 1995. Failures of explanation in Darwinian ecological anthropology: part I. *Philosophy of the Social Sciences* 25: 219–249.

Vayda, Andrew P., and Bonnie J. McCay. 1975. New directions in ecology and ecological anthropology. *Annual Review of Anthropology* 4: 293–306.

Vázquez, Adolfo Sánchez. 1977. *The philosophy of praxis*. Atlantic Highlands, N.J.: Humanities Press.

Wagner, John. 1999. Blue Mountains constantly walking: The re-signification of nature and the re-configuration of the commons in rural Papua New Guinea. RMAP Working Papers, No. 24. Ed. Karen Fisher. Resource Management in Asia-Pacific Project, Division of Pacific and Asian History, Research School for Pacific and Asian Studies, Australian National University, Canberra.

——. 2002. *Commons in Transition: An analysis of social and ecological change in a coastal rainforest environment in rural Papua New Guinea*. Ph.D. dissertation, Department of Anthropology, McGill University.

——. 2003. The politics of accountability: an institutional analysis of the conservation movement in Papua New Guinea. *Social Analysis* 45 (2): 78–93.

Wagner, Roy. 1967. The curse of Souw: Principles of Daribi clan definition and alliance in New Guinea. Chicago: University of Chicago Press.

——. 1969. Marriage among the Daribi. In *Pigs, Pearlshells and women: Marriage in the New Guinea Highlands*, edited by Robert M. Glasse and Mervyn J. Meggitt. Englewood Cliffs, N.J.: Prentice-Hall.

——. 1970. Daribi and Foraba cross-cousin terminologies: A structural comparison. *Journal of the Polynesian Society* 79: 91–98.

——. 1972. *Habu: The innovation of meaning in Daribi religion*. Chicago: University of Chicago Press.

———. 1978. Lethal speech: Daribi myth as symbolic obviation. Ithaca: Cornell University Press.

Wallace, Alfred Russell. 1880. The Malay Archipelago: The land of the orang-utan and the bird of paradise. A narrative of travel, with studies of man and nature. London: Macmillan.

Wallerstein, Immanuel. 1974. Theoretical reprise. In *The modern world-system: Capitalist agriculture and the origins of the European world economy in the Sixteenth century*. New York: Academic Press.

Wanek, Alexander. 1996. *The state and its enemies in Papua New Guinea*. Richmond: Curzon Press.

Wassman, Jurg. 1993. Worlds in mind: The experience of an outside world in a community of the Finisterre Range of Papua New Guinea. *Oceania* 64:117–145.

Watson, Mark, and Smith Asoyama. 2001. Dispersion, habitat use, hunting behavior, vocalizations, and conservation status of the New Guinea Harpy Eagle (Harpyopsis novaeguineae). *Journal of Raptor Research* 35:235–239.

Weber, Max. 1958 [1904–1905]. *The Protestant Ethic and the Spirit of Capitalism*. New York: Scribner's.

Weiblen, George D. 1998. Composition and structure of a one hectare forest plot in the Crater Mountain Wildlife Management Area, Papua New Guinea. *Science in New Guinea* 24: 23–32.

Weiner, James F. 1994. The origin of petroleum at Lake Kutubu. *Cultural Anthropology* 9: 37–57.

Weisgrau, Maxine. 1997. *Interpreting development: Local histories, local strategies*. New York: University Press of America.

Wells, Michael, Katrina Brandon, and Lee Hannah. 1992. *People and parks: Linking protected area management with local communities*. Washington: World Bank, World Wildlife Fund, and U.S. Agency for International Development.

Wells, Michael, Scott Guggenheim, Asmeen Kahn, Wahjudi Wardojo, and Paul Jepson. 1999. *Investing in biodiversity: A review of Indonesia's integrated conservation and development projects*. Washington, D.C.: World Bank.

Werlen, Benno. 1993. *Society, action, and space*. New York: Routledge.

Wesley-Smith, Terrence. 1995. Melanesia in review — issues and events, 1994: Papua New Guinea. *The Contemporary Pacific* 7:364–374.

West, Cathrine Paige. 1994. *Wilderness as defined by human action: Understanding the relationship between culture, praxis, and nature*. Master's thesis, University of Georgia.

———. 1996. *The anthropology of ecological thought: Foundations and new directions*. Field Statement submitted in partial fulfillment for the Ph.D. in anthropology. Rutgers University. Advisor, Bonnie J. McCay.

———. 1997. *Nature and culture in anthropology*. Field Statement submitted in partial fulfillment for the Ph.D. in anthropology. Rutgers University. Advisor, Dorothy L. Hodgson.

West, Catherine Paige. 1999. Is nature to culture as marijuana is to alcohol? Understanding "development" in Papua New Guinea. Paper read at the American Ethnological Society Annual Meetings, Portland, Oregon, 25–28 March.

———. 2000. *The practices, ideologies, and consequences of conservation and development in Papua New Guinea*. Ph.D. dissertation, Department of Anthropology, Rutgers University, New Brunswick, N.J.

———2001. Environmental non-governmental organizations and the nature of ethnographic inquiry. Special issue, *Anthropology and consultancy: Social analysis*, edited by Pamela J. Stewart and Andrew Strathern 45 (2): 55–77.

West, Paige, and James G. Carrier. 2004. Ecotourism and authenticity: Getting away from it all? *Current Anthropology* 45 (4): 483–498.

Westermark, George. 1997. Clan claims: Land, law and violence in the Papua New Guinea Eastern Highlands. *Oceania* 67 (3): 218–233.

Whimp, Kathy. 1997. Governance, law, and sovereignty: Enforcing environmental objectives in Papua New Guinea. In *The political economy of forest management in Papua New Guinea*, edited by Colin Filer. Port Moresby: National Research Institute and International Institute for Environment and Development.

White, Geoffrey M., and Lamont Lindstrom, eds. 1993. Custom today in Oceania. Special edition, *Anthropological Forum* 6.

White, Richard. 1991. *The middle ground: Indians, empires, and republics in the Great Lakes region, 1650–1815*. Cambridge: Cambridge University Press.

Whitehouse, Harvey. 1995. *Inside the cult: Religious innovation and transmission in Papua New Guinea*. Oxford: Oxford University Press.

Whyte, Anne. 1978. Systems as perceived: A discussion of "maladaptation in social systems." In *The evolution of social systems*, edited by Jonathan Friedman and Michael J. Rowlands. Pittsburgh: University of Pittsburgh Press.

Williams, Raymond. 1973. The *Country and the city*. New York: Oxford University Press.

Willis, Katherine, Lindsey Gillson, and Terry M. Brncic. 2004. How "virgin" is virgin rainforest? *Science* 304:402–403.

Wilshusen, Peter R., Steven R. Brechin, Crystal L. Fortwangler, and Patrick C. West. 2002. Reinventing a square wheel: Critique of a resurgent "protection paradigm" in international biodiversity conservation. *Society and Natural Resources* 15:17–40.

Wilson, Alexander 1992. *The culture of nature: North American landscape from Disney to the Exxon Valdez*. Cambridge, Mass: Basil Blackwell.

Wolf, Eric. 1982. *Europe and the people without history*. Berkeley: University of California Press.

Womersley, J. S. and J. B. McAdam. 1957. The Forests and forest conditions in the territories of Papua and New Guinea. Report prepared for the British Commonwealth Forestry Conference in Australia. Territory of Papua New Guinea: Papua New Guinea Forest Service.

World Bank. 1982. *Papua New Guinea: Selected development issues*. Washington, D.C.: World Bank

Worsley, Peter. 1968. *The trumpet shall sound: A study of "cargo" cults in Melanesia*. New York: Stockton.

Worster, Donald. 1993. The shaky ground of sustainability. In *Global ecology*, edited by Wolfgang Sachs. London: Zed Books.

Wright, Debra D. 1997. Preliminary report on the Crater Mountain biological surveys. Unpublished report.

———. 1998. *Fruit choice by the Dwarf Cassowary,* Casuarius bennetti, *over a three year period in Papua New Guinea*. Ph.D. dissertation, University of Miami, Coral Gables, Fla.

Wright, Debra D., J. Heinrich Jessen, Peter Burke, and Hector G. de Silva Garza. 1997. Tree and liana enumeration and diversity on a one-hectare plot in Papua New Guinea. *Biotropica* 29: 250–260.

Wright, Debra D., Andrew L. Mack, E. H. Paxton, and James I. Menzies. 1995. Recent Aproteles bulmerae (Megachiroptera: Pteropodidae) bones found in Eastern Highlands Province, Papua New Guinea. *Mammalia* 59: 163–164.

Wurm, Stephen A. 1957. Preliminary report on the languages of the Eastern, Western and Southern Highlands of Papua New Guinea. Unpublished report. Department of anthropology and sociology, the Australian National University. Canberra, Australian Capital Territory.

———. 1960. The linguistic situation in the Highlands districts of Papua and New Guinea. Canberra: A. J. Arthur, Commonwealth Government Printer.

———. 1961. New Guinea languages. *Current Anthropology* 2: 114–116.

———. 1962. The languages of the Eastern, Western, and Southern Highlands, territory of Papua and New Guinea. In *Linguistic survey of the south-western Pacific*, ed. Arthur Capell. New and rev. edition. Nouméa, New Caledonia: South Pacific Commission.

———. 1964. Australian New Guinea Highlands languages and the distribution of their typological features. Pt. 2. *American Anthropologist* 66: 77–97.

———, ed. 1977. *New Guinea area languages and language study*. Vol. 1, *Pacific Linguistics*. Canberra: Australian National University.

Young, Emily H. 1999. Balancing conservation with development in small-scale fisheries: Is ecotourism an empty promise? *Human Ecology* 27: 581–620.

Young-Whitforde, Dudley. 1950/1951. Report on a patrol to the area south of Mt. Michael: Central Highlands, Bena Bena Sub-district. Unpublished report. Department of District and Native Affairs, Australian Administration. No. 2 of 1950/1951, patrol dates: 5–31 July 1950. Microfilm: A7034, Item 156 (reel 5).

Zerner, Charles. 1994. Through a green lens: The construction of customary environmental law and community in Indonesia's Maluku Islands. *Law and Society Review* 28 (5): 1079–1122.

Index

Land (*continued*)
140; cultural hybridity and, 259 n.9; gazetting for inclusion in WMA and, 37, 145; identity and, 135–36; social relations and, 108–11; trespassing violations and, 176, 177
Larson, P., 36
Leahy, Mick, 128
Leahy, Patrick, 239
Lefebvre, Henri, 27–28, 151, 228–29
Leslie, Ian, 76
Lévi-Strauss, Claude, 273 n.1
Linnekin, Jocelyn, 168
Loney, Matt, 252 n.1
Lowie, Robert, 265 n.62
Lyotard, Jean-François, 160

MacArthur Foundation, 141–42, 144, 190
Mack, Andrew, 42, 130–31, 141, 142, 144, 258 n.20, 270 n.10
MAF (Mission Aviation Fellowship), 14, 73, 76
Maimafu: allocation of services to, 95; artificiality of, 94; bilum making in, 18, 200–212; on cargo cult mentality, 171; changing customs in, 62; conservation projects understood by, 44, 135–38; conversion to Christianity in, 64; the creation story in, 60–62; customs of, exchanged for development, 48–49; dialects of, 13–14; disengagement of, from environment, 185; education in, 15, 114; environmental knowledge of, 116, 181; expatriates in, 271 n.2; family relations in, 67–68, 233–36; group identification in, 53; Harpy Eagle Project in, 192–94; history of, 58–59, 239–41; housing in, 53–54. 258n2; identification of, 10–11, 12–13, 28, 253 n.16; income generating projects in, 275 n.18; information communication in, 152; land claims of, 108–9, 197; leadership in, 66, 164; location of, 7, 8 (map),

10–11, 12, 28; Management Committee of, 44, 220; national resident fieldworkers in, 143; on *neki maha* (bad places), 83; origin stories in, 56–58; Peace Corps volunteers in, 15, 187–88, 240; pigs absent from, 74, 262 n.34; RCF relations with, 77–78, 114–16, 225–26; reciprocity in, 47–48; relationship with the environment, 175–76; research business initiatives and, 189; SDA membership in, 14; sister exchange in marriage in, 265 n.56; as spatial production, 10–11, 28. *See also* Commodification; Conservation-as-development
Marriage: bilum making and, 202–3; coffee gardens and, 106; men's preparation for, 63, 64; SDA church on, 71; sister exchange in, 265 n.56; wedding feasts and, 148–49. *See also* Bride price; Childbirth
Marx, Karl, 183, 184, 185, 212, 265 n.62
Material culture, 156–59, 200–201, 219, 221, 265 n.62
Mauss, Marcel, 46
McArthur, J. R., 12, 62–63
McBride, Sam and Nancy, xiv, xx, 96–97
Mead, Margaret, 172
Melanesia, 259 n.8, 265 nn.60, 62
Melanesian Pidgin, 16, 67, 253 nn.17, 19
Men: big-man status and, 66, 119, 143, 164; childbirth and, 91, 93; clans and, 44, 53, 56–58, 79, 117–18; conservation-as-development projects and, 220; control of, over women's labor, 204, 205, 208; education of, 100, 101, 239; environmental conservation and, 89; group identification of, 53; housing for, 63, 135; hunting practices of, 176, 177; initiation rites for, 63, 81, 82, 166, 260 n.117; labor migrations of, 66–67, 72, 127, 152; leadership criteria for, 66–67, 261 n.22; marriage and, 63, 64; meat consumption by, 95–96; Melanasian